CU00403544

THE MILITARY
AIRFIELDS OF BRITAIN

South-Western England

Channel Islands, Cornwall, Devon, Dorset,
Gloucestershire, Somerset, Wiltshire

THE MILITARY
AIRFIELDS OF BRITAIN
South-Western England

Channel Islands, Cornwall, Devon, Dorset, Gloucestershire, Somerset, Wiltshire

KEN DELVE

THE CROWOOD PRESS

First published in 2006 by
The Crowood Press Ltd
Ramsbury, Marlborough
Wiltshire SN8 2HR

www.crowood.com

© Ken Delve 2006

All rights reserved. No part of this publication may be reproduced or transmitted in any
form or by any means, electronic or mechanical, including photocopy, recording, or any
information storage and retrieval system, without permission in writing from the publishers.

British Library Cataloguing-in-Publication Data
A catalogue record for this book is available from the British Library.

ISBN 1 86126 810 6
EAN 978 1 86126 810 5

Typeset by Textype, Cambridge

Printed and bound in Great Britain by Biddles Ltd, King's Lynn, Norfolk

Contents

Acknowledgements

This series is the result of many years of research in the archives of the RAF Air Historical Branch and without the unstinting help of the staff of that organization this project would have been impossible. There are a number of individuals who have been particularly valuable – indeed, essential – help in this volume: Rod Priddle for his invaluable help with airfields of Wiltshire and clearance to use material from his excellent book *Wings over Wiltshire* (ALD Design & Print), which is highly recommended to readers who are seeking detailed information on airfields and aviation in this county; Ray Sturtivant for a great deal of the Fleet Air Arm material in this series – as an historian of this subject (and many others) Ray is without equal and I am very grateful for his help and advice. Also for permission, along with Mick Davis who drew the plans, to use World War One airfield plans that appeared in *Royal Navy Aircraft Serials and Units 1911–1919* (Sturtivant, Ray and Page, Gordon, Air Britain 1992);

Aldon Ferguson, one of the leading airfield researchers has been a great help in many respects.

Over the years in which I have been researching and writing aviation history I have been helped by a great many people, from veterans to enthusiasts and fellow historians: I thank all those with whom I have had the pleasure to have worked with and apologize to any who think they should have been named in these acknowledgements – sorry guys, the list was too long! However, there are two names I must include: Peter Green who was a co-author on a Canberra book and has very much been an inspiration for my aviation history work, and Andrew Thomas, a fellow RAF-officer who has established a first-class reputation as an aviation historian. Finally, to my son and research assistant – Luke – without whom the project would have been impossible.

RAF Heraldry Trust

During my time as editor and managing editor of *FlyPast* magazine, I was involved in promoting one of the most interesting, useful and necessary historical archive projects. The RAF Heraldry Trust seeks to create an accurate colour archive of every official badge awarded to RAF units, including squadrons, stations, Wings, Groups and Commands. The artist, Mary Denton, accurately recreates in authentic colours the original badges of units and these provide a permanent archived record, presently held by RAF Cranwell. In the absence of official funding and the lack of interest from the Heritage Lottery Fund the project is being funded by private individuals who sponsor one or more badges and can therefore add a dedication to the finished artwork. The project has some 2,000 badges to complete and to date only a few hundred have been painted. More sponsors are needed; for more information contact: Charles M Ross, Chairman of Trustees, RAF Heraldry Trust, Chestnut House Farm, Ludford Road, Binbrook, Market Rasen, Lincs LN8 6DR. Or check out the website at: www.griffon.clara.net/rafh/heraldry.htm

Station Badge for RAF Chivenor; an example of a typical RAF Heraldry Trust record with the Badge in authentic colours plus details of origin of Badge and its motto, along with dedication.

To help support this worthwhile project a percentage of the royalties from the Crowood Military Airfields of Britain series in being donated to the RAF Heraldry Trust to sponsor station badges.

Series Introduction

This series of books examines Britain's Military airfields region by region, covering military aviation from World War One to the present day. There have been two main periods of airfield construction – World War One, when a large number of landing grounds and aerodromes were built for either defensive purposes or training, the majority of offensive operations taking place from airfields in France, and World War Two, when some parts of England housed hundreds of airfields, many of which were 'taking the war to the enemy' on a daily basis. The highpoint of airfields in terms of numbers came in the latter months of 1944, when Britain housed some 1,000 airfields and over 30,000 aircraft, plus a significant number of small or temporary landing strips.

This series is not a detailed history of each and every airfield but rather a 'user-friendly' reference, which, for each airfield, comprises an outline history along with maps, plans, photographs and data tables containing information such as location, units and memorials. Commercial publishing realities mean that even the entries for major airfields have had to be restricted in size and all airfields and landing strips that had no recorded military usage have been excluded.

Note on Sources

It is a well-established misunderstanding that military records are precise, comprehensive and accurate; sadly this is far from the truth and the problems inherent in first locating and then checking documents are not for the faint-hearted researcher. In addressing the history of airfields in the UK, the researcher has a variety of primary sources to consult; for the RAF the most in-depth, at least potentially, is the F540 Operational Record Book (ORB), a series of records now classified in the AIR 28 series by the National Archives at Kew, London. There are, however, two problems with this document: firstly, only RAF Stations, i.e. independent locations with a station headquarters, were required to compile and submit this monthly record and that parameter removed many of the wartime airfields and landing grounds; and, secondly, the quality of record is very variable. The researcher is invariably frustrated by the way in which such records were kept, the compiling officer

was following Air Ministry guidelines, but these took no account of the desires and interests of future historians! An airfield could, for example, have gone from a grass surface to a concrete runway with no mention at all in its ORB, and when you consider more minor building works the chances of a mention are even slimmer. Movements in and out of units may or may not be recorded – and even if mention is made there is no guarantee that the date given is accurate. This might sound strange, however it has to be remembered that these monthly ORBs were not compiled on a daily basis but were invariably put together in retrospect – at best, days after the end of the recorded month but perhaps weeks later.

I spent much of my RAF career compiling ORBs at squadron and station level – as a secondary duty that had to be fitted around my primary aircrew task – and the problems of pulling together information in retrospect, especially from units or individuals that were either too busy or disinterested was a major struggle. The net result was a submission that would get past the signatory (squadron or station commander) and satisfy both the higher command that saw it and the final recipients at Air Ministry/MoD. Because such records were sent via higher commands there was also an element of politics in their content, as few commanders would submit a 'warts and all' record that might ruffle feathers further up the chain. However, even with these constraints and problems, the ORB remains the core historical document at all levels of the RAF organization. To put any appreciable level of detail into the overall research of an airfield requires reference to the ORBs of the based units, those for the flying units being particularly helpful – but with the same set of difficulties outlined above. Squadron ORBs are contained in the AIR 27 series. Other unit records, flying and ground, can also be consulted and, indeed, for some airfields, especially major training units, the unit record is essentially the station record.

The SD161 'location on units' record is an excellent source for unit listings at a particular location for a given month. There is one major drawback, in that it is compiled from other inputs that may not, in themselves, be accurate or up to date; for example, the SD161 might list the presence of a particular squadron or other unit in its monthly entry for an airfield but, in fact, the move of that unit, whilst planned and authorized, might not have taken place or might have occurred at a slightly different time. It is a similar picture with the Secret Organizational Memoranda (SOM) files: these documents were the authorization for units to form, move, change command-allegiance, change name, disband, and so on, and as such they can prove very useful – as long as they are used with care. A planned and authorized action might subsequently be modified or cancelled and the researcher might not have picked up the amendment. An example of this in respect to airfields is the authorization under SOM 79/40 (dated 30 January 1940) for 'the requisitioning of land at Bysshe Court, Surrey as a RLG for Redhill, the site is 2½ miles West of Lingfield'. Two months later, however, SOM 194/40 (dated 11 March) stated 'Redhill is to use Penshurst as an RLG and the site at Bysshe Court is not required.'

For Royal Navy/Fleet Air Arm units the official record system is the Ship's Log, which applies to shore sites as well as floating vessels, and these documents can be even more frustrating, as they vary from diary format, often excellent and including photographs, to minimal factual statements that are of little use.

The USAAF units also submitted regular official reports and, as one airfield usually only housed a single Group, the records of that Group can provide some useful details, although they are primarily concerned with operations and not infrastructure.

It would, of course, be impossible to refer to every one of these sources when compiling a series of books such as the Crowood 'Military Airfields in Britain' series and the author freely acknowledges his debt to other researchers who have ploughed this field and produced excellent reference works. A great many of these secondary sources (a term that is no insult to these authors) have been used during the compilation of the Crowood series and a selection of the major ones is given below:

Halley, James J, *The Squadrons of the Royal Air Force and Commonwealth* (Air Britain)
Jefford, C G, *RAF Squadrons* (Airlife)
Sturtivant, Ray; Hamlin, John; Halley, James J, *RAF Flying Training and Support Units* (Air Britain)
Lake, Alan, *Flying Units of the RAF* (Airlife)
Sturtivant, Ray; Page, Gordon, *Royal Navy Aircraft, Serials and Units* (Air Britain)
Airfield Review, Airfield Research Group magazine (*see* below)
Freeman, Roger, *The Mighty Eighth* (Arms and Armour Press) – the impressive series of books by Roger on the 8th Air Force

Plus the author's own published works, such as *The Source Book of the RAF* (Airlife)

All good historians will confess that everything that appears in print contains errors; some of these are errors repeated from primary or secondary sources, some are typological (1942 and 1943 are a mere keystroke apart) and some are simply omissions where the author has not been able to fill in the gap or has completely missed a document. All of these errors will be found in this series – and I would welcome feedback so that any future updates can be more accurate and complete.

Where aircraft numbers are given as, for example, 16+7, this indicates the establishment of that type of IE (Initial Establishment) and IR (In-Use Reserve); in theory the unit is allocated that total number of the type – but this does not indicate the actual strength.

Photographs and Plans

Photographs and plans are an essential element of the research and presentation of airfield history and this series attempts to bring together one of the most comprehensive pictorial records yet published. For some airfields there is a plethora of plans, whilst for others the search for a period layout draws a blank. It is a great shame that virtually all of the civilian contractors involved in airfield construction did not maintain, or have subsequently disposed of, their records of this work. Official plans (Air Ministry Drawings) exist for various periods, particularly fine sets being available for late-1944 and the mid-1950s, but in both cases the surviving documents have, in typical military fashion, been amended to the latest issue; for example, airfields no longer in use in December 1944 have been removed from that volume. With the exception of the Air Ministry overall-layout drawings, most plans cover only the main infrastructure of the airfield itself – runways, peritrack, dispersal and hangars, ignoring the off-airfield sites such as accommodation and technical.

Most of the airfield plans used in this volume are **Crown Copyright via Air Historical Branch** unless otherwise stated.

Photographs are perhaps an even thornier issue and the quality and number of images varies hugely from airfield to airfield, with training bases being the most poorly represented. The RAF's security-conscious attitude meant that cameras were a real no-no at airfields and, other than occasional official or press sessions, there are massive gaps in the photo coverage. The situation at the USAAF bases was somewhat better, for both official and unofficial photographs; what makes this even

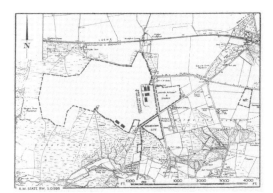

Plan of Warmwell from the 1944 RAF plans series.

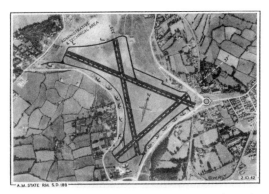

Air photo of Harrowbeer with runway layout emphasized, from the 1944 RAF plans series.

Oblique photo of Filton dated 14 May 1944.

Aerial shot of Dunkeswell showing dispersal area around one of the T2 hangars.

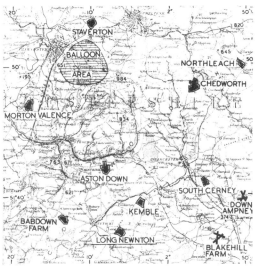

Airfield location map of Gloucestershire region, from the 1944 RAF plans series.

easier from the researcher's point of view is the ease of access to this material at the National Archives building in Maryland.

Wartime air-to-ground images are hard to find and, although it seems likely that every airfield in the UK was photographed on numerous occasions during the war, unearthing these images is never easy. The Luftwaffe produced excellent target folders, including aerial photos, of many British airfields and this source of material is superb when you can find it.

A number of photographic surveys of the UK have been flown over the past sixty years; indeed, according to some sources, the 7th Photographic Group flew a vertical survey of much of Britain during the war and this material would prove invaluable should it be easy to access, which sadly is not the case. Post-1945, airfields have been popular targets for reconnaissance squadrons to practice both vertical and oblique pinpoint-photography and thousands of negatives would have been exposed – but not necessarily printed or preserved. Keele University is the present home for tens of thousands of air-to-ground photos from World War Two onwards and almost every airfield in Britain is likely to be amongst the collection – if you can locate the individual site. There are three main 'national' collections of aviation images in the UK: the Imperial War Museum and RAF Museum, both in London, and the Fleet Air Arm Museum at Yeovilton. For the researcher/author this is a somewhat mixed blessing as, whilst the material can usually be studied by prior arrangement, it is often prohibitively expensive to acquire copies for publication. The majority of illustrations used in this series are from private collections and plans/diagrams are from official sources.

Pubs were a vital part of social life and every group of air force personnel had their preferred watering hole; the Royal Oak was used by personnel from Dunkeswell.

Pubs

For every airfield there is the question of drinking! All RAF aircrew and ground crew had their favourite pubs, and usually they went to different ones; likewise, different squadrons might adopt their own pub or pubs. Whilst regular drinking took place in the messes and the NAAFI, a trip down to the 'local' was an essential part of squadron life, with frequent reference to the 'boys' climbing into the Boss's car and tearing off to the pub. You only have to read any autobiography from a wartime-RAF chap to find reference to these forays – often with humorous results. The Americans were even keener on making use of local pubs and every airfield will have had one or more favourite watering holes. Although reference is made to pubs in some of the entries in this series, we have not included complete lists, as this information is not available. I would like to have included details of wartime pubs in these records but that level of research relies on people with local knowledge and interest – if you know of any pubs that fit this description then let me know and I will update the file!

Messes and Headquarters

Pre-war RAF stations included excellent living accommodation; indeed, one of the great advantages of an expansion-period officers' mess, for example, was that they all followed the same pattern and it was easy therefore to stagger from bar to accommodation wing without getting lost, no matter which airfield you were at! However, with the threat of air attack and with many airfields having little or no accommodation, the military adopted the course of 'acquiring' a suitable local establishment, which in many cases meant a stately home or, at least, very large house.

This type of building was taken over by HQ staff and also for use as officers' messes, with the frequent addition of a hutted 'village' in the grounds. As with pubs, this information is not always readily to hand, other than for major HQ-units, and I would like to hear from local researchers who can add details of houses taken over in this way. Perhaps the best known in the UK is the Petwood Hotel at Woodhall Spa, Lincolnshire, which was used as a mess by the officers of 617 Squadron, and which hosts numerous RAF reunions and is a great place to spend a weekend.

Visiting Airfields

The majority of airfield sites are *out of bounds*, either because they are still active military installations or, more commonly they are in private hands for agricultural or industrial use. While touring the countryside looking for airfields you will come across many variations on the 'KEEP OUT' sign, some couched in pleasant, but firm, tones and others somewhat more vehement in their opinion of any who would dare tread from the public paths. It is worth noting that footpaths exist over many of these airfields and so reference to a good OS Map (which is an essential part of any pack-up for the airfield tourer) will keep you on the straight and narrow. Sadly, the footpaths were not laid out with visiting airfield structures in mind and all too often all that is glimpsed is a building, often partly hidden by vegetation, often at some distance from the marked path. You can always try contacting the landowner to seek permission to enter the airfield site and this is certainly worth a try for a pre-planned visit – although finding contact details for landowners can be tricky. As with all outdoor activities you need to have the right clothing and equipment – stout, waterproof footwear (that is not allergic to mud) is an essential if you plan to walk the ground rather then observe from the side of the road. When it comes to photography, a long lens (up to 300mm) is always worth having, as you may not be able to get close to some structures.

A good military maxim is that 'time spent on reconnaissance is seldom wasted' and this equally applies to the research time you spend before taking to the field – study the maps and diagrams in this book, in conjunction with the OS Landranger map, and you will (hopefully) have a much more productive visit. These books are, of course, equally useful for the 'armchair visitor' and provide a wealth of information for those interested in a particular area or type of airfield.

Memorials

I have always been a 'people person' when it comes to aviation history and, to that end, I find the question of memorials fascinating, as these are a means of providing a visible link with, and recognition of, those who were involved with operations from the airfields. Any student of memorials will soon realize the variations that exist in this recognition – and it should be pointed out that the majority of airfields do not have a memorial. The regional variation is enormous and in large part reflects the type of organization operating in a region; for example, the USAAF bases are generally well represented with memorials, often comprising impressive stones complete with inscriptions, and in many cases twin white flag-poles from which to fly the Stars and Stripes and the Union Jack. This is in large part due to the strength of post-war associations amongst the American Groups and the creation of Anglo-American friendship groups. Likewise, the RCAF units, especially those of No.6 (RCAF) Group in Yorkshire, are well represented with memorials. Of the RAF operational commands only Bomber Command has an appreciable number of memorials at their former airfields, whilst for others, including Fighter Command, the situation is very variable, with some of the London/Kent Battle of Britain airfields having memorials – the one at Croydon is one of the finest in the UK – but with others having nothing. Taking the country as a whole, there have been two major 'memorial building' phases, the early 1980s and the early 1990s; however, over the last couple of years there has been another burst of activity, although not on the scale of the previous ones. It would be great if every airfield was provided with a memorial that recognized the role it and its personnel played in World War Two, and it is this conflict that memorials commemorate, but this laudable aim is unlikely ever to be achieved, although there are still groups and organizations

working towards the creation of such memorials. When looking for memorials it is not always a case of looking in the obvious places, such as the airfield site, as in many cases they are located in the nearby village, either on the village green or in the churchyard (or indeed the church itself). The entries in this airfield series give location details for memorials where appropriate and this will save many an hour of sometimes fruitless searching (been there!); however, I do not claim that I have listed them all or even that they are all where I say they are – so feel free to update our information!

Talking of churches, it is always worth a look in the local church and churchyard – which may not always be the one nearest to the airfield or the village with the same name as the airfield – for additional memorials, such as Books of Remembrance, and for grave stones. Many parish churchyards in the UK include Commonwealth War Grave Commission grave markers, although these do not always relate to the local airfield but might simply be the grave of a local person who had died whilst in military service. Don't, however, simply look for the CWGC markers,

Memorial at the gate of Moreton-in-Marsh airfield.

The control tower at Zeals (now a house) is one of the few surviving buildings at the airfield.

as many graveyards will contain other RAF (and even RFC) stones. Not all graves are in the War Graves plot and not all have the standard stone. I did not visit all local graveyards during this survey and so this information has been omitted – but I would be delighted if researchers were able to piece together these details for their airfields.

Non-Airfield Sites

Airfields are only part of the military aviation story and a variety of other locations played roles in the overall picture, from HQ units to training establishments and storage units. However, despite the importance of such sites, they have been omitted from this series except for passing reference where appropriate in an airfield entry. This has been done for reasons of space, as to include all the 'other' sites would have added a significant number of pages – and cost.

Notes on Using the Series

Unit Tables

There was much debate on how to present the unit tables, with some preferring a numerical list and others a chronological list. The 'solution' that has been adopted is as follows: unit tables are presented in four chronological divisions – Pre-1919 (World War One), 1919–1939 (inter-war), 1939–45 (World War Two) and Post-1945. This is not always ideal, but it does show major utilization of a given airfield by period. Where a unit is appropriate to more than one period it appears in each, although, where the overlap is a matter of months, the periods might overlap with the entry; for example, the following entry for Biggin Hill:

32Sqn   Sep 1932–Jan 1940   Bulldog, Gauntlet,
                                 Hurricane

In this case the squadron subsequently re-appeared at Biggin Hill and has a second entry in the 1939–1945 period.

During World War Two, and particularly at fighter and maritime bases, units moved around frequently and often were at an airfield for a matter of days or with brief periods of absence elsewhere. It would be impractical to list all these changes and so for some entries the symbol '+' appears alongside the entry.

This signifies 'not a continuous period'; for example, 79 Squadron's entry for Biggin Hill:

79Sqn   Mar 1940–10 May 1940;
          21 May 1940–8 Sep 1940+

The squadron spent time at Digby, Hawkinge, Sealand and Acklington during the period 21 May 1940–8 Sep 1940 and these dates bracket its appearance at Biggin Hill.

Within these broad divisions, squadrons are listed in numerical order and other units, listed after the squadrons, are in chronological order, as there is less likelihood that readers will scan these looking for a particular unit. All RAF and Fleet Air Arm units are listed first, followed by USAAF/USAF.

Only the major types on establishment with a unit are listed and the reader will often see reference to 'various': this means that the unit had such a diverse fleet that it has not been practicable to list every type. This is particularly true of training units during World War One, although a glance at the records of a World War Two Spitfire squadron might well reveal a Tiger Moth, Magister or even Hurricane on strength as a 'hack' aircraft.

Airfield Recording

As part of the on-going research into military airfields there is a vital role for local historians and enthusiasts – by becoming 'local experts' they can help fill in the detail. It is the detail, such as grave records, local pubs, present condition of the airfield and its associated structures, preserved material (museums and local collections), and photographs, that helps provide a more complete picture of the airfield and those who were once based there.

The example form provides a standard record-sheet and in conjunction with the Aviation History Centre we are encouraging individuals to become 'local representatives', in order that the detail can be added for every airfield in the UK. This is not, of course, a permit to go marching over fields claiming right of access! The normal procedures have to be followed, but a local representative can take the time to get to know the airfield and its surrounding area, talking to landowners for access and finding out such lost information as the pubs used by various units. This is a people task – asking questions and chasing up little bits of information with which to build the overall picture.

The Aviation History Centre has agreed to provide basic information as a starting point for anyone wishing to become a local representative and they have also pointed out that you do not actually need to be local – it may be that you have a particular interest in an operational Group, squadron or local area and would like to pursue that interest. Individuals are also not restricted to taking on a single airfield, but what is required is a responsible attitude when dealing with the landowners, an interest in finding out accurate information and a desire to share that information.

Airfield Research Group

It is worth considering joining the Airfield Research Group: this organization consists of individuals with an interest in research into and, to some extent, preservation of, airfields in the UK. They publish an excellent magazine (free to members) and the quality of research is superb. For further details contact: Hon. Secretary, Raymond Towler, 33A Earls Street, Thetford, Norfolk IP24 2AB.

AIRFIELD RECORD			
Airfield name		County	
Lat/Long		OS Map	
Nearest town/village		OS Grid	
AIRFIELD SURVEY			
Control Tower			
Hangars			
Runways			
Perimeter Track			
Dispersals			
Technical Buildings			
Admin Buildings			
Domestic Buildings			
Land Ownership			
Public Access			
ASSOCIATED SITES			
Memorial			
Church (graves?)			
Pubs			
House (mess or HQ)			
Museum			
Other Information			
Date of Record			
Recorded By			
NOTES: 1. Permission must be acquired before entering areas that are not public access. 2. Mark positions of buildings, memorials, etc on airfield plan/map. 3. A photo record should also be made.			
Aviation History Centre: navman678@hotmail.com; or via The Crowood Press			

Introduction – South-West England

This region, and in particular Wiltshire, has the historic claim of being at the forefront of the development of British military aviation, for it was in the Salisbury Plain area, long a centre of army training, that the first military airfields were constructed. The airfield at Larkhill is particularly noteworthy, as it was here that the Aeroplane Trials were held in 1912 to determine the aeroplane type best suited for development into the standard for army aviation. With new airfields at Upavon and Netheravon, military aviation was centred on this small area and, whilst aviation soon spread throughout the UK, this region remained at the forefront of the army co-operation role until after World War Two. This is not the place for a detailed history of military aviation in this region, but the following brief notes will help set the scene.

World War One

As with most of the UK, the South-West was not directly involved in operational flying, other than Home Defence and coastal patrol; the major air campaign took place over France and the Low Countries, but airfields such as those in this region played a vital role in training the pilots and observers who were so voraciously consumed by the front-line squadrons.

Thousands of aircrew were trained by the Training (Ex-Reserve) Squadrons, later Training Depot Stations, that sprang up throughout the region from late-1916, with the early airfields such as Netheravon and Upavon playing a major part in this task; Netheravon, for example, playing host to eight Training Squadrons in the period from 1915 to April 1918, when those still at the airfield combined to form two Training Depot Stations. Yatesbury even had two aerodromes adjacent to each other – No.1 and No.2 Camps, both heavily involved with training. This meant that the skies over Wiltshire, the busiest county in the region in terms of training bases, were filled with the buzzing of Avro 504s, BEs of various types, Camels, Snipes, RE8s, and virtually every training and operational type of World War One. It also meant that there were frequent accidents and fatalities, as combining pupil pilots with aircraft invariably led to crashes. The development of airfields in the region was almost constant throughout the war, with new sites and facilities being built almost up to the Armistice; indeed, the period from the formation of the RAF in April 1918 was one of the busiest, as it coincided with the German spring offensive and some of the hardest-fought air battles of the war.

Unlike other parts of England there was no real need for Home Defence, as the German Air Services

Salisbury Plain 1913 with senior officers admiring(?) one of the Army's new aeroplanes.

Line-up of Central Flying School (CFS) aircraft at Upavon in 1914.

did not send their airships or long-range bombers to targets in the region, other than on the occasional foray. The region did, however, play an important role in the maritime campaign to stem the impact caused by the German U-boats. By 1916 the submarines had started to have an effect on Allied coastal shipping and a number of RNAS Stations were created for use by airships or seaplanes. The U-boats continued to have the upper hand and further coastal stations were opened in 1917. The final U-boat offensive of spring 1918 was the most worrying of all and led to a major attempt by the Allies to create a string of airship stations and airfields, to provide cover for all convoys and patrols over likely U-boat hunting grounds. A string of sub-stations was laid out for the major airship base at Mullion, each with one or two Coastal or SS-Type airships and thousands of hours of patrols were flown. The RAF took over the entire system on its formation in 1918 and established a series of Special Duties Flights at a number of the existing airfields, most of these being equipped with the DH6. Nevertheless, in comparison to other parts of Britain, this region was, with the exception of training, almost a backwater in World War One.

Between the Wars

The South-West's airfields did not escape the mass disbandment of units and closure of airfields – by the early 1920s, most of the airfields had returned to agriculture, many had had their buildings removed but, at some places, the structures were left in place and found other uses. However, a number of airfields survived – for example, Netheravon and Old Sarum. The latter became home to the newly formed (at Stonehenge) School of Army Co-operation from January 1921 but, throughout the 1920s and early 1930s, Old Sarum underwent virtually no development in infrastructure, although the part it played in

developing the army co-operation role was to be crucial in the next war. By the early 1930s the hunt was on for new airfields and, whilst the initial phase of the RAF's Expansion Period focused on operational stations further to the east, a number of airfields were put into development in this region. For many, this was still a grass airfield with few facilities – the intended role being training.

World War Two

The geographic area covered in this book ranges from the extreme west of England, along the Atlantic shores of Devon and Cornwall, where the major operational involvement in World War Two was with the maritime campaign, to the southern coast of Dorset, well within range of the enemy's bombers and close enough for Allied tactical aircraft to undertake fighter-bomber operations, to the heartland of Wiltshire and the surrounding counties, which became an important area of airborne operations and housed hundreds of transport aircraft and gliders, both British and American. However, as with World War One, this region was very much involved with flying training and many of its airfields, from major parent-units to satellites and relief landing-grounds, were part of the very large aircrew-training system.

Coastal Operations

The geographic position of south-west England made it ideal for maritime operations and Coastal Command units carried out defensive patrols, anti-submarine operations and offensive anti-shipping strikes from airfields such as Chivenor and St Eval. The period 1942–1943 was particularly intense, as the Battle of the Atlantic had to be fought and won if

Singapore of 209 Squadron at Mount Batten, September 1937.

Boscombe Down in 1934; one of the most impressive inter-war airfields in this region.

Wellington XIV of 407 Squadron at Chivenor in December 1944.

Liberator of VB110 at Dunkeswell; the US Navy flew anti-submarine ops from two airfields in Devon.

the Allied build-up of men and material for the invasion of Europe was to succeed. Without the air campaign over the Bay of Biscay the German U-boats would have been far more effective. The Americans also arrived to take part in the maritime war and a US Navy Group was stationed in Devon, making use of Dunkeswell – 'Mudville Heights' as it was 'affectionately' known – and other airfields. Whilst much of the RAF's maritime war from this region was flown by Whitleys and Wellingtons, the latter's Leigh Light operations from Chivenor being particularly noteworthy, Devon was home to a highly effective Australian Sunderland unit: 10 Squadron RAAF spent much of the war at Mount Batten and had an excellent record, flying thousands of hours on patrols over the grey waters – and making a number of successful attacks on U-boats. With the preponderance of naval bases along the south coast it was also inevitable that the Fleet Air Arm would look for airfields in the region, both for training and as shore bases for disembarked squadrons. Major naval airfields were developed at Yeovilton, Henstridge and elsewhere.

Airborne Operations

When the Allies assaulted Normandy on 6 June 1944, the airborne-operation element was the largest of its kind ever mounted, with thousands of highly trained troops being delivered by parachute or glider. This region played a major part in this offensive, as it was home to both RAF and USAAF transport units.

At 2249 hours on 5 June, seven Dakotas of 271 Squadron left Down Ampney towing Horsa gliders of 'E' Squadron, Glider Pilot Regiment (GPR), destined for LZ 'V' and the assault on the Merville battery. Over the next twenty minutes, Dakota, Halifax and Albemarle tugs lifted Horsas from Blakehill

Farm, Tarrant Rushton, Harwell and Brize Norton as advance parties for the various assault elements. Two groups of transport aircraft carried paratroops to act as pathfinders, dropping on the LZs and marking them for the subsequent glider assault-parties. Amongst these advanced units was that tasked with seizing the two bridges. Three gliders were allocated to each of the bridges, the intention being to land as close to the targets as possible, in the dark, and, with the benefit of surprise, to overpower the defenders and remove any demolition charges. Of the six gliders involved in this *coup de main* operation, five landed spot-on their assigned positions; the sixth, due to an error by the tug aircraft, ended up some eight miles away (although the soldiers managed to fight their way back to the bridges).

The final British part of the airborne assault took place on the evening of 6 June when, under Operation *Mallard*, 256 combinations took off from seven airfields in southern England en route to Normandy. The first aircraft airborne were Dakotas of 271 Squadron from Down Ampney at 1840 hours towing Horsa gliders; over the next one hour and twenty minutes the remainder of the force, comprising 30 Hamilcar and 226 Horsa gliders, took to the air behind their tows: these comprising seventy-four Dakotas from 48 and 271 Squadrons (Down Ampney), 512 Squadron (Broadwell) and 575 Squadron (Broadwell); sixty-nine Stirlings from 190 and 620 Squadrons (Fairford), and 196 and 299 Squadrons (Keevil); eighty-one Albemarles from 296 and 297 Squadrons (Brize Norton), and 295 and 570 Squadrons (Harwell); and, finally, thirty-two Halifaxes from 298 and 644 Squadrons (Tarrant Rushton). Out of this air armada one Horsa crashed on take-off, three broke their tows en route and three were forced to ditch in the Channel; the remaining gliders, including all the Hamilcars with their precious heavy weapons and armoured vehicles, made it safely down to the LZs – the first landings taking place around 2051 hours. A further fifty RAF Dakotas undertook supply-dropping missions. Over the next few days further drops were made, including the all-important re-supply missions, and, despite the problems that had been encountered and the losses suffered, it was, without doubt, an incredible achievement. Many of the region's airborne-forces airfields were back in action again in September 1944 (Operation *Market-Garden*) and in March 1945 (Operation *Varsity*).

Training

Despite the maritime and airborne operations participation it would be fair to say that the region's major role was flying training, largely because it was a bit more out of reach of enemy air attack; although a number of airfields were attacked, these were small-scale raids causing little damage. Training bases, such as South Cerney and Little Rissington, trained hundreds of aircrew and often had over 100 trainers on strength, which meant they had to make use of vari-

ous satellites and RLGs. Bomber training also took place, with No.21 Operational Training Unit at Moreton-in-Marsh providing bomber crews and also contributing to bombing ops from time to time. Training of army co-operation pilots remained a major task for the likes of Old Sarum, but also involved other airfields, such as Oatlands Hill. The skies over the region were seldom quiet, as pupils pounded the circuit or flew navigation exercises.

Other Roles

The South-West also housed a number of aircraft factories, some of pre-war origin and some built as shadow factories to disperse and increase production – typical of the shadow factories was that at South Marston (Swindon), which was used by a number of manufacturers and produced or modified thousands of aircraft. The Westland plants at Yeovil and Weston-super-Mare were busy throughout the war, whilst Glosters (Brockworth) not only produced standard service-types but also developed the RAF's first jet, the Meteor.

Whilst the region was not in the forefront of the

Impressive line-up of Airborne Forces Halifax tugs and gliders at Tarrant Rushton in June 1944 for the D-Day airborne assault.

No.87 Squadron aircrew and aircraft pose at Charmy Down in 1942.

Battle of Britain or the Blitz, it did require fighter defences, although it was late in acquiring them, as the RAF had not expected Britain to be attacked from airfields in France. There was something of a panic in 1940 to acquire airfields for fighter use, especially near the south coast, where there were many attractive targets. Shortage of airfields and shortage of fighters meant that Gladiators flew from Plymouth as one of the city's main air defences. The switch to night attack gave even more problems, as the real night-fighters (Blenheims and Beaufighters) were needed elsewhere – so Defiants and Hurricanes appeared. One squadron in particular, 87 Squadron, had a roving existence that saw it appear at a number of airfields in the region – from the Scilly Isles to Somerset, with Charmy Down one of its main bases. When the RAF turned to the offensive, there were airfields in this region well placed for offensive ops, such as Predannack, Bolt Head and Warmwell; all of these were used by fighter and fighter-bomber detachments and as re-arm and refuel bases.

Cold War and Beyond

The pattern followed that of World War One, with squadrons disbanding and airfields closing, although, in general terms, it was the early 1950s before the first phase of land disposals took place. The Korean War and the Cold War between the Russians and the West led to the re-opening of some airfields and the re-birth of training units to give refresher training to aircrew that had barely had time put on civilian clothes. Many of the airfields that had been used for training in World War Two were brought back into this use, but it was all very short-lived and by the late-1950s the panic was over and the post-war RAF (and FAA) settled down to the real Cold War. The Americans had taken over a number of airfields for use by detachments of nuclear-armed bombers from Strategic Air Command, Fairford being one of the locations for this, but, by the early 1960s, most of this was over.

Throughout the 1970s and 1980s the region was involved in various aspects of the Cold War, from transport operations out of Lyneham to monitoring Soviet naval activity from St Eval and St Mawgan. The most recent set of defence cuts (1990s) saw the axing of a number of bases and, by the turn of the Millennium, there were only a handful of bases left in service, such as Lyneham (the only significant RAF location in Wiltshire but now scheduled to close in 2010–2012), Yeovilton (the Fleet Air Arm's sole jet-operating base), Fairford (with no based units but increasingly busy with operational detachments), Boscombe Down (one of the bright spots, in that it is still used for trials and evaluation) . . . and that's about it for major airfields.

The following counties are covered in this volume:

Channel Islands (CI)
Cornwall (Corn)
Devon (Dev)
Dorset (Dors)
Gloucestershire (Glos)
Somerset (Som)
Wiltshire (Wilt)

Great public relations shot May 1964, Yeovilton with Buccaneers and Sea Vixens.

Operational Period Matrix

Site	World War One	World War Two	Post-1950[1]	Site	World War One	World War Two	Post-1950[1]
Alton Barnes (Wilt)	—	X	—	Northleach (Glos)	—	X	—
Aston Down (Glos)	—	X	—	North Stoke (Glos)	—	X	—
Babdown Park (Glos)	—	X	—	Oatlands Hill (Wilt)	—	X	—
Barnsley Park (Glos)	—	X	—	Okehampton (Dev)	—	X	—
Barnstaple (Dev) – see Chivenor	—	—	—	Old Sarum (Wilt)	—	X	—
Bibury (Glos)	—	X	—	Overley (Glos)	—	X	—
Blakehill Farm (Glos)	—	X	—	Overton Heath (Wilt)	—	X	—
Bolt Head (Dev)	—	X	—	Padstow (Corn)	X	—	—
Boscombe Down (Wilt)	—	X	X	Perranporth (Corn)	—	X	—
Brockworth (Glos)	—	X	X	Portland (Dors)	X	X	X
Bude (Corn) — see Mullion	X	—	—	Portreath (Corn)	—	X	—
Castle Combe (Wilt)	—	X	—	Prawle Point (Dev)	X	—	—
Charlton Horethorne (Som)	—	X	—	Predannack (Corn)	—	X	—
Charmy Down (Som)	—	X	—	Ramsbury (Wilt)	—	X	—
Chedworth (Glos)	—	X	—	Rendcombe (Glos)	X	—	—
Chickerell (Dors)	—	X	—	Roborough (Dev)	—	X	X
Chivenor (Dev)	—	X	X	Rollestone (Wilt)	X	X	—
Cleave (Corn)	—	X	—	St Eval (Corn)	—	X	X
Clyffe Pypard (Wilt)	—	X	—	St Justs (Corn)	—	X	—
Colerne (Wilt)	—	X	X	St Marys (Scilly Isles)	—	X	—
Culdrose (Corn)	—	X	X	St Mawgan (Corn)	—	X	X
Culmhead (Som)	—	X	—	St Merryn (Corn)	—	X	X
Davidstow Moor (Corn)	—	X	—	Sandbanks	X	—	—
Down Ampney (Glos)	—	X	—	Shrewton (Wilt)	—	X	—
Down Farm (Glos)	—	X	—	South Cerney (Glos)	—	X	X
Dunkeswell (Wilt)	—	X	—	South Marston (Wilt)	—	X	X
Everleigh (Wilt)	—	X	—	Southrop (Glos)	—	X	—
Exeter (Dev)	—	X	X	Staverton (Glos)	—	X	—
Fairford (Glos)	—	X	X	Stoke Orchard (Glos)	—	X	—
Falmouth (Corn)	X	X	—	Stonehenge (Wilt)	X	—	—
Filton (Glos)	—	X	X	Tarrant Rushton (Dors)	—	X	X
Guernsey (CI)	—	X	—	Thruxton (Wilt)	—	X	—
Haldon (Dev)	—	X	—	Tilshead (Wilt)	—	X	—
Hamworthy (Dors)	—	X	—	Toller (Dors) – see Mullion			
Harrowbeer (Dev)	—	X	—	Torquay (Dev)	X	—	—
Henstridge (Som)	—	X	—	Townsend (Wilt)	—	X	—
High Post (Wilt)	—	X	—	Trebelzue (Corn) – see St Mawgan			
Hullavington (Wilt)	—	X	X	Treligga (Corn)	—	X	—
Jersey (CI)	—	X	—	Tresco (Scilly Isles)	X	—	—
Keevil (Wilt)	—	X	—	Upavon (Wilt)	X	—	—
Kemble (Glos)	—	X	—	Upottery (Dev)	—	X	—
Laira (Dev) – see Mullion	—	—	—	Upton – see Mullion			
Lake Down (Wilt)	X	—	—	Warmwell (Dors)	—	X	—
Larkhill (Wilt)	X	X	—	Weston super Mare (Som)	—	X	X
Leighterton (Glos)	X	—	—	Weston Zoyland (Som)	—	X	—
Little Rissington (Glos)	—	X	X	Westward Ho! (Dev)	X	—	—
Long Newnton (Glos)	—	X	—	Whitchurch (Som)	—	X	—
Lulsgate Bottom (Som)	—	X	—	Windrush (Glos)	—	X	—
Lyneham (Wilt)	—	X	—	Winkleigh (Dev)	—	X	—
Manningford (Wilt)	—	X	—	Worth Matravers (Dors)	—	X	—
Merifield (Corn)	X	—	—	Wroughton (Wilt)	—	X	—
Merryfield (Som)	—	X	—	Yate (Glos)	—	X	—
Minchinhampton (Glos) – see Aston Down				Yatesbury (Wilt)	X	X	—
Moreton (Dors)	X	—	—	Yeovil (Som)	—	X	—
Moreton-in-Marsh (Glos)	—	X	—	Yeovilton (Som)	—	X	X
Moreton Valence (Glos)	—	X	X	Zeals (Wilt)	—	X	—
Mount Batten (Dev)	—	X	—				
Mullion (Corn)	X	—	—				
Netheravon (Wilt)	X	X	—				
Newlyn (Corn)	X	—	—				
New Zealand Farm (Wilt)	—	X	—				

[1]Post-1950 has been chosen as many airfields were not abandoned until 1946–47 and most sites not actually disposed of until the early 1950s. This refers to airfields operational during the Cold War period of the 1950s–1970s.

ALTON BARNES

County: Wiltshire

UTM/Grid: OS Map 163 – SU100620
Lat/Long: N51°21.23 W001°51.23
Nearest Town: Devizes 5 miles to west

The grass airfield at Alton Barnes was hard to distinguish from its surroundings, but the canal helped.

HISTORY

The airfield at Alton Barnes was used as an RLG for the Central Flying School, based at Upavon, from August 1940 to around September 1941 and was one of three local airfields performing this function during this period. Actually, the site had been in use since late-summer 1935 by CFS as a practice forced-landing ground and the farmer was paid an annual 'rent' for this use, although at this stage it was still literally a field – with a windsock. At the end of August 1939, the farmer was told that the land was being requisitioned for use as an RLG, which also involved additional surrounding land to provide a large-enough area. It remained little more than a field until late-1941, when development into a 'standard' RLG

was undertaken; however, the Germans has already taken note of its position and, by mid-1940, Alton Barnes had a Luftwaffe target-folder complete with aerial photo.

With the end of CFS use, Alton Barnes was allocated as an RLG for No.29 EFTS, based at Clyffe Pypard; the Tiger Moths and Magisters of this unit made use of the airfield from December 1941 to July 1945. The RLG upgrade took place from December 1941 to June 1942 and land was cleared to provide a roughly rectangular landing-area, bounded to the south by the Kennet and Avon canal and on the other three sides by roads. Actually, it was provided with excellent accommodation – far better than many

RLGs – with a range of buildings around the sides of the airfield but mainly to the east. The site underwent further development during the war and, by the time of the 1944 survey, it was using four grass-strips and had ten Blister hangars; there was also a Sommerfeld Track perimeter track and, whilst the data sheet says that no dispersals were provided, the plan shows twenty-four dispersals, with many of these having a Sommerfeld Track surface. The tracking was laid down over the winter of 1943–1944 in an attempt to alleviate the waterlogging problems that had dogged the airfield.

From its re-opening on 3 June 1942, Alton Barnes was used by 'A' and 'B' Flights of the EFTS, with Tiger Moths undertaking basic pilot-training. May brought a change of 'customer', with the emphasis being on training Army glider pilots, as the airborne force build-up began in earnest. However, this was short-lived and, by the end of the year, the usual routine of RAF pilot training was once more in place. It was not the end of glider involvement, as the Operational and Refresher Training Unit (ORTU) from Thruxton used the airfield for a few weeks in early 1944.

The navy arrived in October 1944, with the EFTS taking on some naval-pilot training; the pupil pilots travelled daily from Clyffe Pypard, as accommodation at Alton Barnes was limited. Pupil pilots continued to 'bash' the circuit at Alton Barnes and carry out general handling in the local area to the end of the war, although numbers started to decline in early 1945. By the end of the first week of July all aircraft had left and, on 9 July, the airfield was reduced to Care and Maintenance – although little of either actually took place. Two years later the site was released and returned to agriculture, with most buildings soon vanishing. There is now little trace of the RAF airfield of Alton Barnes.

UNITS

1939–1945

CFS	Aug 1940–Sep 1941	various
29 EFTS	Dec 1941–9 Jul 1945	Tiger Moth, Magister
ORTU	Jan–Feb 1944	various

MEMORIAL

1. Plaque mounted on air raid shelter, inscribed:

This memorial on the only surviving air raid shelter marks the site of RAF Alton Barnes which was used as an airfield for training between 1939–45, CFS-Upavon operated here until 1941 when the site was transferred to No.29 EFTS Clyffe Pypard. The memorial is

The main occupants of the airfield were Tiger Moths, primarily with No.29 EFTS (via Rod Priddle)

AIRFIELD DATA DEC 1944

Command:	Flying Training Command	Runway surface:	Grass
Function:	EFTS RLG	Hangars:	Standard Blister × 6, Extended-Over Blister × 4
Runways:	NE/SW 1,100yd	Dispersals:	Nil
	E/W 870yd	Personnel:	Officers – Nil
	NW/SE 870yd		Other Ranks – 130
	N/S 820yd		

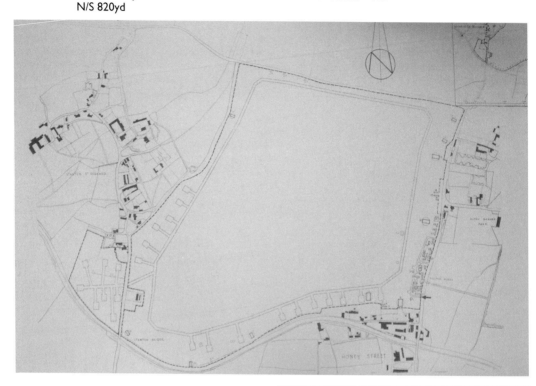

dedicated to those who lost their lives whilst training here:

P/O K J Holmes DFC RAF 18th June 1941
P/O A Gibbons RAFVR 18th June 1941
Sgt K O Bate RAFVR 18th June 1941
Sq Ldr W B Beale RAF 4th September 1941
P/O G H Brown RAFVR 4th September 1941
'Sunward I've climbed and joined the tumbling. . . Put out my hand and touched the face of God.' WHMS

The memorial was unveiled on 18 September 1999 by Group Captain Mark Stevens from Boscombe Down.

2. Near the canal is a stone cairn with a plaque marking the crash of an Albemarle from Keevil – see Keevil entry for details.

Located on one of the air raid shelters, the memorial records names of those killed training at the airfield.

ASTON DOWN
(Minchinhampton)

County: Gloucestershire

UTM/Grid: OS Map 163 – SO912010
Lat/Long: N51°42.30 W02°07.45
Nearest Town: Stroud 4 miles to north-west

Aston Down airfield is in good condition, as this recent air view shows, and is now home to a very active glider club.

HISTORY

For twelve months in the latter part of World War One, the airfield at Minchinhampton was one of the main training bases for the Australian Flying Corps (AFC). The airfield was situated between Stroud and Gloucester, near the village of Aston Down, and 170 acres of land were acquired in late-1917 for the construction of what was to be No.1 Station of the AFC. With a large rectangular flying-area bounded by a range of buildings, including four General Service sheds of 170 × 100ft, the airfield was, for the period, well equipped. The first of the training squadrons was listed in the RFC sequence – No.33 Training (Ex-Reserve) Squadron – but this arrived at Cirencester in mid-1917, as its intended base at Minchinhampton was not ready. Indeed, it is unclear if the squadron moved to the new airfield before being re-designated as No.8 (Training) Squadron, Australian Flying Corps in January 1918. It was under the latter designation that it became the first unit to use Minchinhampton. As with all training units, it used a variety of aircraft types, although the Avro 504 was one of the main trainers.

This squadron departed to Leighterton after a few

During World War One the site was known as Minchinhampton SE5; this shot shows SE5As of No.6 (Training) Squadron of the Australian Flying Corps.

weeks but, in April, the airfield received two training squadrons: No.5 from Shawbury and No.6 from Ternhill. These, too, operated a variety of types, including operational types such as the Pup, DH6, Camel and SE5a. By mid-1918 it was a busy airfield, with fifty or sixty aircraft on strength, plenty of flying and a number of crashes. The training units were tasked with keeping the AFC's front-line squadrons in France topped-up with pilots and, during the intense battles of 1918, this meant a steady stream of pilots. However, with the sudden end to the war, the training requirement came to an end and the Australians were keen to return home. The two training units disbanded in May and June 1919 and the airfield was sold-off the following year, the ground once more becoming fields.

Fifteen years later the RAF was searching for new sites and, as was often the case, interest was shown in World War One locations. A parcel of land at Aston Down was acquired in the mid-1930s for development into an airfield, the reasonably flat and well-drained Downland being ideal for rapid development.

No.7 Aircraft Storage Unit formed here in 1938, but was re-designated as No.20 Maintenance Unit in October the same year, as part of No.24 Group. The role was, initially, equipment storage, but this was soon changed to aircraft storage and the preparation of aircraft for delivery to squadrons. This remained one of the major roles for Aston Down throughout its RAF career, although 'ownership' changed through various Wings and Groups. The MU used a number of SLGs during its time at Aston, the last of these, Abbots Bromley, going out of use in 1949. Finally, in September 1960, Aston Down's MU role came to an end when its task was absorbed by No.5 MU at Kemble.

Fighter Command's No.12 Group formed a Group Pool unit at the airfield in September 1939 and Gladiators and Hurricanes were used to give pilots continuation flying after they had finished their training, in order to maintain a pool of pilots ready for sending to front-line units. The station was officially transferred to Fighter Command and additional buildings were constructed. No.5 Operational Training Unit was formed from the Group Pool on 15 March 1940, its role being to train fighter pilots for No.10 Group, for which task it was initially equipped with Gladiators and Blenheims. On 1 November it was re-designated as No.55 OTU, by which time its strength had grown to over eighty aircraft, the majority being Hurricanes and Blenheims, along with Masters and a few Defiants. The Blenheims and Defiants were passed to No.54 OTU at Church Fenton for training night-fighter crews and, in March, the rest of the unit moved to Usworth. By this time, construction of hard runways was underway, but Aston Down had only a short break before its next training unit arrived, the primarily Hurricane-equipped No.52 OTU moving in from Debden in August. This unit continued to grow and, subsequently, operated satellites at Chedworth (from August 1942) and Charmy Down (from August 1943), with Spitfires becoming the major type from late-1941.

There was an intensive two-year use by this OTU and Aston trained a great many pilots in this period, the facilities at the airfield undergoing periodic improvement to suit the increasing training workload.

August 1943 brought one of Fighter Command's most important, yet little known, units to the airfield, the Fighter Leaders School moving in from Charmy Down. The name was attached to the resident OTU as No.52 OTU (FLS) and the aircraft establishment was based on more than thirty Spitfires, although the FLS used a variety of types as part of its training. The designation was changed in October 1943 to No.52 OTU (Fighter Command School of Tactics). By the time it moved to Millfield in January 1944, the unit had over sixty Spitfires, plus a number of Typhoons and Hurricanes, in addition to Masters and other support types.

As the unit list shows, various other training and support units operated from Aston Down, including the Anson air ambulances of No.1311 Flight, as well as at least two operational squadrons. Mitchells of 180 Squadron used Aston Down as a detachment airfield from their home base at Dunsfold, from summer 1943 to spring 1944. The experienced army co-operation unit, 4 Squadron, arrived from Sawbridgeworth in January 1944, bringing its Mustangs and, unusually for an AC unit, Mosquito XVIs. In January, the squadron also acquired Spitfire XIs. However, in March they returned to Sawbridgeworth.

However, it was training units that remained most

A poor quality view of circa 1943 with inked-in runways and hangars.

Aston was used by a number of Typhoon-equipped training units from summer 1944; this is not an Aston Down picture.

important and, from summer 1944, the major unit was No.3 Tactical Exercise Unit – whose main role was teaching ground-attack, including rocket-projectile ops, to Typhoon pilots. Whereas Spitfires had once dominated the dispersals, their place was now taken by the Typhoons and, by October, the unit had an establishment of sixty-four of these, plus ten Mustangs and assorted other aircraft. In December the TEU was renamed as No.55 OTU and the training commitment was increased and diversified, although ground-attack remained the major task. This unit saw out the rest of the war at Aston Down and, at one point, its impressive establishment included 107 Typhoons, fourteen Masters and five Martinets. The unit disbanded on 14 June 1945. The data sheet for 1944 indicates how the airfield had grown; its facilities included fifty hangars, although twenty-three of these were Robins and the large number is mainly due to the presence of the MU.

In the immediate post-war period the airfield was home to No.2 Ferry Pool, this unit being part of No.41 Group and forming at Aston Down on 1 December. It operated a variety of types as required by No.20 MU, although Ansons were the main transport type for ferrying of crews. For the 'casual observer' Aston Down would have appeared a strange place in the post-war years, as it became a major aircraft-storage site, with around 1,000 'no longer needed' aircraft on-site. The fate of most of these aircraft was as scrap, but some were used for experiments in open-storage preservation. Aircraft were given an all-over protective covering but, unlike dry storage-areas such as Davis Montham in the USA, temperate Gloucestershire was not as forgiving and the technique was a failure.

The MU and its associated ferry organization were kept busy. The designation changed, in February 1952, to No.2 Home Ferry Unit and, in June, it became part of Transport Command. However, on 1 February 1953, the Home Ferry Unit was raised to squadron status as 187 Squadron, initial equipment being Anson C.19s, although these were subsequently joined by Anson C.12s and Varsity T.1s. The unit finally disbanded in September 1957 and the MU closed in 1960. Some of the facilities continued to be used by No.5 MU from Kemble and September 1966 saw CFS transfer its Jet Provost task-work from Fairford to Aston Down, but this was primarily as an RLG and not a based arrangement. This latter remained in force until 1976.

Aston Down, which still appears in pristine condition (with the exception of one of the runways, which has all but vanished), is now home to the Cotswold Gliding Club and some of the hangars are still used for storage.

DECOY SITE

Q   Horsley   ST865963

Lancaster making a low fly-by, probably early 1946.

UNITS

Pre-1919

8 (T) Sqn AFC	14 Jan 1918–25 Feb 1918	various
5 (T) Sqn AFC	2 Apr 1918–May 1919	various
6 (T) Sqn AFC	25 Apr 1918–Jun 1919	various

1939–1945

4 Sqn	3 Jan 1944–3 Mar 1944	Mustang, Mosquito, Spitfire
180 Sqn det	Aug 1943–Apr 1944	Mitchell
12 Gp Pool	15 Sep 1939–6 Mar 1940	Gladiator, Hurricane
5 OTU	15 Mar 1940–1 Nov 1940	
55 OTU	1 Nov 1940–14 Mar 1941	Blenheim, Defiant, Hurricane
52 OTU	25 Aug 1941–25 Jan 1944	Spitfire, Master
9 FPP	Sep 1941–Jun 1945	Anson
81 Gp CF	22 Dec 1941–15 Apr 1943	various
FLS	16 Aug 1943–26 Jan 1944	Spitfire + various
84 Gp SU	14 Feb 1944–10 Jul 1944	
1311 Flt	21 May 1944–10 Jul 1944	Anson
27 Gp CF	May 1944–22 Jan 1945	various
5 OADU	5 Jun 1944–31 Jan 1945	Anson
3 TEU	Jul 1944–Dec 1944	Typhoon
55 OTU	18 Dec 1944–14 Jun 1945	Typhoon, Master

Post-1945

187 Sqn	1 Feb 1953–2 Sep 1957	Anson, Varsity
2 FP	1 Dec 1945–7 Feb 1952	various
2 HFU	7 Feb 1952–1 Feb 1953	Anson
1689 Flt	6 Mar 1946–8 Apr 1953	Wellington, Harvard, Oxford
83 GS	13 Oct 1946–1955	Cadet, Sedbergh
CFS	19 Sep 1966–Feb 1976	Jet Provost

AIRFIELD DATA DEC 1944

Command:	Fighter Command	Runway surface:	Hardcore and tarmac
Function:	Tactical Exercise Unit, Parent	Hangars:	Robin × 23, Blister × 8, Bellman × 6, Type E × 6, Type D × 4, Type L × 2, Type C × one
Runways:	036 deg 1,600 × 50yd	Dispersals:	44
	094 deg 1,100 × 50yd	Personnel:	Officers – 95 (11 WAAF)
	164 deg 1,100 × 50yd		Other Ranks – 2,240 (399 WAAF)

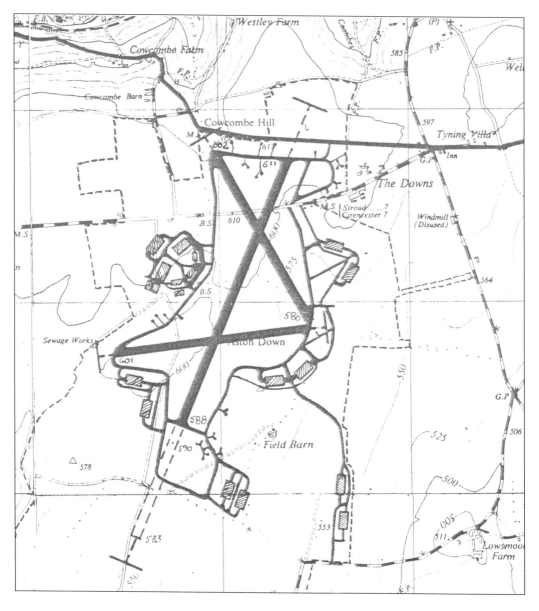

BABDOWN FARM

County: Gloucestershire

UTM/Grid: OS Map 163 – ST845938
Lat/Long: N51°38.34 W002°13.27
Nearest Town: Tetbury 3 miles to east

HISTORY

Babdown Farm spent the first part of the war as a Relief Landing Ground for Hullavington, which was home to the diverse training fleet of No.9 Flying Training School. The airfield, named after the nearby farm and situated on a wide, flat area just west of the village of Beverston, was laid out in late-1939 and early 1940, becoming available for use in summer 1940. The airfield was initially used for night flying from the parent station and, for some strange reason, it specialized in this activity for the first period of its existence. This was a simple grass field with few facilities when it first opened, but improvements were gradually made, which, subsequently, included hangars and accommodation.

The FTS operated a variety of trainer types, but the night flying was initially carried out by Audaxes and Harts, these delightful bi-planes now performing in the training role. As with most RLGs the intensity of use is often hard to determine and the records are often lost within the records of the parent unit. The FTS also operated Hurricanes and Masters and these, too, appeared at Babdown, as did the Harvard, which from May 1940 was meant to be the main trainer but which was in short supply. In February 1942, the FTS became No.9 (Pilots) Advanced Flying Unit, but little else changed and the Oxford and Harvard remained the main types, with Babdown still operating as an RLG for Hullavington. In August, the PAFU moved north to Errol in Scotland, but the sound of Oxfords continued, as Babdown became a satellite airfield for No.3 Flying Instructors School (Advanced), whose main base was at Castle Combe.

AIRFIELD DATA DEC 1944

Command:	Flying Training Command	Runway surface:	Grass
Function:	(Pilot) Advanced Flying Unit, Parent	Hangars:	Blister × 4, 'C' Type (?) × 2
Runways:	343 deg 1,203yd	Dispersals:	Nil
	123 deg 1,013yd	Personnel:	Officers – 72 (4 WAAF)
			Other Ranks – 720 (217 WAAF)

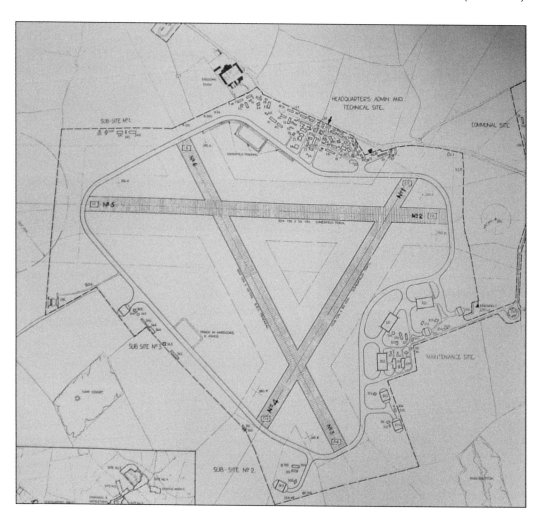

However, the period from February onwards appears to have been one of reduced usage, as Babdown underwent construction to bring it to full RLG status; this included laying two Sommerfeld Track runways in place of the previous grass strips. It is interesting to note that the 1944 survey states there were two grass runways but, in fact, the airfield appears to have been given three Sommerfeld strips in the standard triangu-lar pattern, along with a connecting perimeter track.

The main work was completed by August 1942 and the FIS was able to take full advantage of the new facilities, although once again the focus was on night flying. Although now designated for use by the Spitfires of No.52 OTU as an RLG, there was proba-bly little use by that unit during this period.

The FIS made use of Babdown to September 1943

and was followed by No.3 (P)AFU for a few weeks in September and October 1943 but, in the latter month, No.15 (P)AFU moved to the airfield from Andover. The PAFU remained in residence for the rest of the war and its establishment of over 100 Airspeed Oxfords certainly kept the circuit at Babdown busy. The unit used a main RLG at Castle Combe from November 1943, but also made limited use of Bath Racecourse as an RLG the following spring. No.1532 Beam Approach Training Flight, also equipped with Oxfords, was attached to the PAFU throughout the period.

The airfield was not immediately abandoned in the post-war period but, with the departure of its flying unit, was allocated as a sub-site for No.7 Maintenance Unit. This MU was headquartered at Quedgeley and used Babdown from July 1945 to September 1950.

With the exception of the technical area centred on the hangars, little now remains of Babdown Farm airfield; the general pattern can be seen from the air, as part of the perimeter track survives on the north side and soil and crop marks still show where the rest of the perimeter track ran.

UNITS

1939–1945

9 FTS	3 Aug 1940–14 Feb 1942	various
9 PAFU	14 Feb 1942–Aug 1942	Harvard, Oxford
3 FIS(A)	8 Aug 1942–30 Sep 1943	Oxford
1532Flt	13 May 1943–15 Jun 1945	Oxford
15 (P)AFU	28 Oct 1943–19 Jun 1945	Oxford

BARNSLEY PARK

County: Gloucestershire

UTM/Grid: OS map 163 – SP075075
Lat/Long: N51°45.97 W001°53.56
Nearest Town: Cirencester 4 miles to south-west

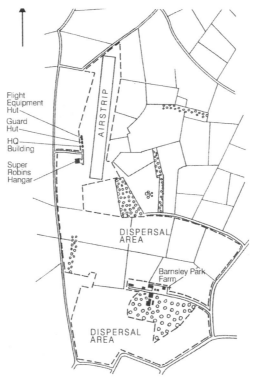

The small strip at Barnsley Park was roughly North-South, with extensive dispersal areas in the fields to the South. (Airfield Research Group).

HISTORY

Barnsley Park was developed as No.22 Satellite Landing Ground for No.6 Maintenance Unit, an Aircraft Storage Unit (ASU) based at Brize Norton. The airfield opened on 1 July 1941 and remained in use to September 1945, having changed ownership to No.5 MU in August 1942. As with many of the SLGs, it frequently appears unnamed in the records, simply being recorded as No.22 SLG. It was a typical site, although originally intended as a temporary measure, in that it had an area of wooded parkland in which aircraft could be dispersed and a reasonable field for take-off and landing. The landing strip, which was eventually 1,200yd long, was situated at the north end of the site and, along with a few minor buildings, there was also a single Super Robin hangar. Aircraft then taxied south to the dispersal areas around Barnsley Park Farm.

The plan for temporary use was changed, but before Barnsley Park could be accepted as a full-time SLG, it required some improvement work. The site was closed from November 1941 to August 1942 and,

as mentioned above, it was allocated to No.5 MU (Kemble) when it re-opened. The work had included laying areas of steel meshing to improve the surface conditions and the construction of a number of buildings. The SLG was now cleared to accept fighter types and twin-engine types and, from late-1943 onwards, it received a steady stream of aircraft. By late-1944 the SLGs were holding a large number of aircraft, as production and delivery outstripped the needs of the operational units. Unlike many SLGs, Barnsley Park does not appear to have undertaken any significant modification work on its aircraft and was very much a storage site.

With the end of the war the SLGs were surplus to requirements – as were most of their charges, a large number of which ended up as scrap – and SLG No.22 was out of use by late-1945, being returned to its original, peaceful, rural setting the following year. There is little left of this wartime site, other than the bungalow that had been constructed as the SLG headquarters building.

BIBURY

County: Gloucestershire

HISTORY

Nimble Harts, relegated from their day-bomber role to that of trainer, and Oxfords, both of No.3 Service Flying Training School, were the first users of Bibury. The SFTS was based at South Cerney but, because of the hectic nature of its training role, it made use of a number of Relief Landing Grounds. Operational types – Hurricanes and Spitfires – also made an appearance at Bibury in summer 1940, when the airfield was used by a detachment from 87 Squadron, followed by a detachment of 92 Squadron. The airfield was laid out on Ablington Down, north of the village of Bibury, with an odd-shaped grass airfield created by the removal of hedge boundaries. It was intended as an RLG, for use by one of the many training schools in the area, and was initially allo-

cated to No.3 SFTS. Facilities at the airfield were limited when it first opened but were gradually improved, with Bibury eventually having two runways with Sommerfeld Track surfaces (mid-1942), plus an assortment of Blister hangars and even a T-type hangar. A number of communal sites were built in the fields just to the west of the airfield.

After one brief period of excitement on 19 August 1940, when a Ju88 strafed the airfield, causing some damage and one fatality, but then being shot down by Spitfires that scrambled in pursuit, Bibury settled down to an existence as a training airfield, although the last fighters did not leave until the end of 1940. Over the next two years the SFTS aircraft kept the circuit busy. The school was re-designated in March

Airfield Data Dec 1944

Command:	Maintenance Command	Runway surface:	Sommerfeld Track
Function:	Storage Unit	Hangars:	Double Blister (65ft) × 4, Single Blister (65ft) × one, T.2 × one
Runways:	100 deg 1,180yd	Dispersals:	Nil
	040 deg 1,060yd	Personnel:	Officers – 83 (4 WAAF)
			Other Ranks – 560 (96 WAAF)

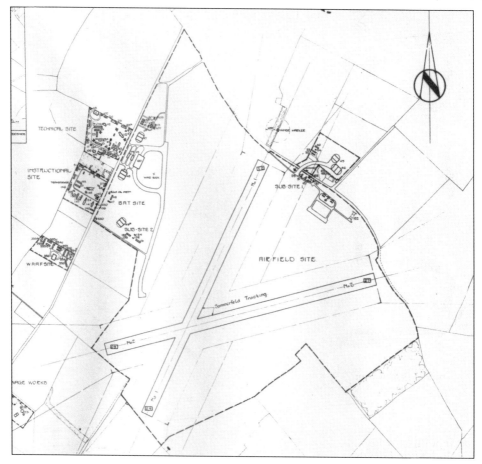

1942 as No.3 (Pilot) Advanced Flying Unit, still parented at South Cerney, and retained use of Bibury as an RLG to November 1944. In July 1943, the Oxfords of No.1539 Beam Approach Training Flight moved in, this unit being affiliated to the PAFU.

The end of flying operations saw the airfield become part of the Quedgeley-based No.7 Maintenance Unit. The MU was an Equipment Supply Depot, a not very glamorous role but, nevertheless, an important one. They had little real need of the airfield, but retained its

use to February 1950. Various airfield buildings survive, including two Blister hangars.

Units

1939–1945

87 Sqn det	Jul 1940–Dec 1940+	Hurricane
92 Sqn	Aug 1940–Sep 1940	Spitfire
3 SFTS	6 Jul 1940–1 Mar 1942	Hart, Oxford
3 PAFU	1 Mar 1942–15 Nov 1944	
1539 Flt	13 Jul 1943–15 Nov 1944	Oxford

BLAKEHILL FARM
(Station 459)

County: Gloucestershire

UTM/Grid: OS Map 173 – SU073907
Lat/Long: N51°37.23 W001°53.15
Nearest Town: Swindon 7 miles to south

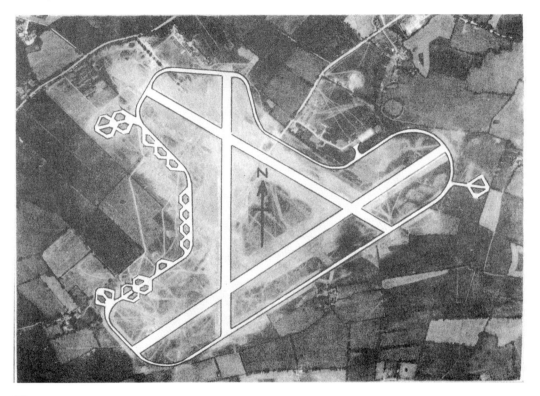

HISTORY

The site for this airfield was only acquired in early 1943, as part of the final airfield-construction programme, and it was built to the, by then, standard layout with three surfaced runways at 60-degree angles, all connected by a perimeter track along which, or off of which, were various dispersals. The majority of the latter were on the west side of the airfield, whilst the two T.2 hangars were on the east side. The site was a large flat area by the River Key and the airfield took its name from Blakehill Farm, which lost much of its land but remained standing adjacent the southern taxiway. There was a large group of communal sites to the north-east of the airfield. Construction was reasonably straightforward and no major problems were reported, although the area of PSP laid at either end of the NE/SW runway was unusual. The exact date when this was laid is uncertain, but it may have been in connection with the requirement, in 1944, to array tugs and gliders

ready for a mass departure.

The airfield opened in February 1944 and was immediately transferred from Air Defence of Great Britain (a temporary name adopted by Fighter Command) to No.46 Group of Transport Command. From spring 1944, Blakehill Farm was a Dakota base, with a detachment of 271 Squadron in residence from February, being supplemented by the arrival of 233 Squadron in March 1944. A Glider Servicing Echelon arrived that month, as did a detachment of the Glider Pilot Regiment, and Blakehill started training for what would be its sole wartime role – airborne operations. Horsas began arriving in numbers during April, for both training and storage, and a second GSE was added, No.16 joining No.11.

Blakehill Farm was nominated as the base hospital for the Group, to which casualties from the invasion would be returned for initial treatment and allocation to hospitals. All transport aircraft that would

AIRFIELD DATA DEC 1944

Command:	Transport Command	Runway surface:	Concrete and wood chippings
Function:	Operational Parent	Hangars:	T.2 × 2
Runways:	240 deg 2,000 × 50yd	Dispersals:	46 × Loop
	130 deg 1,400 × 50yd	Personnel:	Officers – 231 (7 WAAF)
	190 deg 1,400 × 50yd		Other Ranks – 2,470 (115 WAAF)

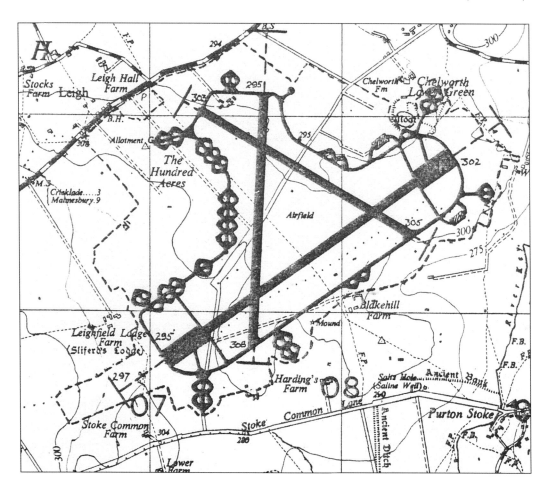

operate into the Normandy area had CASEVAC as a role and it was expected that a large number of casualties would arrive at the airfield. Aircraft were prepared by having stretcher points added, along with the ability to quickly change the interior to suit the role, and a number of 'flying nurses' (Air Ambulance Orderlies) were trained. In the meantime, training for the invasion continued. First off from the Blakehill runway late on 5 June 1944 were six combinations from 233 Squadron. They were followed by a

further twenty-four Dakotas; two of which didn't return from the D-Day mission. Further airborne ops were flown over the next few days and, before long, aircraft were landing at the rough temporary strips being carved out of the French countryside, enabling them to pick up casualties.

A second Dakota squadron was formed at the airfield in September, the Canadian 437 Squadron becoming operational with some crews just before the next airborne operation. The airfield played a

Blakehill Farm housed two Dakota squadrons, whose main task was glider tow for Horsas; although this typical scene of a jeep being loaded into a Horsa would have been seen at Blakehill, this is not a Blakehill photograph.

major role in the airborne drop for Operation *Market-Garden*, the squadrons flying the following missions:

- 233 Sqn: seventy-three Dakotas, comprising forty-two glider-tow and thirty-one re-supply missions; three aircraft failed to return.
- 437 Sqn: forty-five Dakotas, comprising sixteen glider-tow and twenty-nine re-supply missions; five aircraft failed to return.

The squadrons continued to train for any future airborne operation and took part in the final such assault, the crossing of the Rhine, Operation *Varsity*, in March 1945, although they deployed to Birch for this operation. Transport aircraft were in heavy demand and Blakehill Farm remained busy with supply missions and, as the war neared its end, the bringing home of prisoners of war.

Gliders re-appeared over Blakehill in June 1945 with the arrival of No.22 Heavy Glider Conversion Unit from Keevil, the main role of the unit being to train Hadrian pilots for deployment to the Far East theatre, where the war was still going on. The main tug-type was the Albemarle and glider pilots flew type conversion and tactical-assault practice. However, after the end of the war with Japan, training ceased in October 1945 and the unit disbanded in November. The smaller Horsa glider had also been present in some numbers, with 100 of the type allocated to Blakehill for storage; although the HGCU had discontinued main course training on this type, they were still used from time to time. From December 1945 to July 1946, but with a break of two months in spring, the airfield was the base for No.1555 Radio Aids Training Flight, equipped with Austers to train transport pilots, in radio-aids procedures. The last of the operational Dakota squadrons left in January 1946, when 575 Squadron, which had only arrived the previous November, departed to Bari in Italy, and the station closed on 1 December 1946.

Blakehill Farm survived the post-war disposal rush and in spring 1948 became an unmanned satellite airfield for the newly-reformed No.2 Flying Training School (and later the Central Flying School), whose main base had moved to South Cerney in April 1948. This type of use continued to 1957 and, in 1963, Blakehill then passed to the Government Communications Headquarters (GCHQ) for use as a radio listening-post. The site is now a wildlife conservation area and, whilst a number of buildings survive, the runways have gone – although their lines are still quite clear from the air.

UNITS

1939–1945

233 Sqn	5 Mar 1944–8 Jun 1945	Dakota
271 Sqn det	Feb 1944–Aug 1945	Dakota
437 Sqn	1 Sep 1944–7 May 1945	Dakota
575 Sqn	24 Nov 1945–31 Jan 1946	Dakota
GPR	Mar 1944–?	
22 HGCU	21 Jun 1945–Nov 1945	Albemarle, Hadrian

Post-1945

1555 Flt	17 Dec 1945–1 Feb 1946	Oxford
	30 Apr 1946–Jul 1946	
2 FTS	Apr 1948–1952	Tiger Moth, Harvard, Prentice

MEMORIALS

1. To 437 Squadron, dedicated 25 Sep 1994, a stone pillar with a plaque inscribed:

> When you pause to see the time of day remember the Canadians who flew from this airfield brave and courageous, some never returned, others returned with lifetime memories. Dedicated by the members of 437 (T) Husky Squadron with the gracious help of the people of Cricklade on 25th September 1994. No.437 Squadron Royal Canadian Air Force RAF Blakehill Farm 14 Sept 1944–7th May 1945.

2. It was another ten years before a matching memorial was raised to 233 Squadron; this was dedicated on 25 Apr 2004.

The memorial area has stone obelisks to the two squadrons, although there was 10 years between the erection of the two memorials.

BOLT HEAD

County: Devon

UTM/Grid: OS Map 201 – SX713373
Lat/Long: N50°13.23 W003°48.08
Nearest Town: Salcombe 1 mile to north-east

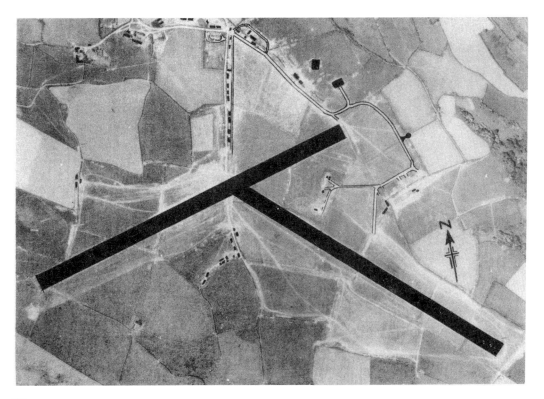

HISTORY

Spitfires were the main based-type at Bolt Head from summer 1942 to the end of the war and, as the unit list shows, there were a number of squadrons that passed through the airfield, initially as detachments, that were not always in permanent residence.

This very basic airfield was laid out on the headland of the same name near Devon's most southerly point – which meant that it was as close as could be to enemy-held territory. It was thus ideally placed for use by offensive aircraft operating over the sea areas and the near Continent. The airfield opened for Fighter Command in summer 1941 and the first definite use of what was still a basic airfield was by a detachment of 16 Squadron Lysanders. The same type was used by a detachment of 276 Squadron, probably from late-1941, although these were employed in the air-sea rescue role – for which Bolt Head was ideally situated. The airfield underwent expansion and improvement during 1942, which included the laying of two

Sommerfeld Track runways, a number of dispersals on the northern side of the airfield and two Blister hangars; the runways were subsequently lengthened to that shown in the 1944 survey.

The air photo clearly shows the unusual layout of runways and other facilities, but this was dictated by the restricted nature of the site on its headland. With the improvements made, the airfield became an operational satellite rather than a forward airfield, this change taking place in April 1942, and it was from summer 1942 that the airfield usually housed a fighter squadron. The initial detachment comprised Spitfire Vs from 421 Squadron, whose main base was at Exeter; this unit using Bolt Head as a detachment base for a month and then being replaced by the similarly equipped 310 Squadron. The main role of the fighters was providing escort to the medium bombers on *Circus* missions and, even though Bolt Head was officially a single-squadron airfield, it was not unusual

AIRFIELD DATA DEC 1944

Command:	Fighter Command	Runway surface:	Sommerfeld Track
Function:	Operational Satellite	Hangars:	Blister × 2
Runways:	237 deg 1,400yd	Dispersals:	5 × Single-Engine
	293 deg 1,300yd	Personnel:	Officers – 40 (1 WAAF)
			Other Ranks – 567 (132 WAAF)

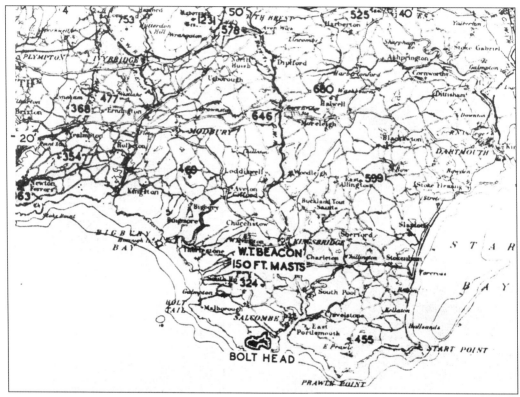

This regional map shows the isolated position of Bolt Head.

for more than one squadron to be present for a day or so for a particular mission. The fighters also flew offensive ops and, from September, Typhoons started using the airfield – flying defensive (to counter hit-and-run raids) and offensive sorties. The unit list shows that there was seldom a time when the airfield was without a unit; what it does not show is the forward-airfield usage, whereby one or more squadrons would move to the airfield for one day. With the departure of the Czech detachment the airfield received the whole of 610 Squadron, who brought their Spitfire VCs from Perranporth. This unit remained in residence to mid-December 1943 but, with their departure, the sound of Merlins died and Bolt Head became fairly quiet for a number of

months. Aircraft from the airfield had scored a number of successes on air and ground targets and had suffered some losses but, despite its exposed position, Bolt Head was itself only attacked twice, on 7 March 1942 and 1 May 1942, both ineffective hit-and-run attacks.

The airfield came to life once more in the build-up period to D-Day, the first, brief, occupants being Typhoons of 266 Squadron, who spent a few days here in early March 1944. A few days after they departed, the Spitfire VIs of 234 Squadron arrived from Coltishall, departing the following month when replaced by 41 Squadron. Typhoons re-appeared, courtesy of 263 Squadron, in mid-June and stayed for four weeks. Their departure in July was followed by a six-week presence of 611 Squadron and its Spitfire LFVBs. The final based-squadron was 275 Squadron; this unit arrived in August 1944, taking over the ASR role from 276 Squadron, and stayed to October 1944, when it moved to Exeter. However, it retained a detachment at Bolt Head and continued to do so to February 1945, despite another move of the main base to Harrowbeer.

Bolt Head was reduced to Care and Maintenance on 25 April 1945, the date of the last major bombing raids over Germany, and was retained on the books into 1947. Some parts of the structure, including the steel matting, had been removed in this period and the area was soon returned to agriculture.

Private flying operations now take place at the grass strip of Bolt Head, using a single 620m runway (11/29), but parts of the wartime airfield remain, including the taxiway and a number of dispersal points. The comment made in the current Flight Guide is one that would have been appropriate during the airfield's wartime use: 'Aerodrome becomes boggy in winter. Due to proximity of the sea and nearby cliffs, coastal weather effects can be expected, including sea mist and downdrafts'. Indeed, the sea mists had caused one of the greatest losses of aircraft to a Bolt Head operation when five aircraft of 317 Squadron – forward-deployed from Exeter – were lost, having run short of fuel when sea mist rolled over Bolt Head (two other Spitfires from the squadron managed to sneak back in to the airfield).

Supermarine Walrus ASR aircraft were operated by 276 Squadron out of Bolt Head.

The Squadron also operated other types, including a number of Spitfires with equipped to drop survival equipment.

Its extreme southerly position made it ideal for certain types of fighter operation and a number of Spitfire squadrons were based here.

UNITS

1939–1945

16 Sqn det	summer 1941	Lysander
41 Sqn	29 Apr 1944–19 Jun 1944+	Spitfire
234 Sqn	18 Mar 1944–29 Apr 1944	Spitfire
257 Sqn det	Sep 1942–Jan 1943	Typhoon
263 Sqn det	Mar 1943–Jun 1943	Whirlwind
263 Sqn	19 Jun 1944–10 Jul 1944	Typhoon
266 Sqn	7–12 Mar 1944	Typhoon
275 Sqn	7 Aug 1944–15 Feb 1945	Anson, Spitfire
276 Sqn det	1941–1943?; May 1944–?	Lysander, Spitfire, Warwick
310 Sqn det	Jul 1942–Sep 1942	Spitfire
421 Sqn det	Jun 1942–Jul 1942	Spitfire
610 Sqn	26 Jun 1943–19 Dec 1943; 16–24 May 1944	Spitfire
611 Sqn	17 Jul 1944–30 Aug 1944	Spitfire
10 Gp CF det	Feb 1943–Apr 1945	various

BOSCOMBE DOWN

County: Wiltshire

UTM/Grid: OS Map 184 – SU178401
Lat/Long: N51°09.38 W001°44.30
Nearest Town: Amesbury 2 miles to north-west

HISTORY

The War Office requisitioned 333 acres of land in late-1916 for the construction of one of a series of new airfields in the Salisbury Plain area, all of which were intended for training or experimental purposes. The site was an odd shape and the main area of buildings was placed on the west side, leaving a large grass area for flying operations, although, as the plan shows, the layout did not perhaps make best use of the available areas. At this stage Boscombe was still intended as a wartime-only airfield, but it was provided with reasonable facilities, the number and quality of which was improved over the next year. The original Bessonneau and other temporary hangars and aircraft sheds were gradually replaced by more permanent structures, including six large aeroplane sheds and one aeroplane repair-shed (all 100 × 180ft) and various other support buildings on the technical site. The domestic site included messes and accommodation. However, not all of this work had been completed by the end of the war.

As far as users were concerned, No.6 Training Depot Station formed at Boscombe Down in October 1917, its three Flights having been 'donated' by other units; the airfield was known as 'Red House Farm' for its first days of use, but then the name Boscombe Down was adopted – after the area of land on which it was built. The TDS was part of 36th (Training) Wing at Upper Croft, Thruxton, although in November 1918 it transferred to 33rd Wing as part of the post-war reorganization. As with all training units the aircraft fleet was very diverse, with Avros, BEs and DHs of various types being used. Boscombe was also home to the United States Air Service, with training being provided for a number of American units before they went off to France.

The end of the war did not bring an end to Boscombe's work and, indeed, for a few months, the airfield acquired additional units, with No.10 and No.14 Training Depot Stations moving in, although the latter was only a cadre unit. However, the almost total collapse of the RAF training system in 1919 included the demise of Boscombe's role and the airfield was reduced to Care and Maintenance on 15 May 1919. The site remained in use for aircraft storage to 1 April 1920 and was then sold back to the original landowner.

The decision to sell proved premature and, in 1926, the site was re-acquired (at a far higher price) for development into a permanent bomber-station with the standard complement of two squadrons. Restoration of some of the old buildings, the erection of new buildings and work on the overall landing area meant that RAF Boscombe Down did not open until 1 September 1930 – and even then construction work was still underway. The Virginias of 9 Squadron were first to take up residence, arriving from Manston in November; they were joined in April 1931 by 10 Squadron, equipped with Hyderabads, although this quickly gave way to the Hinaidi and then the Virginia. This gave Boscombe its two established squadrons with Wessex Bombing Area. The routine was one of training and exercises and the station settled into a peacetime routine. However, from 1935 the pace increased and, as the unit list shows, a number of bomber squadrons were present at Boscombe Down in the latter part of the 1930s. In 1935, two new squadrons formed, using what became the standard Bomber Command method of forming new units: 214 Squadron was created using 'B Flight' of 9 Squadron and 97 Squadron from 'B Flight' of 10 Squadron. The same year saw the RAF's latest bomber – the Heyford – arrive at Boscombe and the following year the RAF underwent a re-organization, which included the formation of Bomber Command

and allocation of Boscombe Down to No.3 Group.

The bombers left in January 1937 and the station became part of No.16 Group of Coastal Command, with 224 Squadron arriving in February and 217 Squadron forming in March. Within weeks, both were flying the Anson, one of the Command's main operational types. Further unit movements took place and, on 1 July, the station was back under Bomber Command.

A Special Duties Flight was formed in 1938 to work with the Civil Defence Experimental Establishment at Porton and it seems likely that the main task of this unit was to investigate the air delivery of poison gas. This is a subject that is buried deep in RAF records, but it is known that a number of Lysanders were equipped with canisters for this task. This was very much a sideline and Boscombe was still an operational station as war approached and there is some evidence that the Group formed an Experimental Flight in summer 1939, although details of its work and period of service are sketchy (it may in fact be one and the same as the Special Duties Flight). The significance for Boscombe's history is that this was the first type of unit in what was to become the airfield's future in test and evaluation. Another of the 'sketchy' units was the Lysander Flight, formed in November 1939 to undertake special-duties operations in France.

The two resident Battle squadrons, 88 and 218, were formed into No.75 Wing in August 1939, as part of the preparation for forward deployment to France with the Advanced Air Striking Force. The move came on 2 September, the Wing moving its

In the latter part of World War One and into the early 1920s, Boscombe was a sprawling camp with a mixture of permanent and temporary buildings and hangars, and extensive tentage. (Aldon Ferguson)

AIRFIELD DATA DEC 1944

Command:	Flying Training Command	Runway surface:	Concrete (240 deg), grass
Function:	Experimental Station	Hangars:	Blister (69ft) × 12, GS Shed
Runways:	240 deg 3,000 × 100yd		(204 × 173ft) × 3, GS Shed
	WNW/ESE 1,400yd		(174 × 100ft) × one,
	SSE/NNW 1,400yd		Type A × one, Type C × one
		Dispersals:	14 × Loop (BRC Fabric), 2 × Concrete
			circular (100ft diam), one × Concrete
			square (150 × 150ft)
		Personnel:	Officers – 118 (7 WAAF)
			Other Ranks – 2,529 (559 WAAF)

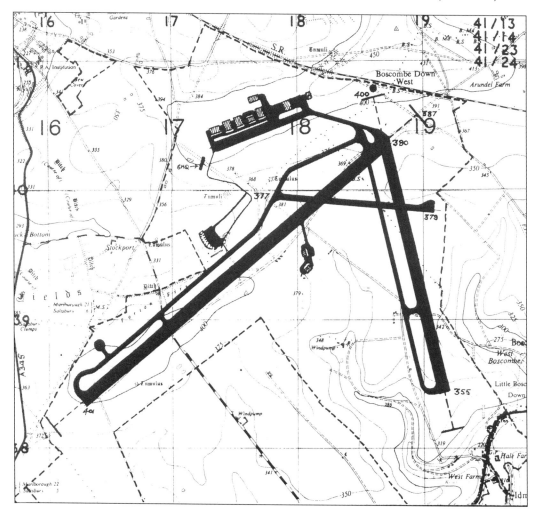

headquarters to Auberive-sur-Suippe. Boscombe was still a grass airfield at this stage and had four notional strips, the longest being 1,400yd, but it was apparent that these were not long enough and that hard surfaces would eventually be required. The airfield was to undergo various periods of development, which, by 1944, provided it with one long (3,000yd) hard runway and two grass strips, in addition to a variety of hangars and dispersal areas. Although work on the concrete runway had started in early 1945, it was not fully open until October. As with most major airfields, it is difficult to trace the building of support facilities, as these are invariably not mentioned in station records.

The Blind Approach Training and Development Unit (BATDU) formed here in mid-September 1939 with a small number of Ansons and, although it had a brief (one week) disbandment in June 1940, it remained at Boscombe to December, having been renamed the Wireless Intelligence Development Unit at the end of October. On 6 November, the small, but significant, Bomber Development Unit (BDU) had formed with an establishment of one Blenheim, one Hampden, one Wellington and one Whitley. This organization was tasked to 'undertake trials from the operational point of view of new items of bombing equipment and to assist Bomber Command in the elucidation on bombing problems'. The WIDU was a fascinating unit, in that its role was to investigate German radio beams in what were the first moves of the radio-countermeasures war – without detailed knowledge of radio frequencies and parameters no estimate could be made of their capabilities and no effective counters developed. The importance of this work was soon recognized and the unit was given squadron status, as 109 Squadron, in December

Virginia of 9 Squadron; the unit was here from 1930 to 1935.

The Battles of 218 Squadron were here for a year, leaving on the outbreak of World War Two.

Aerial view of Boscombe Down, 1934 (via Rod Priddle).

1940. This squadron is better known for its later operational exploits with the Mosquito, but the years it spent at Boscombe Down made a vital contribution to the air war.

However, the most important development in autumn 1939 was the arrival from Martlesham Heath of the Aeroplane and Armament Experimental Establishment (A&AEE), the move taking place in order to base this important organization at a safer location than its Suffolk coastal site (too close to the enemy). The A&AEE was a complex organization and under its umbrella title it included a number of specialist flights and squadrons, with an, at times, bewildering array of titles. In its early days at Boscombe it comprised two main elements – Flight Performance Testing, which had three Flights, and Flight Armament Testing, which had two Flights. Throughout the war new sub-units came and went, sometimes operating detachments at other airfields: these included the Armament Testing Squadron, Performance Testing Squadron, Gunnery Flight (Jun 1940–?), Handling Squadron (Nov 1940–Aug? 1942), High Altitude Flight (Dec 1940–Sep 1944) and the Intensive Flying Development Squadron (1941–?).

But we need to step back to 1940 to mention one incident in the station's history. Boscombe is not famed as a fighter station and yet it was the only airfield to have a Fighter Command VC winner – Flight Lieutenant James Nicolson of 249 Squadron. On 16 August 1940 Nicolson led Red Section into combat and, in the subsequent battle, his courageous attack on a Bf110 led to the award of Fighter Command's only Victoria Cross. His citation read:

> During an engagement with the enemy near Southampton on 16th August 1940 Flight Lieutenant Nicolson's aircraft was hit by four cannon shells, two of which wounded him whilst another set fire to the gravity tank. When about to abandon his aircraft owing to flames in the cockpit he sighted an enemy fighter. This he attacked and shot down, although as a result he displayed exceptional gallantry and disregard for the safety of his own life.

Boscombe was one of the most secret and most interesting of airfields for the rest of the war and it is impossible in this brief history to even scratch the surface of the work it did, or list all the units and sub-units of the A&AEE. Suffice it to say that virtually every aircraft type was evaluated here, as were most weapon and avionics systems – it truly was at the centre of the RAF's operational development. Surprisingly, the Luftwaffe made very few appearances and the attacks that did take place were small scale and generally ineffective. In 1944 the Flying Division, which covered all

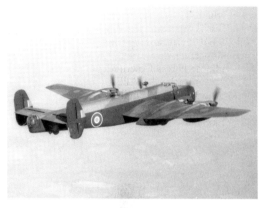

As home to the A&AEE, Boscombe was an incredibly important airfield and was temporary home to almost every type of RAF aircraft as they passed through on test and evaluation. This selection illustrates just three of the many hundreds: Spitfire MB878 October 1943, Halifax IA, Spitfire RB146.

the sub-units with flying duties, was re-organized into A, B, C and D squadrons, each with specific responsibilities. One of Boscombe Down's most famous units is the Empire Test Pilots' School (ETPS) and the precursor of this unit formed at Boscombe in June 1943 as the Test Pilot's School, an element within the A&AEE. The following January it was raised to independent status and, in July 1944, had the name Empire added to its title, continuing to operate a very diverse fleet of aircraft, some on establishment and some borrowed. It remained in residence to October 1945, when it moved to Hullavington; it would be over twenty years before it returned. Boscombe not only handled a diverse range of aircraft, it handled a large number of aircraft; for example, it had 176 aircraft on charge in August 1945.

Although the original plan had been that the A&AEE would only use Boscombe as a temporary (wartime) home, the decision was taken that it would become the permanent place of residence. Its role remained the same but, in November 1946, a Civil Aircraft Test Section was added, with responsibility, with the Civil Aviation Authority, of issuing transport aircraft with a Certificate of Airworthiness.

The Airborne Forces Experimental Establishment was absorbed into the A&AEE in September 1950 and, in April 1954, the Handling Squadron arrived from Manby, initially as a lodger unit but eventually to be absorbed by the based units. Handling

Squadron is yet another of those little-known but vital RAF units and its main task was, as its name suggests, to determine the handling characteristics of RAF aircraft and to be the sponsor for the all-important Pilots' Notes/Flight Reference Cards and other material used by aircrew. These functions remain part of Boscombe's activities.

During the early 1950s, Boscombe Down underwent a total rebuild and it was at this time that the huge 'weighbridge hangar' was added. This massive structure, featuring a clear span of no less than 250ft (76m), was originally designed to accommodate the Bristol Brabazon airliner and although this project was abandoned the hangar has gone on to provide an invaluable facility to the aviation testing industry.

It was fairly common for special units to form to handle any particularly important trials and evaluation, an example of this was the Joint Services Trials Unit that moved from Upavon to Boscombe in June 1962 to continue its work on evaluation of the Red Top air-to-air missile, for use by the RAF and Fleet Air Arm. This unit disbanded in July 1967, the main

Boscombe Down's Argosy with its distinctive colour scheme and markings – seen here arriving at Finningley for an airshow.

VC10 taxies out past the HAS site that was added to the airfield in the 1980s.

The A&AEE 'Raspberry Ripple' scheme on Sea King ZF115, June 1990.

The airfield's central role in trials and testing continues; this Harrier from Boscombe's Operational Evaluation Unit (OEU) was visiting the airshow at Waddington.

Red Top work having concluded, but No.22 Joint Services Trials Unit had formed at Boscombe in January 1966, using the same aircraft – established, such as a Sea Vixen, and borrowed – and continued to operate until December 1974. The Empire Test Pilots' School moved in to Boscombe from Farnborough in January 1968, although its precursor – the Test Pilots' School – had formed at Boscombe as part of the A&AEE in June 1943.

In the late-1970s NATO undertook a major airfield-hardening programme to provide Hardened Aircraft Shelter (HAS) sites and operations blocks; although Boscombe was not home to operational tactical aircraft it was designated as a deployment airfield, mainly for the planned influx of USAF aircraft in the event of war with the Warsaw Pact, and, as such, was part of the hardening programme.

With the introduction to service in 1982 of the Tornado, the RAF had need of a specialist unit to undertake operational trials and evaluation of the aircraft's weapon systems; this led to the formation of the Tornado Operational Evaluation Unit (TOEU) in September 1983, the unit using aircraft borrowed from other units. The success of this unit led to the adoption of the same principle for all tactical types. The Strike/Attack Operational Evaluation Unit was formed in October 1987, using a mix of borrowed aircraft with which to evaluate all aspects of the operational employment of air weapons and defensive systems.

As part of the seemingly endless re-organizations, A and B squadrons became the Fixed-Wing Test Squadron in February 1988, with D Squadron becoming the Rotary-Wing Test Squadron under the same change. In April 1992, the long-established name of the Aircraft and Armament Experimental Establishment was changed to the Aircraft and Armament Evaluation Establishment, the famous initials of A&AEE remain the same, as does the role (pretty much) – but evaluation did more accurately express the role of the organization. I am less happy with the change that took place in April 1996 to the Assessment and Evaluation Centre; this reflects the role but loses the historic connection with A&AEE, another slice of British military aviation history to bite the dust with Boscombe becoming a commercial, but still highly classified, operation. At this point the AEC remained part of DERA (Defence Evaluation and Research Agency), which had been created in April 1995, with three main components at Boscombe: Fast-Jet Test Squadron, Heavy-Aircraft Test Squadron and Rotary Test Squadron, as well as parenting responsibilities for ETPS.

The airfield is now operated by QinetiQ – one of those dreadful 'with-it' corporate titles – and remains at the forefront of military aircraft and systems evaluation. Boscombe Down (EGDM) operates two main hard-runways, the longest being 3,212m (05/23), as well as two short, parallel runways and various helicopter landing areas.

DECOY SITE

Q	South Newton	SU096356

UNITS

HQ Units at Boscombe Down

No.75 Wing	24 Aug 1939–2 Sep 1939	88, 218Sqn

Pre-1919

6 TDS	12 Oct 1917–15 May 1919	various
11 TDS	Nov 1918–Apr 1919	various
14 TDS	Nov 1918–Mar 1919	various

1919–1939

9 Sqn	26 Nov 1930–15 Oct 1935	Virginia
10 Sqn	1 Apr 1931–25 Jan 1937	Hyderabad, Hinaidi, Virginia, Heyford
51 Sqn	24 Mar 1937–20 Apr 1938	Anson, Whitley
58 Sqn	24 Mar 1937–14 Feb 1940	Anson, Whitley
78 Sqn	1 Nov 1936–1 Feb 1937	Heyford
88 Sqn	17 Jul 1937–Sep 1939	Hind, Battle
97 Sqn	26 Sep 1935–7 Jan 1937	Heyford
150 Sqn	8 Aug 1938–3 Apr 1939	Battle
166 Sqn	1 Nov 1936–20 Jan 1937	Heyford
166 Sqn det	Jun 1939–Sep 1939	Whitley
214 Sqn	16 Sep 1935–15 Oct 1935	Virginia
217 Sqn	15 Mar 1937–7 Jun 1937	Anson
218 Sqn	22 Apr 1938–2 Sep 1939	Battle
224 Sqn	15 Feb 1937–9 Jul 1937	Anson
4 Gp EF	Jul 1939–?	Hind

1939–1945

35 Sqn	7–20 Nov 1940	Halifax
56 Sqn	1 Sep 1940–29 Nov 1940	Hurricane
58 Sqn	?–14 Feb 1940	Whitley
109 Sqn	10 Dec 1940–19 Jan 1942	Whitley, Anson, Wellington
109 Sqn det	Jan 1942–Apr 1942	Anson, Wellington
249 Sqn	14 Aug 1940–1 Sep 1940	Hurricane
A&AEE	9 Sep 1939–1 Apr 1992	various
BATDU	18 Sep 1939–30 Oct 1940	Anson
LysanderFlt	20 Nov 1939–?	Lysander
W(I)DU	30 Oct 1940–10 Dec 1940	Anson, Whitley
HAF	30 Dec 1940–Sep 1944	Spitfire, Wellington

BDU	Nov 1940–1 May 1941	
Handling Sqn	8 Nov 1940–22 Aug 1942; 12 Apr 1954–?	
IFDU/F	15 Nov 1941–	various
AGME	23 Nov 1941–29 Jan 1942	various
MRF	1942–?	
ETPS	21 Jun 1943–Oct 1945	various

Post-1945

810 OEU FAA	27 Jul 1993–current?+	Sea King
826 OEU FAA	Jul 1992–27 Jul 1993+	Sea King
893Sqn FAA	30 Jun 1967–24 Aug 1967	Sea Vixen
899 OEU FAA	1 Jun 1993–30 Sep 1993	Sea Harrier
Handling Sqn	12 Apr 1954–?	
HF/S	12 Apr 1954–current	various
JSTU	1 Feb 1962–14 Jul 1967	Sea Vixen
22 JSTU	1 Jan 1966–31 Dec 1974	Sea Vixen
A&AEE	?–1 Apr 1992	various
ETPS	29 Jan 1968–current	various
29 JSTU	1 May 1980–15 Sep 1980	Lynx
TOEU	1 Sep 1983–5 Oct 1987	Tornado
SAOEU	5 Oct 1987–current	various
AAEE	1 Apr 1992–1 Apr 1996	various
SUAS	2 Apr 1993–current	Bulldog, Tutor
MRF	1994–Mar 2001?	Hercules
AEC	1 Apr 1996–current	various

MEMORIALS

1. Located near the old control tower is a stone pillar, with relief carving of a Hurricane, and plaque to James Nicolson VC dedicated 16 August 1990; inscribed:

> In memory of James Nicolson VC 1917–1945. On the 16th of August 1940 Flight Lieutenant James B. Nicolson was leading Red Section of No. 249 Squadron from RAF Boscombe Down. An attack by enemy aircraft whilst over Southampton left Nicolson wounded and his Hurricane on fire. When about to bail out he sighted and shot down one of the attacking aircraft, only then did he abandon his own aircraft. For this deed of gallantry Nicolson was awarded the Victoria Cross, the only member of Fighter Command to be so honoured during the war.

2. The on-site Boscombe Down museum (limited access by prior arrangement) includes various items relating to the history of the station and its units.

A.M. STATE RM. S.D. 93.

Airfield plan 1944

BROCKWORTH
(Hucclecote)

County: Gloucestershire

UTM/Grid: OS Map 163 – SO882160
Lat/Long: N51°50.54 W002°10.36
Nearest Town: Gloucester 2 miles to west

Aerial view dated 18 June 1959.

HISTORY

Brockworth will always have a place in aviation history as the location for the first flight, on 8 April 1941, of the Gloster E28/39. Strictly speaking this was a taxi trial, during which PEG Sayer briefly lifted the aircraft off the ground; the *true* first flight took place at Cranwell on 15 May. Of greater import for the war effort was the production of 2,750 Hurricanes and 3,330 Typhoons.

This site, on the outskirts of Gloucester and adjacent to the village of Brockworth, was originally known as Hucclecote and was, at first, little more than a flat field from which aircraft could be test flown. This activity commenced in late-1915 and the aircraft in question came from H H Martyn & Co Ltd in Cheltenham, one of many firms to take-on aircraft contract work in World War One – in this case for Airco (the Aircraft Manufacturing Company). The factory was at Sunningend and a steady stream of aircraft was taken by road to the 'airfield' for testing. In June 1917 this activity was taken over by the

Gloucestershire Aircraft Company and, at some point in mid- to late-1918 an Aircraft Acceptance Park was formed at the airfield; the site was frequently referred to as Hucclecote or Brockworth, although 'official' adoption of the latter name does not appear to have occurred until post-1945. The AAP was formed to handle all Gloucestershire aircraft and its part of the airfield was provided with an array of hangars and sheds. The Armistice of November 1918 brought a rapid end to the lucrative wartime contracts and the AAP disbanded – whilst the Gloucestershire Aircraft Company endeavoured to survive in the harsh post-war aviation market. In November 1926 they changed their name to the more manageable Gloster Aircraft Company and acquired the airfield and its buildings.

Life was still difficult and, despite having formed a design team and acquiring some work, as well as developing new designs, Glosters could not survive on their own; in May 1934, they were absorbed by the Hawker Aircraft Company, although they retained the Gloster name. This brought immediate work, with the very successful Hart family of biplanes, and an expansion of the site with a new factory complex on the east side. With the Hurricane having been chosen as one of the RAF's main fighters and with massive orders under the late-1930s expansion plans, the site was further expanded when a shadow factory was authorized in August 1938. Although this factory was not fully operational until late-1940, the Brockworth site launched its first Hurricane in autumn 1939.

A single, hard runway was laid over the winter of 1941/42 – the previous winter having revealed how waterlogged the airfield could become. Production of Hurricanes gradually gave way to Typhoons and the factories achieved a peak monthly production of 130 aircraft (the peak for Hurricanes had been 160). As an important manufacturing facility Hucclecote was marked on the Luftwaffe's target maps, but it was never successfully attacked; only on two occasions did single bombs cause any damage or casualties.

The promise shown by the Gloster E28/39 was followed by the production of the RAF's first operational jet, the Gloster Meteor. This was, without doubt, one of the classic aircraft of the late-1940s and early 1950s and was a great success with the RAF and numerous overseas air forces. It was produced in a large number of variants – and the runway at Brockworth was totally unsuitable. Whilst production continued at the factory and most aircraft departed from here, the bulk of flight testing was transferred to the nearby airfield at Moreton Valence. The same was true of the next major product, the Javelin, and it was a Javelin that made the last significant flight from Brockworth on 8 April 1960. By the end of that year, aviation activity had virtually ceased at the factory and, although it remained a production works for a few more years, this was not aviation-related. The factory site was disposed of by Glosters in April 1964 to become an industrial trading estate. Many of the airfield buildings, including hangars and assembly halls, survived and were turned into industrial units but, sadly, the remains of the airfield are scheduled to disappear under 1,400 houses and the Gloucester Business Park and a plan for an aviation museum on-site has had to be abandoned (the Jet Age Museum will eventually re-establish itself at Staverton).

DECOY AIRFIELDS

	Badgeworth	SO903180
	Birdlip	SO925135
QF	Shurdington	SO920180

Typhoon at Brockworth in January 1943. (Peter Green Collection)

The E28/39 made its first 'hop' at Brockworth.

White Meteor of the RAF's first jet unit, 616 Squadron; this shot was taken in early 1945 when the Squadron was operating in Europe. The Meteor was Gloster's most successful post-war product.

UNITS

Pre-1919

90Sqn	15–29 Jul 1918	Dolphin

MEMORIAL

Plaque on the site where the E28/39 was built.

CASTLE COMBE

County: Wiltshire

UTM/Grid: OS Map 173 – ST850770
Lat/Long: N51°29.50 W002°13.04
Nearest Town: Chippenham 5 miles to south-east

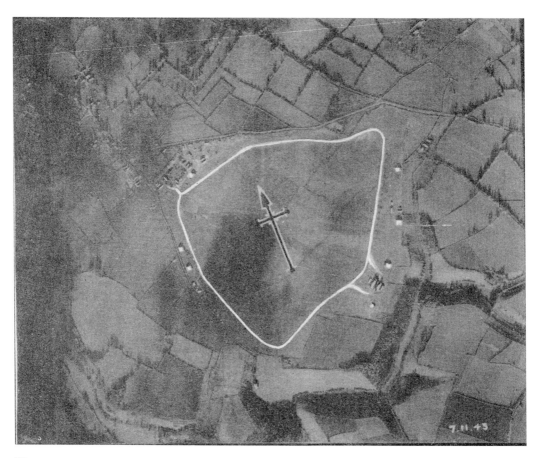

HISTORY

The airfield at Castle Combe was four miles to the south-west of Hullavington and was first used as a satellite landing ground by No.9 Flying Training School from that station. The school's Audax and Hart trainers began using the site in the immediate pre-war period, although the date of first use is uncertain, at which time it was little more than a field. However, in the latter part of 1940, Castle Combe was upgraded to a Relief Landing Ground and the surface and facilities were improved. This work took place over the winter, but the airfield still saw some use during the period before it officially re-opened with its new status in May 1941.

The school changed title and function in February 1942 to become No.9 (Pilots) Advanced Flying Unit

and continued to use Castle Combe as one of its RLGs until August, when the unit moved to Errol. During this period, naval types such as the Albacore and Swordfish also made an appearance, as the unit took on naval pilot training. The departure of the PAFU saw Castle Combe attract a based unit when No.3 Flying Instructors School moved here from Hullavington, equipped with Masters and Oxfords.

The airfield surface remained a problem because of waterlogging and further development took place in 1942, which included Sommerfeld Track for at least one of the two runways: the 1944 data sheet suggests that only one runway was tracked, whereas other sources suggest that both were tracked. Improve-

AIRFIELD DATA DEC 1944

Command:	Flying Training Command	Runway surface:	Sommerfeld Track (313 deg), grass
Function:	Pilot Advanced Flying Unit, Satellite	Hangars:	Blister (65ft) × 5, T.2 × one
Runways:	NE/SW 1,085yd	Dispersals:	Nil
	313 deg 930yd	Personnel:	Officers – 109 (4 WAAF)
			Other Ranks – 853 (152 WAAF)

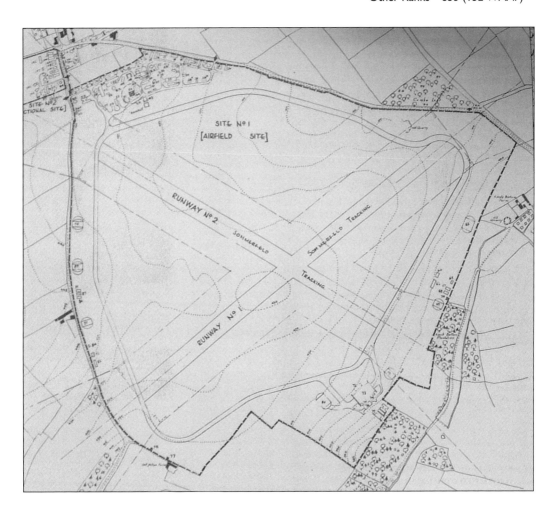

ments also included a concrete perimeter track and additional hangars that took the total to six – five Blisters and one T.1, although again sources vary, with some suggesting a total of seven Blisters. There were a number of remote domestic and admin sites to the north-west of the airfield, some of which still have huts surviving – another example of how rugged these temporary structures have proved to be.

The FIS remained in residence to October 1943, during which time it trained a great many flying instructors and also suffered the inevitable fatal crashes that were part of wartime flying training. When the FIS departed to Lulsgate Bottom, its place at Castle Combe was taken by No.15 PAFU, the first Flight of which arrived in November. The main training type was the Oxford and the parent base was at Babdown Farm, with Castle Combe used

Fine wartime shot of the airfield showing the grass oval with its surrounding concrete perimeter track. (via Rod Priddle)

as the main RLG, although this included actual basing of aircraft and personnel. The airfield surface continued to cause problems, but an even bigger problem was caused on 14 March 1944 when a Stirling made a forced landing, ran off the end of the runway and had part of its load of sea mines explode. The explosion caused some damage but, fortunately, no casualties – it was the single most dramatic event at the airfield, although not the only emergency landing. The PAFU continued to use the airfield to June 1945 but, with their departure, Castle Combe was placed under Care and Maintenance. The following year a ground unit handling Polish resettlement arrived; this stayed until June 1948 and, on 18 October that year, the airfield was put up for disposal.

It was not long before it was acquired and, like a number of other airfields, it was turned into a motor-racing circuit, the perimeter track making an ideal race-track. The first meet on the race circuit was held on 8 July 1950 and it has been an active track for the past fifty-five years; the present owner – Howard Strawford – has maintained many of the airfield buildings and also erected a memorial in 1996.

UNITS

1939–1945

9 FTS/SFTS	?–Feb 1942	various
9 PAFU	Feb 1942–Aug 1942	Master, Hurricane
3 FIS	8 Aug 1942–1 Oct 1943	Oxford, Master
15 PAFU	Nov 1943–Jun 1945	Oxford

MEMORIAL

Located near the control tower is a stone pillar with inscribed plaque: 'RAF Castle Combe 1940–1946. To commemorate all those who served here. Unveiled by Michael Shekleton 11th November 1996.' Squadron Leader Michael Shekleton had served at the airfield.

CHARLTON HORETHORNE (HMS *Heron II*)

UTM/Grid: OS Map 183 – ST643244
Lat/Long: N51°01.00 W002°30.00
Nearest Town: Yeovil 6 miles to south-west

County: Somerset

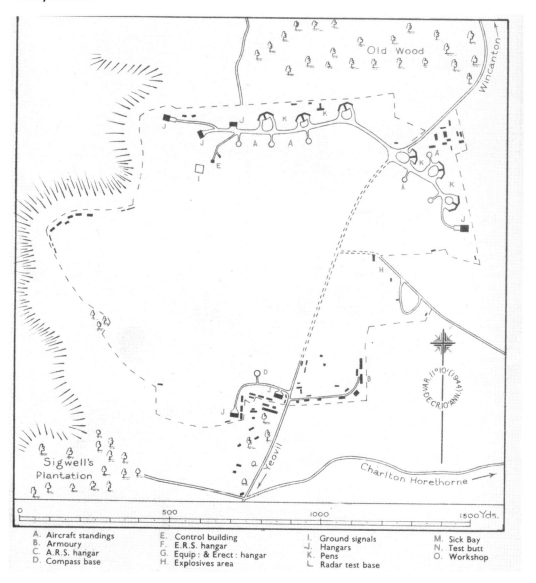

A. Aircraft standings
B. Armoury
C. A.R.S. hangar
D. Compass base
E. Control building
F. E.R.S. hangar
G. Equip: & Erect: hangar
H. Explosives area
I. Ground signals
J. Hangars
K. Pens
L. Radar test base
M. Sick Bay
N. Test butt
O. Workshop

HISTORY

Although Charlton Horethorne spent most of its war as a training base, its initial occupants were a series of Fleet Fighter units from summer 1942 to early 1943. As shown in the unit list, most of these were equipped with the Fulmar, although a number had Sea Hurricanes as their main type. As was usual with this type of squadron at this period of the war, the average strength was six to ten aircraft and so the airfield was never particularly busy. Fulmars and Oxfords were delivered to the airfield in summer

1942 to form 790 Squadron to train Fighter Direction Officers, the squadron being attached to the Fighter Direction School. In June 1944, the Fulmars gave way to Fireflies as the fighter side of the training; other than a short detachment to Culmhead in summer 1944, the squadron was resident at Charlton Horethorne to April 1945, when it moved to Zeals and, as such, was the longest-serving unit at the airfield. It was not, however, the only unit: for short periods the airfields was quite busy.

This naval domination of the airfield had not been the original plan – Charlton Horethorne was intended as a fighter satellite for Exeter and was laid out as such, as a grass airfield, in 1941. However, by the time it neared completion, the RAF's requirements had decreased, whilst those of the Fleet Air Arm had increased and when the airfield opened in May 1942 it had switched allegiance to the Navy, becoming HMS *Heron II* because of its attachment to RNAS Yeovilton (HMS *Heron*). The unit list shows the presence of a number of squadrons; both training and operational.

October 1943 brought 780 Squadron from Lee-on-Solent to act as a pilot-training unit, for which it primarily used Harvards and Masters, although a number of other types were also on strength, including operational types such as the Swordfish. A few weeks later, the training strength at Charlton Horethorne increased again with the arrival of 794 Squadron, whose mixed fleet of aircraft acted as an air-firing training unit and provided target towing. By the time this squadron disbanded in June 1944, its more usual title was No.1 Naval Air Firing Unit. In February 1944, No.765 Squadron reformed at Charlton Horethorne as a 'Travelling Recording Unit', whose main task was assessing the efficiency of radar units. The squadron operated a small number of Wellingtons, but Charlton proved inadequate and initial flying was done from Manston; the unit moved to Lee-on-Solent in mid-March.

Charlton Horethorne remained a grass field, eventually sporting four grass strips – the Navy preferred four strips to the RAF's three – and a range of other facilities dispersed around the edge of the flying area, with fighter pens and hangars on the north side and a group of technical buildings on the south-east corner.

When the Fleet Air Arm left at the end of the war, the airfield reverted to Maintenance Command of the RAF and was used as a sub-site by No.11 Maintenance Unit at Chilmark. This ammunition storage role lasted from April 1945 to June 1948, but for the last few months of that period the airfield appears to have been inactive, the stored material having been moved elsewhere. The site was quickly disposed of and agriculture returned, making use of a number of the buildings for storage. Whilst the old

grass airfield is hard to distinguish from the air today, many of the buildings survive.

Units

1939–1945

Squadron	Dates	Aircraft
765 Sqn FAA	10 Feb 1944–18 Mar 1944	Wellington
780 Sqn FAA	9 Oct 1943–28 Nov 1944	Master, Harvard
790 Sqn FAA	27 July 1942–1 Apr 1945+	Fulmar, Oxford, Firefly
794 Sqn FAA	1 Dec 1943–30 Jun 1944	various
804 Sqn FAA	6 Apr 1943–20 Jun 1943	Sea Hurricane
808 Sqn FAA	11 Dec 1942–8 Jan 1943	Seafire
809 Sqn FAA	26 Nov 1942–9 Dec 1942	Fulmar
879 Sqn FAA	10 Oct 1942–18 Nov 1942	Fulmar
886 Sqn FAA	10 Jul 1942–11 Aug 1942	Fulmar
887 Sqn FAA	10–25 Jul 1942	Fulmar
891 Sqn FAA	11 Aug 1942–9 Sep 1942	Sea Hurricane
893 Sqn FAA	9 Sep 1942–6 Oct 1942	Fulmar
895 Sqn FAA	31 Dec 1942–23 Feb 1943	Sea Hurricane
897 Sqn FAA	11 Jan 1943–22 Mar 1943	Sea Hurricane

CHARMY DOWN
(Station 487)

County: Somerset

UTM/Grid: OS Map 173 – ST764700
Lat/Long: N51°25.38 W002°20.31
Nearest Town: Bath 2 miles to south

HISTORY

Approval was given in January 1940 for the acquisition of land at Charmy Down for the creation of an RLG for Filton, with the proviso that it would subsequently be developed as a satellite for Colerne (SOM 81/40). Construction of a fighter station with three hard runways, connecting perimeter track, fighter pens and other (limited) facilities took place during 1940, but any use by Filton units is indeterminate. Charmy Down officially opened in November and its prime role was air defence of the Bristol area, with night air-defence a particular priority, as the Luftwaffe tended to use night raids when penetrating this far into England. A detachment of Hurricanes from 87 Squadron (Colerne) moved in during November and spent a frustrating time trying to work with moonlight or searchlights in order to locate enemy aircraft – these 'Cat's Eye' ops by single-engine types were notable more for landing incidents (especially Spitfire squadrons) than successful intercepts.

Charmy Down was one of the many airfields in the area to house the Westland Whirlwind, an interesting but not wonderfully successful fighter; 137 Squadron formed here on 20 February 1941, equipping with Whirlwind Is. The unit worked-up and became operational and eventually departed to Coltishall in November. In August it had been joined by the RAF's other operational Whirlwind unit, 263 Squadron arriving from Filton. The Defiants of 125 Squadron arrived from Colerne in early August 1941, but departed again in late-September to continue their work-up; the squadron re-appeared in 1942, when it detached Beaufighters to the Somerset base from its main base at Colerne.

The Hurricanes of 87 Squadron returned in January 1942 for another eleven-month stint at Charmy Down, having become specialists in the 'Cat's Eye' night-fighting role, although also undertaking other fighter roles. The same month saw the formation of No.1454 Flight with the Turbinlite Havoc; these spe-

AIRFIELD DATA DEC 1944

Command:	Flying Training Command	Runway surface:	Tarmac
Function:	Pilot Advanced Flying Unit, Satellite	Hangars:	Blister × 12
Runways:	310 deg 1,450 × 50yd	Dispersals:	45
	250 deg 1,350 × 50yd	Personnel:	Officers – 137 (USAAF)
	012 deg 933 × 50yd		Other Ranks – 1,325 (USAAF)

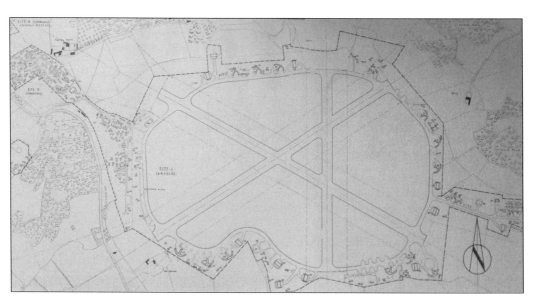

cialist flights were an attempt to boost the night defences and involved a fighting pair – a Havoc, with its nose-mounted searchlight, working with a Hurricane in a 'hunter-killer' team controlled by ground radar. The idea was for the ground radar to position the hunters behind the enemy and, at an appropriate range, the Havoc would illuminate the target for the Hurricane to swoop forward and make the kill. Despite much practice and a great deal of patience the technique was never a success; nevertheless, in September 1942, the Flight was raised to squadron status as 533 Squadron.

However, by early 1943, the airfield's operational career had come to a close – the enemy were no longer close enough – and Charmy Down initially became a training base. It was used by the Fighter Leaders School element of No.52 Operational Training Unit. Equipped with Spitfires and responsible for passing on tactical lessons, the school was here from February to August 1943 as part of No.10 Group, moving to Aston Down on 16 August. The move was initiated because Charmy Down had been allocated to the Americans, who were in the process of acquiring a large number of airfields in this region, primarily for airborne forces. The airfield was used by

the 8th Air Force from November 1943 to October 1944, with the main role being that of a Tactical Air Depot, which meant no appreciable flying activity. However, the P-61s of the 426th Night Fighter Squadron, and possibly the 423rd NFS, may have spent a short period here in June 1944.

The 1944 survey showed Charmy Down with three tarmac runways, connected by a peri track, off which were forty-five dispersals and twelve Blister hangars, one large group of which was situated at the end of a taxiway at the north-east side of the airfield (the area shown as Hartley Farm on the modern OS map).

With the departure of the Americans, the airfield was transferred to No.23 Group, Flying Training Command for use by South Cerney's No.3 PAFU as an RLG, a role it held to December 1945. The Harvards and Oxfords of the parent unit made some use of Charmy but it was not ideal, as there were other busy airfields nearby (such as Colerne – only two miles away). When the trainers left in late-1945, the airfield's only flying was carried out by No.92 Gliding School, but this was short-lived and the airfield was de-requisitioned in the late-1940s.

Despite sixty years of neglect the airfield is still easy

The Hurricane-equipped 87 Squadron spent nearly two years (in two periods) at Charmy Down, specialising in night fighter operations.

to spot from the air, the pattern of runways, no longer surfaced, still being quite clear, as is the perimeter track.

DECOY SITE

Marshfield ST785782

UNITS

1939–1945

87 Sqn	Nov 1940–7 Aug 1941; 27 Jan 1942–2 Nov 1942	Hurricane
88 Sqn	Apr–Jun 1943	Boston
125 Sqn	7 Aug 1941–24 Sep 1941	Defiant
137 Sqn	20 Feb 1941–8 Nov 1941	Whirlwind
234 Sqn	23–30 Aug 1943	Spitfire
245 Sqn	26 Oct 1942–29 Jan 1943	Typhoon
247 Sqn det	summer 1942	Hurricane
263 Sqn	7 Aug 1941–28 Jan 1942	Whirlwind
286 Sqn det	spring 1942	various
417 Sqn	27 Nov 1941–26 Jan 1942	Spitfire
421 Sqn	30 Nov 1942–4 Dec 1942	Spitfire
533 Sqn	8 Sep 1942–25 Jan 1943	Havoc, Boston, Hurricane
1454 Flt	21 Jan 1942–Sep 1942	Havoc
52 OTU	Feb 1943–10 Aug 1943	Spitfire, Master
3 PAFU	Oct 1944–Dec 1945	Harvard, Oxford

USAAF

425th NFS	Jun 1944–?	P-61
423rd NFS??		

Post-1945

92 GS	Jun 1945–20 Feb 1948	Cadet, Sedbergh

CHEDWORTH

UTM/Grid: OS Map 163 – SP042131
Lat/Long: N51°48.99 W001°56.42
Nearest Town: Cheltenham 6 miles to north-west

County: Gloucestershire

HISTORY

No.3 Pilots Advanced Flying Unit at South Cerney had almost 200 Airspeed Oxfords on establishment by early 1944 and, to cope with its training load, it used a number of relief landing grounds; Chedworth was in use for this purpose by the PAFU between February 1943 and some time in early 1944 and many a student pilot would have flown circuits around this airfield on its Gloucestershire ridge. The land for the airfield had been acquired in 1941 and a 'general use' airfield laid out in 1942, the intention being that it could be allocated for any suitable use – hence, its cruciform pattern of two runways connected by a perimeter track, but with very few other facilities. It was initially brought into use in April 1942 as a satellite for Aston Down and the first users were from the parent station's No.52 Operational Training Unit. Spitfires from the OTU arrived in late summer. This unit remained the main user into 1944 although, from January 1943, the main resident was the Fighter

Leaders School, formed out of (at Chedworth) and technically still part of No.52 OTU. Spitfires continued to operate over and around Chedworth and, as the FLS's role was to teach tactics, this involved some 'interesting displays' over the airfield. The school moved to Charmy Down in February and, although it remained an RLG/satellite for the OTU to early 1944, Chedworth was used by various training units over the next few months.

The Oxfords of 3 PAFU (*see* above) were joined by a detachment from No.6 PAFU, which used Chedworth between August and October 1943 from their parent base at Little Rissington.

Operational types returned in late-1943, when Chedworth was used by a sub-unit (Combined Gunnery Squadron) of Nos.60 and 63 OTUs. This was formed from the gunnery flights of the two OTUs and notionally operated Mosquitoes and Martinets, although Beaufighters appear to have been on

AIRFIELD DATA DEC 1944

Command:	Fighter Command	Runway surface:	Tarmac
Function:	Tactical Exercise Unit, Satellite	Hangars:	Extra-Over Blister × 2
Runways:	035 deg 1,400 × 50yd	Dispersals:	25
	115 deg 1,300 × 50yd	Personnel:	Officers – 22 (1 WAAF)
			Other Ranks – 650 (65 WAAF)

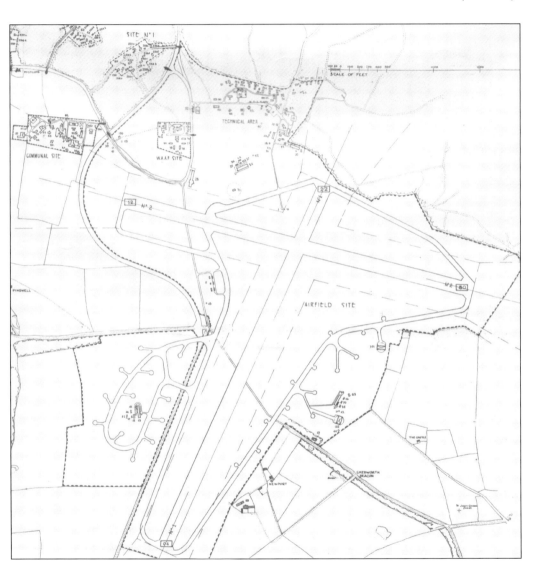

strength. The aircraft returned to their respective parents in January and February 1944 but, in April, No.3 Tactical Exercise Unit moved south from Annan and used Aston Down and Chedworth, with the latter becoming home to 'C Squadron' with its Mustangs. At the end of the year, the airfield was allocated as a satellite to the Typhoon-equipped No.55 Operational Training Unit, whose parent base

The airfield layout is still distinct from the air and a number of buildings (huts of various types and an impressive pill box) still survive.

was Aston Down and which had re-formed by renumbering the TEU. This commitment lasted to May 1945 and, between the two airfields, the OTU operated over 100 Typhoons.

Chedworth was immediately reduced to Care and Maintenance; in December, it was transferred to Admiralty control, although little use appears to have been made of the site. The runways were maintained in good condition for some time and the exact date at which Chedworth passed back into civil hands is uncertain. This probably occurred in the early 1950s and roads that had been closed since the construction of the airfield were re-opened. Traces of both runways survive (the airfield is very easy to spot from the air) and one of the roads follows the line of the old peri track on the west of the airfield. Various buildings survive on the airfield and in the surrounding woods.

Units

1939–1945

Unit	Dates	Aircraft
52 OTU	25 Aug 1942–25 Jan 1944	Hurricane, Master, Spitfire
FLS	Jan–Feb 1943	Spitfire
3 PAFU	Feb 1943–Jan 1944?	Oxford
6 PAFU	Aug 1943–Oct 1943	Oxford
60/63 OTU	Oct 1943–Feb 1944	Mosquito, Martinet
55 OTU	18 Dec 1944–29 May 1945	Typhoon, Master

CHICKERELL

County: Dorset

UTM/Grid: OS Map 194 – SY655796
Lat/Long: N50°36.90 W002°29.33
Nearest Town: Weymouth 1½ miles to south-east

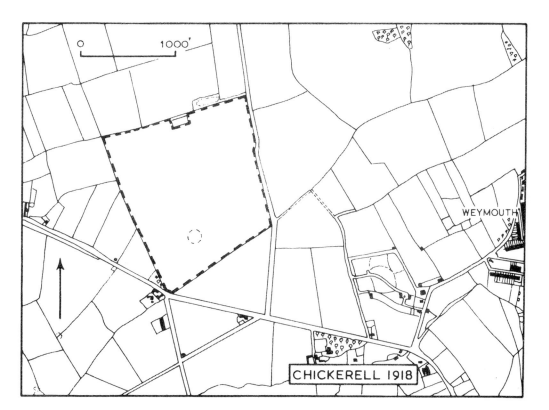

CHICKERELL 1918

HISTORY

In early 1918 the outcome of World War One was still in the balance and amongst the renewed German offensives was that by U-boats to try to strangle Allied shipping movements. In response to this a series of new landing grounds was created, to bolster those already operational and for which the primary role would be anti-submarine patrols. The intention was to provide frequent, if not constant, air cover around coastal waters. The site at Chickerell, close to the coast by Weymouth, was one such site and simply comprised a square field with virtually no facilities other than a hutted camp on the east side. In June 1918, No.513 Flight formed at Chickerell as part of the RAF's re-organization of coastal air defences; the Flight became part of 253 Squadron (as 'D Flight'), transferring to 241 Squadron in August. The Flight operated the DH6, the standard coastal type, and finally disbanded in January 1919.

For most of these landing grounds that would have been the end, but Chickerell's proximity to Weymouth led to attempts to make it into a civil airfield. Early 'commercial' flights with converted HP 0/400s were not a great success and there appears to have been little use of the airfield in the 1920s, although some private flying may have taken place. The military re-appeared from time to time; for example, using Chickerell as a detachment base for aircraft exercising with naval units from Portland (late-1920s) or using the Chesil Bank ranges (1937 onwards). The 1930s were, perhaps, more notable for appearances by the Cobham Flying Circus, a connection still marked by one of the roads on the housing estate that now covers the site – Cobham Drive – although one wonders how many residents know what this means.

The convenient location of the strip close to the

Chickerell in April 1929, a period when it was used by aircraft working with Navy units off the south coast.

weapon ranges kept Chickerell in use throughout World War Two as an emergency-landing airfield for aircraft that got into trouble whilst using the range and also for occasional detachments, although these seldom feature in records. Indeed, Chickerell is something of a mystery site (a good subject for a researcher). Fleet Air Arm units would also have made intermittent use of the airfield, because of its location close to major naval installations and training areas, but again this is poorly recorded. This type of usage continued into the post-war period and one of the few definite detachments from squadron records was that by helicopters of 705 Squadron for a

few months in early 1953. Naval use appears to have ended in 1955 and the long-lived but seldom used Chickerell was passed out of military service in 1959. As mentioned above, the site has now vanished under housing.

UNITS

Pre-1919

513Flt	7 Jun 1918–23 Jan 1919	DH6

Post-1945

705Sqn FAA det	15 Jan 1953–27 Mar 1953	various

CHIVENOR

County: Devon

UTM/Grid: OS Map 180 – SS492344 (Barnstaple SS503345)
Lat/Long: N51°05.18 W004°09.00 (Barnstaple N51°05 W004°08)
Nearest Town: Barnstaple 3 miles to east

HISTORY

North Devon is best-known for the airfield at Chivenor and the pre-war civil airfield at Barnstaple, which was on the same site, is all but forgotten. In late-1933 the Barnstaple and North Devon Flying Club was formed to provide pleasure-flying and flying training and the small field adjacent to the River Taw to the west of the town was officially given the grandiose title of North Devon Airport on 13 June 1934. Passenger flights took tourists to the island of Lundy (famous for its Puffins) and, over the next few years, a number of other passenger services were added.

The small landing ground at Barnstaple was used in 1939 by two detachments of No.1 Anti-Aircraft Co-operation Unit from its main base at Watchet in Somerset, X Flight from January to the end of the year and Z Flight for a few weeks in November and December: both Flights operated Queen Bee target-drones. The following year Atlantic Coast Airlines became part of the Civilian Repair Organization and, from August 1940, handled a wide range of small aircraft: from Magisters to Prefects, as well as a number

of Oxfords. However, the airfield was of very limited use and, when RAF Chivenor opened, the airfield at Barnstaple was closed.

With the Atlantic destined to be a major battlefield it was evident that airfields would be needed on the west and south-west coasts of England and, in May 1940, reconstruction work started, to turn the small grass airfield of Barnstaple into a fully equipped operational station. A classic three-runway layout was adopted on the flat area of land bounded by the river estuary and the Barnstaple to Ilfracombe railway line, with the main runway oriented east/west and with all support facilities on the north side. Approaches to the runways were not ideal, with the estuary providing the usual hazards of birdstrikes and the large hill just to the north often being masked in low cloud or sea mist. The technical site eventually comprised a group of eight hangars, in pairs, with a large hutted camp – much of which still survives. Like most major airfields, Chivenor underwent almost constant development and, by the 1944 sur-

AIRFIELD DATA DEC 1944

Command:	Coastal Command	Runway surface:	Concrete (carpet-coated)
Function:	Operational Parent	Hangars:	Bellman × 4, Hinaidi × 4, Extra-Over Blister × one
Runways:	102 deg 2,000 × 50yd	Dispersals:	45 × Concrete Spectacle, 5 × 150ft diam
	242 deg 1,460 × 50yd	Personnel:	Officers – 268 (2 WAAF)
	162 deg 1,170 × 50yd		Other Ranks – 2,743 (331 WAAF)

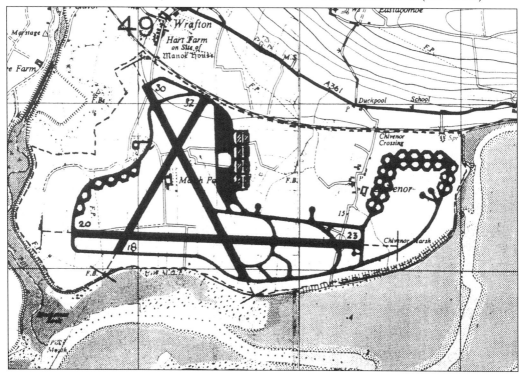

vey, its main runway was 2,000yd and the extensive area of dispersals included a loop at the east end, around what had been the Barnstaple Airport site (the latter area of dispersals being constructed in 1944, when Chivenor became home to three Wellington squadrons, as well as transient traffic).

RAF Chivenor had opened on 12 October 1940, with building work still underway, and its initial employment was for training. No.3 (Coastal) Operational Training Unit formed at Chivenor on 27 November 1940 with responsibility for Anson and Beaufort aircrew training (both ex-No.1 OTU) plus Wellington and Whitley training. The plan did not unfold in this way because of shortage of facilities and only the Beaufort element was fully established at Chivenor. This element was re-designated as No.5 (C)OTU in August 1941, as part of No.17 Group, and its initial establishment was 18+6 Beaufort, 6+2

Anson/Oxford and 3+1 target-tow types. The unit spent almost a year at Chivenor and its pupils learnt navigation and weapons before being sent to their squadrons. The OTU moved to Turnberry, its original intended home, in May 1942 and Chivenor spent the rest of the war as an operational station. As the unit list shows, operational squadrons had been using the airfield from its earliest days, but these were here either for conversion training or as short-term operational detachments, and it was not until early 1942 that the station truly began to take on the enemy. The author's mother was a WAAF (parachute packer) at Chivenor and she remembered the night in November 1941 when a Ju88 landed here in error; the aircraft eventually joined the RAF's 'Enemy Air Circus'.

January 1942 saw the formation of No.1417 (Leigh Light) Flight, to develop and employ anti-submarine tactics using the high-power Leigh Light searchlight, the aircraft homing on its target at night using ASV (radar) and, when close to the target, switching on the searchlight to illuminate it and complete the attack. The Flight became 172 Squadron in April and this unit played a major role in the campaign over the Bay of Biscay, denying the U-boats the opportunity to surface at night to recharge batteries and purge air. It is always difficult to single-out individual squadrons for the part they played in the war, but 172 Squadron is one of those units worthy of special mention.

The Battle of the Atlantic, and particularly the U-boat war, was not going well for the Allies in early 1942 and, in mid-1942, Bomber Command loaned a number of Whitley squadrons to Coastal Command to provide extra aircraft – one of those units was 51 Squadron and it moved its Whitley Vs from Dishforth to Chivenor in May. The same period saw the similarly equipped 77 Squadron, also on loan, operating from Chivenor. Chivenor had become a No.19 Group station in May 1942, the departure of the OTU having finalized this transfer to operational status. With Coastal Command becoming increasingly effective over the Bay of Biscay, the Germans employed fighters to harass the attackers and, in response, the Command started sending Beaufighters to counter this problem. The Beaufighters of 235 Squadron arrived from Docking in mid-July 1942 and flew escorts and patrols in what was becoming a very intense battle that both sides had to win. The Whitley squadrons flew anti-submarine and maritime patrols, but returned to the bomber war in October; this move was made because of their unsuitability for the Biscay campaign, pressure from 'Bomber' Harris for the return of his squadrons and the need for space at Chivenor to use the airfields as a staging point for the air route to North Africa, where Operation *Torch* was launched in November.

The unit list shows various movements in the 1943–1944 period but, in essence, Chivenor's main role was for night attacks on German submarines and, for this, its based units primarily used the GR Wellington with ASV and Leigh Light. Coastal Command B-17 Fortresses of 59 Squadron spent a few months here in early 1943 and various Beaufighter squadrons operated their patrols over Biscay, but it was the Wellington that fought the bulk of Chivenor's war. The station was operating with an average of three such squadrons; of these, the most successful in terms of recorded attacks were 172 Squadron and 304 Squadron, both of which scored U-boat 'kills'. The actual making of an attack was, of course, important, but equally important was the fact that the German submariners could never relax or let down their guard whilst transiting the Bay and the thousands of hours of patrol time by the Wellingtons ensured that Coastal Command dominated this battlefield; this was particularly crucial in the summer of 1944, with

235 Squadron plus Beaufighter, October 1942.

Blenheims of 21 Squadron on detachment in April 1941.

December 1944, Wellington XIV of 407 Squadron.

the invasion of Europe by the Allied armada.

The Allied advance in France eventually captured the key Biscay U-boat bases, such as Lorient, and the scale of operations from Chivenor reduced from autumn 1944, which brought about another change round of units. The basic task remained the same, with Wellingtons flying long patrols over vast areas of sea, but it was very seldom that any sightings were made. This routine continued to the end of the war.

Chivenor had been selected as one of the post-war stations for Coastal Command and, as such, the initial plan was for a two-squadron Strike Wing. The Beaufighters and Mosquitoes of 248 and 254 Squadrons duly arrived in summer 1945 – but the plan was almost immediately changed and within

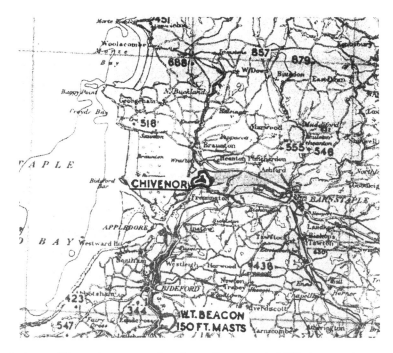

months they had gone. The station was transferred to Fighter Command on 1 October 1946 and its initial use was by 691 Squadron on anti-aircraft co-operation work. Significant users between the end of the war and the arrival of Chivenor's main training unit (No.229 OCU in March 1951) included No.203 Advanced Flying School, followed by the Overseas Ferry Unit (during whose time the station was under the control of Transport Command). However, it was the arrival of the OCU from Leuchars in March 1951 that gave Chivenor its post-war career.

The OCU, with its component shadow squadrons (*see* unit list for an attempt at sorting-out the bewildering changes of shadow-squadron numbering), remained at Chivenor to September 1974, having used the Vampire, Meteor and, for most of the period, the Hunter as its main trainer. Training included tactics and weapons and Chivenor was an ideal base for this type of activity, with plenty of free airspace and no shortage of weapon ranges. The decision to move the unit to Brawdy was hotly debated and much criticized, but the Welsh airfield was home to the other tactical training unit and so the move took place. It was not the end for Chivenor, as the SAR helicopter detachment of 22 Squadron remained in place, not so much to provide the military rescue cover for which these SAR units had been created but as a public relations and 'local service' commitment for rescuing tourists who got stranded on beaches or floated out to sea in small boats! Rescue helicopters had first appeared at Chivenor with a detached flight of 257 Squadron's

Sycamores in 1957; the commitment was subsequently taken over by 22 Squadron and this squadron has remained in residence, with the standard flight of two helicopters, ever since. Their main role, as mentioned, was to pull downed aircrew out of the water or from wherever they ended up but, other than on exercises (the regular sea dinghy-drills that all RAF aircrew 'suffered'), this was, fortunately, seldom required for real.

Training was certainly intense and there were aircraft and aircrew losses during Chivenor's forty years as a fast-jet training base.

The move to Brawdy was a mistake and the fast jets returned to Chivenor in April 1981 as No.2 Tactical Weapons Unit. The two Hawk squadrons were given shadow numbers as 63 Squadron and 151 Squadron; the author was posted to the former for a fast-jet refresher course in 1982 and has kept the posting signal, as it says 633 Squadron (of film 'fame') – a slip or was someone passing on a message? The TWU was renamed as No.7 Flying Training School (a far less 'punchier' title and one that was not well received by the instructors) but it only lasted two years. Despite the extensive rebuilding work that had taken place in the early 1980s before the station re-opened, which included one of the most modern officers' messes in the RAF (although a soulless building when compared with the classic 1930s messes), RAF Chivenor was axed again in October 1994.

The Royal Marines knew a good thing when they saw one and, on 1 October 1995, Chivenor became a Royal Marines barracks (as RMB Chivenor). The RAF

Hawks at RAF Chivenor

maintains a toehold, courtesy of the SAR Sea Kings of 'A Flight' 22 Squadron and the Vigilant T1 gliders of No.624 Volunteer Gliding School. The latter provides air experience gliding for the Air Training Corps and it was in an ATC glider at Chivenor in 1968(ish) that the author made his first solo – a quick circuit for his ATC gliding certificate!

DECOY SITE

Q	Braunton Burrows	SS454338

UNITS

1939–1945

14 Sqn	24 Oct 1944–25 May 1945	Wellington
36 Sqn	26 Sep 1944–9 Mar 1945	Wellington
51 Sqn	6 May 1942–27 Oct 1942	Whitley
59 Sqn	Dec 1942–27 Mar 1943	Fortress
77 Sqn	6 May 1942–5 Oct 1942	Whitley
172 Sqn	4 Apr 1942–1 Sep 1944	Wellington
179 Sqn	6 Sep 1944–1 Nov 1944+	Wellington
235 Sqn	16 Jul 1942–21 Jan 1943	Beaufighter
252 Sqn	1 Dec 1940–6 Apr 1941	Blenheim, Beaufighter
272 Sqn	3 Apr 1941–28 May 1941	Blenheim, Beaufighter
304 Sqn	19 Feb 1944–21 Sep 1944	Wellington
404 Sqn	22 Jan 1943–2 Apr 1943	Beaufighter
407Sqn	1 Apr 1943–29 Jan 1944+	Wellington
407 Sqn	28 Apr 1944–28 Aug 1944; 11 Nov 1944–4 Jun 1945	Wellington
459 Sqn	10 Mar 1945–10 Apr 1945	Baltimore
547 Sqn	10 Dec 1942–22 Jan 1943; 2 Apr 1943–31 May 1943	Wellington
612 Sqn	25 May 1943–9 Sep 1944+	Wellington
1 AACU	Jan 1939–Dec 1939	Queen Bee (as Barnstaple)
3 (C) OTU	27 Nov 1940–Aug 1941	Beaufort
5 (C) OTU	1 Aug 1941–16 May 1942	various
1417Flt	8 Jan 1942–4 Apr 1942	Wellington
ASVTF/U	Jan 1944–20 Jun 1945	Wellington

Post-1945

5 Sqn	26 Oct 1949–13 Mar 1951	various
17 Sqn	11 Feb 1949–13 Mar 1951	various
19 Sqn	1 Sep 1992–1 Oct 1994	Hawk (7 FTS)
22 Sqn	c1958–current	Whirlwind, Wessex, Sea King
26 Sqn	23 Sep 1946–23 Oct 1946	Tempest
63 Sqn	1 Jun 1963–Sep 1974	Hunter (229 OCU)
63 Sqn	Apr 1981–Apr 1992	Hunter, Hawk (2 TWU)
63 Sqn	1 Apr 1992–1 Sep 1992	Hawk (7 FTS)
79 Sqn	Jan 1967–Sep 1974+	Hunter (229 OCU)
92 Sqn	1 Sep 1992–1 Oct 1994	Hawk (7 FTS)
127 Sqn	Nov 1957–Nov 1958	(229 OCU)
131 Sqn	Oct 1958–Nov 1958	(229 OCU)
145 Sqn	Nov 1958–1 Jun 1963	(229 OCU)
151 Sqn	Sep 1981–Apr 1992	Hunter, Hawk (2 TWU)
234 Sqn	Nov 1958–Sep 1974	Hunter (229 OCU)
248 Sqn	19 Jul 1945–30 May 1946	Mosquito
254 Sqn	29 Jun 1945–26 Nov 1945	Beaufighter, Mosquito
275 Sqn det	1957–?	Sycamore, Whirlwind
517 Sqn	30 Nov 1945–21 Jun 1946	Halifax
521 Sqn	3 Nov 1945–31 Mar 1946	Fortress, Halifax
691 Sqn	4 Oct 1946–11 Feb 1949	various
CCFATU	6 Jan 1946–21 Feb 1946	Martinet, Spitfire
203 AFS	15 Oct 1947–19 Jul 1949	Spitfire
OFU	17 Jul 1950–19 Mar 1951	various
229 OCU	28 Mar 1951–2 Sep 1974	Vampire, Sabre, Hunter (see squadrons)
624 VGS	3 Sep 1965–current	various
2 TWU	1 Apr 1981–1 Apr 1992	Hunter, Hawk (see squadrons)
7 FTS	1 Apr 1992–1 Oct 1994	Hawk (see squadrons)

CLEAVE

County: Cornwall

UTM/Grid: OS Map 190 – SS205125
Lat/Long: N50°53.08 W004°33.00
Nearest Town: Bude 4 miles to south

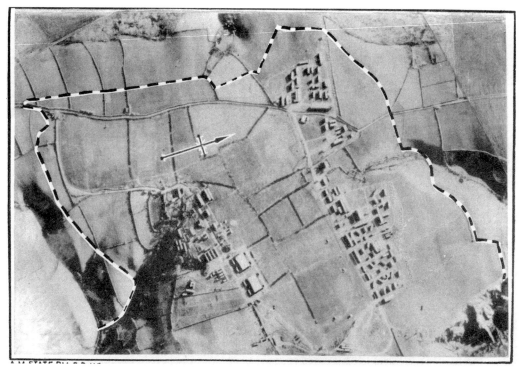

HISTORY

Cleave was an unusual airfield in that it was designed for, and spent the whole war as, a base for anti-aircraft co-operation-unit use, although this could in part be explained by the large number of ranges in the area and the fact that South-West England was a major training area – although this site on the cliff-tops near the seaside resort of Bude was not perhaps the best place for this function. The simple grass field was laid out in early 1939 for No.22 Group (to Army Co-operation Command when it formed at the end of 1940) and its first occupants arrived in May: 'G Flight' of No.1 Anti-Aircraft Co-operation Unit bringing its Wallaces all the way from Usworth and 'V Flight' of the same unit forming with Queen Bees from the former Pilotless Aircraft Flight at Henlow. The former were tasked to work with No.12 LAAPC (Light Anti-Aircraft Practice Camp) at Penhale and the latter with No.6 HAAPC (Heavy AAPC) at Cleave. The catapult-launch system for the QBs was ready by June and by mid-summer both Flights were

fully occupied. No.1 AACU either formed or sent other Flights to Cleave over the next few months to operate with a number of ranges and practice camps, making Cleave one of the busiest airfields performing this essential role. The airfield was home to a variety of aircraft types, from the pilotless Queen Bees to various target-tow types, such as the Henley, Wallace, Lysander and others.

Two roving Ju88s found and bombed the airfield on 26 August 1940, damaging a number of aircraft and creating a certain amount of disturbance at this remote and essentially 'peaceful' airfield.

Cleave had undergone fairly constant development, with the hutted areas – one on the north side and one on the south side – growing to cope with the increasing number of units. The hutted camp on the north side also housed army personnel attending gunnery courses, including American personnel. The 1944 survey showed three hangars, with two Bellmans and one Blister. The operating surface

AIRFIELD DATA DEC 1944

Command:	Fighter Command	Runway surface:	Grass
Function:	Anti-Aircraft Co-operation Unit	Hangars:	Bellman × 2, Blister × one
Runways:	ENE/WSW 900yd	Dispersals:	Nil
	N/S 750yd	Personnel:	Officers – 13 (2 WAAF)
			Other Ranks – 486 (78 WAAF)

remained grass, with two notional strips (although one plan shows four strips), and there were times when this caused problems because of waterlogging. There is even some suggestion that the airfield was closed, or at least restricted in use, for a few months in 1942. The AACU had four of its Flights at Cleave from 1940 to 1942 and, in November 1942, they were all re-designated as numbered Flights in the 1600 series (*see* unit list). The following June the

station transferred to Fighter Command when that organization absorbed elements of the disbanded Army Co-operation Command, but this was only a paper transaction and Cleave's role and units were unchanged. No.1618 Flight was disbanded in autumn 1943 and the three remaining Flights were brought together in December 1943 to form 639 Squadron; this unit, operating Henley IIIs and Hurricane IVs, remained at Cleave for the rest of the war. The squadron disbanded at the end of April 1945 and the station was put into Care and Maintenance the following month, finally closing in November.

There is little to see from the air of what was once RAF Cleave – but the area of the old camp is now dominated by a series of domes (weather-covered radio antennae), as it is a listening post and relay station for the Combined Signals Organization, notionally Anglo-American but more of the latter. The site is now referred to as Morwenstow, after the nearby village.

UNITS

1939–1945

639 Sqn	1 Dec 1943–30 Apr 1945	Henley, Hurricane
1 AACU:		
GFlt	15 May 1939–1 Nov 1942	Wallace, Henley
VFlt	15 May 1939–1 Nov 1942	Queen Bee
DFlt	6 Sep 1939–1 Nov 1942	various
KFlt	26 Aug 1940–6 Sep 1940	various
OFlt	5 Nov 1940–1 Nov 1942	various
1602 Flt	1 Nov 1942–1 Dec 1943	Henley (ex-DFlt)
1603 Flt	1 Nov 1942–16 Dec 1942; 27 Jan 1943–1 Dec 1943	Henley (ex-GFlt)
1604 Flt	1 Nov 1942–1 Dec 1943	Henley (ex-OFlt)
1618 Flt	1 Nov 1942–autumn 1943?	Queen Bee, Tiger Moth (ex-VFlt)

CLYFFE PYPARD

County: Wiltshire

UTM/Grid: OS Map 173 – SU071770
Lat/Long: N51°28.45 W001°54.00
Nearest Town: Swindon 8 miles to north-east

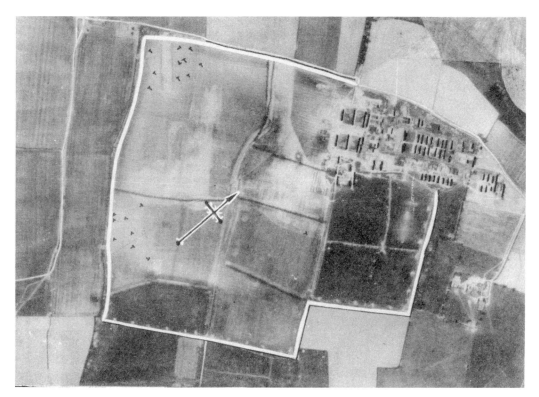

HISTORY

The grass airfield at Clyffe Pypard was unusual in that it had only one resident for its entire period of use – No.29 Elementary Flying Training School. By 1940 the need for pilots was far greater than the capacity of the existing training schools and the RAF needed to find and man training schools in the UK – in the west of the country, as far from enemy interference as practicable, and overseas. Clyffe Pypard was one of those sites.

The airfield was laid out on a large area of farmland to the south of the village after which it was named. Construction took place during early 1941, with field boundaries being removed from the operating area (but, as the air photo shows, they were 'replaced' as part of the camouflage scheme for the airfield) and a hutted camp constructed on the north corner, with technical site (hangars and workshops) alongside the accommodation and domestic buildings in neat rows. In June 1941, Marshalls Flying Schools (Cambridge) were asked to take on responsibility for

the formation and running of a new Class A school to be based at Clyffe Pypard and No.29 EFTS duly opened on 8 September 1941 within No.50 Group. As a Class A school it was given an establishment of 48+24 aircraft to be organized in four flights to handle 120 pupil pilots. No.1 course started on 15 September with seventy pupils and the Tiger Moths were soon pounding the circuit and trying to find clear airspace for general handling. There is some confusion as to the initial size of the school but, at some point, it was raised to Class A+2, which gave it an establishment of seventy-two Tiger Moths and thirty-six Magisters, although this may not have taken place until June 1942.

Inevitably there were accidents and, equally inevitably, some of these were fatal – all too often they involved mid-air collisions. It was a very busy training establishment and so made use of a number of RLGs, including Alton Barnes and Penkridge, as

AIRFIELD DATA DEC 1944

Command:	Flying Training Command	Runway surface:	Grass
Function:	EFTS, Parent	Hangars:	Standard Blister ×
Runways:	E/W 1,333yd		14, Bellman × 4,
	NE/SW 1,116yd		Over Blister × one
	N/S 1,100yd	Dispersals:	Nil
	NW/SE 1,050yd	Personnel:	Officers – 48
			Other Ranks – 580

Tiger Moths – in large numbers – were operated by No.29 EFTS. (via Rod Priddle)

A very quiet-looking Clyffe Pypard in late 1947. (via Rod Priddle)

well as using Manningford as an emergency landing ground. From May 1942, the school acquired a commitment to train army glider pilots. Establishment was changed in January 1943 to 108 Tiger Moths and the Magisters were withdrawn, but the training cycle continued to be hectic. The task increased in October 1944 with the start of grading courses for Fleet Air Arm pupil pilots – the first course of which started on 13 October with 245 pupils! And so the routine continued to the end of the war, although pupil numbers had started to dwindle in the New Year, which was just as well, as the winter weather had caused runway serviceability problems (as it had in previous winters). The airfield had kept a four grass-runway layout, the longest of which was 1,333 yards – plenty for a Tiger Moth, but not enough for the odd four-engined bomber that had tried to land here.

The last of the RLGs, Alton Barnes, returned its detached Flights to the parent airfield in July and the EFTS was virtually halved in size, to sixty aircraft in four Flights, each with fifteen aircraft. The training routine continued post-war, although in October 1946 the Navy commitment ended. However, the following February the Army commitment increased,

with the school taking over glider and AOP pilot training from No.22 EFTS; this added a small number of Austers to the school establishment. The end came in October 1947, when the school was disbanded and its training task taken over by No.21 EFTS at Booker. This was not quite the end of Clyffe Pypard as an RAF facility, as its domestic area was used as an out-station by Lyneham, due to a lack of accommodation at that airfield and the fact that it was only three miles to the north-west. This usage continued to June 1961.

The site was quickly returned to agriculture, but a significant number of buildings have survived and, whilst there is little to see from the air, a ground visit is worthwhile.

UNITS

1939–1945

29 EFTS	13 Sep 1941–5 Nov 1947	Tiger Moth, Oxford, Anson

COLERNE (Station 353)

County: Wiltshire

UTM/Grid: OS Map 173 – ST810720
Lat/Long: N51°26.45 W002°16.45
Nearest Town: Bath 6 miles to south-west

Formation rehearsal over Colerne, 1953.

HISTORY

The advanced element of the opening-up party arrived at Colerne on 25 September 1940, the intention being for the station to be ready by 1 October (SOM 857/40). This delightful airfield is best-known for its post-war use as a transport base and its origins as an Aircraft Storage Unit and its wartime role as a fighter base are often forgotten. This area of land on the outskirts of the village of Colerne, a few miles to the north-east of Bath, was surveyed and accepted in 1936 and, whilst at first glance it might not have seemed ideal – being bounded by roads and with deep valleys on all sides of the plateau on which it stood, the surface was good and development was expected to be straightforward. Work did not commence until

June 1939, by which time the Air Ministry had acquired a site of around 900 acres. The builders had a few farm buildings to demolish, plus field boundaries to be removed and some levelling of the ground where runways would be constructed, but progress was initially rapid, although it slowed over the winter because of poor weather.

The still far from complete airfield opened on 1 January 1940, for use by Maintenance Command for aircraft storage, a temporary grass strip being used and the first of the dispersal areas having been made ready. No.39 Maintenance Unit had a cadre of personnel on site from late-1939, but did not officially form until 1 January 1940 within No.41 Group and was not officially open for aircraft storage until May. For much of its wartime occupation of Colerne it also used a number of satellite landing grounds: No.1 (Slade Farm), No.2 (Starveall Farm) and No.28 (Barton Abbey). The MU handled a diverse range of aircraft, from Ansons and Fulmars to Spitfires, Tomahawks, Liberators and Wellingtons. The airfield plans clearly show four main dispersal areas, each centred around two or more hangars, this unusual pattern being a result of the airfield's construction as an ASU. The decision was taken, in summer 1940, to construct a standard pattern of three surfaced runways and for Colerne to be handed to Fighter Command, with the MU remaining as a lodger unit. The same month brought a decision to form No.4 Aircraft Assembly Unit, tasked with the erection of Curtiss aircraft (such as the Mohawk and Tomahawk) and this unit was probably in residence, working closely with the MU, from late-1940 (although some records suggest it did not actually form until 1941); it became No.218 MU on 1 March 1942 and, in August that year, took on the highly-important task of fitting SI (Secret Installation) equipment – namely, radar.

But we have moved ahead of ourselves, as Colerne had become a Fighter Command station in October 1940, to house operational squadrons and a Sector HQ for No.10 Group. The first of the hard runways was open for business in September, but it was some months before all three were in use and the Sector Ops Room was not fully operational until April 1941. When complete, the airfield had a neat triangle of runways linked by a perimeter track and with taxiways leading off to the MU dispersal areas, the bulk of which were to the north. As with most major airfields, the runways underwent modification – either to surface or length – from time to time but the overall structure of the airfield, despite additions or alterations to buildings, remained little changed into the post-war years. By 1941, the most important element of air defence for this region was night defence and, to fulfil this role, the Hurricanes of 87 Squadron arrived in late-November from Exeter. However, the bulk of the squadron soon ended up at the satellite airfield of Charmy Down and Colerne remained, from an operational point of view, fairly quiet. Defiants arrived with 256 Squadron in early February but, in March, they changed places with the similarly equipped 307 Squadron at Squires Gate. The Poles were here for only a few weeks, but managed a number of engagements, with at least one confirmed 'kill' – but the two Defiant squadrons had lost far more aircraft and aircrew in accidents. April brought two Spitfire squadrons to Colerne and on the 10th it brought a few German bombs, with a lone aircraft dropping three small bombs that damaged a hangar and caused one fatality.

Night-fighter capability was increased in late-April with the arrival of AI-equipped Beaufighters and Blenheims of 600 Squadron – who scored their first success from Colerne a month later. Night-fighter strength was boosted in June 1941, when 125 Squadron formed with Defiants, although the squadron was still on work-on when it moved to Charmy Down in August; it returned in January 1942, still with Defiants, but began receiving Beaufighter IIFs in February. The unit list shows the large number of fighter squadrons, and a number of support units, that used Colerne in the wartime period, with a mix of single and twin-engined types. Night defence remained the most important role and Colerne was one of the stations to be given a Turbinlite Flight – an attempt to make better use of single-engined fighters by combining them with AI-equipped aircraft that would home the hunter-killer pair and then illuminate the target with a Helmore searchlight. It seemed a good idea in theory and even on exercise, but was never a real success. Colerne had two such Fighter Flights, No.1454 and No.1457. Hurricanes and Spitfires acted as 'Cat's Eye' fighters, relying on moonlight or searchlights to help them find their prey, and in 'moon periods' the fighter strength at the airfield was sometimes increased by a detachment of such aircraft; for example, 19 Squadron for a few days in July 1942.

A strange fighter appeared in September with the arrival of the 27th Fighter Squadron of the 1st Fighter Group, USAAF and their P-38 Lightnings. The squadron was part of 12th Air Force and was here to work-up for the North African campaign, Operation Torch, which meant that they only stayed a few weeks. By 1943, the night-defence commitment had reduced and Colerne began to take on a more offensive role, flying night-intruder ops over enemy territory as well as day rangers; the Mosquitoes of 151 Squadron flew this type of mission from late-April 1943. The overall pace of operations for the station increased in the early part of 1944 as Allied air power prepared for D-Day; the unit list shows the large number of squadrons to have passed through Colerne in this period. However, the list is deceptive, in that squadrons sometimes had only a flight of aircraft at the base, whilst some squadrons that had aircraft here on a temporary basis do not appear at all in the list: for example, on the eve of D-Day, a joint Mosquito unit assembled at Colerne with aircraft from 85 Squadron (twelve), 151 Squadron (four), 605 Squadron (three), 29 Squadron (three) and 410 Squadron (four), all under the command of Group Captain John Cunningham and tasked to fly stopper patrols to prevent any night-time interference with the landings. And so the war continued for Colerne; of particular note was the arrival in January 1945 of 616 Squadron, an experienced fighter squadron and now the first RAF squadron with the Meteor jet fighter. This was very much a work-up period for the squadron,

Personnel (plus dog) of No.39 MU's test flight.

Typhoon EK139 of 175 Squadron at Colerne in May 1943.
(Peter Green Collection)

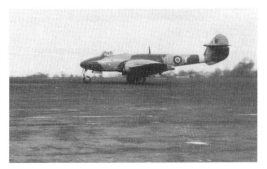

The Meteors of 616 Squadron spent a brief period here in
early 1945.

Buckmaster RP201; the type was operated by No.238
OCU. (via Rod Priddle)

but a few weeks later they departed to Andrews Field.

Jets returned the following month, when Colerne became home to the first jet training unit, No.1335 Conversion Unit, with 504 Squadron arriving in April to be converted to Meteors. In May, the station was transferred to No.11 Group and Colerne entered the post-war period as a jet-fighter base; but it was still an MU and, whilst the RAF's new jet-fighters were a sign of the future, the arrival – and destruction by scrapping – of hundreds of unwanted aircraft was a sign of the past. The year following the end of the war had not been a good one, as there had been a number of fatal Metcor crashes; on 1 November 1946 the station ended its fighter period and was handed back to Maintenance Command. The unit list indicates the diversity of units here during the late-1940s and early 1950s, including Auster AOP Flights, a gliding school and a number of Communications Flights.

Fighter Command took-over again on 15 May 1952 and for the next five years Colerne was back in the training business, firstly with the Airborne Interception School and then with No.238 OCU (as the AIS became in June). The unit primarily used AI-equipped Brigands and its main role was training navigators in the use of airborne radar. Meteors returned to Colerne in 1956, but it was short-lived, as the OCU departed to North Luffenham in January

36 Squadron parade in front of one of their Hastings.

1957. It was all change for the Wiltshire airfield, with Transport Command taking control on 1 January. The Hastings of 24 Squadron arrived the same day from Abingdon and, a few months later, they were joined by 511 Squadron. However, September 1958 saw 511 Squadron renumber as 36 Squadron, the crews and aircraft taking on their new identity overnight. The Squadron's Hastings spent nearly ten years operating worldwide from here. A year after the change of number, the Hastings strength was boosted

AIRFIELD DATA DEC 1944

Command:	Fighter Command	Runway surface:	Tarmac
Function:	Sector Airfield	Hangars:	L Type × 8, K Type × 3, J Type × 2, Over Blister × one
Runways:	256 deg 1,930 × 50yd	Dispersals:	16 × Twin-Engine, one × Fortress
	196 deg 1,175 × 50yd	Personnel:	Officers – 167 (24 WAAF)
	302 deg 1,000 × 50yd		Other Ranks – 3,173 (261 WAAF)

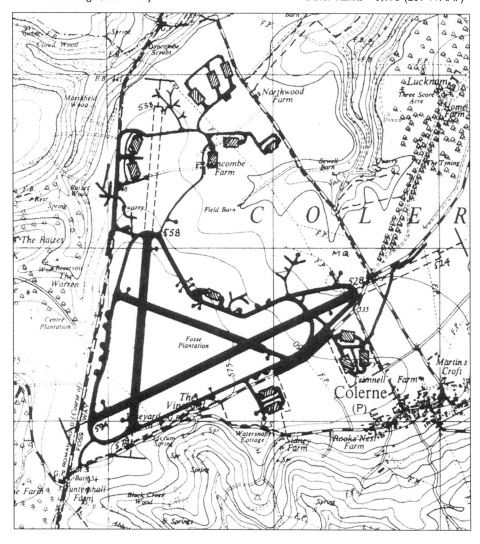

by the formation of 114 Squadron (April 1959), which operated C.1s and C.2s to September 1961, when it disbanded. The transport era was a busy but short-lived one for Colerne and the reduction in strength started in 1967, with 36 Squadron moving to Lyneham to convert to the C-130 Hercules. However, Colerne had been allocated as the RAF's major servicing base for the new transport type, a role it retained for eight years. By early 1968 the squadrons had gone, but the airfield was increasingly busy with its engineering role.

The Defence White Paper of 1975 listed Colerne as

one of the many airfields to close, with its engineering task to be moved to the Hercules base at Lyneham. RAF Colerne closed its gates on 31 March 1976, but immediately became Azimghur Barracks with the army. During its thirty years of army 'occupation', the base has been used for a number of activities, from Junior Leader training to communications centre; aircraft and helicopters appeared from time to time on exercise or visits and the airfield was maintained in operational condition. Since 1993 there has been a permanent RAF flying presence by No.3 Air Experience Flight, joined in 1994 by Bristol University Air Squadron. To the casual observer the airfield is a well-preserved picture of an RAF station of the late-war and immediate post-war period.

There is one final aspect of Colerne worthy of note: from the late-1940s to 1975 the station acquired aircraft for what became known as the Colerne Aircraft Museum and, whilst this had started informally as a way of preserving operational types, it grew to include a number of 'one-offs', such as the prone-position Meteor and the Handley Page 115 research aircraft. When the collection was finally put up for auction in June 1975 it comprised thirty-three airframes.

Note: For those wanting a more detailed history of Colerne – and the other Wiltshire airfields – Rod Priddle's *Airfields of Wiltshire* is highly recommended: the Colerne entry is 35,000 words long with a good selection of pictures.

DECOY SITES

	Marshfield	ST785782
Q/QF	Monkton Farleigh	ST820661
Q	West Littleton	ST767764

UNITS

HQ units at Colerne

No.149 (LRF) Wing	28 Jul 1944–Sep 1944
No.27 (Signals Training) GP	15 Sep 1949–20 Jul 1953

1939–1945

19 Sqn	23–31 Jul 1942	Spitfire
29 Sqn	22 Feb 1945–11 May 1945	Mosquito
87 Sqn	28 Nov 1940–18 Dec 1940; 7 Aug 1941–27 Jan 1942	Hurricane
89 Sqn	25 Sep 1941–19 Nov 1941	Beaufighter
118 Sqn	5–9 Apr 1941	Spitfire
124 Sqn det	spring 1943	Spitfire
125 Sqn	16 Jun 1941–7 Aug 1941; 25 Jan 1942–14 May 1942	Defiant, Beaufighter
131 Sqn	10–22 Feb 1944	Spitfire
137 Sqn	2 Jan 1944–4 Feb 1944	Typhoon
151 Sqn	30 Apr 1943–16 Aug 1943; 17 Nov 1943–25 Mar 1944	Mosquito
165 Sqn	10 Feb 1944–10 Mar 1944	Spitfire
175 Sqn	8 Apr 1943–29 May 1943	Typhoon
183 Sqn	24 Mar 1943–8 Apr 1943; 30 May 1943–5 Jun 1943	Typhoon
184 Sqn	1 Dec 1942–1 Mar 1943	Hurricane
219 Sqn	26 Mar 1944–1 Apr 1944	Mosquito
256 Sqn	6 Feb 1941–26 Mar 1941	Defiant
263 Sqn	28 Jan 1942–10 Feb 1942; 15 Aug 1942–13 Sep 1942	Whirlwind
264 Sqn	1 May 1942–30 Apr 1942	Mosquito
285 Sqn det	1943–1944	various
286 Sqn	30 Dec 1941–10 Oct 1942+; 20 May 1944–28 Jul 1944	various
307 Sqn	26 Mar 1941–26 Apr 1941	Defiant

Aerial view dated 26 September 1958.

Most of Colerne is still in good condition and in part still in military use (by the Army).

316 Sqn	18 Jun 1941–2 Aug 1941	Hurricane
317 Sqn	26–27 Jun 1941	Hurricane
402 Sqn	4–17 Mar 1942	Hurricane
406 Sqn	17 Sep 1944–27 Nov 1944	Beaufighter
410 Sqn	28 Jul 1944–9 Sep 1944	Mosquito
417 Sqn	26 Jan 1942–24 Feb 1942	Spitfire
456 Sqn det	Dec 1942; 17 Aug 1943– 17 Nov 1943	Beaufighter
488 Sqn	3 May 1944–9 Oct 1944+	Mosquito
501 Sqn	9 Apr 1941–25 Jun 1941	Spitfire
504 Sqn	28 Mar 1945–10 Aug 1945	Meteor
587 Sqn det	summer 1944	various
600 Sqn	27 Apr 1941–6 Oct 1941+	Beaufighter
604 Sqn	13 Jul 1944–6 Aug 1944	Mosquito
616 Sqn	17 Jan 1945–28 Feb 1945	Meteor
10 Gp CF	1 Jul 1940–17 Apr 1945	various
2 ADF	18 Mar 1941–23 Jul 1943	various
1454 Flt	27 Jun 1941–26 Jan 1942	Havoc
1457 Flt	15 Sep 1941–15 Nov 1941	Havoc
1487 Flt det	3 Jan 1943–Feb 1943	Lysander
1498 Flt	14 Aug 1943–12 Sep 1943	Lysander
1335 CU	8 Mar 1945–27 Jul 1945	Meteor

USAAF units

1st FG/27th FS	15 Sep 1942–6 Nov 1942	P-38

Post-1945

24 Sqn	1 Jan 1957–5 Jan 1968	Hastings
36 Sqn	1 Sep 1958–1 Jul 1967	Hastings
74 Sqn	16 May 1946–14 Aug 1946+	Meteor
114 Sqn	13 Apr 1959–30 Sep 1961	Hastings
245 Sqn	10 Aug 1945–16 Aug 1946	Meteor
511 Sqn	1 May 1957–1 Sep 1958	Hastings
662 Sqn	1 Feb 1949–10 Mar 1957	Auster
1335 CU	8 Mar 1945–15 Aug 1946	Meteor
62 Gp CF	7 Jan 1948–30 Jul 1952	various
92 GS	20 Feb 1948–1 Sep 1955	Cadet, Sedbergh
1956 Flt	1 Feb 1949–10 Mar 1957	Auster
1963 Flt	1 Feb 1949–10 Mar 1957	Auster
81 Gp CF	1 Jan 1952–15 Apr 1958	various
AIS	12–15 Jun 1952	Brigand
238 OCU	15 Jun 1952–1 Jan 1957	Brigand, Buckmaster, Meteor
RAFCCS	1 Aug 1952–1 Jul 1957	
228 OCU det	1 Jan 1957–31 May 1957	Valetta
24 Gp CF	1 Jan 1960–1 Apr 1964	Anson
Bristol UAS	Nov 1994–current	Bulldog, Tutor
3 AEF	Aug 1993–current	Chipmunk, Bulldog, Tutor

MEMORIAL

It is shameful that such an important RAF station does not have a proper memorial (see note in the introduction regarding airfield memorials) and all that exists is a lead shield in the church of St John the Baptist; the shield depicts the Station Badge. The graveyard contains forty-three RAF graves (RAF, WAAF, RCAF, RNZAF).

The graveyard contains 43 RAF graves (actually RAF, WAAF, RCAF and RNZAF).

CULDROSE
(HMS *Seahawk*)

County: Cornwall

UTM/Grid: OS Map 203 – SW675258
Lat/Long: N50°05.02 W005°15.13
Nearest Town: Helston 1 mile to north-west

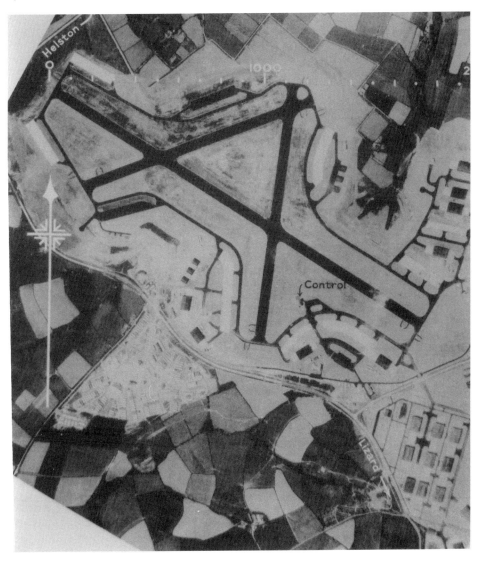

HISTORY

Culdrose is now the Navy's main helicopter base and houses a wide variety of units; it is one of only two surviving main Fleet Air Arm flying stations (along with Yeovilton) – and it is unusual in that it did not open until after World War Two. The site for Culdrose, on a remote peninsula in Cornwall, was acquired in early 1944 and the original intent was to build RNAS Helston (the nearest town) and open it as HMS *Chough* for training purposes. Development was slow and the airfield eventually opened on 17

AIRFIELD DATA DEC 1944

Command: Fleet Air Arm   Runway surface: Tarmac on concrete, concrete ends
Function: Observer and Air Signal School   Hangars: Pentad (185 × 105ft) × 17, Mainhill
                                                                      (84 × 60ft) × 6
Runways: 12/30 6,000 × 150ft   Dispersals: Aprons × 10
              01/19 3,450 × 150ft   Personnel: Officers – 239 (11 WRNS)
              07/25 3,300 × 150ft   Other Ranks – 1,798 (340 WRNS)

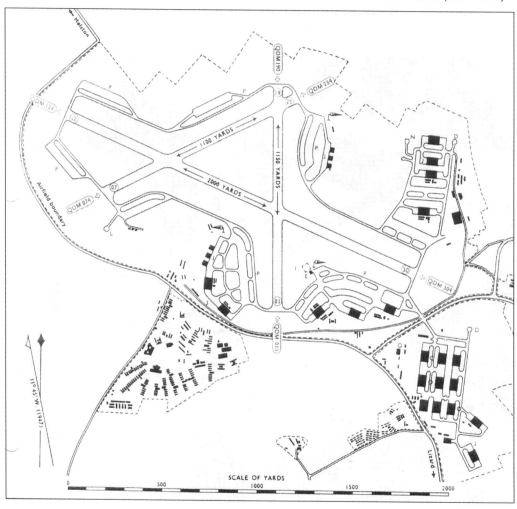

April 1947 – one of the few entirely post-war airfields – as RNAS Culdrose, HMS *Seahawk*. Constructed on a large flat area to the south-east of Helston and within two miles of the sea, the airfield was laid out with three hard runways to standard wartime dimensions, the longest being 2,000 yards, and with the usual excellent naval provision of hangars, mainly comprising Pentad and Mainhill types. The hangars were arranged in groups on the south and east sides of the airfield, along with other technical and support buildings, whilst the domestic site was to the south. The air photo of May 1946 shows Culdrose in its pristine, almost completed, condition with all the major buildings in place; it is also evident from the photo

Skyraider AEW I of 849 Squadron. (Ray Sturtivant)

Sea Fury of 736 Squadron (Ray Sturtivant)

The Gazelles of the Sharks helicopter display team were famed throughout Europe for their superb display routine.

Jetstream of 750 Squadron used to train naval observers.

how many field boundaries had to be removed to make room for the airfield and the fact that a number of minor roads or tracks were cut.

The initial plan was for the new airfield to house the squadrons that formed the Naval Night Fighter School but, as the unit list shows, many of the units that arrived here in 1947–1948 did not survive long. Late-May 1947 brought 780 Squadron from Donibristle to operate its Harvards and Oxfords as the Naval Instrument Flying School, a task it performed from here until disbanded in November 1949. In late-August 1947, the Seafire F.XVIIs of 807 Squadron landed at Culdrose and the squadron spent a few weeks here re-equipping with the Sea Fury F.10, before moving to Eglinton to complete its work-up. This was the other function of Culdrose, as it was for most naval flying stations: to act as shore-base for disembarked squadrons for training, re-equipment or simply a rest period. The unit list shows that Culdrose was used extensively for this purpose.

January 1948 saw the formation of 792 Squadron as a Night Fighter Training Unit, using Firefly NF.1s and a number of Ansons equipped with AI (radar). Sea Hornets replaced the Fireflies two years later, but the squadron disbanded in August 1950. No.809 Squadron had reformed at Culdrose on 20 January 1949 with Sea Hornets, to operate as a night fighter

and strike squadron and, having converted to type, it undertook its first embarked deployment on HMS *Vengeance*. Culdrose remained its shore base and it spent various periods here before disbanding in May 1954; the Sea Hornet had not proved a great success aboard ship. The strength at Culdrose continued to increase: 762 Squadron, a twin-engine conversion unit, arrived from Ford in May 1948, bringing with it Oxfords and Mosquitoes – but it too was destined to have a short life here, disbanding in December 1949. In February 1950 the station had become No.1 Naval Air Fighter School (NAFS) and new squadrons started to arrive to fulfil this role. The major component of this was 736 Squadron, which was equipped with fifty Sea Furies – and a few Seafires – and duly arrived at Culdrose on 1 February from St Merryn. The squadron was split a few months later, with half going to form 738 Squadron. August 1952 brought another change, with 738 taking on the piston-engine role, whilst 736 reformed, out of 702 Squadron, as an Advanced Jet Flying School, for which it acquired Attackers and Meteors. The donor unit, 702 Squadron, had reformed at Culdrose on 4 April 1949 as the Naval Jet Evaluation and Training Unit, with an initial establishment of four Sea Vampire F.20s; these were soon joined by Meteor T.7s and the unit began intensive trials, including carrier evaluation. Supermarine Attackers joined 702 in March 1952 and, a few months later, the change of number-plate took place.

Four Skyraider AEW.1s arrived in November 1951 to form 778 Squadron, the Fleet Air Arm's AEW (Airborne Early Warning) squadron; this was an ugly aircraft, with its great pendulous belly housing the radar, but it had a vital role in protecting carrier task-forces. The squadron disbanded in July 1952, but only so that it could join 849 Squadron at Brawdy. This latter squadron, or rather a Flight of this squadron, subsequently moved to Culdrose and, over the next few years, operated AEW Skyraiders followed by Gannets. In the meantime, the squadrons of the Naval Air Fighter School moved to Lossiemouth in November 1953 and Culdrose became the Naval Observer and Air Signals School, initially with 766 and 796 squadrons, but joined the following year by 750 Squadron. As the unit list shows, various squadrons came and went during this period, a mix of training units and operational units, the latter including 816, 817 and 825 Squadrons, which re-equipped and trained here. However, a few years later the decision was taken to make Culdrose a helicopter base; the Observers School moved to Malta in October 1959 – by which time the first helicopters had arrived. No.705 Squadron had moved across from Lee-on-Solent in January 1958 as a helicopter training unit and was equipped with a mixed fleet of Dragonfly, Hiller HT.1 and Whirlwind helicopters. This squadron is still at Culdrose and, since March 1974, has been operating the Gazelle as its main type in the Basic Helicopter Training role. The squadron became famous for its impressive 'Sharks' helicopter display team (sadly now disbanded).

A great many other helicopter units have used Culdrose: in order of their first appearance at the station they included 700H, 706, 700W, 700V, 824, 826, 771, 810 and 849. The role has remained primarily that of training, but a number of the units have been involved with the evaluation of new types or tactics: for example, 700H formed in April 1960 to act as the Intensive Flying Trials Unit for the Wessex 1 in the ASW role. All the main naval helicopter types have passed through Culdrose, the latest being the EH101 Merlin and, over the years, the station has undergone a number of major rebuilds; not to the flying infrastructure – the airfield looks very much as it did when it opened – but to the support facilities, both technical and domestic. For much of the 1970s, the focus of training was on the Sea King and, in addition to FAA pupils, Culdrose also trained a number of foreign air arms, starting in 1971 with the Indian Navy. Between July 1972 and November 1976 the Royal Navy Foreign Training Unit undertook this role at Culdrose; since then the work has continued as and when, but not using a dedicated training organization. There have even been attempts to co-ordinate RAF and FAA Sea King training and engineering, but with mixed results!

Fixed-wing aviation also returned, with 750 Squadron coming back to Cornwall as the Royal Naval Observer School in September 1972, equipped with Jetstreams. The nearby airfield of Predannack (six miles to the south) has been used as a satellite for many years. RNAS Culdrose (EGDR) still operates all three runways: 12/30 (1,830m), 18/36 (1,051m) and 07/25 (1,042m), along with a number of helicopter landing spots. The station is now home to nine flying units: 700 Sqn operates as the Merlin Operational Evaluation Unit; 750 Sqn Jetstreams for Observer training; 771 Sqn; 792 Sqn with unmanned drones; 814 Sqn with the ASW Merlin; 820 Sqn with ASW Sea King/Merlin; 824 Sqn for Merlin Operational and Advanced Training; 829 Sqn with Merlin; and 849 Sqn with ASW Sea Kings.

UNITS

Post-1945

700 Sqn FAA	– current	Merlin
700 GSqn FAA	17 Aug 1959–1 Feb 1960	Gannet
700 HSqn FAA	1 Jun 1959–27 Aug 1959	Whirlwind
700 SSqn FAA	1 Jul 1969–29 May 1970	Sea King
700 VSqn FAA	29 Oct 1963–7 May 1964	Wessex
700 WSqn FAA	4 Jun 1963–4 Mar 1964	Wasp
702 Sqn FAA	4 Apr 1949–26 Aug 1952	Sea Vampire, Meteor, Attacker
705 Sqn FAA	7 Jan 1958–current	various
706 Sqn FAA	4 Jan 1962–?	Wessex, Wasp, Sea King
706 BSqn FAA	7 Jan 1964–5 Feb 1964	Wessex, Hiller
707 Sqn FAA	9 Dec 1964–15 May 1972	Wessex
736 Sqn FAA	1 Feb 1950–4 Nov 1953	Sea Fury
738 Sqn FAA	1 May 1950–9 Nov 1953	Sea Fury
744 Sqn FAA	1 Mar 1954–23 Oct 1954	Firefly
745 Sqn FAA	6–16 May 1957	Avenger
750 Sqn FAA	30 Nov 1953–13 Oct 1959	Sea Prince
750 Sqn FAA	26 Sep 1972–current	Jetstream
751 Sqn FAA	27 Sep 1957–1 May 1958	Sea Venom
759 Sqn FAA	16 Aug 1951–28 Nov 1953	Seafire, Firebrand, Sea Vampire, Meteor
762 Sqn FAA	1 May 1948–8 Dec 1949	Mosquito, Oxford
765 Sqn FAA	7 Feb 1955–25 Mar 1957	Firefly, Oxford, Sea Balliol
766 Sqn FAA	3 Oct 1953–25 Nov 1954	Firefly, Seafire
771 Sqn FAA	4 Sep 1974–current	various

Culdrose is now a major operator of the Sea King.

778 Sqn FAA	5 Nov 1951–7 Jul 1952	Skyraider
780 Sqn FAA	27 May 1947–16 Nov 1949	Harvard, Oxford
790 Sqn FAA	13 Dec 1947–15 Nov 1949	various
792 Sqn FAA	15 Jan 1948–16 Aug 1950	various
792 Sqn FAA	–current	unmanned drones
796 Sqn FAA	9 Feb 1954–1 Oct 1958	Firefly, Gannet
802 Sqn FAA	9 Mar 1949–5 Dec 1951+	Sea Fury
804 Sqn FAA	3 Jul 1952–17 Nov 1952+	Sea Fury
807 Sqn FAA	19 Aug 1947–29 Sep 1947; 13 Mar 1948–4 May 1948	Sea Fury
807 Sqn FAA	2 May 1950–15 Jun 1950	Sea Fury
809 Sqn FAA	20 Jan 1949–10 May 1954+	Sea Hornet
810 Sqn FAA	20 Apr 1959–12 Jul 1960+	Gannet
810 Sqn FAA	15 Feb 1983–?	Sea King
812 Sqn FAA	19–24 Aug 1948	Firefly
813 Sqn FAA	15 Dec 1947–25 Mar 1949+	Firebrand
814 Sqn FAA	9 Mar 1949–15 Jan 1952	Firefly
814 Sqn FAA	– current	Merlin
815 Sqn FAA	22 Jan 1954–12 Jan 1962+	Avenger, Gannet, Whirlwind
815 Sqn FAA	20 Dec 1964–7 Oct 1966+	Wessex
816 Sqn FAA	15 Aug 1955–29 Feb 1956	Gannet
817 Sqn FAA	18 Aug 1955–29 Feb 1956	Gannet
819 Sqn FAA	Jan 1964; May 1971; Sep 1980; Sep 1983; May 1985	Wessex, Sea King
820 Sqn FAA	3 Nov 1959–3 Oct 1960; 23 Sep 1964–1 Dec 1964	Whirlwind, Wessex
820 Sqn FAA	22 Aug 1966–18 Jul 1967; 18 Jun 1968–current+	Wessex, Sea King, Merlin
824 Sqn FAA	27 Jan 1954–12 Mar 1954; 7 May 1956–20 Jul 1987+	Sea King
824 Sqn FAA	–current	Merlin
825 Sqn FAA	4 Jul 1955–9 Sep 1960+	Gannet
825 Sqn FAA	3 May 1982–17 Sep 1982+	Sea King
826 Sqn FAA	18 Mar 1966–27 Jul 1993+	Wessex, Sea King
829 Sqn FAA	4 Mar 1964–1 Dec 1964	Whirlwind
829 Sqn FAA	–current	Merlin
831 Sqn FAA	28 Oct 1957–Jan 1964	various
845 Sqn FAA	10 Apr 1962–Jun 1973+	Wessex, Wasp, Whirlwind
846 Sqn FAA	8 May 1962–Dec 1975+	Whirlwind, Wessex
849 ESqn FAA	29 Jan 1954–Dec 1964+	Skyraider, Gannet
849 Sqn FAA	–current	Sea King
1830 Sqn FAA	Jul 1953	Firefly
1832 Sqn FAA	May–Jul 1948	Seafire
1833 Sqn FAA	Aug 1958	Seafire
1843 Sqn FAA	Jul 1954	Corsair
ATDU	18 May 1956–31 Aug 1958	

CULMHEAD
(Church Stanton)

County: Somerset

UTM/Grid: OS Map 193 – ST208154
Lat/Long: N50°55.95 W003°07.70
Nearest Town: Taunton 5 miles to north

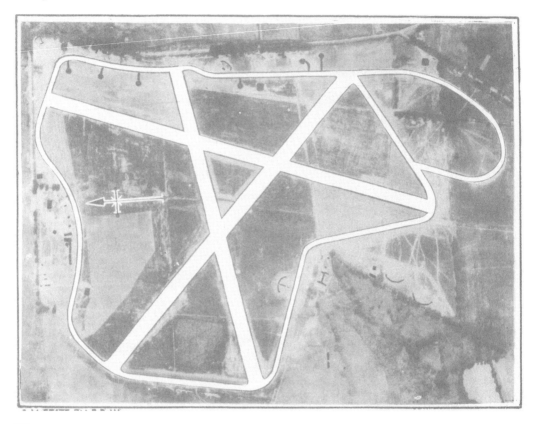

HISTORY

This Somerset fighter base is best known as Culmhead, but for the first two years of its existence it was RAF Church Stanton, after the group of buildings – and church – just to the south-west of the airfield site; the change of name took place on 22 December 1943 and was, perhaps, an attempt to reduce the number of airfields with the prefix 'Church', although it was a bit late in the war to be making such a change. Constructed on the edge of the Black Down Hill to the south of Taunton, the land at Church Stanton, around Tricky Warren Farm – a name that locals sometimes used for the airfield – was acquired in 1940 and, by summer 1941, a standard fighter-airfield had been laid out. This comprised a triangle of three runways with linking perimeter track, off which were a number of dispersals of either fighter-pen type or frying pan. The air-

field was initially provided with a number of Blister hangars and by 1944 it had had ten Blisters and one T.2. There was a small group of support buildings on the north side but, as usual at this period, most admin and domestic sites were 'off airfield' in remote sites two or three miles away. All three runways were surfaced and the 1944 survey shows the longest to have been 1,410 yards.

The first units arrived in early August 1941, the station having opened on 1 August; 302 Squadron moved in from Jurby and 316 Squadron from Colerne. Both were Polish units, the former with Hurricanes and the latter initially with Hurricanes but re-equipping with Spitfires from October. Together they operated as No.2 Polish Fighter Wing and their main task was air defence, although they also undertook convoy patrols, bomber escort and

AIRFIELD DATA DEC 1944

Command:	Fighter Command	Runway surface:	Asphalt
Function:	Operational	Hangars:	Extra-Over Blister × 6, Over Blister × 4, T.2 × one
Runways:	216 deg 1,410 × 50yd	Dispersals:	27 × Single-Engine, 9 × Twin-Engine
	330 deg 1,320 × 50yd	Personnel:	Officers – 23 (10 WAAF)
	276 deg 1,350 × 50yd		Other Ranks – 1,414 (291 WAAF)

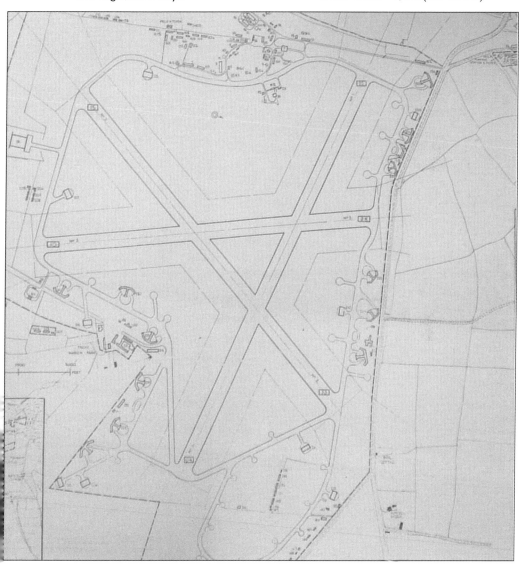

occasional fighter sweeps. The Polish Wing, with 306 Squadron having replaced 316 Squadron, left Church Stanton in summer 1942 to be replaced by Czech units, initially 313 Squadron from June 1942, being joined in October by 312 Squadron to make a Czech Wing. The requirement for air defence for this part of the south-west had reduced to almost nil by late-1942, but there was an increasing need for offensive flights over the Continent and Culmhead's units took part in such missions, often using refuel airfields nearer the coast in order to extend their operational range. The unit list shows a number of changes of unit in this period of 1942–1944, with Spitfires as the main type, although Fleet Air Arm Seafires of No.24 Naval Wing operated from here for a few weeks in April–May 1944. This was the D-Day build-up period and Culmhead, as it was by then, was in its busiest period of operations.

Of particular significance was the presence of 616 Squadron. This unit arrived in mid-May from Fairwood Common with Spitfire VIIs but, during its stay at Culmhead, became the RAF's first jet fighter squadron when it re-equipped with Meteors. The first Meteor Is arrived in mid-July but, by the later part of the month, most of the unit had moved to Manston. On the subject of unusual units: one of the more unusual of the Royal Aircraft Establishment (RAE) sub-units was based at Culmhead for two years from spring 1942; the Research Department Flight had formed in late-1939 to investigate the effects on aircraft of barrage-balloon cables and then develop counters. The unit used a variety of types, such as the Hurricane and Wellington.

By late summer all the major flying units had left Culmhead and No.10 Group, Fighter Command had no further interest in this remote airfield. After a few weeks of inactivity Culmhead was transferred to No.23 Group for training use. No.3 Glider Training School (Stoke Orchard) used Culmhead as a satellite from 9 December 1944 to late-July 1945, the initial

Spitfires of 610 Squadron operated from Culmhead from early April to mid May 1944.

presence being motivated by the poor condition of the airfield at Stoke Orchard. The school used Masters as tugs for Hotspur training gliders. From January, the Glider Instructors Flight was affiliated to the school at Culmhead. However, by July, this last period of flying activity was over and the airfield was reduced to Care and Maintenance.

In the immediate post-war period, No.67 Maintenance Unit made use of Culmhead; the MU was operated by Morris Motors Ltd and had been based in Taunton since forming in October 1940. The period at Culmhead lasted from September 1945 to the disbandment of the unit in April 1946. This once-busy fighter airfield was then closed and its role in the introduction of jet fighters to the RAF was promptly forgotten. The site was not returned to agriculture and was retained in official hands, subsequently being developed into a W/T station as part of the so-called Composite Signals Organization, an Anglo-American activity for communications and intelligence.

The airfield is still very distinctive from the air, as its basic structure has not changed, although the centre of the airfield is now dominated by a group of buildings. A number of the 'off-airfield' sites have also survived.

Units

1939–1945

66 Sqn	28 Jun 1943–10 Aug 1943	Spitfire
126 Sqn	22 May 1944–3 Jul 1944	Spitfire
131 Sqn	17 Sep 1943–10 Feb 1944;	Spitfire
	24 May 1944–28 Aug 1944	
154 Sqn	7 May 1942–7 Jun 1942	Spitfire
165 Sqn	17 Sep 1943–10 Feb 1944;	Spitfire
	10 Mar 1944–2 Apr 1944	
234 Sqn	26 Jun 1943–8 Jul 1943	Spitfire
286 Sqn	10 Apr 1944–20 May 1944	various
302 Sqn	7 Aug 1941–5 Sep 1941	Hurricane
306 Sqn	12 Dec 1941–3 May 1942	Spitfire
312 Sqn	10 Oct 1942–24 Jun 1943+	Spitfire
313 Sqn	8 Jun 1942–28 Jun 1943	Spitfire
316 Sqn	2 Aug 1941–13 Dec 1941	Hurricane, Spitfire
504 Sqn	30 Jun 1943–14 Aug 1943	Spitfire
587 Sqn	10 Apr 1944–1 Oct 1944	various
610 Sqn	7 Apr 1944–16 May 1944	Spitfire
616 Sqn	16 May 1944–21 Jul 1944	Spitfire, Meteor
790 Sqn FAA	10 Aug 1944–26 Sep 1944	various
887 Sqn FAA	18 Apr 1944–15 May 1944	Seafire
894 Sqn FAA	28 Apr 1944–15 May 1944	Seafire
RDF	Mar 1942–Mar 1944	various
3 GTS det	9 Dec 1944–24 Jul 1945	
GIF	31 Jan 1945–?	Master, Hotspur

DAVIDSTOW MOOR

County: Cornwall

UTM/Grid: OS Map 201 – SX150850
Lat/Long: N50°38.05 W004°37.02
Nearest Town: Launceston 10 miles to east

HISTORY

The remote airfield at Davidstow Moor was in operational use for two years and, despite a few periods of intense activity, was one of Coastal Command's lesser-used airfields. It is a fascinating site to fly over today as, with the exception of an area of forestry on the south side, it looks frozen in time and one could almost imagine the Beaufighters or Wellingtons sitting at dispersal. On the north edge of bleak Bodmin Moor and within five miles of the coast, Davidstow Moor airfield was laid out on a plateau area whose contour line was 290m (around 970ft), making it one of the highest airfields in Britain and making it very prone to being covered in cloud rolling in from the Atlantic; indeed, the choice of site is somewhat surprising, other than the fact that airfields were desperately needed in this area and there were few suitable sites. The land was acquired in 1941 and construction took place in the first half of 1942, to provide a three-runway airfield with extensive dispersal areas – but few other facilities. Despite the moorland conditions,

construction was reasonably straightforward, although it did involve the removal of various field boundaries, the closure of minor roads and some drainage work.

Davidstow Moor was brought into temporary use before completion as a staging post for operations in connection with Operation *Torch*, the Allied invasion of North Africa, and, on 8 November 1942, it was used by two Bomb Groups of the 8th USAAF (the 44th and 93rd), whose B-17s were attacking naval installations in France. Over the next few weeks this routine was repeated, whilst construction of the airfield continued. Cleave-based No.1603 Flight used the airfield from December 1942 to January 1943 for its Henley target-towers, but this was very much a temporary expedient, although the same month the first Coastal Command unit arrived. Hudsons of 53 Squadron arrived on 1 January and must have wondered what they had come to – the unit had returned from the British West Indies to a Cornish winter! They were probably delighted to

AIRFIELD DATA DEC 1944

Command:	Coastal Command	Runway surface:	Concrete
Function:	Operational, Parent	Hangars:	T.2 × 3
Runways:	304 deg 2,000 × 50yd	Dispersals:	50 × Concrete 130ft diam
	248 deg 1,400 × 50yd	Personnel:	Officers – 302 (4 WAAF)
	210 deg 1,400 × 50yd		Other Ranks – 2,958 (508 WAAF)

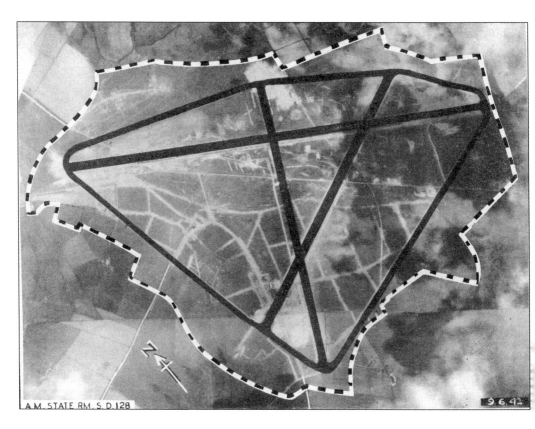

A.M. STATE RM. S.D.128   9 6 42

move six weeks later to Docking in Norfolk. Davidstow Moor was now fully operational with No.19 Group, Coastal Command and its main role was that of providing anti-submarine patrols over the Atlantic and Bay of Biscay, as part of the still-desperate battle against the U-boats. Wellingtons of 304, 547 and 612 squadrons spent time here from summer 1943, searching the waters by day and night, especially by night, to keep the U-boats on the defensive. Most of these sorties involved hours of searching vast areas of sea – and, over the Bay of Biscay, keeping a very good look-out for the roving German fighters – with few sightings and very few attacks.

The operational squadrons had gone by late-1943 and, for a few months, the airfield's primary role was

that of air-sea rescue. Within a few weeks of its arrival at Davidstow Moor in January 1944, 269 Squadron had given up some of its aircraft and experienced crews to form 282 Squadron. The Warwick Is of this unit remained at the station to September, working alongside a detachment from their parent squadron.

In the period leading up to D-Day the operational strength of the station was boosted by a number of new units; the importance of providing a maritime screen capable of detecting and destroying German naval activity was a key part of the invasion strategy. The unit list shows the presence of a number of Wellington units, but does not reflect the occasional use of the airfield as a forward base by other maritime squadrons. April saw the formation of another

304 Squadron operated Wellingtons from Davidstow Moor for six months in late 1943; this is a Mark XI of that squadron seen some time in 1944.

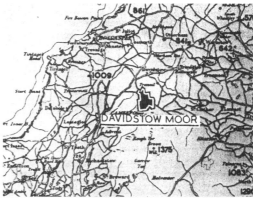

Beaufighters of 404 Squadron at Davidstow Moor.

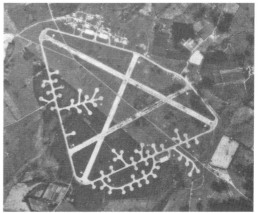

The airfield as photographed by 543 Squadron on 13 June 1967 – more than 20 years after the RAF had left.

Wellington unit, 524 Squadron reforming with Wellington XIIIs – the definitive version with the highly effective Leigh Light. The Wick Strike Wing of Beaufighter Xs from 144 and 404 squadrons arrived in early May to boost offensive capability in the D-Day period. The 'Beaus' justified their presence by making a successful attack on a German naval force on 6 June.

With the Allies ashore and seizing German naval bases in France, the role of the coastal stations reduced and Coastal Command undertook a re-organization of units, which saw Davidstow Moor empty of squadrons. The station was reduced to Care and Maintenance on 20 September 1944 – and that was the end of its RAF flying career. The airfield had been in use by ground units, primarily the RAF Regiment, since the summer and this continued to October 1945, with the final abandonment of the airfield taking place in December.

A 1.85 mile circuit of taxiway and runway was used as a Grand Prix circuit between 1953 and 1955, but this wartime airfield has spent most of the last sixty years forgotten, which is, of course, why it is so well preserved. Part of the airfield is now used by the Moorland Flying Club, with a 1,550m section of runway 12/30 in use, along with short sections of the other two wartime runways. This is primarily a microlight airfield, although gliding also takes place.

UNITS

1939–1946

53S qn	1 Jan 1943–18 Feb 1943	Hudson
144 Sqn	10 May 1944–1 Jul 1944	Beaufighter
206 Sqn	18 Mar 1944–12 Apr 1944	Fortress, Liberator
269 Sqn	8 Jan 1944–8 Mar 1944	Hudson, Walrus
281 Sqn det	Dec 1943–Feb 1945?	Warwick
282 Sqn	1 Feb 1944–19 Sep 1944	Warwick
304 Sqn	7 Jun 1943–13 Dec 1943	Wellington
404 Sqn det	8 May 1944–Sep 1944+	Beaufighter
524 Sqn	7 Apr 1944–1 Jul 1944	Wellington
547 Sqn	31 May 1943–25 Oct 1943	Wellington
612 Sqn	12 Apr 1943–25 May 1943	Wellington
1603 Flt	16 Dec 1942–27 Jan 1943	Henley

MEMORIAL

There is a memorial on Site No.4 near the airfield to those who served at Davidstow Moor.

DOWN AMPNEY
(Station 458)

County: Gloucestershire

UTM/Grid: OS Map 163 – SU100965
Lat/Long: N51°40.03 W001°51.40
Nearest Town: Cirencester 6 miles to north-west

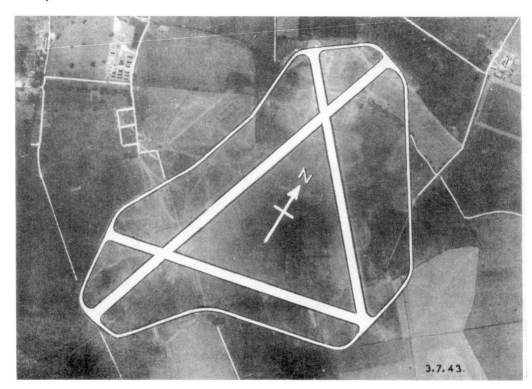

3.7.43.

HISTORY

Down Ampney had a short but active operational career as one of the airborne forces airfields to participate in the crucial drops over Normandy in the early hours of D-Day. It was a very late airfield and opened only a few months before the historic events in which it participated. A flat area of farmland was acquired on the outskirts of this quiet Gloucestershire village in 1943 and a three-runway airfield was constructed during the winter, the main aim being to lay three concrete runways of standard length as quickly as possible. The runways were laid in a near-perfect pattern, with the main (2,000 yard) strip having additional width at each end for the forming-up of the tug-glider combinations that were part of airborne ops, it also had additional feeder taxiways from the perimeter track for the same purpose. The runway ends were by a perimeter track on which were three dispersal areas, with a total of fifty loop-type dispersals; the southern group were used by 48 Squadron

and the eastern group by 271 Squadron. Both squadrons were equipped with Dakotas and both arrived in late-February 1944; 48 Squadron coming from Bircham Newton, where it had started its conversion from Hudsons to Dakotas, and 271 Squadron moving in from Doncaster, having been a Dakota operator since August 1943. For both it was a new role and, as part of No.46 Group's airborne forces, a very intense period of training commenced immediately.

There was no real technical area as such, as the two T.2 hangars were on opposite sides of the airfield, but the major group of – temporary buildings – was on the north-west side, close to one of the T.2s, and this is shown on some plans as the '271 Squadron maintenance area'. Communal sites were dispersed in the fields to the west of the airfield. Very little of the airfield, other than the runways and perimeter track, were complete when the squadrons arrived and, as at

AIRFIELD DATA DEC 1944

Command:	Transport Command	Runway surface:	Concrete
Function:	Operational, Parent	Hangars:	T.2 × 2
Runways:	030 deg 2,000 × 50yd	Dispersals:	50 × Loop
	090 deg 1,400 × 50yd	Personnel:	Officers – 261 (12 WAAF)
	150 deg 1,400 × 50yd		Other Ranks – 2,168 (272 WAAF)

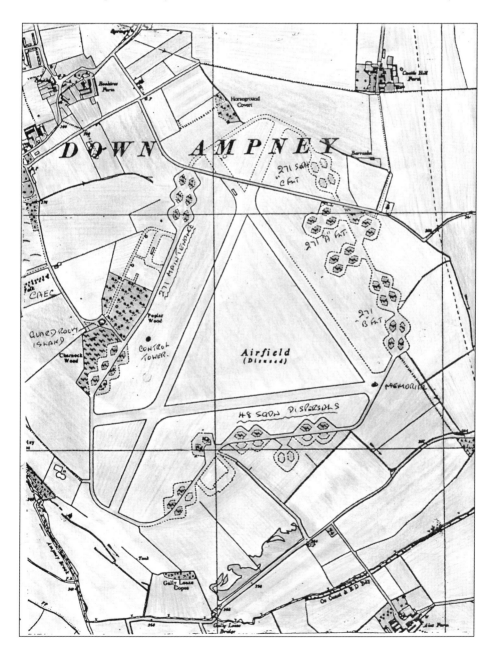

many wartime 'airfield building sites', mud was the order of the day. The squadrons participated in a series of build-up exercises to confirm the readiness of all parts of the airborne force and, considering the intense nature of the flying, there were very few incidents; by late-May Down Ampney was ready.

On the evening of 5 June 1944, the station despatched seven Dakota-Horsa combinations in the first wave of the assault; these were followed by thirty-seven more combinations. Only one 'Dak' was lost, ditching in the Channel. The next few days were spent on supply dropping and, as soon as landing grounds were available in Normandy, the Dakotas commenced another of their roles – casualty evacuation.

Under a policy agreed in February, Down Ampney was nominated as a Main Base Airfield (MBA) – along with Broadwell, Blakehill Farm and Watchfield. 'Only in an emergency were casevac aircraft to land at any other airfield. Once a casualty had arrived at an MBA he would be transferred by road to an appropriate medical facility.' One of the main RAF units was 271 Squadron, whose 'Sparrow' aircraft formed an Ambulance Flight. The fact that Down Ampney was an MBA meant that aircraft of various squadrons arrived with casevacs and the airfield was incredibly busy, with, at times, what seemed like an endless stream of stretchers and ambulances. It is hard to imagine this scene when you stand today on this quiet piece of farmland.

Within weeks the squadrons were focusing once more on training to sharpen their skills for the next airborne assault; this came in September with Operation *Market-Garden* over Holland, the RAF squadrons dropping 1st British Airborne Division over the Dutch town of Arnhem to seize the Rhine crossing. It was both heroic and tragic. Over the few days from 17 September, the squadrons initially dropped troops (and gliders) and then flew re-supply missions in the face of increasingly fierce German defences. On 19 September a Dakota of 271 Squadron was shot-down by anti-aircraft fire, its pilot, Flight Lieutenant Lord, keeping the burning aircraft on track in order to drop its load of supplies. This act brought a posthumous Victoria Cross; the citation reads:

Flight Lieutenant David Samuel Anthony Lord, DFC, 271Sqn RAF.

Flight Lieutenant Lord was pilot and captain of a Dakota aircraft detailed to drop supplies at Arnhem on the afternoon of the 19th September, 1944. Our airborne troops had been surrounded and were being pressed into a small area defended by a large number of anti-aircraft guns. Air crews were warned that intense opposition would be met over the dropping zone. To ensure accuracy they were ordered to fly at 900 feet when dropping their containers. While flying at 1,500 feet near Arnhem the starboard wing of Flight Lieutenant Lord's aircraft was twice hit by anti-aircraft fire. The starboard engine was set on fire. He would have been justified in leaving the main stream of supply aircraft and continuing at the same height or even abandoning his aircraft. But on learning that his crew were uninjured and that the dropping zone would

The Station was involved in the last airborne assault of the war – Operation *Varsity* in March 1945; gliders litter the landing site.

be reached in three minutes he said he would complete his mission, as the troops were in dire need of supplies. By now the starboard engine was burning furiously. Flight Lieutenant Lord came down to 900 feet, where he was singled out for the concentrated fire of all the anti-aircraft guns. On reaching the dropping zone he kept the aircraft on a straight and level course while supplies were dropped. At the end of the run, he was told that two containers remained. Although he must have known that the collapse of the starboard wing could not be long delayed, Flight Lieutenant Lord circled, rejoined the stream of aircraft and made a second run to drop the remaining supplies. These manoeuvres took eight minutes in all, the aircraft being continuously under heavy anti-aircraft fire. His task completed, Flight Lieutenant Lord ordered his crew to abandon the Dakota, making no attempt himself to leave the aircraft, which was down to 500 feet. A few seconds later, the starboard wing collapsed and the aircraft fell in flames. There was only one survivor, who was flung out while assisting other members of the crew to put on their parachutes. By continuing his mission in a damaged and burning aircraft, descending to drop the supplies accurately, returning to the dropping zone a second time and, finally, remaining at the controls to give his crew a chance of escape, Flight Lieutenant Lord displayed supreme valour and self-sacrifice.

No.109 (Transport) Operational Training Unit at Crosby-on-Eden detached a few aircraft and crews here in September to augment the squadrons following losses in the Arnhem operation. The squadrons were training again for the next operation and were also bringing back a regular stream of casualties; Down Ampney received its 20,000th casualty in December 1944.

On 24 March the station participated in the third of the airborne assaults, Operation *Varsity*, the Rhine crossing, sending sixty Dakotas. Then, all of a sudden, the war in Europe was over; transport duties kept the squadrons busy, but both moved out in August, their place being taken by two Canadian transport squadrons, both of which stayed to early 1946. The station closed almost immediately and was one of the first series of disposals in the 1950s, returning to agriculture. The layout of the airfield is still distinct from the air, even though part of the peri track and one runway have been removed (they are still easily visible as 'marks'). On the ground there is little to see other than crumbling concrete, although traces of a few buildings remain.

UNITS

1939–1945

48Sqn	23 Feb 1944–14 Aug 1945	Dakota
271Sqn	29 Feb 1944–10 Aug 1945	Dakota, Harrow (Sparrow)

Post-1945

435Sqn	29 Aug 1945–31 Mar 1946	Dakota
436Sqn	29 Aug 1945–4 Apr 1946	Dakota

MEMORIALS

1. The original memorial stone on one of the runways carried a plaque with the inscription:

> From this airfield in 1944–45 Douglas Dakotas from 48 and 271 Squadrons, RAF Transport Command, carried the 1st and 6th Airborne Divisions, units of the Air Dispatch Regiment and Horsa gliders of the Glider Pilot Regiment to Normandy, Arnhem and the crossing of the Rhine operations. We will remember them. 18.IX.1977.

This memorial has since been replaced (moved?).

2. Down Ampney church includes a memorial stained-glass window, beneath which, on the exterior wall, is a plaque inscribed: 'RAF Garden of Remembrance. Down Ampney'.

DOWN FARM (SLG No.23)

County: Gloucestershire

UTM/Grid: OS Map 172 – ST855906
Lat/Long: N51°36.84 W002°12.64
Nearest Town: Stroud 9 miles to north

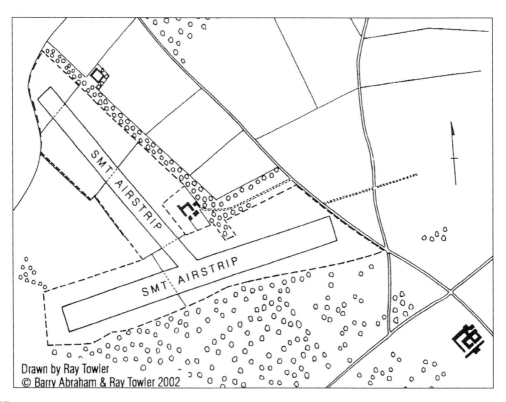

Drawn by Ray Towler
© Barry Abraham & Ray Towler 2002

HISTORY

Opened on 1 May 1941, Down Farm was Satellite Landing Ground (SLG) No.23 and was used by No.10 Maintenance Unit, a civil-manned Aircraft Storage Unit based at Hullavington. As with all the ASUs, this MU needed dispersal fields at which to store aircraft prior to delivery to units or whilst they were not required for immediate use. In the early years of the war, the ideal was a site close to the parent MU and with a reasonable grass surface for take-off and landing and adjacent wooded areas to make camouflage of dispersed aircraft a realistic proposition. The site at Down Farm, part of Westonbirt Park near Tetbury, was highly suitable and was adopted in spring 1941, the initial assessment taking place in April.

The site was originally scheduled to handle Defiants, Venturas and Wellingtons but, like most of these sites, the actual occupants seldom matched the plan, although the first aircraft into Down Farm were Defiants. A plan to develop the site into a major air-field was abandoned and it remained an SLG throughout the war, with the number of aircraft in storage varying from around 100 in the middle years of the war to an impressive 182 aircraft in the months after the war. Like all SLGs, it was provided with a minimum of facilities, although the two runways were given SMT (Square Mesh Track) surfaces and a number of SMT dispersals were laid when the site took storage of four-engined 'heavies', such as the Stirling.

Of the nearly 200 aircraft in store in summer 1945 very few would have survived more than a few months, as this was the period of mass destruction of unwanted airframes; it is not certain how many were actually broken up at the SLGs although, in most cases, they were flown back to their parent MU for this ignominious end. Down Farm was cleared of aircraft during January 1946 and handed back to its original owners the following month.

DUNKESWELL
(Station 173, Station 804)

County: Devon

UTM/Grid: OS Map 193 – ST134078
Lat/Long: N50°51.79 W003°13.91
Nearest Town: Honiton 4 miles to south

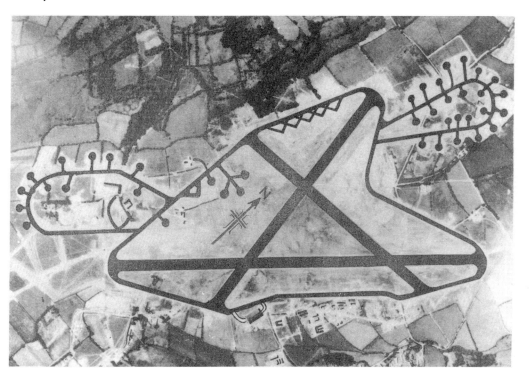

HISTORY

The airfield at Dunkeswell in South-East Devon was unusual in that it housed an operational United States Navy unit, the 7th Fleet Air Wing. Indeed, this was something of an American enclave, as the nearby airfield at Upottery (less than three miles to the north-east) housed a Troop Carrier Group.

The airfield was constructed on an area of farmland to the west of the village of Dunkeswell and the original intention was for it to be a fighter airfield; it was under No.10 Group during the initial construction period, but was transferred to Coastal Command in May 1942, before construction was complete. The airfield was given the standard triangle of three surfaced runways, with a linking perimeter track and dispersal areas. Coastal Command requested provision for three squadrons and this involved constructing two taxiway loops to accommodate the large number of dispersal points, each of which had to be capable of being used by large coastal types. Hangar provision was limited to three T.2s (although a later plan shows

five hangars) and, with the exception of one or two key buildings, such as the control tower, all other structures were 'huts, various'. Construction appears to have been completed in late autumn 1942, but Coastal Command had no immediate use for the airfield and it remained empty for some months.

Dunkeswell was eventually 'opened for business' in June 1943 when it was allocated to the USAAF, the first occupants being the 479th Anti-Submarine Group B-24s, which had been allocated on a temporary basis to the Air Force Anti-Submarine Command, pending the arrival of dedicated units for this role. At least two squadrons of this Group, the 4th and 19th, moved to the new airfield in August and much of the support elements of the station were provided by the RAF. Operations commenced on 13 July and, a month later, two more squadrons arrived to join the Group, the 6th and 22nd. However, by that time, the squadrons of Fleet Air Wing 7 had started to arrive in Devon, with VB103 being later

AIRFIELD DATA DEC 1944

Command:	Coastal Command for USNAF	Runway surface:	Concrete with ¾in asphalt carpet
Function:	Operational, Parent	Hangars:	T.2 × 3
Runways:	230 deg 2,000 × 50yd	Dispersals:	44 × Tarmac on concrete
			125ft diam, 6 × Tarmac on
			concrete spectacle
	360 deg 1,470 × 50yd	Personnel:	Officers – 262 (10 WAAF)
	270 deg 1,270 × 50yd		Other Ranks – 2,770 (450 WAAF)

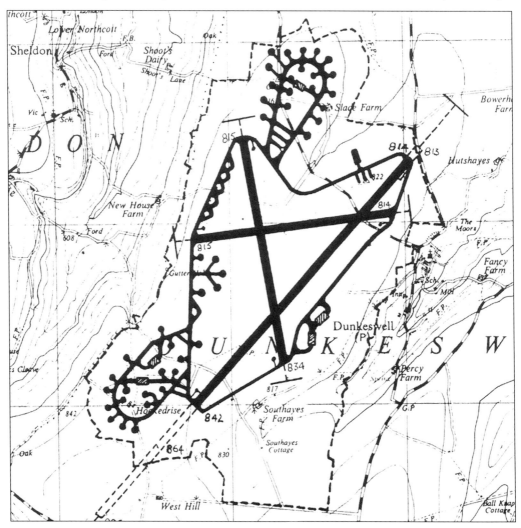

joined by VB105 and VB110. The 479th ASG started to move out to Hardwick and Alconbury, but it was early November before they had all gone.

The main type used by the FAW squadrons was the PB4Y-1 variant of the B-24 Liberator and the Wing was operational and flying AS patrols over the Bay of Biscay within weeks of taking up residence. The squadrons played a full part in the maritime war and, in common with their Coastal Command colleagues, were particularly busy during the D-Day

Liberator of VB110 taxies out for an anti-submarine mission.

Great cartoon (by Stil) of VB103, one of the units of FAW7.

The sign says it all – 'Mudville Heights'.

The northern dispersal loop with its single T2 hangar.

period. In addition to the Liberators, the Wing also operated a number of Catalinas and, at one period, a number of British-marked Seafires could be seen on one part of the airfield, housed in canvas hangars. These aircraft had been allocated to the Wing for evasion training, but how long they remained is uncertain.

In March 1944, the United States Navy took over administration of the station from the RAF and, under the command of Commander Thomas Durfee USNR, the American flag was run up and Dunkeswell was commissioned as a US Naval Air Facility. FAW7 remained operational from Dunkeswell to the end of the war, having flown hundreds of sorties and thousands of hours. Most sorties saw nothing but sea, some made sightings of U-boats or schnorkels and a number of attacks were made. The run-down of American units was rapid and by late-July the US Navy had said farewell to 'Mudville Heights' – as they had called Dunkeswell.

In the immediate post-war period the airfield was transferred to Transport Command and used by Ferry Units. No.11 Ferry Unit arrived from Talbenny in early August 1945, but almost immediately was disbanded into No.16 Ferry Unit. The latter formed at Dunkeswell on 15 August from No.11 FU and No.3 Aircraft Preparation Unit. The new FU operated a mix of aircraft and remained at Dunkeswell until April 1946, when it moved to St Mawgan for its last few months of existence. No.265 Maintenance Unit (Grove) used Dunkeswell as a sub-site in the late-1940s and appears to have disbanded here in December 1948. The airfield was reduced to Care and Maintenance and spent a few quiet years. It was allocated as an RLG for 208 Advanced Flying School (Merryfield) from November 1951 to June 1954; the school operated Meteors and Vampires for pilot training but how much use they made of the RLG is uncertain. The final few months of 1954 saw the airfield allocated to No.9 FTS for the same purpose.

Dunkeswell (EGTU) is now an active general aviation airfield operated by Air Westward, with two of the wartime runways still in use – 05/23 (968m) and 17/35 (644m). Major operators include the Devon School of Flying and Somerset Microlights. The Dunkeswell Memorial Museum Trust is trying to acquire the old control tower and operations building as the centre for a museum, as both buildings are under threat.

The English Heritage list of key airfields records Dunkeswell as:

> This is the best preserved of all the sites in the west of Britain associated with the strategically vital Battle of the Atlantic. Begun in 1941, the US Navy Fleet Air Wing was based here from 1942 until 1945. Dunkeswell exemplifies the highly dispersed planning and temporary fabric of contemporary airfields. Among the surviving original buildings are the operations block and control tower.

UNITS

1943–1945
USAAF units

479th ASG (479th BG)

Squadrons:	4th, 6th, 19th, 22nd Sqns

Aircraft:	B-24
Dates:	6 Aug 1943–30 Oct 1943

USN units
FAW7

Squadron:	VB103, VB105, VB110
Aircraft:	Liberator, Catalina
Dates:	Sep 1943–Jul 1945

Post-1945

11 FU	9–15 Aug 1945	various
12 FU	15 Aug 1945–26 Apr 1946	various
208 AFS	Nov 1951–Jun 1954	Meteor, Vampire
9 FTS	Jul 1954–Dec 1954	Vampire

MEMORIAL

1. The village church contains a Roll of Honour.
2. Propeller mounted an a stone memorial and flanked by two flagpoles; no inscription.

Briefing room used by VB105.

EVERLEIGH (No. 31 SLG)

UTM/Grid: OS Map 173 – SU190556
Lat/Long: N51°17.95 W001°43.73

County: Wiltshire

Nearest Town: Upavon 2 miles to east

HISTORY

The site at Everleigh was ideal for a satellite landing ground, as it comprised a large open field surrounded by wooded areas (Everleigh Ashes woods) and it was opened on 22 November 1941 as No.31 SLG for use by No.15 Maintenance Unit at Wroughton. The site had actually been in use since late-1940 as a practice forced-landing (PFL) area by the training aircraft from Upavon-based Central Flying School. It was probably this early use of what was simply a large field that identified the site as suitable for development into an SLG. The main grass strip was laid out in December 1941 and oriented north/south with a landing run of 1,600 yards, a second strip at almost 90 degrees was subsequently added (May 1942). As was usual with SLGs, aircraft for storage were taxied to the surrounding wood and parked along the edges of the wood, the trees providing some degree of camouflage. Very few support buildings were provided, although Everleigh fared better than most and had a Super Robin hangar (1943) and a variety of other buildings, including an armoury (an unusual feature for an SLG – but the site also had a small-arms range).

The SLG was used for a number of airborne assault exercises in 1942: a tragic demonstration in April – witnessed by Prime Minister Churchill – resulted in a number of deaths, and a somewhat more successful exercise in September. In the latter month Everleigh was transferred to No.33 MU (Lyneham), although the aircraft storage role remained unchanged. The site was kept on the books of No.33 MU for the rest of the war, but was also used on an opportunity basis by No.10, No.15 and No.39 MUs, as it was suitable for virtually all types of aircraft and had plenty of dispersal capacity. The Hullavington-based No.10 MU began to send Stirlings to the site from December 1943 and, at one stage, the fields around Everleigh Ash housed eighty-seven of the four-engined aircraft. In the latter part of 1944 the Stirlings left and the main type under storage was the Harvard.

By spring 1945 the number of aircraft had dwindled and the SLG was closed for aircraft storage in the autumn. The military did not, however, release the whole of the site back to agriculture; part of it remains MoD land and is still used by the army for exercises.

EXETER (Station 463)

County: Devon

UTM/Grid: OS Map 192 – SY002938
Lat/Long: N50°44.00 W003°25.18
Nearest Town: Exeter 3 miles to west

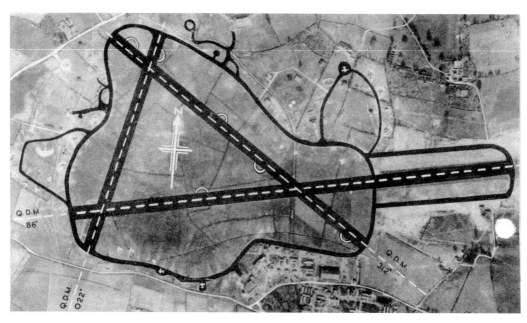

HISTORY

Exeter Airport is currently a thriving regional airport, providing holiday charters and scheduled flights to Europe, and will celebrate its seventieth anniversary in 2007. The site to the east of the city was chosen in early 1932 and it would have been one of the earliest municipal airports, except for the fact that the landowners (Waterslade Farm) did not want to sell the land. It took some while for the legalities – and compulsory purchase – to be resolved and it was not until May 1937 that the Air Ministry was able to grant a licence to Exeter Airport, the airport opening to traffic on the last day of the month. An operating company had been formed by the London-based Straight Corporation to operate the airport on behalf of the City Council and the first commercial 'airliner' to use Exeter Airport was a DH86 of Jersey Airways. The airport was not formally opened until 20 July 1938, by which time the terminal building was ready, although some construction was still taking place. The RAF was delighted that an airfield had been built in this area as, with a European war now inevitable, it was looking for suitable airfields throughout the UK. Indeed, Vildebeests of 42 Squadron had made a brief stay at the airport in July 1937 during exercises with the navy.

The Straight Corporation had launched the Exeter Flying Club and this was soon attracting numerous members, many of whom also became part of the Civil Air Guard scheme when this was introduced in 1939. That same year, the Corporation was also authorized to form No.37 ERFTS at Exeter, this taking place in July and being accompanied by construction of a new hangar for the school aircraft – but, as with all these schools, it was disbanded at the outbreak of war on 3 September. Exeter became one of the airports requisitioned to be part of the National Air Communications network – requisitioned airlines and airfields to provide communication within the British Isles. It became a major NAC airfield and, as such, underwent expansion. However, the airport's remote location also appealed to a number of trials establishments that were seeking new homes; first of these was the Research Department Flight from Farnborough, which arrived on 14 September to work with the Washington-Singer laboratories in Exeter. The Flight's main role was development of systems to protect aircraft from balloon cables and they operated from here until moving to Church Stanton in early 1942.

'The Central Gunnery School moved to Exeter on

AIRFIELD DATA DEC 1944

Command:	Fighter Command	Runway surface:	Asphalt
Function:	Sector Station, Night Fighter	Hangars:	Over Blister × 6, Extra-Over Blister × 4, Hinaidi × one
Runways:	266 deg 2,000 × 50yd	Dispersals:	19 × Twin-Engine, 5 × Single-Engine
	312 deg 1,450 × 50yd	Personnel:	Officers – 224 (14 WAAF)
	200 deg 1,000 × 50yd		Other Ranks – 2,777 (639 WAAF)

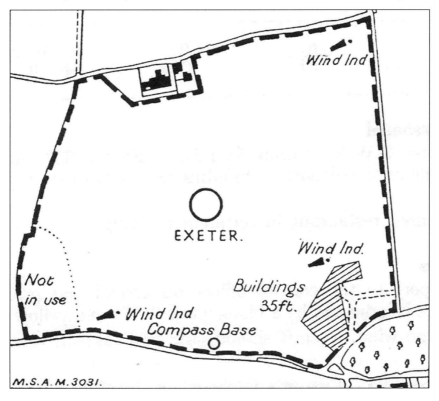

1 May 1940 and pending completion of the permanent buildings, personnel were housed in a tented camp on the south side of the airfield.' This move, as recorded in Secret Organizational Memorandum 205 of 1940, may not actually have taken place but, in June, the Gunnery Research Unit (GRU) of the Royal Aircraft Establishment did move in. The work of the GRU was fascinating and vital to the development of effective guns and gun systems and in the four years it spent at Exeter it was involved in a large number of trials, worthy of a book in its own right.

The RAF had formally taken charge of the airfield on 1 June, initially with Flying Training Command. However, on 6 July, control was transferred to No.10 Group of Fighter Command and, whilst non-operational units such as the RDF and GRU were to

remain in residence for some years, Exeter was now given operational status as a key part of the air defence of South Devon. Exeter's first fighters arrived in mid-June, when Hurricanes of 213 Squadron flew in from Biggin Hill. This unit stayed nearly three months and, in July, had been joined by the Hurricanes of 87 Squadron. The fighters were soon involved in patrols over coastal shipping as well as holding standby or scrambling from their home base. Temporary accommodation was soon replaced with more permanent buildings and the airfield's infrastructure also continued to evolve. August 1940 was a particularly hectic month for the Exeter squadrons, with some successes but also many losses. Bombs were dropped near the airfield on 21 August, killing a number of army personnel; Exeter Airport stood out from the surrounding fields, as major construction work was underway to provide three hard runways and associated facilities, including additional fighter pens. The airfield had also become part of the Civilian Repair Organization (CRO), with Air Service Training taking over a Bellman hangar (and workshops in the City), with the later addition of two more hangars, in order to provide engineering and maintenance for Spitfires.

The unit list shows the rotation of fighter squadrons in 1940 and 1941; of particular note was the presence of Whirlwinds of 263 Squadron from December 1940 – this unusual fighter making its operational debut from Exeter on shipping attacks – and the arrival of dedicated night-fighter units. The Defiants of 307 Squadron arrived from Colerne on 26 April 1941 to provide night defence for the Exeter area. The airfield had received a number of visits from the Luftwaffe that same month (at least four significant raids), which had caused severe damage and destroyed a number of aircraft. Beaufighter IIFs arrived in August 1941, to give the Poles a much improved capability, with Beaufighter VIFs taking over the following May. As a Sector Station, Exeter played a key role in the defences and, by summer 1941, was controlling Bolt Head, Church Stanton, Charlton Horethorne and Harrowbeer. The Luftwaffe had renewed its interest in Exeter and made a number of attacks on the airfield in April–May 1942, but this time the defenders had the better of it and the night fighters made a number of claims.

The unit list also shows the large number of units to have rotated through Exeter during the wartime period and, whilst day and night air-defence remained a major role into early 1943, the station's squadrons were playing an increasing offensive role, either on bomber escort or fighter sweep. Anti-ship-

ping work was equally important and the Fleet Air Arm based aircraft here in 1942–1943 for this purpose. For a short period in 1944 this became Station 463 of the USAAF, its location being considered ideal for airborne operations connected with the invasion. Four squadrons (eighty C-47s) of the 440th Troop Carrier Group duly arrived in April and, for the next six months, the airfield and surrounding area were dominated by the Americans. On D-Day (6 June) the Group despatched forty-seven C-47s with paratroops of the 101st Airborne Division; three aircraft failed to return. The Group effectively left Exeter in August, except for a brief re-appearance the

Hurricane P2798 of 87 Squadron at Exeter in September 1940; the 'LK' code of this squadron was seen at a great many of the fighter bases in the south-west as it led a peripatetic life in the early years of the war. (Andy Thomas)

following month, but the airfield remained in American hands to late-October. The RAF returned and the airfield was used mainly by the anti-aircraft co-operation aircraft of 286 Squadron, and the air-sea rescue Spitfires and Walruses of 275 Squadron. The last few months of the war saw a mixture of units based here, the largest of which was No.3 Glider Training School.

RAF Exeter had been transferred to Flying Training Command on 1 January, its operational career over, and the GTS moved in with its various tugs and gliders; this was a large unit and it needed to make use of Culmhead as a satellite. This was, however, short-lived and the GTS had gone by early summer – the station having returned to Fighter Command once more in July 1945, although now part of No.11 Group (No.10 Group having disbanded in May). Spitfires of 329 Squadron spent a few weeks in late summer, the Frenchmen getting ready to return home, with the somewhat more sedate 691 Squadron joining in with the parties. The Spitfires left in November but, as Exeter was now a permanent fighter base, it received a Wing of two squadrons, day-fighter Meteors with 222 Squadron and night-fighter Mosquitoes with 151 Squadron. By early 1946 the plan had changed; the Exeter Sector Station was closed and the squadrons moved on, leaving RAF Exeter to close down in October 1946.

Exeter Airport was transferred to the Ministry of Civil Aviation on 1 January 1947, but it was not until 1952 that commercial flights were re-started, by Jersey Airways. In the interim, the airport was used by a number of organizations, including a flying club and an aircraft manufacturer. The latter was the little-known Chrislea Aircraft Corporation, which took

Sqn Ldr G F Brown was CO of 257 Squadron from September 1942 to April 1943.

Winter weather as a Whirlwind of 263 Squadron is prepared for another sortie, Exeter February 1941.

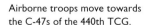

Airborne troops move towards
the C-47s of the 440th TCG.

over the AST buildings. The only products of note
were the Super Ace and the Flying Jeep, neither of
which was produced in significant numbers. When
the company was taken over by C E Harper Aircraft
production ended; the new company focused its
efforts on engineering and became a sub-contractor
for Vickers. Military flying returned in April 1949
with the formation of No.10 Refresher Flying School,
with the first course training on Tiger Moths from
16 May. Two Ansons were also acquired and
Chipmunks eventually replaced the Tiger Moths; the
school was disbanded in June 1954. Of more significance was the presence, from March 1951, of No.2
Civilian Anti-Aircraft Co-operation Unit, which
was operated by Exeter Airport Ltd and which was in
existence for ten years. The CAACU formed on 18
March for No.25 Group and was initially equipped
with Beaufighters, Mosquitoes and Spitfires,
although it subsequently operated a wide variety of
types, including the Vampire, Meteor and Hunter. In
July 1954 it had combined with No.4 CAACU
(Llandow) to officially become No.3/4 CAACU at
Exeter. It was eventually disbanded in December
1971 and its role taken on by the Canberras of No.7
Squadron at St Mawgan.

The Ministry of Defence had acquired the airport
from the Council in 1958 but, in 1964, it was leased to
Air Holdings to act as an operating company. Finally,
the Devon County Council acquired the site in 1974.
Ten years later, management of the site was taken on
by British Airports Ltd (later UK Airports Ltd) but,
since 1991, the operating company has been Exeter
and Devon Airport Ltd. The main runway was

Vampire of No.2 CACU at Exeter, probably October
1967.

extended and strengthened in 1981 and, during the
1980s, a number of other infrastructure improvements
took place. Major development work continued in
the 1990s, with a new arrivals area in June 1999 and a
new departure lounge in June 2003. Following a 70
per cent increase in passengers over the year, the
period to November 2004 saw Exeter Airport exceed
an annual total of 500,000 passengers a year.
Although now dominated by the long east/west
(08/26 at 2,073m) runway, the only one still in use,
Exeter International Airport (EGTE) retains its basic
wartime layout, with the main area of buildings,
including the terminal area, on the south side.

The author has fond memories of No.4 Air
Experience Flight and its Chipmunks, as he waddled
from the hut to the aircraft, parachute strapped to his
backside, as an Air Cadet. The AEF was based here
from September 1958 to December 1995.

DECOY SITES

Q	Aylesbeare Common	SY056902
Q	Clyst Hydon	ST056012
Q/QF	Clyst St Mary	SX993917
QF	Woodbury	SY048882
Q	Woodbury Common	SY037869

UNITS

HQ units at Exeter

50th TCW	26 Apr 1944–1 Oct 1944
Western Sector	16 Jan 1945–15 Jul 1946
No.62 (Southern Reserve) Gp	15 May 1946–2 Jul 1946

1939–1945

16 Sqn	spring 1942	Mustang
19 Sqn det	autumn 1943	Spitfire
21 Sqn det	autumn 1942	Ventura
26 Sqn	8 Dec 1944–14 Jan 1945	Spitfire
66 Sqn	24 Feb 1941–27 Apr 1941	Spitfire
87 Sqn	5 Jul 1940–28 Nov 1940	Hurricane
93 Sqn det	early 1941	Havoc
124 Sqn det	spring 1943	Spitfire
125 Sqn	15 Apr 1943–14 Nov 1943	Beaufighter
131 Sqn	26 Jun 1943–16 Aug 1943	Spitfire
165 Sqn	30 Jul 1943–8 Aug 1943	Spitfire
213 Sqn	18 Jun 1940–7 Sep 1940	Hurricane
225 Sqn det	summer 1940	Lysander
247 Sqn	Dec 1941–21 Sep 1942	Hurricane
257 Sqn	21 Sep 1942–8 Jan 1943	Spitfire
263 Sqn	28 Nov 1940–24 Feb 1941	Hurricane, Whirlwind
266 Sqn	8 Jan 1943–21 Sep 1943	Typhoon
275 Sqn	22 Oct 1944–12 Jan 1945	Spitfire
278 Sqn det	early 1945	Spitfire, Walrus
282 Sqn det	autumn 1944–early 1945	various
307 Sqn	26 Apr 1941–15 Apr 1943	Beaufighter, Mosquito
308 Sqn	1 Apr 1942–7 May 1942	Spitfire
310 Sqn	7 May 1942–26 Jun 1943+	Spitfire
317 Sqn	21 Jul 1941–1 Apr 1942	Hurricane, Spitfire
329 Sqn	30 Aug 1945–17 Nov 1945	Spitfire
406 Sqn	15 Nov 1943–14 Apr 1944	Beaufighter
421 Sqn det	29 Jun 1942–8 Jul 1942	Spitfire
504 Sqn	18 Dec 1940–21 Jul 1941	Hurricane
536 Sqn det	late 1942	Havoc, Hurricane
601 Sqn	7 Sep 1940–17 Dec 1940	Hurricane
610 Sqn	4 Jan 1944–7 Apr 1944	Spitfire
616 Sqn	17 Sep 1943–18 Mar 1944+	Spitfire
803 Sqn FAA	15–23 Mar 1939	Skua
816 Sqn FAA	20 May 1943–25 Jun 1943	Seafire, Swordfish
825 Sqn FAA det	30 Dec 1942–1 Feb 1943	Swordfish
834 Sqn FAA	9 Feb 1943–Apr 1943	Swordfish
841 Sqn FAA det	9 Jul 1943–25 Nov 1943	Swordfish
37 ERFTS	3 Jul 1939–3 Sep 1939	Anson, Tiger Moth
RDF	14 Sep 1939–Mar 1942	various
416 Flt det	May–Jun 1940	Lysander
GRU	3 Jun 1940–14 Apr 1944	various
Exeter UAS	20 Aug 1941–1943	Tiger Moth
1487 Flt det	Mar 1942–Aug 1943	Lysander
3 GTS	Jan 1945–Jul 1945	Master, Hotspur

USAAF units
440th TCG

Squadrons:	95th, 96th, 97th, 98th TCS
Aircraft:	C-47
Dates:	18 Apr 1944–1 Oct 1944

Post-1945

151Sqn	19 Apr 1946–11 Jul 1946	Mosquito
222Sqn	11 Dec 1945–8 Jul 1946+	Meteor
691Sqn	1 Aug 1945–29 Apr 1946	various
84 GS	Jun 1945–1 Sep 1955	Cadet, Sedbergh
10 RFS	Apr 1949–20 Jun 1954	Tiger Moth, Anson, Chipmunk
2 CAACU	18 Mar 1951–31 Dec 1971	
624 VGS	1 Sep 1955–3 Sep 1965	various
4 AEF	8 Sep 1958–27 Dec 1995	Chipmunk

FAIRFORD (Station 457)

County: Gloucestershire

UTM/Grid: OS Map 163 – SU149983
Lat/Long: N51°40.53 W001°46.30
Nearest Town: Lechlade 3 miles to east

3.7.48

HISTORY

Fairford is frequently in the news, as strategic bombers of the USAF use it as a deployment base for operations, the most notable instances in recent years having included heavily laden B-52s en route to attack targets in Bosnia as part of Operation *Allied Force*. Whilst much of its history has been associated with the USAF, it was originally constructed as a Transport Command airfield. A large area of land to the south of the village of Fairford, and only two miles east of Down Ampney, was acquired in 1943 for construction of a standard runway. Construction involved the closure of a number of roads, demolition of buildings and the removal of numerous hedges, followed by some grading and levelling, although drainage was not a problem. The main 2,000 yard runway was roughly NE/SW and, like the others, was concrete with, at least partial, asphalt covering. A perimeter track linked the runways and, as at the other transport – which really meant airborne forces– airfields, the ends

of the main runway were widened and given additional linking taxiways. Loop dispersals were distributed around the peri track and there were two T.2 hangars, one of these being on the north-west side as part of the main group of support buildings. The dispersed communal areas were just to the north of the airfield.

Although still un-finished, RAF Fairford was declared ready to receive units by late-January 1944, although the site had been in use from the previous autumn. The night-flying flight of No.3 (Pilots) Advanced Flying Unit at South Cerney made some use of Fairford from autumn 1943 to March 1944. However, the airfield remained fairly quiet, although in March, as part of the increase in airborne assault units in this area, Fairford became home to No.3 and No.4 Glider Servicing Echelons of No.38 Group, their main responsibility being Horsa gliders. The airfield was also one of those allocated for glider storage, the notional figure being 100 Horsas.

AIRFIELD DATA DEC 1944

Command: Flying Training Command
Function: Heavy Glider Conversion Unit, Satellite
Runways: 230 deg 2,000 × 50yd
        280 deg 1,400 × 50yd
        330 deg 1,400 × 50yd

Runway surface: Asphalt and concrete
Hangars: T.2 × 2
Dispersals: 52 × Spectacle
Personnel: Officers – 180 (8 WAAF)
           Other Ranks – 2,518 (308 WAAF)

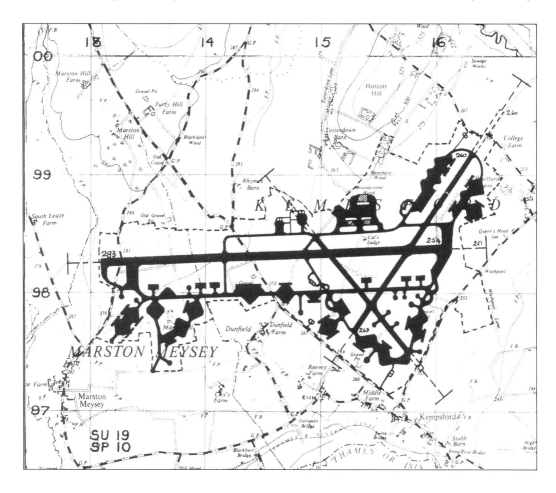

More significantly, two operational squadrons arrived in March, both equipped with Stirlings; 620 Squadron and 190 Squadron came from Leicester East and started intensive training for the airborne role. The squadrons also flew sorties for the Special Operations Executive (SOE) as part of the increased delivery of agents and supplies to France in advance of the invasion. On the evening of 5 June the station sent forty-five Stirlings to Normandy as part of Operation *Tonga*, with three of 620's aircraft failing to return. The following days saw more such missions, although the major effort was on supply-dropping and the ground crew had to work hard to repair the all too frequent flak damage. After a few weeks to rest, refit and keep training, the squadrons were off on the next airborne op, dropping and then supporting British airborne forces at Arnhem for *Market-Garden*. This bold move was ultimately a failure and, for the Fairford squadrons, it was a disaster. Having lost five aircraft in the early missions the squadrons were airborne again on 21 September on another re-supply mission. The formation was intercepted by German

This would have been a common activity with No.22 HGCU – a Horsa glider being towed behind an Albemarle (this is probably not a 22 HGCU shot).

Stirling LJ566 of 620 Squadron, one of the two airborne forces squadrons to operate from Fairford in 1944.

B-52 taking-off from Fairford during Operation *Allied Force*; the airfield has hosted various operational detachments by USAF strategic bombers in recent years.

fighters and, in a short space of time, 190 Squadron lost ten Stirlings and 620 lost two. To lose such a large percentage of a single squadron was a devastating blow and Fairford must have been a sombre place that night – but the war continued and so too did the operational missions. On October 10 the squadrons sent thirty-two Stirling-Horsa combinations to Rome as Operation *Molton*, in connection with the Italian surrender. Then, in mid-October, both left Fairford and the station's operational career was over.

In October Fairford became a satellite for the Keevil-based No.22 Heavy Glider Conversion Unit (HGCU), whose main task was to train glider pilots for the Horsa, although a number of glider types were used. The main tug aircraft was the Albemarle and, in addition to basic training, Fairford was also used to practise glider assaults. The parent unit moved to Blakehill Farm in June 1945, but Fairford was retained as a satellite until October, the HGCU disbanding the following month. The post-war period has seen two major uses for Fairford; firstly, as a RAF transport base, the high-point of which was in the late 1960s and, secondly, as a forward-deployment base for the United States Air Force.

For a short period in 1947–48 the station was home to four transport squadrons but, in December 1948, it was reduced to Care and Maintenance. However, the decision had been taken to improve the airfield, which included extending the main runway and, when the station re-opened in summer 1950, it was the Americans who took an interest, taking over the airfield the following July as Station 457.

Fairford had become a Strategic Air Command deployment base and the first visitors arrived in February 1954, the B-36 Peacemakers from Carswell Air Force Base arriving for the first of what would become rotational detachments, each of which lasted a few weeks or months. Over the next ten years, a number of SAC units, primarily equipped with the B-36 or B-47, took their turns at Fairford. The rotations ended in 1964, having been reducing in frequency for some time, and Fairford was returned to the RAF. It was now a well-equipped airfield and, after a brief usage by the Central Flying School, it was returned to operational status for Transport Command. No.53 Squadron reformed here on 1 January 1966 to operate the Belfast C.1, although it moved to Brize Norton in May 1967. Other transport squadrons followed but, by February 1971, the last of the Hercules squadrons had moved to Lyneham and the station became an RLG for Brize Norton.

American interest revived in the mid-1970s and by 1978 the airfield was being used by detachments of KC-135 tankers. Over the last thirty years the airfield's career has seen a number of ups and downs but in general terms it has been maintained by the USAF, with ground units based here to support what, in recent years, have become increasingly frequent detachments. From an aviation enthusiast point of view a third notable activity has been the use of Fairford for hugely impressive air displays (International Air Tattoo).

UNITS

1939–1945

190 Sqn	25 Mar 1944–14 Oct 1944	Stirling
620 Sqn	18 Mar 1944–18 Oct 1944	Stirling
22 HGCU	Oct 1944–Oct 1945	Albemarle, Horsa, Hotspur, Hadrian

Post-1945

10 Sqn	1 Jul 1966–23 May 1967	VC10
30 Sqn	1 May 1968–1 Feb 1971	Hercules
47 Sqn	1 Mar 1968–1 Feb 1971	Hercules
53 Sqn	1 Jan 1966–23 May 1967	Belfast
113 Sqn	1 May 1947–1 Sep 1948	Dakota
295 Sqn	10 Sep 1947–1 Nov 1948	Halifax
297 Sqn	21 Aug 1947–1 Nov 1948	Halifax
1555 Flt	15 Sep 1945–30 Apr 1946; Jul 1946–31 Oct 1946	Oxford
1556 Flt	Dec 1945–1 Apr 1946	Oxford
1528 Flt	1 Feb 1946–4 Mar 1946	Oxford
1529 Flt	27 Jan 1946–16 Feb 1946	Oxford
27 Gp CF	late 1946–Sep 1947	various
CFS	Nov 1964–Aug 1966	

FALMOUTH

County: Cornwall

UTM/Grid: OS Map 204 – SW815334
Lat/Long: N50°09.61 W005°03.63
Nearest Town: Falmouth Harbour

HISTORY

A small number of moorings were placed in Falmouth Harbour for use by RAF flying boats in the months immediately after the outbreak of war. The same general area had been used by floatplane detachments in the latter part of World War One and, indeed, the harbour had seen periodic visits by seaplanes during the 1920s and 1930s, although not to a regular RAF facility. In truth, there was little more here than a few moorings, although a number of local buildings were used on a temporary basis. Initial wartime use was by a detachment for 240 Squadron, who sent three London IIs here in late-September from their main base at Invergorden. The Londons were replaced a few weeks later by Stranraers of 209 Squadron but they, too, spent only a few weeks here before being withdrawn. The RAF retained the moorings under Care and Maintenance until December 1941, but very little use was made of these.

UNITS

1939–1945

209Sqn det	Oct–Nov 1939	Stranraer
240Sqn det	Sep–Oct 1939	London

FILTON (Station 803)

County: Gloucestershire

UTM/Grid: OS Map 172 – ST595802
Lat/Long: N51°31.20 W002°34.43
Nearest Town: Bristol 4 miles to south

Aerial shot dated 22 June 1944.

History

Although there is one unit that has a particular association with Filton – No.501 (City of Bristol/County of Gloucester) Squadron, which spent a total of twenty-one years at the airfield, including four months during World War Two – the airfield is best-known for its aircraft manufacturing activities with the Bristol Aeroplane and Engine Company (and its successors).

The British and Colonial Aeroplane Company had taken over premises at Filton in 1910 and, by November, their first major aircraft, the Bristol Boxkite, was in production, with military orders being placed the following year. The company acquired an adjacent piece of land as a landing ground for flight test and delivery, anticipating an increase in military contracts. With the outbreak of World War One, the factory underwent massive expansion and was turning out hundreds of aircraft,

AIRFIELD DATA DEC 1944

Command:	Transport Command	Runway surface:	Concrete and tarmac
Function:	Operational, Parent	Hangars:	23 × Old Type (wood), Type B
Runways:	101 deg 1,500 × 50yd		(4-bay) × one, Type B (single bay) × one
	030 deg 1,338 × 50yd	Dispersals:	Aprons and hardstands for 45–63 aircraft
		Personnel:	Officers – 77 (4 WAAF)
			Other Ranks – 844 (170 WAAF)

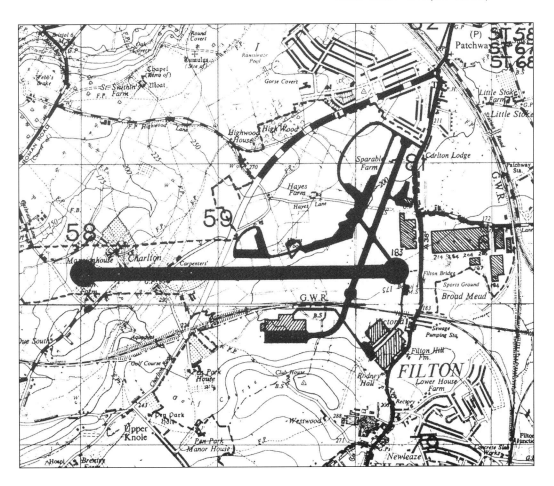

which also involved component manufacture at sites throughout the area. No.5 Aircraft Acceptance Park (AAP) was formed at Filton in early to mid-1917 to accept aircraft from local manufacturers, the main types being Bristol F2b, DH9 and DH9a, and the Filton works being the major provider. In December 1917 the name was changed to No.5 (Bristol) AAP and it operated as this until some time in 1919.

As the unit list shows, a number of Royal Flying Corps operational and training squadrons used Filton between late-1915 and 1919, most only staying for a few days or weeks.

The inter-war period was a difficult one for all aircraft manufacturers, but Bristols had branched out into flying training and, as part of this, received a contract to operate a reserve school. This opened at Filton in May 1923. In 1935 the school was re-designated as No.2 Elementary and Reserve Flying Training School (ERFTS) and continued to use a diverse fleet of trainers, including Audax, Hart and

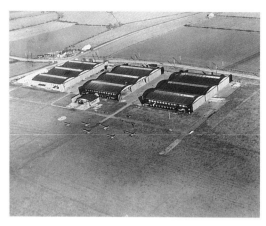

1920s shot of Filton showing the World War One AAP hangars. (Rolls-Royce)

The 'Bristol' Flying School of the 1930s. (Rolls-Royce)

Tiger Moth. Filton was unusual, in that it operated two such schools; No.10 ERFTS had formed at Filton on 1 January 1936 for the same basic role and used Filton and Whitchurch until disbanded in September 1939. As with all such units, No.2 ERFTS was disbanded on 3 September 1939 – but it immediately reformed, still under the Bristol Aeroplane Co., as No.2 EFTS. It was part of No.50 Group and was designated a Class B unit capable of handling ninety pupils and with 36+18 aircraft on establishment. Tiger Moths were the aircraft of choice and for nearly a year the pupil pilots used Filton for their basic training. The school subsequently moved to Staverton and Worcester in August 1940.

By the mid-1930s, the aircraft manufacturers had started to receive massive orders from the RAF as part of the panic expansion schemes and Bristol types, such as the Blenheim, Beaufort and Beaufighter, were to play major roles in World War Two. The airfield underwent major expansion to cater for the increased production and, in addition to the factory facilities, two hard runways were laid out (late-1941), along with various hangars and dispersals.

The Air Transport Auxiliary (ATA) staffed No.2 Ferry Pilots Pool from its formation at Filton on 16 January 1939, the task being delivery of new aircraft to the Aircraft Storage Units. The FPP had its own Anson ferry aircraft to collect and deliver pilots. During 1940 this unit underwent a number of name changes, initially to No.4 FPP and then adding, and losing, 'Continental' in its title. By November it had become HQ Service Ferry Pools.

At the outbreak of war, the airfield's 'own' fighter squadron was recalled from detachment. No.501 (County of Gloucester) Squadron had formed at Filton as a special reserved squadron on 14 June 1929,

initially in the light-bomber role with the DH9a. In May 1936, it had been transferred to the Auxiliary Air Force, still as a bomber unit but now with Hawker Harts. It eventually became a fighter squadron in March 1939 with Hurricanes and, at the outbreak of war, was on annual camp at Manston. No doubt the people of Bristol and the workers at Filton were pleased to see the Hurricanes dispersed around the airfield, but they had little to do, as the war had not yet arrived over England. The squadron moved to Tangmere in late-November – but was back a year later.

It was from here that 263 Squadron left with its Gladiators in April 1940 en route to Norway with HMS *Glorious*; the campaign they fought from the frozen surface of Lake Lesjeskog was courageous but futile and disaster struck for the survivors when *Glorious* was sunk. The squadron returned to Filton in April 1941, by which time they were equipped with the interesting but ineffective Westland Whirlwind.

The unit list details the various operational squadrons and support units that were based at Filton during World War Two; the operational period was short-lived and as soon as the German air threat receded, so too did the fighter presence. Considering its importance, the Bristol factory complex received little attention from the Luftwaffe, the only effective attacks taking place on 25 September 1940 and 11 April 1942.

Aircraft production and the delivery of those aircraft remained the main purpose of Filton and, in addition to the work of the FPP, No.2 Overseas Aircraft Preparation Unit (OAPU) formed in December 1942 to handle the main Bristol types – Beaufort, Beaufighter and Blenheim – as well as the Anson, Albemarle and Mosquito. The Unit lost the 'Overseas' part of its title in July 1944, but continued the same basic role until becoming part of No.15 Ferry Unit the following July. The new unit only lasted until October, when it was disbanded.

In the latter part of the war Filton also became Station 803 of the USAAF as, in autumn 1943, the IXth Air Force started to use the airfield for the assembly and preparation of aircraft. This was a period of rapid expansion for the USAAF and large numbers of aircraft were being shipped to the UK – and needed stripping of their protective coatings, assembly, checking and delivery. Having erected a series of Butler Combat Hangars, the USAAF technicians handled a variety of types, including the main fighters (P-38, P-47, P-51), medium bombers (A-20) and support types, such as the T-6. The unit was here to support IXth Air Force and when that organization moved to the Continent in mid-1944 the Filton facil-

ity was closed.

In the post-war period Bristols once more took on a flying training role for the RAF, operating No.12 Reserve Flying School from April 1948 to March 1953. By this time the appearance of the airfield had undergone a major change, with near-doubling of length of the main runway, as well as greatly increasing its width. Bristols had turned their attention to civil airliners and the aircraft that caused this runway extension was the Brabazon. Construction was not popular in the local area, as it involved closing a major road and demolishing a number of buildings. This work commenced in March 1946 and, in August, the airfield was transferred to the Ministry of

One of the most significant of the Filton products was the Blenheim; this 1937 shot is of an early Blenheim – a time when the performance of the aircraft was a revelation for a light bomber.

Bombay L5808 at Filton.

The Luftwaffe target folder of November including this aerial photo.

The camouflaged Bristol Works during World War Two. (Rolls-Royce)

The American presence at Filton, all April 1944: A-20s; removing the grease coat from a Mustang; removing protective coverings on P-51s. (US National Archives)

Supply. The 8,150ft runway was of little use to the Brabazon, as the aircraft did not enter production, but it did ensure the future of Filton as an aircraft production facility into the 1990s.

For over thirty years from September 1958 the Chipmunks, and later Bulldogs, of No.3 Air Experience Flight operated from Filton; the unit moved to Hullavington in June 1989. Bristol University Air Squadron managed nearly fifty years (in two periods) at Filton; the squadron formed in Bristol in February 1941 and was attached to the airfield from April, using aircraft of the based EFTS. This arrangement continued to July 1946, when BUAS disbanded. It reformed at Filton in December 1950 and remained here until transferring to Hullavington in March 1992.

On 26 November 2003 one of Filton's most famous products returned to the airfield for the final time; Concorde G-BOAF arrived from Heathrow to 'retire'

– the Concorde era having come to a sudden and sad end. Bristol/Filton (EGTG) is still operated by BAe Systems and its single runway (09/27 of 2,467m) is used by visiting aircraft on company business, as well as two flying clubs, a police helicopter unit and an air charter company. The main activity at the BAe site is now connected with maintenance and support for the Airbus.

UNITS

HQ units at Filton

| No.21 Wing | 9 Aug 1916–2 Sep 1916 |
| No.110 (AAC) Wing | 3 May 1940–5 May 1941 |

Pre-1919

19 Sqn	29 Mar 1916–30 Jul 1916	various
20 Sqn	15 Dec 1915–16 Jan 1916	BE2c, JN4
33 Sqn	12 Jan 1916–29 Mar 1916	BE2c

42 Sqn	1 Apr 1916–8 Aug 1916	BE2d, BE2e
62 Sqn	8 Aug 1916–17 Jul 1917	various
66 Sqn	24 Jun 1916–2 Jul 1916	BE types
101 Sqn	18 Mar 1919–11 Oct 1919	FE2b
121 Sqn	10–17 Aug 1918	various
35 TS	1–16 Feb 1917	various
51 TS	30 Dec 1916–8 Jan 1917	various
55 TS	15–22 Nov 1916	various

1919–1939

501Sqn	14 Jun 1929–27 Nov 1939	DH9a, Wapiti, Wallace, Hart, Hind, Hurricane
RS	May 1923–1935	various
2 ERFTS	1935–3 Sep 1939	various
10 ERFTS	1 Jan 1936–3 Sep 1939	

1939–1945

25 Sqn	14 Sep 1939–4 Oct 1939	Blenheim
118 Sqn	20 Feb 1941–7 Apr 1941	Spitfire
145 Sqn	9–10 May 1940	Hurricane
236 Sqn	25 May 1940–14 Jun 1940	Blenheim
263 Sqn	2 Oct 1939–24 Apr 1940	Gladiator
263 Sqn	10 Apr 1941–7 Aug 1941	Whirlwind
286 Sqn	17 Nov 1941–30 Dec 1941	various
501 Sqn	17 Dec 1940–9 Apr 1941	Hurricane

504 Sqn	26 Sep 1940–18 Dec 1940	Hurricane
528 Sqn	15 Jun 1943–15 May 1944	Blenheim, Hornet Moth
2 FPP	16 Jan 1939–1 Apr 1940	Anson
2 EFTS	3 Sep 1939–1 Nov 1941	Tiger Moth
4 FPP	1 Apr 1940–7 Nov 1940	Anson
8 AACU	29 Apr 1940–6 Aug 1940	various
7 RMU	Jul 1940–Aug 1940	Hornet Moth
Bristol UAS	25 Feb 1941–15 Jul 1946	Moth, Tiger Moth
10 Gp AACF	5 May 1941–17 Nov 1941	Blenheim, Lysander
10 Gp TTF	Oct 1941–Nov 1941	Lysander
2 OAPU	1 Dec 1942–5 Jul 1944	Anson
2 APU	5 Jul 1944–1 Jul 1945	various
15 FU	1 Jul 1945–10 Oct 1945	various

Post-1945

501Sqn	10 May 1946–10 Mar 1957	Spitfire, Vampire
12 RFS	1 Apr 1948–31 Mar 1953	various
Bristol UAS	1 Dec 1950–6 Mar 1992	Tiger Moth, Harvard, Chipmunk, Bulldog
3 AEF	8 Sep 1958–Jun 1989	Chipmunk, Bulldog

April 1963 and the experimental Bristol T188 (XF926) – looking somewhat strange as the fin of the chase Hunter appears to be growing out of the fuselage of the T188!

Vulcan being used a Olympus test-bed by Bristol.

GUERNSEY

County: Channel Islands

UTM/Grid:
Lat/Long: N49°26.08 W002°36.12
Nearest Town: St Peter Port 3 miles to north-east

HISTORY

Guernsey is one of only two British airfields to have been used by the RAF and the Luftwaffe, with the latter making the most operational use of the airfield. The Channel Island of Guernsey had an air link provided by flying boat from the early 1920s but, in May 1939, an airport – a small grass airfield with few facilities – was opened a few miles from St Peter Port. Guernsey Airways started limited commercial services and the RAF decided that it would make an excellent forward base for Coastal Command, a detachment of Ansons from 48 Squadron arriving in early September. The outbreak of war brought restrictions to civil flying; meanwhile, the Ansons started flying coastal patrols, although these ceased in early October.

The School of General Reconnaissance moved its Ansons to Guernsey from Thorney Island in late-April 1940 but, with the German invasion in the west the following month, which was followed by a rapid collapse of the Allied forces in France, it was decided to move to a safer location. By mid-June the school had departed to Hooton Park. The airfield was used as a refuelling stop by Bomber Command in June for a series of attacks on Italy, but it was evident that the German advance would make the islands untenable. The Luftwaffe duly arrived on 1 July, bringing an advance guard of the occupation force. For the next five years Guernsey Airport was an operational Luftwaffe airfield and was, initially, used as an advanced fighter base, the first residents being Bf109s for the Battle of Britain, with both JG27 and JG53 spending periods here. Units rotated during the rest of the war and the fighters were called on to defend German targets on the islands as the RAF took the opportunity to bomb, for example, shipping in St Peter Port. The Germans eventually left the island on 9 May 1945 and, with British re-occupation of the Channel Islands, Guernsey became home to No.160 Staging Post from May to October 1945. The primary role of these organizations was, as their name suggests, providing facilities for the refuel, and sometimes maintenance of, transit aircraft. They were usually situated at convenient places on long-range transit routes and Guernsey was part of the network of such locations used by No.46 Group of Transport Command.

Commercial aviation returned to the airport but development was slow over the next few decades and it was not until 1960 that a surfaced runway was laid, enabling aircraft with better performance to use the airport and overcoming the problem of waterlogged grass areas. Private and corporate aviation has also been a feature of the airport and, although the main commercial connections have been with the UK, traffic has continued to grow. The official title is now the States of Guernsey Airport (EGJB) and the single asphalt runway (09/27) is now 1,463m. A new terminal opened in April 2004 at a cost of £19 million and passenger figures are now around one million a year. In addition to commercial services, the airport is used by corporate and private aviation, the latter including the Guernsey Aero Club.

UNITS

1939–1945

17Sqn det	June 1940	Hurricane
48Sqn det	summer 1939	Anson
SoGR	Apr 1940–Jun 1940	Anson

HALDON (HMS *Heron II*)

County: Devon

UTM/Grid: OS Map 192 – SX915765
Lat/Long: N50°34 W003°31

Nearest Town: Teignmouth 2 miles to south-east

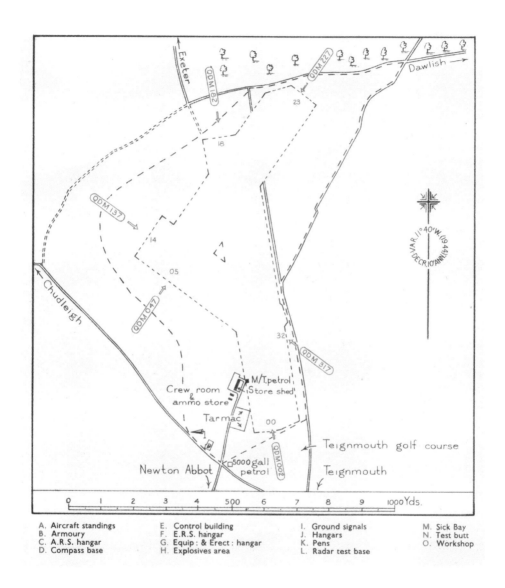

A. Aircraft standings
B. Armoury
C. A.R.S. hangar
D. Compass base

E. Control building
F. E.R.S. hangar
G. Equip: & Erect: hangar
H. Explosives area

I. Ground signals
J. Hangars
K. Pens
L. Radar test base

M. Sick Bay
N. Test butt
O. Workshop

HISTORY

Haldon Airport was established as a private airfield in 1928 by Bill Parkhouse; having acquired a stretch of land at Little Haldon, he developed it into a simple grass airfield and acquired an Avro Avian with which to promote aviation and give flying lessons. The story of this private airfield and its various characters is an interesting one, but outside the scope of this military study.

Haldon Airport, Teignmouth was requisitioned in early April 1940 for use by the RAE's Research Department at Exeter (SOM 250/40). This particular element of the RAE was unofficially known as the Balloon Barrage Flight and part of its work involved trials work on cable-cutting devices. The unit was equipped with Wellesleys, Battles and Wellingtons, but it seems unlikely that these spent much time at Haldon.

The airfield, also known as Haldon Moor, was a grass airfield laid out in an irregular shape with a maximum run of around 1,000 yards for the north/south strip. The airfield had very few facilities, other than a small group of buildings on the south end of the site.

The airfield spent much of its war as a satellite for Yeovilton and the first naval presence appears to have been 794 Squadron from mid-1940. The squadron used a variety of aircraft and its primary role was target-towing. Over the next two years the airfield was used by at least two other Yeovilton-based training squadrons, both operating in the Fleet Fighter training role. As usual with satellites, the scale of actual usage is hard to determine. The official transfer to Admiralty control took place on 18 August 1941, with Haldon becoming HMS *Heron II* to reflect its relationship with Yeovilton. The Fleet Air Arm made little use of the airfield, although at least two support squadrons spent periods here to work with the nearby weapon ranges in Lyme Bay. The main role was that of towing targets for naval

gunners and Masters and Skuas were initially used for this task. Haldon underwent some improvement work in 1942 to provide better operating surfaces, which included the laying of Sommerfeld Track. However, the site was still not ideal and Haldon was reduced to Care and Maintenance in May 1943 and the ship name was transferred to Charlton Horethorne. The RAF resumed control, but had no significant use for this very limited grass field; however, in August 1944, No.84 Gliding School formed at Haldon and was equipped with the standard training glider, the Cadet. The unit remained at the moorland site for two years, but moved to Exeter in June 1946.

UNITS

1939–1945

RAE	1939–1940?	Battle, Wellesley, Wellington
84 GS	Aug 1944–Jun 1945	Cadet, Sedbergh
759Sqn FAA	1942	various
761Sqn FAA	1941–1942?	various
794Sqn FAA	1940–?	various

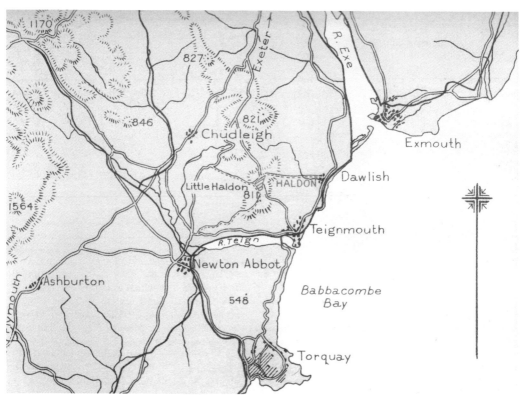

HAMWORTHY

County: Dorset

UTM/Grid: OS Map 195 – SZ035900
Lat/Long: N50°42.57 W001°57.10
Nearest Town: Poole Harbour

HISTORY

Although the flying-boat base at Hamworthy did not open until 1 August 1942, flying-boat operations had been taking place from Poole Harbour since 1939; Imperial Airways had become part of the National Air Communications network at the outbreak of war and had moved its 'boats' from Hythe to Poole in September 1939. This was something of an ad hoc arrangement, as the mooring site near Brownsea Island was not ideal and the airline kept its maintenance and support at Hythe. In April 1940, it was joined by the newly formed British Overseas Airways Corporation (BOAC). Routes included North America, via Ireland, and North Africa and the service provided by BOAC was of major importance in moving vital personnel and material (documents).

Coastal Command's need for additional flying-boat bases led it to look at Poole Harbour and a site – far from suitable – was developed in the first half of 1942, the moorings being located to the north of the Wareham Channel, which would become the 'waterway' for take-off and landing. A slipway was constructed, but there was little available land on which to develop the support facilities and local buildings had to be requisitioned. The RAF continued to search for a better site but, in the meantime, the first operational aircraft flew in. The Australians of 461 Squadron brought their Sunderlands from Mount Batten to Hamworthy in early September 1942 and for the next few months flew anti-submarine and maritime patrol operations from the Dorset base. When they departed to Pembroke Dock in April 1943, their place was taken by 210 Squadron, equipped with Catalinas. The latter unit found a much improved site, as the RAF had managed to take over the Salterne Pier area, but it was still far from ideal – and the busy harbour was little short of a nightmare for pilots. There may have been some compensation in that the officers' mess was the 'Harbour Heights Hotel' and, with personnel living in Poole, the often dreary RAF base-life could be avoided. Operationally it remained a problem and in December 1943 the squadron disbanded (but

reformed the following day at Sullom Voe by renumbering 190 Squadron).

The Poole Harbour site was handed to Transpor[t] Command for use by BOAC Sunderlands and RA[F] Hamworthy closed on 1 May 1944. The boats [of] BOAC remained active from Poole until Marc[h] 1948.

Units

1939–1945

210Sqn	21 Apr 1943–31 Dec 1943	Catalina
461Sqn	5 Sep 1942–20 Apr 1943	Sunderland

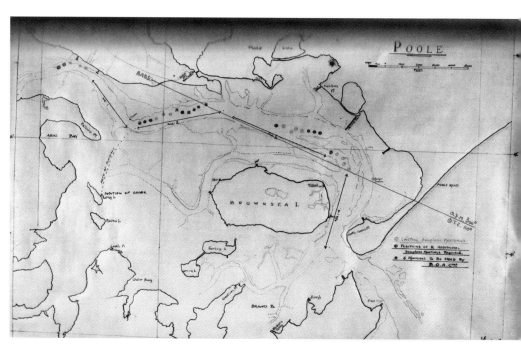

HARROWBEER

County: Devon

UTM/Grid: OS Map 201 – SX513680
Lat/Long: N50°29.27 W004°05.42
Nearest Town: Plymouth 8 miles to south

HISTORY

Authority was given in late September to requisition land at Roborough Down for development as a fighter station. The name was changed to Harrowbeer in late-October, to avoid confusion with the other Roborough at Plymouth. Although the site was only a mile or so from the edge of Dartmoor (and it is still a bleak location), its construction involved diverting a major road, and even then it was squeezed in by roads on all sides, and demolishing a number of buildings. Three runways were laid down but, at only 900yd, one of these was particularly short; this was not a problem, as the airfield was intended as a fighter airfield with No.10 Group, initially with the defence of Plymouth in mind. RAF Harrowbeer opened in August 1941 and the first based-occupants were the Spitfires of 130 Squadron, which arrived from Portreath in late-October to work-up with their

new aircraft. They stayed just over a month and, as the unit list shows, were the first of a long list of fighter units to spend time at Harrowbeer, most of which were involved in offensive operations, with fighter-bombing becoming something of a speciality.

The airfield was also well-placed to provide air-sea rescue cover and, in October 1941, a special unit, 276 Squadron, formed here for this role. The squadron was initially equipped with the Hurricane and Lysander, but the following January it received the Walrus, an excellent ASR type to which many downed aircrew owed their survival. The squadron remained operational from Harrowbeer to April 1944, having also run detachments at other airfields, and its fleet list during this time was diverse.

Only one fighter squadron was actually formed at Harrowbeer, with personnel and aircraft coming

AIRFIELD DATA DEC 1944

Command:	Maintenance Command	Runway surface:	Asphalt
Function:	Storage Unit	Hangars:	Over Blister × 8, Bellman × 2
Runways:	110 deg 1,300 × 50yd	Dispersals:	18 × Twin-Engine
	166 deg 1,100 × 50yd	Personnel:	Officers – 76 (7 WAAF)
	229 deg 900 × 50yd		Other Ranks – 1,623 (224 WAAF)

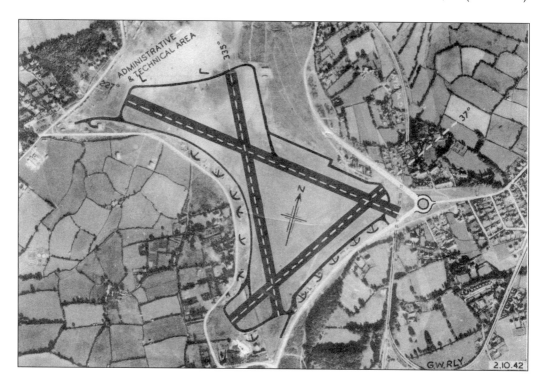

together in December 1942 to form 193 Squadron. The squadron was designated as a Typhoon unit but its initial equipment, which arrived in January, included a few Hurricanes to help with the work-up until the full complement of 'Tiffies' had been received. A year later the squadron hosted a special event at Harrowbeer, as it had become a 'sponsored' squadron – the 'Fellowship of the Bellows' – money for the aircraft having been raised by this organization in Brazil. Amongst the VIPs was the Brazilian Ambassador, but the planned flypast to mark the occasion was marred by the, not unusual, low cloud – one of the penalties of building an airfield on the edge of Dartmoor.

No.229 Maintenance Unit had formed at Harrowbeer in October 1942 as a Mobile Equipment Park within No.40 Group, something of a strange use for this airfield, but there was a shortage of RAF facil-

ities in this region and, at this period, the airfield was underutilized. In April 1943, the MU became part of No.83 Group, as part of the re-structuring of the RAF's tactical air organization for the invasion of Europe, and became an Air Stores Park. The Admiralty had lodger facilities at Harrowbeer, but the only significant use came in the middle of 1944, when 838 Squadron moved in with its Swordfish from Macrihanish for anti-submarine operations with No.156 (General Reconnaissance) Wing. The twelve aircraft were equipped with ASV and provided a valuable boost to Coastal Command's anti-U-boat capability during the D-Day period. With Allied forces securely ashore, the Wing disbanded and units re-deployed, the Swordfish departing for Northern Ireland. Harrowbeer had been very busy in the period either side of D-Day, with anti-shipping operations, fighter sweeps and fighter-bomber ops

Spitfire of 126 Squadron, probably at Harrowbeer; the Squadron was one of many fighter units to operate on very short-term detachments from the Devon base.

Harrowbeer was also an ASR base and was used as such by at least three specialist squadrons.

but, with the invaders safely ashore, the airfield was suddenly no longer required and it was reduced to Care and Maintenance in late summer. The 1944 airfield survey showed that Harrowbeer was officially a storage unit of Maintenance Command and that it had ten hangars, the majority being Blister type. It also showed that two of the runways could be extended to 1,450 yards 'with light demolition'.

The last few months of 1944 saw some use for communications flights, Plymouth housing a number of headquarters, and in January the airfield was transferred to Flying Training Command and returned to full active service. Walrus ASR aircraft were first to return, 275 Squadron arriving from Exeter – but disbanding a few weeks later. Other squadrons passed

through in the early months of 1945, but there was little real interest and RAF Harrowbeer was closed on 13 May 1946. The site was transferred to the Ministry of Civil Aviation for consideration as a civil airport, which would have been all but impossible, but nothing came of this plan. No.19 Group based its Comms Flight here for a few months in 1948 and No.82 Gliding School used the airfield for two years, eventually leaving when the RAF finally lost all interest.

Little of the airfield remains, although a number of fighter pens have survived and, as it is a park area, you can pull your car into a fighter pen and have a picnic! The overall structure of the airfield is still clear from the air, for although the runways have gone the pattern is still visible.

UNITS

HQ units at Harrowbeer

No.156 (GR) Wing	22 Apr 1944–8 Aug 1944	838Sqn

1939–1945

1 Sqn	20–22 Jun 1944	Spitfire
19 Sqn det	late 1942	Spitfire
26 Sqn	14–21 Jan 1945; 3 Apr 1945–23 May 1945+	Mustang
64 Sqn	26 Jun 1944–30 Aug 1944	Spitfire
126 Sqn	3 Jul 1944–30 Aug 1944	Spitfire
130 Sqn	25 Oct 1941–30 Nov 1941	Spitfire
131 Sqn	24 Mar 1944–24 May 1944	Spitfire
165 Sqn	20–22 Jun 1944	Spitfire
175 Sqn	10 Oct 1942–9 Dec 1942	Hurricane
183 Sqn	5 Jun 1943–4 Aug 1943	Typhoon
193 Sqn	18 Dec 1942–17 Aug 1943	Hurricane, Typhoon
263 Sqn	20 Feb 1943–15 Mar 1943	Whirlwind
263 Sqn	19 Mar 1944–19 Jun 1944	Typhoon
266 Sqn	21 Sep 1943–15 Mar 1944+	Typhoon
275 Sqn	12 Jan 1945–15 Feb 1945	Walrus, Spitfire
276 Sqn	21 Oct 1941–4 Apr 1944	various
286 Sqn det	spring 1942	various
302 Sqn	1 Nov 1941–5 May 1942+	Spitfire
312 Sqn	2 May 1942–10 Oct 1942+	Spitfire
329Sqn	19 Jun 1945–16 Jul 1945	Spitfire
414 Sqn	26 May 1943–4 Jun 1943	Mustang
610 Sqn	24 May 1944–19 Jun 1944	Spitfire
611 Sqn	24 Jun 1944–3 Jul 1944	Spitfire
616 Sqn	15–18 Mar 1943	Spitfire
691 Sqn	21 Feb 1945–1 Aug 1945	various
834 Sqn FAA det	Apr 1943	Swordfish
838 Sqn FAA	Apr 1944–Aug 1944	Swordfish

Post-1945

19 Gp CF	15 Dec 1947–29 Jul 1948	various
82 GS	19 Feb 1948–16 Aug 1950	Cadet, Sedbergh

MEMORIAL

Granite stone near the 'Leg of Mutton' pub; inscribed

RAF Harrowbeer operational 1941–1949. From this station flew pilots of many Commonwealth and Allied countries including Britain, Canada, Czechoslovakia, France, Poland, Rhodesia and the United States of America with the support of their ground crew and airfield defence units. This stone is in memory of all who served here and especially of those who gave their lives. Many local residents helped build and maintain the airfield. Unveiled by the first Station Commander, Group Captain The Honourable E F Ward on 15th August 1981, the fortieth anniversary of the opening of this station.

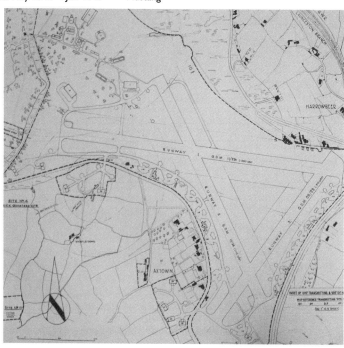

HENSTRIDGE
(HMS *Dipper*)

County: Dorset (now Somerset)

UTM/Grid: OS Map 183 – ST752205
Lat/Long: N50°59.00 W002°21.28
Nearest Town: Yeovil 10 miles to south-west

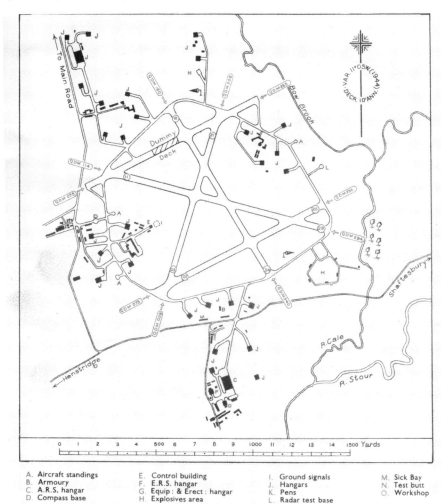

A. Aircraft standings
B. Armoury
C. A.R.S. hangar
D. Compass base

E. Control building
F. E.R.S. hangar
G. Equip: & Erect: hangar
H. Explosives area

I. Ground signals
J. Hangars
K. Pens
L. Radar test base

M. Sick Bay
N. Test butt
O. Workshop

HISTORY

Henstridge was commissioned, as HMS *Dipper*, on 1 April 1943, for use by No.2 Naval Air Fighter School (NAFS). The school was made up of various numbered squadrons and the airfield had a notional capacity of 120 aircraft – making it one of the Fleet Air Arm's major training bases. One of the core squadrons was 761 Squadron, which moved in from Yeovilton to form the NAFS and used Seafires and Spitfires, in addition to a small number of Masters, to provide pilot training, including deck-landing. The squadron had arrived with a number of Fulmars, but these vanished within the first few weeks as the unit built-up its strength of fighters. The squadron remained at Henstridge to January 1946 and, over that period, operated a number of Seafire/Spitfire Marks and, by mid-1944, its strength was around seventy fighters.

The site at Henstridge, named after the nearby village, was acquired in 1941 and was a large flat area bounded on two sides by the Bow Beck and with roads on the other two sides. Development of an airfield with five runways was called for by the Navy and it was quite a planning feat to fit them into the area and also provide the support infrastructure for what was intended as a major training base. Development was slower than expected, but by the time the airfield opened it was well equipped with runways, although the longest was only 1,200 yards, a linking perimeter track and various dispersal areas, most of which were on taxiway extensions to the north and south, along with associated hangars. At least one of the runways was rigged out as a carrier deck, complete with markings and arrester wires.

June 1944 saw the formation of 718 Squadron to operate as an Army Co-operation Training Unit, for which it used training types, such as the Harvard, and operational types, such as the Seafire and Spitfire. The unit provided role training, which included photo reconnaissance and tactical reconnaissance, as well as air combat training. By October, the unit was more usually referred to as the Army Co-operation Naval Operational Training Unit (ACNOTU). A further change of name came in April 1945 to the School of Naval Air Reconnaissance (SoNAR).

A number of operational squadrons also used Henstridge, albeit usually for short periods; for example, the Seafires of 885 and 886 Squadrons spent a few weeks here in spring 1944. They were part of Lee-on-Solent's Air Spotting Pool – a specialist grouping training to work with naval bombardment during the invasion of Europe. Other disembarked squadrons came here for rest or refit; for example, 894 Squadron came off HMS *Illustrious* in October 1943 and received Seafire IIBs, trained with these, joined up with 887 Squadron, and left again in January.

The unit list shows the various movements at Henstridge, the busiest period being 1944. In mid-December 1945, the Sea Otters of 'C Flight' 799 Squadron arrived for refresher and conversion training but, early the following year, the Flight rejoined the parent unit at Lee-on-Solent. The airfield was paid-off on 11 October 1946, but was brought back into service in 1949 to act as a satellite for Yeovilton, a role it retained, but not continuously, to 1957. Civil helicopter operations had taken place at the airfield from the early 1950s and in 1955 Bristow Helicopters formed with its headquarters at Henstridge, but three years later they moved to Redhill and, with no further aviation use, the remaining buildings were sold-off, becoming an industrial estate.

The occasional private flying that took place from part of the airfield was eventually formalized in 1986

with the opening of Henstridge Airfield, now a licensed airfield (EGHS) operated by EGHS Ltd. The airfield occupies the most northerly of the old wartime runways and the adjacent peri track; runway 07/25 is now 750m and the concrete dummy deck is still there. Most of the rest of the airfield is also still visible from the air and numerous buildings survive (but ground visitors beware, the occupants of the industrial estate are NOT friendly!)

Units

1939–1945

718Sqn FAA	5 Jun 1944–17 Aug 1945	various
748Sqn FAA	4 Feb 1944–9 Mar 1944	various
761Sqn FAA	10 Apr 1943–16 Jan 1946	various
794Sqn FAA	22 Nov 1943–1 Dec 1943	various
808Sqn FAA	7 Mar 1944–22 Apr 1944+	Seafire, Spitfire
885Sqn FAA	31 Mar 1944–22 Apr 1944	Seafire
886Sqn FAA	11 Mar 1944–25 Apr 1944	Seafire
887Sqn FAA	13 Dec 1943–8 Jan 1944	Seafire
894Sqn FAA	19 Oct 1943–8 Jan 1944	Seafire
897Sqn FAA	2 Mar 1944–6 May 1944+	Seafire

Post-1945

760Sqn FAA	27 Dec 1945–23 Jan 1946	Seafire
767Sqn FAA	4 Jan 1952–20 Sep 1952	Firefly, Sea Fury
799Sqn FAA	17 Dec 1945–23 Jan 1946	Sea Otter

HIGH POST

County: Wiltshire

UTM/Grid: OS Map 184 – SU145372
Lat/Long: N51°08.03 W001°47.64
Nearest Town: Salisbury 4 miles to south

The hotel at High Post in its camouflaged finish and having 'grown' a control tower on top. (via Rod Priddle)

HISTORY

High Post opened as a private airfield in May 1931 for the Wiltshire Light Aeroplane and Country Club and was, literally, a field. Over the next few years the club changed its name to Wiltshire School of Flying and the airfield was provided with a clubhouse and hangar; in 1935 a major and impressive development was agreed – to create the High Post Aerodrome Hotel, which incorporated an 'observation tower' on its roof. The previous year High Post had held an 'Empire Air Day', the only civil airfield to do so.

The airfield was closed to civil flying in September 1939 and was taken over for military use. Initial use was by army co-operation aircraft, with 'D Flight' arriving from Old Sarum in February 1940. This was followed in June by 112 Squadron, RCAF, who took great delight in moving in to the hotel as an officers' mess, although much of the squadron had to make do with tented facilities. The Canadians moved to Halton on 13 November and, in the same month, the

trainers from No.1 SFTS at Netheravon started making use of High Post as a daytime RLG. This continued to late-1943 but was then terminated, because of the hazard of having trainers flying circuits at High Post, as they were too close to the more important airfield (and circuit) at Boscombe Down. However, by this time the remote airfield had taken on a far more important task and its grass surfaces were being used by Spitfires. As part of the dispersal plan for Spitfire production, sites in Salisbury were being used for production and sub-assembly; the aircraft were then taken to High Post (or Chattis Hill) for final assembly, flight testing and despatch. The first Spitfire to fly out of High Post was Spitfire I X4497, which flew on 12 January 1941. At first the assembly shed was only able to take three completed aircraft at one time, a major restriction on the output, which ran at an average of six aircraft a week. However, the old flying club hangars remained in use until June

1944, when a double B.1 hangar was erected and used for aircraft assembly, thus boosting capacity. This was essential, as the production capacity in Salisbury had also increased, with the provision of a new facility. The original grass field was far too small and additional land was obtained, hedges removed and grass strips laid out; this involved closure of a minor road to give a 1,760yd north/south strip. Of the other two runways, one was 2,000yd and one 1,500yd – an impressive collection of runways for this type of airfield, but High Post was playing a major role in Spitfire production.

By mid-1944, High Post was a busy airfield, with various marks of Spitfire and Seafire on site; when testing was complete aircraft were collected by ferry pilots for transit to Maintenance Units and it was not unusual for twenty to thirty aircraft to be present at any one time. The prototype Spiteful, a developed Spitfire, made its first flight from here on 30 June 1944 in the hands of that great Spitfire Test Pilot, Jeffrey Quill. June 1944 saw the Supermarine Flight Test Department move to High Post from Worthy Down, a situation that continued into the post-war period. The rush for Spitfires had come to a sudden halt in the latter months of the war, but

Supermarines were already working on future projects. One of these was the Attacker F1 for the Royal Navy, the first purpose-built jet for the Fleet Air Arm. Although the prototype made its first flight from Boscombe Down (27 July 1946) it then moved to High Post – and grass runways – to continue the flight-test programme. The company, however, took the opportunity to acquire Chilbolton, partly because of the threat from expansion of Boscombe Down, and abandoned High Post in 1947. The final year of the airfield's existence had also seen a brief return by the Wiltshire Flying Club (from April 1946) and the Royal Artillery Flying Club.

Some of the buildings were subsequently removed, including the double B.1 hangar to Boscombe Down, whilst others have been modified and are still in use. From the air the site is not at all distinct and you need to know exactly where to look or you miss it.

UNITS

1939–1945

112Sqn RCAF	6 Jun 1940–13 Nov 1940	
1 SFTS	29 Nov 1940–Sep 1943	various

High Post played a very significant part in the testing and delivery of Spitfires; Spitfire XII MB878 may have passed through High Post but it is seen here with the A&AEE on trials.

HULLAVINGTON

County: Wiltshire

UTM/Grid: OS Map 173 – ST900810
Lat/Long: N51°31.38 W002°08.02
Nearest Town: Chippenham 4 miles to south

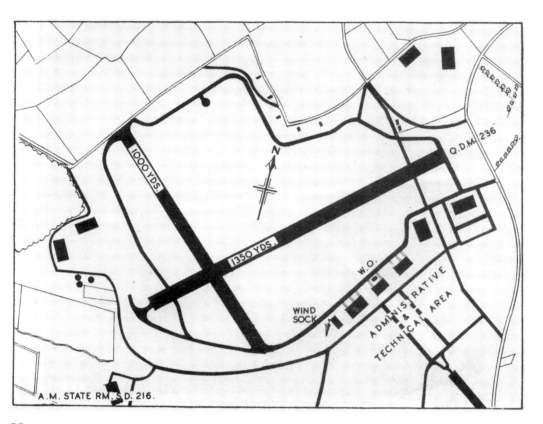

HISTORY

Hullavington is listed as one of the key airfields by English Heritage, due to the state of preservation of its historic buildings, although this does not necessarily imply any level of legal protection of those structures! An area of land on the Duke of Beaufort's estate between the villages of Hullavington and Stanton St Quintin was acquired in 1935 for an expansion period airfield. The site was perfect in size and shape and the plan was to develop a dual-role site for a major training airfield and an Aircraft Storage Unit, the latter with a notional capacity of 400 aircraft. As was standard at the time, the station was given a large open area of well-surfaced grass as an operating area and a comprehensive collection of well-constructed support buildings for technical and administrative use, these being positioned on the east side of the airfield. With Cotswold stone being handy

and reasonably cheap, many of the buildings used this material, making the buildings at Hullavington some of the most attractive of their type. The ASU was given five dispersed sites on the edges of the airfield, each centred on two hangars, along with a HQ site. The latter included one of the four C-Type hangars, the other three being part of the main airfield technical site.

RAF Hullavington opened on 14 June 1937 and, in early July, received its first unit, No.9 Flying Training School from Thornaby. Equipped with the Hart, Audax and Fury, the school was tasked with training pilots, with forty pupils on each course, for single-engine aircraft. The trainers were soon using the four grass strips, which varied between 1,000 and 1,300 yards in length, and Hullavington was, without doubt, a delightful airfield at this time. Ansons

AIRFIELD DATA DEC 1944

Command:	Flying Training Command	Runway surface:	Tarmac over concrete
Function:	Empire Central Flying School	Hangars:	Blister × 11, Type E × 6, Type C × 4,
Runways:	235 deg 1,350 × 50yd		Type L × 2, Type D × 2, Bellman ×
	140 deg 1,130 × 50yd		one, ARS × one, Type B.1 × one
		Dispersals:	Nil
		Personnel:	Officers – 192 (14 WAAF)
			Other Ranks – 1,299 (348 WAAF)

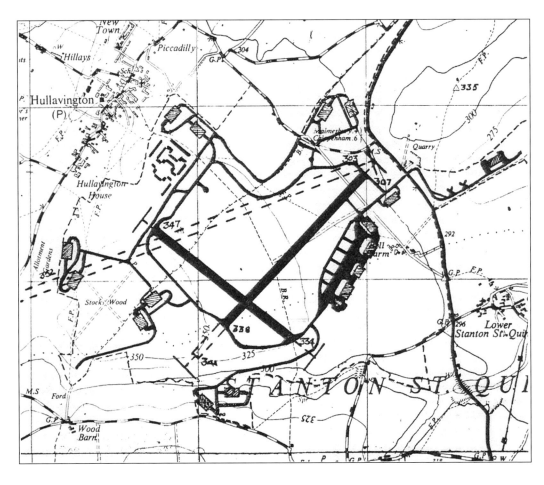

arrived in March 1938, when the school acquired a commitment to train pilots for multi-engine aircraft.

The allocated Maintenance Unit, No.9 MU, formed at Hullavington on 8 July 1938, but at first was only handling Motor Transport. A change of number to No.10 MU (to avoid confusion with the resident FTS) early the following year coincided with the arrival of the first aircraft from storage, but not all

the ASU dispersed sites were complete and some aircraft were stored in the open.

Both the ASU and the FTS were operational when war broke out and there was little change to the daily routine at Hullavington – pilots still needed to be trained and aircraft still needed to be stored. The school received Oxfords to boost its training but, within days of arriving, one was involved in a fatal accident. This had not, of course, been the first fatality at the airfield – accidents and fatalities were an all too frequent part of flying training.

The outbreak of war also brought operational aircraft on dispersal under the Scatter Scheme. Blenheims of 114 Squadron from Wyton, joined later by a few aircraft of 139 Squadron, spent a few days here in September. By May 1940, the FTS had over 100 aircraft on strength – sixty-three Ansons and forty-five Harvards – and training continued an ever-increasing pace by day and night, which meant that Hullavington was allocated the use of a number of RLGs, such as Babdown Farm (officially from July) and Long Newnton (from September), whilst the MU was also over-crowded and used sites at Yatesbury and Townsend. During the summer, the training task was changed to that of single-engine pilot training and No.9 FTS was given a new establishment of 76+36 Masters, to be effective by November.

Audax trainers were part of No.9 FTS when it commenced flying at Hullavington. (via Rod Priddle)

In the meantime, the war arrived at Hullavington. The airfield was allocated to the newly formed No.10 Group of Fighter Command for temporary use for lodger fighter detachments. The first such usage was by 92 Squadron in the first week of July, the squadron sending aircraft over from Pembrey each day to hold night standby from Hullavington – a far from ideal role for the section of Spitfires given the task. They were soon replaced by a permanent detachment from 87 Squadron, flying Hurricanes. This squadron had a peripatetic career during this period, providing night defence from a variety of airfields in this region.

Hullavington also had its own Station Defence Flight, equipped with a small number of Hurricanes and flown by FTS instructors, as part of the emergency attempts to boost fighter defence of the region. These too flew night patrols and scrambles, but with no success. The Luftwaffe was somewhat more successful and the bombs dropped by a single He111 on 14 August 1940 caused four deaths, damage to buildings and various degrees of damage to sixteen aircraft, including two of the Defence Flight aircraft that had just landed from a patrol. The RAF patch in the cemetery at St Giles in Stanton St Quinton continued to grow, as flying accidents claimed pupils and instructors at a steady rate.

By now the MU was storing a wide range of aircraft types, with the Stirling being the largest, and to help with the aircraft delivery programme No.8 (Service) Ferry Pilots Pool formed in November 1940, although it and its successor, No.10 (Polish) Ferry Flight, had become part of the Kemble-based Service Ferry Flight by summer 1941. The MU acquired two satellite landing grounds in 1941: No.14 SLG (Overley) from April and No.23 SLG (Down Farm) from May, with Castle Combe, also in use by No.10

Part of the impressive collection of types operated by the Empire Central Flying School. (via Rod Priddle)

MU, being upgraded to RLG status. The main tasks of the MU during this period were preparation of Wellingtons for overseas units and Hudsons and Spitfires for UK-based units, although storage rather than modification work also involved other types.

The grass surfaces were proving inadequate for the intensity and type of flying and work started, in October 1941, to lay two hard runways, although grass strips continued to be used in the meantime. Only two runways were laid, at 90 degrees to each other, the final lengths being 1,130yd and 1,350 yd.

The scale of training at Hullavington continued to increase, with the navy sending pilots – and Swordfish aircraft – to the airfield in January 1942. The following month the school was re-designated as No.9 (Pilots) Advanced Flying Unit, although all flying was transferred to the satellite at Castle Combe; the HQ remained at Hullavington to July. No.3 Flying Instructors School formed here on 1 August 1942, but its Oxfords and Masters moved to Castle Combe a week later; however, the engineering aspects of the unit remained at Hullavington and the airfield itself was also used for night flying. The major unit to use Hullavington from April 1942 to the end of the war was the Empire Central Flying School (ECFS), which formed here on 1 April, the nucleus being provided by CFS at Upavon. This was an important and fascinating unit with students from virtually every Allied nation and a very diverse fleet of aircraft; the bulk of the establishment comprised trainers, such as the Harvard and Anson or Oxford, but the school had access to just about every type in service with the RAF and USAAF. The main role of ECFS was to standardize flying instruction by training and standardizing flying instructors, but it also had a research and handling role.

Having been attacked in 1940 and 1941 by hit-and-run raiders, the 'annual' attack for 1942 took place on 27 July, when a Do217 dropped four bombs between two hangars causing damage to buildings and to three Horsa gliders. Gliders had become a major part of the work of the MU, the Horsas arriving in bits and being assembled before being flown out behind a tow aircraft. The purpose-built MAP hangar that was erected in June 1943 was subsequently used for this work. However, by May 1943, the focus of attention on operational types was on the Mosquito and Stirling; storage of the latter became a problem and 110 were sent to Down Farm, with others going to the SLG at Everleigh when this became available. These tasks continued to the end of the war; with the end of the war, Hullavington's MU and its associated SLGs became a magnet for unwanted aircraft, with row upon row of Defiants, Lancasters and other types, very few of which were destined to survive the scrap man. The MU finally disbanded on 31 December 1959.

The ECFS survived into the post-war period but, on 7 May 1946, became the Empire Flying School, with its main task being the introduction of all-weather flying (most of the new generation of fighters under development being designated as AW). This period lasted three years, before the unit was absorbed into the RAF Flying College at Manby (July 1949). The same month saw the arrival of No.1 Air Navigation School from Topcliffe, opening another sixteen-year chapter of flying training for Hullavington. The ANS initially operated Ansons and Wellingtons, these being replaced by the Varsity and Valetta before the unit disbanded in May 1954. Their place was taken by No.2 Flying Training School from Cluntoe (Northern Ireland), who used Provosts and Chipmunks for basic pilot training. In September 1955, the school became the first to introduce an all-jet route for flying training, by introducing the Jet Provost as the basic trainer. The first course passed-out at Hullavington on 2 July 1956.

Once again, an RLG was needed to cope with the rate of flying and Keevil was used from January 1955 to November 1957, the end date corresponding with the departure of the FTS from Hullavington to Syerston.

The following month 'flying pigs' returned, when No.1 Air Electronics School arrived from Swanton Morley, initially with the Anson but with the Varsity ('pig') being added soon after. It became the Air Electronics School a few years later and, in January 1962, moved to Topcliffe. November 1958 had seen the formation of an unusual unit at Hullavington, when 114 Squadron reformed with Chipmunk T.10s, a rare instance of a squadron being equipped with this type of aircraft. The unit departed for Nicosia, Cyprus the following month.

The final major training unit to operate from Hullavington was No.2 Air Navigation School – with more 'pigs' – which arrived from Thorney Island in January 1962. The navigation school moved to Gaydon in 1965 and Hullavington was without a major based flying unit. The station had another nearly thirty years of RAF occupation – finally closing on 1 April 1993 – but the whole of that time was spent with ground units, with the exception of the AEF and gliders. Various parachute and balloon units moved into Hullavington in the late-1960s, combining in July 1967 to become the Parachute Support Unit. Under various guises this continued into the 1990s and played an important role in developing air-dropping of loads, working closely with the Lyneham-based Hercules and with Hullavington (and Keevil) being used as a drop zone for trials. The arrival of the RAF Regiment in August 1980 boosted the strength of the station and this association continued to March 1992.

RAF Hullavington is now Buckley Barracks and is home to the No.9 Supply Regiment of the Royal Logistic Corps. The RAF's current presence at Hullavington comprises the Viking gliders of 625 Volunteer Gliding School that provides flying for cadet forces. The five Grob Viking T.1s use one of the old wartime Blister hangars.

The English Heritage list of key airfields records Hullavington as:

> Hullavington, which opened in 1937 as a Flying Training Station, embodies to a unique degree the improved architectural quality associated with the post-1934 Expansion Period of the RAF. Most of the original buildings have survived and form a particularly coherent and well-ordered ensemble. The flying field remains, bounded by groups of hangars.

Spitfire of the Empire Flying School, June 1948. (Peter Green Collection)

A 1997 view of the tower and hangars – at what almost looks like a deserted airfield. (Rod Priddle)

DECOY SITE

Q	Allington	ST885768

UNITS

1919–1939

9 FTS	9 Jul 1937–14 Feb 1942	Oxford, Battle, Harvard, Anson

1939–1945

87 Sqn det	summer 1940	Hurricane
92 Sqn	1–9 July 1940	Spitfire
9 FTS	?–14 Feb 1942	Oxford, Battle, Harvard, Anson, Hurricane
8 (S)FPP	5 Nov 1940–27 Mar 1941	Anson
3 FIS	1–8 Aug 1942	Oxford, Master
9 (P)AFU	14 Feb 1942–Jul 1942	Master, Harvard
ECFS	1 Apr 1942–7 May 1946	
1427Flt	18 May 1942–5 Sep 1942	Stirling, Halifax
1532Flt	15 Oct 1942–13 May 1943	Oxford
HandlingSqn	22 Aug 1942–31 Jul 1949	

Post-1945

114Sqn	20 Nov 1958–15 Dec 1958	Chipmunk
EFS	7 May 1946–31 Jul 1949	

88 GS	28 Sep 1947–May 1948	Cadet
1 ANS	7 Jul 1949–1 May 1954	Wellington, Anson
2 FTS	1 Jun 1954–18 Nov 1957	Provost, Chipmunk
1 AES	23 Dec 1957–14 Jan 1962	Anson
2 ANS	15 Jan 1962–1 Sep 1965	
3 AEF	Jun 1989–1993	
Bristol UAS	Mar–Nov 1992	Bulldog
625 VGS	1992–current	Viking
621 VGS	30 Jun 1993–current	Viking
622 VGS	Apr 1997–?	Viking, Valiant

MEMORIAL

1. Stone post near old RAF Fire Station with plaque, inscribed: 'No. 10 Maintenance Unit (Civilian manned Aircraft Storage Unit). Loyal and willing servant to the operational Commands 1939–1959.'

2. Next to Guardroom a brick memorial with a number of pictorial and inscribed plaques. One side of the memorial has a carved stone tablet showing the Wessex dragon and torch. The other side has three plaques showing a plan of the airfield and listing the units that served here 1937–1993. The memorial was unveiled on 1 April 1993 by Air Commodore A J Stables CBE.

JERSEY (St Helier)

County: Channel Islands

UTM/Grid:
Lat/Long: N49°12.48 W002°11.73
Nearest Town: St Helier 4 miles to east-south-east

HISTORY

As a Channel Islands airfield, Jersey was one of only two UK airfields to be used by both the RAF and the Luftwaffe in World War Two, the former for a few days and the latter for five years. The original flying-boat service to St Aubins Bay was supplemented, then replaced by the airport built a few miles from St Helier. Jersey Airport opened on 10 March 1937 and, in the two years prior to the war, Jersey Airways and Air France established a number of routes. Civil flying was terminated when war broke out, although Jersey Airways was allowed to continue a limited and controlled service for a short while. The Navy acquired the airport in May 1940 but, between then and the fall of the islands in June, there was very little military activity. A detachment of Albacores of 826 Squadron spent a week here in late-May for training, followed in June by its use as a refuel point by Bomber Command Whitleys en route to targets in Italy and, finally, by two Hurricane squadrons as part of the withdrawal from France. They were not here to defend the island but were providing air cover for the British evacuation from France. The Hurricanes of 17 and 501 squadrons spent a few days here in June 1940 having retreated from Dinard in France; however, there was no time to unpack bags as the squadron moved back to the mainland.

On 1 July the first German aircraft arrived; although ZG76 used the airfield for a while in the Battle of Britain, it was not to be a main operational airfield for the Luftwaffe. The Germans undertook extension and improvement work, but the airfield's main role was an air bridge to France for communications duties.

The British took control once more on 9 May 1945 and a staging post was established, Jersey and Guernsey Airports being useful as refuel points. Civil aviation returned the same month, although it was a a few weeks before Jersey Airways restarted services. In the sixty years since the war, the airport has undergone a number of developments; a hard runway was laid down in 1953 and this has been extended a number of times since then. The States of Jersey Airport (EGJJ) now operates a 1,706m runway (09/27), with a single taxiway on the southern side and a large parking apron around the terminal building. As passenger numbers have continued to increase, work has also taken place on terminal and support buildings, a large-scale extension to the terminal taking place in 1997.

UNITS

1939–1945

17Sqn	Jun 1940	Hurricane
501Sqn	19–21 Jun 1940	Hurricane

KEEVIL (Station 471)

County: Wiltshire

UTM/Grid: OS Map 173 – ST922571
Lat/Long: N51°18.43 W002°06.48
Nearest Town: Trowbridge 4 miles to west

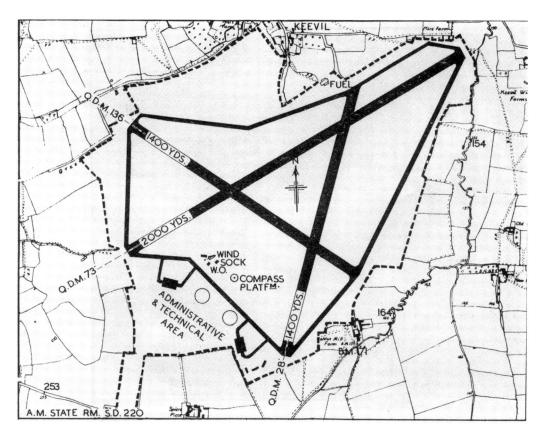

HISTORY

The airfield at Keevil is still used by the RAF, although with no based units, and transport aircraft still fly overhead, releasing stores and, occasionally, paratroops. This airborne operations connection is a very relevant one, as the airfield's most significant use in World War Two was a few months in 1944 when Allied airborne forces participated in the invasion of Europe – Keevil played its part in D-Day and subsequent airborne operations such as Arnhem (*Market-Garden*).

Land was acquired in 1941 between the villages of Keevil and Steeple Ashton, the original plan being for a fighter Operational Training Unit. Field boundaries removal but no major earthworks, were required. The airfield was given three hard runways of standard length, the main 2,000yd runway oriented NE/SW; the ends of all the runways were con-

nected with a perimeter track, with two T.2 hangars on the south-west corner – but there were also nine Blister hangars around the airfield, distributed amongst the dispersal sites. The pattern of dispersals was unusual – as can be seen from a glance at the plan. The layout was actually that of a bomber OTU, but there does not appear to have been any plan to position such a unit here. Construction was complete by late-September 1942 – and the airfield was promptly allocated to the Americans, as the XIIth Air Force was looking for airfields in the UK to build-up for the North Africa campaign, Operation *Torch*. As Station 471, it received the 62nd Troop Carrier Group (TCG), under the command of Colonel Samuel J Davis Jr. By early October, all four squadrons of the Group were in residence and were training for the airborne operations connected with

AIRFIELD DATA DEC 1944

Command:	Flying Training Command	Runway surface:	Concrete and wood chippings
Function:	Parent Heavy Glider Conversion Unit	Hangars:	Extra-Over Blister × 9, T.2 × 2
Runways:	075 deg 2,000yd × 50yd	Dispersals:	41 × 125ft diam, 9 × 150ft diam,
	132 deg 1,400yd × 50yd		one × 75ft diam
	204 deg 1,400yd × 50yd	Personnel:	Officers – 165 (10 WAAF)
			Other Ranks – 2,377 (439 WAAF)

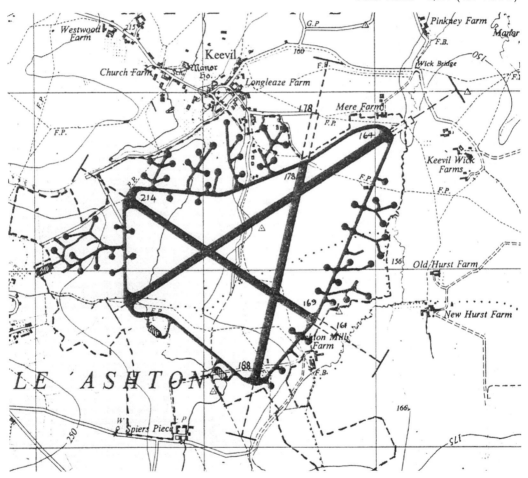

Torch. The Group moved out in the latter part of November and Keevil was handed back to the RAF, with No.70 Group placing it under Care and Maintenance.

The Americans took it back again on 1 June 1943, but it was August before there was any significant use – and even then it was initially as a supply base for the Membury-based 67th Observation Group. The 153rd Observation Squadron moved in and was to remain at Keevil, in various guises, until spring 1944.

The major change for the airfield came in August, with agreement that Vickers could erect an assembly shed and undertake flight-testing of Spitfires. A taxiway extension was laid on the west side, towards the sub-site near Steeple Ashton, where an apron was built and a MAP (Ministry of Aircraft Production) B.1 hangar erected. Actual construction took place at various locations in and around Trowbridge and sub-assemblies arrived at Keevil for final assembly, test and despatch. The Vickers site handled most of the later marks of Spitfire, from the VII to the XIX, and around 600 were completed here.

Meanwhile, the 153rd had continued to operate from Keevil, the main type being the Boston and the main task being photographic survey of the French coastline, all part of the invasion preparation. However, in October, the unit was re-designated as a Liaison Squadron and returned to Membury to equip with L-4 Grasshoppers, before returning to Keevil in late-November, although Bostons still appear to have been in the majority! The unit was assigned to the 9th Air Force from mid-December 1943 and, on 23 December, was joined at Keevil by the 363rd Fighter Group. Under the command of Colonel John R Ulricson, the fighter unit was here to equip and train for the bomber escort role. Its allocated P-51s did not arrive until early January, so pilots made use of Spitfires borrowed from the 67th Tactical Reconnaissance Group. As soon as the Mustangs arrived there was an intensive period of training, followed by a move to Rivenhall on 22 January 1944 to commence operations. The 153rd remained in residence to 13 March, when they departed to New Zealand Farm. Keevil had been officially handed back to the RAF on 10 March and, a few days later, Stirlings of 196 Squadron arrived from Tarrant Rushton, along with 299 Squadron from Stoney Cross. The move was made with most aircraft towing loaded Horsa gliders, both for practice and as a way of moving squadron equipment, a routine that was followed for a few days. Airborne operations had arrived at Keevil and intensive training, from single aircraft to mass exercise with thirty plus aircraft and glider combinations, was the order of the day. In addition to training, 196 Squadron flew a number of missions on behalf of the Special Operations Executive (SOE), dropping supply containers over France. This role was soon adopted by both units and, when not engaged on preparation or execution of major airborne operations, this was their main operational task.

Keevil's initial contribution to D-Day was to send an impressive forty-six Stirlings as part of Operation *Tonga*, a paratroop-drop to secure key points. The paratroops were from the 12th Battalion of British 6th Airborne Division and they climbed aboard the closely parked Stirlings in the late evening of 5 June. Successful drops were made in the early hours of D-Day; each squadron lost one aircraft. The second mission, Operation *Mallard*, was flown on the evening of D-Day and involved thirty-three Keevil aircraft towing Horsas, with the 2nd Ox and Bucks Light Infantry as reinforcements for the paratroops; one aircraft of 299 Squadron failed to return.

For the next few months the main operational task

The Albemarle was one of the types used by the HGCU for glider training.

Glider Pilot Regiment personnel at Keevil in September 1944. (via Rod Priddle)

Stirlings arrayed along the main runway awaiting the D-Day airborne operation.

was supply dropping, to ground troops and to SOE/SAS units. Training continued, as it was likely that further airborne assaults would take place. Keevil's squadrons were involved in Operation *Market-Garden*, the British element of which was Arnhem, the most famous battle of British airborne forces. Keevil had a stock pile of 130 Horsas and fifty of these were airborne behind Stirlings on 17 September, each squadron contributing an impressive twenty-five aircraft – although five of 196 Squadron's aircraft had to abort and three of 299's combinations lost their gliders whilst over England. In the end, forty-two gliders were delivered to the LZ and no Stirlings were lost. The second lift, the following day, involved forty-four aircraft-glider combinations, with thirty-nine being safely delivered to the LZ. The third lift took place on 19 September and involved sixteen gliders, with a further thirty-three Stirlings making supply drops. The latter was a disaster, with most of the supplies ending up with the Germans and four Stirlings being lost. The next day was more successful, in that supplies landed on British troop areas – but six Stirlings were lost. And so it continued to the end of the month, the Stirlings flying re-supply and suffering a number of losses. After an intense, generally effective, but often tragic period, the two squadrons departed to Wethersfield on 9 October 1944.

A few days later the station took on a glider training role with the formation of No.22 Heavy Glider Conversion Unit out of No.86 OTU and the HGCU at Brize Norton. The main role was training of glider pilots on the Horsa, although training for the Hadrian was also conducted, and the unit was given an initial establishment of twenty-nine Albemarles and twenty-three Horsa/Hadrians, although the establishment was subsequently increased to fifty-eight Albemarles and forty-six gliders. Fairford was allocated as a satellite airfield and training – and losses – began almost immediately. No.22 HGCU remained at Keevil to June 1945. Their departure to Blakehill Farm was followed by the arrival of No.61 OTU from Rednal. This unit operated Mustangs and Spitfires to convert pilots to type, as well as running a number of special courses, such as Fighter Reconnaissance. It also operated a small number of other aircraft, including the Hurricane, Harvard and Master. The OTU had two years of existence at Keevil before being re-designated as No.203 Advanced Flying School, within No.12 Group, on 1 July 1947. The task continued as before but, in October, a move was made to Chivenor.

Keevil was placed into Care and Maintenance in 1947 but, as was often the case, little of either took place and Keevil deteriorated, although it was still in good condition when used as an RLG by Hullavington's No.2 Flying Training School (January 1955 to November 1957). The Americans also expressed an interest and, for a number of years, Keevil was a standby base for possible deployment of 3rd Air Force units. Some private flying has taken place and for thirty years it was used by the Bath and Wilts Gliding Club, although the current glider occupants are military – the Bannerdown Gliding Club, which now makes use of the wartime T.2 hangar. Parts of the airfield structure were renewed in the early 1970s and in 1990, but the future of Keevil is uncertain, as it is one of the airfields being looked at in yet another review of defence estate; this 2005 review will almost certainly recommend another round of base closures and although Keevil is not a major airfield for the RAF it still performs a useful function.

UNITS

HQ units at Keevil

100th FW	13 Jan 1944–15 Apr 1944	
84th FW	29 Jan 1944–4 Mar 1944	
70th FW	17 Apr 1944–9 Jun 1944	

1939–1945

196 Sqn	14 Mar 1944–9 Oct 1944	Stirling
299 Sqn	15 Mar 1944–9 Oct 1944	Stirling
22 HGCU	15 Oct 1944–21 Jun 1945	Albemarle, Horsa
VISTREFlt	1 Aug 1946–16 Nov 1947	Anson

USAAF units

62nd TCG

Squadrons:	4th, 7th, 8th, 51st TCS
Aircraft:	C-47, C-53
Dates:	Sep 1942–15 Nov 1942

67th OG

Squadron:	153rd OS
Aircraft:	Boston, L-4, Spitfire
Dates:	Aug 1943–Mar 1944+

363rd FG

Squadrons:	160th, 161st, 162nd FS
Aircraft:	P-51
Dates:	23 Dec 1943–Jan 1944

Post-1945

61 OTU	21 Jun 1945–1 Jul 1947	Spitfire, Mustang
203 AFS	1 Jul 1947–15 Oct 1947	Spitfire, Harvard

Spitfires parked-up near the Vickers site and awaiting flight test.

MEMORIAL

1. Stone cairn with plaque bearing the RAF badge and the inscription:

> Royal Air Force Keevil. Keevil airfield had a significant role in World War II, particularly in its contribution to the D-Day and Arnhem Operations in 1944. Many nationalities served here and, sadly, many who flew from here lost their lives. The village is proud of its association with the airfield over more than 50 years. 'Lest we forget . . .' The Keevil Society 24th September 1994.

2. Located near Alton Barnes airfield is a stone memorial to the crew of an Albemarle from No.22 HGCU, which crashed near that airfield. The plaque shows an Albemarle side-view and the inscription:

> This memorial is dedicated to Flt. Sgt. Thomas C. Newton R.A.F.V.R. – Pilot Sgt. John A.C.

Wilson R.A.F.V.R. – W.Op. /Air Gunner who lost their lives when their Albemarle Bomber V1755 of No.22 H.G.C.U. RAF Keevil crashed near here on the 25th October 1944. At the going down of the sun and in the morning we will remember them.

KEMBLE

County: Gloucestershire

UTM/Grid: OS Map 163 – ST960965
Lat/Long: N51°40.00 W002°03.17
Nearest Town: Cirencester 4 miles to north-east

HISTORY

A station headquarters opened at RAF Kemble in late-September 1940, the airfield being part of No.41 Group (SOM 896/40). The opening of a SHQ made Kemble an independent unit and reflected its growing size rather than any immediate change of role. The airfield had started life two years before in a role that it retained throughout its RAF career – Maintenance Unit.

No.6 Aircraft Storage Unit formed here at the beginning of 1938 but, by early summer, it had become No.5 Maintenance Unit. This was a civilian-manned Aircraft Supply and Storage Depot. RAF Kemble and No.5 MU maintained this role, with minor variations, into the 1980s, but it was frequently much more than just a storage unit, as it also undertook aircraft servicing and modification work. The author delivered and collected Canberra PR.9s of 39 Squadron to and from Kemble; the engineers undertook mods to the aircraft in the late-1970s – such as the fitting of radar warning equipment. The most famous residents of the Gloucestershire base

were, of course, the Red Arrows, but the airfield had a far wider history than as a home base for the RAF's showpiece aerobatic team.

Land to the west of the village of Kemble was acquired in 1937 and, although constrained to north and south by major roads and a railway, there was plenty of room to the west for future expansion, an option that was taken-up in late-1939, although this meant closing a part of the Fosse Way. The main technical site was laid out on the south side and was given three large hangars plus various smaller buildings. It was not long, however, before Kemble began to sprout dispersed sites, most of which included hangars. Indeed, the development of the site is a complex one, as can be seen from the various plans and air photos, with numerous extensions and additions both during the war and after.

Kemble was immediately busy and by late-1939 had some 500 aircraft in storage – a wonderful target at what was virtually an undefended site but, fortunately, the Luftwaffe was occupied elsewhere. The

AIRFIELD DATA DEC 1944

Command:	Transport Command	Runway surface:	9in Hardcore with 6in concrete and asphalt layer
Function:	Parent Station	Hangars:	Robin × 8, Lammella × 4, Type D × 4,
Runways:	270 deg 2,000 × 50yd		Super Robin × 4, Type E × 2, T.2 × 2,
	320 deg 1,300 × 50yd		Blister × 2, Type C × one
		Dispersals:	20 × Spectacle
		Personnel:	Officers – 40 (4 WAAF)
			Other Ranks – 1,154 (168 WAAF)

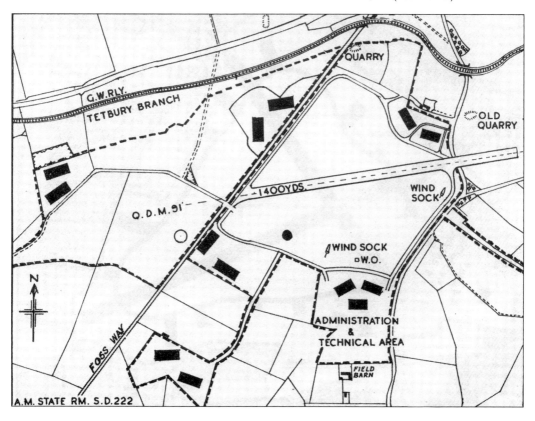

need to ferry aircraft to deployed units in France led to the formation of No.4 (Continental) Ferry Pilots Pool at Filton in April 1940, with a number of Flights from this unit operating at Kemble from June. The HQ of the Service Ferry Pools formed at Kemble out of No.4 (Continental) Ferry Pilots Pool on 7 November 1940 to administer and control the various FPPs and, over the next few months, it absorbed a number of the pools. However, in July 1941, its responsibility was changed to overseas ferrying, another of the little recognized but important roles. In November it became the Ferry Training Unit and moved to Honeybourne.

As was the case at other MUs, there was concern over air defence and a Station Defence Flight was formed using a small number of Hurricanes; these flew standing patrols and scrambles – an early success (25 July) was marred by the loss of the victorious Hurricane and its pilot. Two German bombers attacked the airfield on 14 August but with little result, other than damage to a number of stored Whitleys. Kemble remained a very busy airfield and, like most parent MUs, it had to make use of satellite landing grounds for aircraft storage: No.5 (Berrow) from November 1941 to September 1942; No.12 (Beechwood Park) from May 1941 to March 1943;

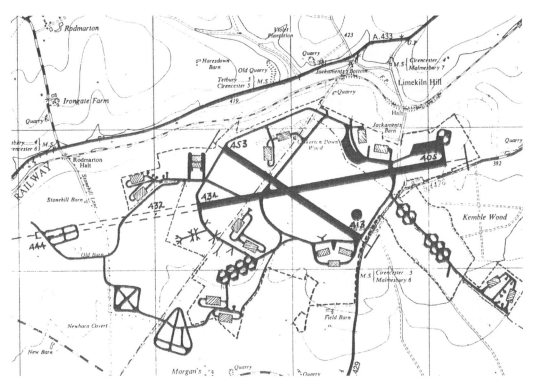

Oblique of Kemble taken on 14 April 1944, the shot shown on page 2 was taken on the same day.

No.44 (Bush Barn) from September 1941 to February 1943; and No.22 (Barnsley Park) from August 1942 to 1945. It also made temporary use of a number of other sites. The airfield needed a hard runway to cope

with the level of traffic and a 4,200ft east/west strip was open for use by spring 1942; as the 1944 data panel shows, this was subsequently lengthened to 2,000yd (6,000ft) and a second hard runway was also provided. The data list also shows the proliferation of hangars by number and type.

The Maintenance Unit also handled a large number of gliders and there was an intention to form a Glider Test and Ferry Flight at the airfield to flight test and then deliver Horsas assembled by the MU. However, whilst some GTFFs were formed as planned, that at Kemble appears to have been given a limited role and an establishment of only a couple of Whitleys when it formed in January 1942.

The Overseas Aircraft Despatch Flight (OADF) was formed at Kemble in September 1940, being upgraded to a Unit (as OADU) the following August, by which time ferry training had been added to its task. From summer 1941, it used Portreath as a satellite, this airfield being a convenient refuel stop before the long journey to the Mediterranean. In November, the OADU moved to Portreath and Kemble took on the role of preparation of aircraft for the trip overseas; the Overseas Aircraft Preparation Flight (OAPF) was formed at Kemble. Two of this unit's Flights operated from Kemble: No.1 (Wellington) and No.2 (Hurricane and 'other types'), with two other Flights based at Filton. The

Kemble Flights became No.1 OAPU in December 1942 and the following year handled Halifax, Hudson, Mosquito and Wellington preparation. The work continued into 1944, with the Halifax and Wellington as the main types. In July 1944, the 'Overseas' part of the title was dropped and the unit handled Beaufighter, Halifax, Warwick and Wellington aircraft. However, a few months later, it moved to Pershore. RAF Kemble was transferred to Transport Command in January 1945 and, by August, transport types, such as the Lancastrian, were arriving at Kemble for work to be carried out by No.2 Transport Aircraft Modification Unit, which formed here that month – but only existed to April 1946. The overseas ferrying role continued into the post-war period with the Overseas Ferry Unit, whose parent station was Abingdon. At Kemble this became No.1 Long-Range Ferry Unit in December 1952 but, the following year, it became part of 147 Squadron when that unit formed at Abingdon.

Kemble was one of a number of relief landing grounds allocated to the Central Flying School and it maintained this role from October 1955 to April 1976. From 1957 it operated a Hunter Flight from Kemble – an appropriate connection with one of the current occupants of the airfield, as Kemble now specializes in the maintenance of a growing fleet of privately owned Hunters. However, in terms of flying units, the post-war period very much belonged to the Red Arrows. The team formed at Fairford in March 1965, but moved with its Gnat T.1s to Kemble in August 1966. The Arrows departed to Scampton in 1982 and Kemble's role as a servicing and modification unit was transferred to the USAF, one of the major types to pass through being the A-10 Warthog.

Kemble (EGBP) is now a licensed airfield and, in addition to the growing collection of private owners and GA operations, it is expanding its heritage element and, in January 2005, announced development of a major heritage site to include a 50,000sq ft museum. It has, for some time, been home to the finest collection of jet warbirds, centred on Delta Jets' own aircraft and those they maintain for private owners, and its Classic Jets airshows have become a highlight in the increasingly reduced and mundane UK airshow calendar. The airfield still operates both wartime runways – 09/27 at 1,833m and 13/31 at 810m – along with two short grass strips. It has also been the venue in recent years for the annual Popular Flying Association air meet, attracting hundres of light aircraft.

The English Heritage list of key airfields records Kemble as:

> Kemble is the most strongly representative – by virtue of its range of hangar types – of 24 Aircraft Storage Unit sites planned and built by the Air Ministry between 1936 and 1940. The hangars are dispersed in pairs around the airfield and include the most advanced Air Ministry hangar types of parabolic form and concrete construction.

DECOY SITE

Long Newnton	ST921925

UNITS

1939–1945

286Sqn det	spring 1942	various
7 (S)FPP	5 Nov 1940–1 Feb 1941	Anson
HQ SFP/S	7 Nov 1940–11 Nov 1941	Hector
OADU	15 Aug 1941–5 Nov 1941	various
OAPF/U	5 Nov 1941–1 Dec 1942	various
GTFF	3 Jan 1942–15 Apr 1944	Whitley
1 OAPU	Dec 1942–29 Jul 1944	various
1 APU	29 Jul 1944–29 Sep 1944	various

Post-1945

2 TAMU	1 Aug 1945–28 Mar 1946	
LRFU	Dec 1952–Feb 1953	
Red Arrows	1 Aug 1966–1982	Gnat, Hawk

The Red Arrows, with their Gnats, were perhaps the most famous occupants of Kemble.

LARKHILL

County: Wiltshire

UTM/Grid: OS Map 184 – SU144437 (Larkhill/Durrington Down); SU127453 (Larkhill/Knighton Down)

Lat/Long: N51°11.54 W001°47.71 (Larkhill/Durrington Down); N51°12.40 W001°49.17 (Larkhill/Knighton Down)

Nearest Town: Amesbury 2 miles to south-east

HISTORY

Larkhill is best known in military circles today for its army connection and especially the firepower demonstrations that take place in this part of the Salisbury Plain ranges; from an aviation perspective its claim to fame is as the first military airfield in Britain and for the first military air trials that took place here in 1912. As the grid reference indicates there have been two airfields in the Larkhill area.

Larkhill/Durrington Down

In July 1909, Horatio Barber erected a tin shed on a small piece of land at the Hill of Larks, Durrington Downs and, having acquired a Valkyrie, taught himself to fly. This was very much army territory and balloon trials had been underway for some time, so this new aeroplane idea was of immediate interest to some, if not all, army officers. An additional shed was erected by the War Office, under an agreement with C S Rolls to teach army officers to fly; Rolls was killed in July 1910 before this became effective, but the shed was used by Captain J Fulton of the Royal Artillery to house a Blériot he had acquired. By spring 1911, four more sheds had been added and the Bristol School of Flying was in full swing, training pilots and also helping with flight-testing of aircraft. Larkhill had also been further developed by the army, with trials into aerial reconnaissance taking place in late-1910 and the decision, in 1911, that the old Balloon School would, in future, look after aeroplanes, airships, kites and balloons. This officially became the Air Battalion Royal Engineers on 28 February 1911, with No.1 Company (Airships) at Farnborough and No.2 Company (Aeroplane) at Larkhill, the changes being effective from April. On 13 May 1912, the latter became 3 Squadron, Royal Flying Corps.

In August 1912, the airfield was the scene of frenzied activity and twenty temporary hangars had been erected alongside the road; the reason for this activity was the British Military Aeroplane Trials, to determine the most suitable aircraft for development. British and foreign manufacturers were invited to participate and prizes were awarded, in addition to the potential for lucrative contracts. The overall winner was 'Colonel' Samuel Cody, but it proved to be a poor decision and the aircraft was never developed; a Bristol monoplane was second but this, too, proved a disaster and, after wing failure, resulted in a lengthy – and ridiculous – ban on military monoplanes for the RFC and RAF. The final choice settled on the BE2 (Blériot Experimental), an aircraft that could not even enter as it was a product of the Government Royal Aircraft Factory!

The trials were followed by the annual military manoeuvres, with aircraft being involved for the first time – with some success and to the annoyance of many senior (cavalry) generals. Larkhill had always been viewed as temporary, as it was difficult to develop and, with the opening of Upavon and Netheravon, the decision was taken to transfer flying to the new airfields, although it was early summer 1913 before 3 Squadron left for its new home at Netheravon. The Bristol School carried on to 2 June 1914, when it moved to Brooklands. The airfield site at Larkhill was absorbed by expansion of the Bulford Camp.

Larkhill/Knighton Down

This new site was just over a mile north of the earlier airfield and came into incidental use during the 1920s by aircraft taking part in the numerous exercises with the army – and with this area as home to the artillery and the main role of aeroplanes being reconnaissance and 'fall of shot' for the guns, it was a logical connection. Various army co-operation squadrons used the site and, by January 1936, it was officially recognized as RAF Larkhill. Nevertheless, it remained a rough and primitive site, although at least one hangar was erected in the early 1940s. The first based-unit was 'D Flight' from the School of Army Co-operation and, for the next two years, it operated types such as the Taylorcraft, Stinson and Lysander. Air Observation Post (AOP) courses were run for newly qualified army pilots and this training role was important in the development of AC tactics. The Flight became No.1424 (AOP) Flight on 20 September 1941, with a training and trials role; the latter included use of a number of Tiger Moths with R/T for control of shoots. The Flight operated an increasingly diverse fleet of aircraft, which, by the end of the year, included Austers; in recognition of its size and importance it became No.43 Operational Training Unit on 1 October. This was followed in November by a move to the airfield with which the

The all-important aeroplane
trials that took place at
Larkhill in 1910.

Blériot monoplane at
Larkhill. (via Rod Priddle)

'Colonel' Cody with his
winning aircraft – the
Army did not, however,
proceed with acquisition
of the Cody biplane. (via
Rod Priddle)

OTU is most associated, Old Sarum.

That essentially brought RAF Larkhill to an end. As this area is still dominated by army camps, aviation has not totally vanished, as helicopters are regular visitors for exercises or visits but, as such sites do not involve a recognized airfield, they fall outside the scope of this study.

UNITS

Pre-1919

3Sqn	13 May 1912–16 Jun 1913	various

1939–1945

DFlt	1 Feb 1940–20 Sep 1941+	various
1424Flt	20 Sep 1941–1 Oct 1942	Taylorcraft, Tiger Moth
43 OTU	1 Oct 1942–19 Nov 1942; Aug 1944–?	various

MEMORIAL

Plaque by roadside marking Larkhill as first aerodrome in Britain; inscribed:

> On this site the first aerodrome for the Army was founded in 1910 by Capt. J D B Fulton RFA and Mr G B Cockburn. This later became 2 Coy Air Bn RE. The British and Colonial Aeroplane Company forerunners of the Bristol Aeroplane Company established their flying school here in 1910. The first military air trials were held here in 1912.

The memorial was unveiled on 12 February 1968 by Brigadier R S Streatfield MC.

LITTLE RISSINGTON

County: Gloucestershire

UTM/Grid: OS Map 163 – SP215190
Lat/Long: N51°52.14 W001°41.34
Nearest Town: Stow-on-the-Wold 4 miles to north

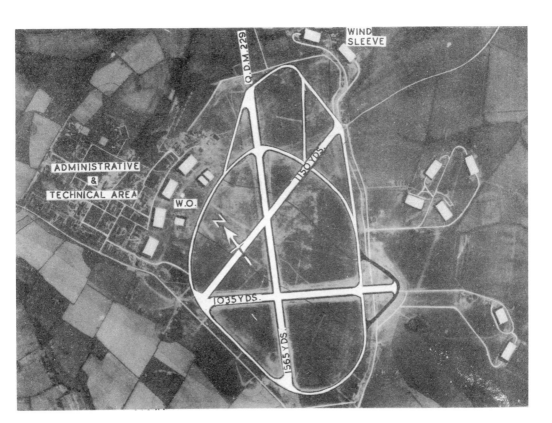

HISTORY

Little Rissington's most notable usage was as a long-term home to the Central Flying School (CFS), with this important RAF organization spending thirty years at 'Rissie' following World War Two. This was an expansion-period airfield and, as such, was laid-out on its Cotswold plateau with a large grass landing area, with four C-Type hangars on the east side as part of a well-established technical area, behind which a pattern of roads was fronted by the usual array of workshops, barrack blocks, messes and other support buildings. As the aerial photo shows, the airfield underwent various changes over the next few years, with additional groups of hangars on the north and east sides, three surfaced runways and a linking perimeter track. The plateau area on which the airfield was built was a limited area of flat (actually, gently rolling) land, which meant that expansion was a problem and restricted the length of the runways.

Little Rissington was intended for dual use as an Aircraft Storage Unit and as a Flying Training Station. The latter arrived first, with No.6 Flying Training School (FTS) moving in from Netheravon in August 1938; by the following year it had an establishment of thirty-eight Ansons and twenty-six Harvards and had become a Service FTS. The actual strength rarely reflected the establishment and the number of Harvards was limited, with pupil pilots having to make do with Audax, Hart and Fury bi-planes – delightful aircraft, but not ideal as training for the front-line types.

No.8 Aircraft Storage Unit formed in December 1938 but, the following February, was re-designated as No.8 Maintenance Unit. The MU was largely civilian manned and it remained at Little Rissington to July 1957. The primary role was aircraft storage and modification and, for most of its existence, it was

AIRFIELD DATA DEC 1944

Command: Flying Training Command
Function: Parent (Pilots) Advanced Flying Unit
Runways: 050 deg 1,565 × 50yd
100 deg 1,150 × 50yd
140 deg 1,035 × 50yd

Runway surface: Concrete covered with tarmac
Hangars: Blister (65ft) × 10, Blister
(69ft) × 7, Bellman × 3,
C-Type × 2, ARS × one; on
MU site: Robin × 8, E-Type × 6,
Super Robin × 3, D-Type × 2, C-
Type × 2
Dispersals: Nil
Personnel: Officers – 223 (11 WAAF)
Other Ranks – 1,988 (391 WAAF)

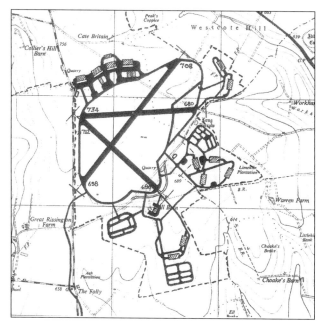

part of No.41 Group Maintenance Command as a lodger unit on the airfield. It handled a variety of aircraft types although, by the latter part of the war, it was specializing in Hamilcar gliders and various marks of Wellington. The MU was allocated use of a number of satellite airfields although, with the exception of No. 3 SLG (Middle Farm), No.28 SLG (Barton Abbey) and No.34 SLG (Woburn Park), this was short-term usage. In the post-war period the main SLGs were Honeybourne and Long Marston. The closure of No.8 MU in 1957 was followed by the formation of No.250 MU, to operate as a Motor Transport servicing unit, although this only lasted from March 1957 to October 1959.

The SFTS made use of a number of RLGs from early 1940, such as Chipping Norton, Hullavington and Windrush. By May 1940, the establishment was

over 100 aircraft – hence the need for the RLGs – and the bi-planes had largely gone. The school lost its single-engine types in June to focus on twin-engine training, with Ansons and Oxfords the main types; at one point in early 1942 the school had 112 Oxfords and thirty-nine Ansons. When you also consider that the MU often had over 100 aircraft on its books, then Little Rissington must have been an amazing sight, as pupil pilots flew circuits and the odd Spitfire or Hampden nipped in and out for the MU.

No.6 (Pilots) Advanced Flying Unit formed at Little Rissington on 1 April 1942, by renaming the SFTS, as part of No.23 Group's pilot training organization and it was this unit that remained the airfield's main wartime occupant. The primary training type was the Oxford but, as usual with these schools, various other aircraft were also on the books, including

Oblique shot of the hangars and the somewhat sprawling technical and domestic areas; date uncertain.

Anson, Harvard and Tiger Moth. The school was busy and so used RLGs at Akeman Street, Chipping Norton, Moreton Valance and Windrush, all of these being allocated for most of the wartime period. At the height of its training work the school had over 100 Oxfords on strength. The other long-term resident was No.1523 Blind Approach Training Flight (BATF), which formed in October 1941 and was affiliated to the PAFU throughout the war. This, too, used the Oxford as its main training type.

Throughout 1945 the training load decreased and, in December, the school became No.6 Service Flying Training School (SFTS), with the Harvard as its primary training type. It was still a busy unit and had over fifty Harvards on strength, which meant that RLGs were still needed – Akeman Street and Southrop being used for this purpose. However, in April 1946, the school moved to Ternhill. There was a brief period when the Harvard-equipped No.7 Flying Instructor School was the main user, but within months this had been disbanded.

The Central Flying School reformed at Little Rissington on 7 May 1946, as a result of the break-up of the Empire Central Flying School (ECFS); the new organization being based upon aircraft and staff from No.7 Flying Instructors School (Advanced) and No.10 Flying Instructors School (Elementary) – the primary aim remaining that of training flying instructors. The Western Union Examining Squadron (WUES) was a short-lived and strange 'unit', whose task it was to examine instructors from the Western Union air forces of UK, France, Belgium and Holland.

It formed at Little Rissington in June 1950, but disbanded in October 1951. It probably formed here to take advantage of the skills and knowledge of the CFS. By May 1951, the Little Rissington part of the CFS had been re-organized into a Ground Training Squadron, two Harvard squadrons, a Meteor Flight and the Examining Wing. Other parts of the school were based at South Cerney and Moreton-in-Marsh; indeed CFS was such a busy organization that it used a number of satellite airfields and these included: Moreton-in-Marsh (1949–1951), Wellesbourne Mountford (1951), Aston Down (1960–1964), South Cerney (late-1940s–1964), Kemble (1955–1976), Fairford (1964–1966) and Aston Down (1966–1976).

A further re-organization occurred in May 1952 with 'Little Ris' (another of the unofficial names for the airfield) becoming home to CFS (Advanced), with CFS (Basic) forming at South Cerney. This meant some moving around of aircraft types, but CFS always operated a wide range of contemporary types. This decision to split was reversed in June 1957, when both elements were brought together again at Little Rissington. The history of CFS is complex and during this thirty-year sojourn at the Gloucestershire base various specialist elements came and went, such as the Helicopter Flight, Meteor Flight and the Communication Flight.

After thirty-years of the 'laying-on of hands' (a term used to refer to the teaching of new instructors) and of providing 'trappers' (CFS examiners who toured training units to make sure that standards were maintained), this vital RAF unit bade farewell to its established base and moved to Cranwell. The

Meteor for the Egyptian Air Force at Little Rissington in 1955.

The Central Flying School was here 30 years in the post-war period; the Gnat was just one of many types operated by the CFS.

Jet Provost display team.

Vigilant motor-glider of No.637 VGS; the ATC glider unit has been here since 1977.

DECOY SITE

Q	Farmington	SP146171

UNITS

1919–1939

6 FTS	26 Aug 1938–1 Apr 1942	Anson, Harvard

1939–1945

1523Flt	Oct 1941–17 Dec 1945	Oxford
6 (P)AFU	1 Apr 1942–17 Dec 1945	Oxford, Harvard

Post-1945

7 FIS	24 Apr 1946–7 May 1946	
CFS	7 May 1946–12 Apr 1976	various
1537Flt	May 1946–4 Apr 1947	Oxford
WUES	1 Jun 1950–31 Oct 1951	various
Oxford UAS	12 Jan 1959–26 Sep 1975	Chipmunk
637 VGS	29 Nov 1977–?	various

departure, in April 1976, brought an era of RAF history to an end – CFS continued but 'Little Ris' vanished. The army recognized a good thing and acquired the airfield, which became Imjim Barracks. A Royal Air Force presence was restored when the gliders of No.637 Volunteer Gliding School arrived from Gaydon in November 1977 and, in the nearly thirty years since then, they have provided flying experience to cadet forces, the current type being the Vigilant powered-glider. The Americans have also made use of the airfield: during the 1980s they took over some of the hangars for possible use as an emergency hospital in the event of a major war in Europe. However, this was the last decade of the Cold War and the facility was closed in 1992.

LONG NEWNTON

County: Gloucestershire/Wiltshire

UTM/Grid: OS Map 173 – ST929920
Lat/Long: N51°37 W002°06
Nearest Town: Tetbury 2 miles to north-west

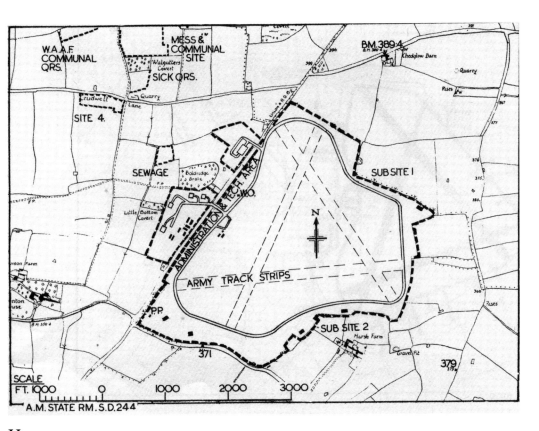

HISTORY

The site at Long Newnton was initially used as a sub-site for No.11 MU (Chilmark) for ammunition storage for a few months from late-1939. However, the following year it was allocated as a decoy Q site for Kemble (three miles to the north) – the ammunition having moved out! The buildings that had been used by the MU helped make the site look more authentic but the field, as laid out, was also promising for actual use and, from September to November 1940, it was used as a relief landing ground for the trainers of Hullavington's No.9 Service Flying Training School. This was the first of a number of such uses of the airfield, as shown in the unit list; the gap months in early 1942 were for the construction of two Sommerfeld Track runways, as the utilization of the airfield was restricted by the poor surface and water-logging; both runways were 1,335 yards by the stan-

dard 50 yards wide and they were linked by a perimeter track; interestingly, the plan for this period suggest three 'Army Track' runways, but the data lists two. A number of Blister hangars were erected on dispersals off the peri track and there was a technical area, with more such hangars and a single T-type hangar, on the west side, but on the other side of the Fosse Way. The remote domestic and support sites were located to the north-west of the airfield.

The airfield re-opened in May 1942 and No. 3 (Pilot) Advanced Flying Unit from South Cerney started using what was a very well-equipped RLG – in reality it was a satellite and the PAFU moved some of their Oxfords here. When the unit left, it was immediately replaced by No.15 (P)AFU; this unit remained in residence to June 1945, when it disbanded. After a few weeks of Care and Maintenance,

AIRFIELD DATA DEC 1944

Command:	Flying Training Command	Runway surface:	Sommerfeld Track
Function:	Pilots Advanced Flying Unit, Satellite	Hangars:	Blister (69ft) × 6, Blister (65ft) ×
Runways:	272 deg 1,185yd		4, T.2 × one
	214 deg 1,140yd	Dispersals:	Nil
	270 deg 2,000 × 50yd	Personnel:	Officers – 86 (3 WAAF)
			Other Ranks – 680 (140 WAAF)

UNITS

the airfield was once more given back to No.11 MU as a sub-site. This role continued to January 1950, when the RAF finally withdrew and the land was returned to agriculture.

Many of the buildings survive and the airfield can still be clearly seen from the air.

1939–1945

Used as RLG by:

9 SFTS (Hullavington)	Sep 1940–Nov 1940
3 SFTS (South Cerney)	Feb 1941–Aug 1941
14 FTS (Lyneham)	16 Aug 1941–26 Jan 1942
3 (P)AFU (South Cerney)	May 1942–Sep 1943
15 PAFU (Andover)	30 Sep 1943–15 May 1945

LULSGATE BOTTOM

County: Somerset

UTM/Grid: OS Map 182 – ST504651
Lat/Long: N51°22.53 W002°42.40
Nearest Town: Bristol 6 miles to north-east

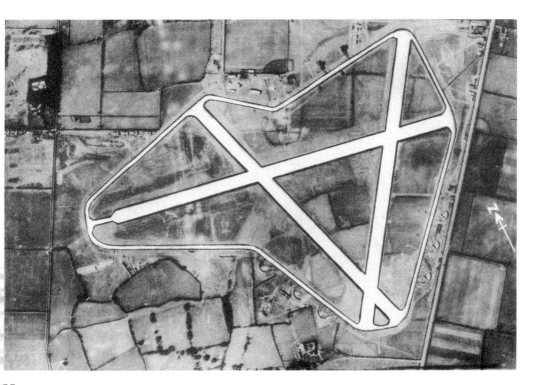

HISTORY

There were three airfields in the vicinity of Bristol – Filton on the Northern edge, Whitchurch on the Southern edge and Lulsgate Bottom, usually just referred to as Lulsgate, a few miles to the south-west and named after the adjacent small village. The latter of the three was the only one outside of Bristol's extensive balloon barrage and, as far as post-war development was concerned, far enough away from the expanding suburbs of the city.

A small site was acquired near the village for development into an RLG for nearby flying training units, Lulsgate Bottom opening in August 1940 as a grass field with few facilities and used by the Tiger Moths of No.10 EFTS at Weston-super-Mare. There were very few airfields in the area, so the pupil pilots found Lulsgate a useful airfield – less than ten miles from their home base and ideal for circuit practice. The amount of use made of the site is uncertain, as it often is with such RLGs, but no actual basing appears to have taken place. This was probably a good idea, as

one of the Bristol 'Starfish' sites (city decoy) was close by.

Fighter Command needed more airfields in the south-west and the decision was taken to develop the RLG into a fighter station for the new No.10 Group, although construction work did not commence until June 1941. The airfield was laid out with three runways and, during construction, one of these received a very welcome visitor – from the RAF intelligence point of view – when a Ju88 landed, in the mistaken belief by the crew that they were in France. The aircraft was soon part of the RAF's evaluation fleet and joined the 'Enemy Air Circus'.

During the construction phase the airfield was referred to as Broadfield Down, after the area of land on which it was built, but this was soon changed back to Lulsgate Bottom. The new airfield opened in January 1942, complete with three tarmac runways, eight hangars and various dispersals – but No.10 Group was no longer interested, as the previous dire

AIRFIELD DATA DEC 1944

Command:	Flying Training Command	Runway surface:	Tarmac
Function:	Flying Instructors School, Parent	Hangars:	Blister (69ft) × 4, Double Blister
Runways:	100 deg 1,300 × 50yd		(69ft) × 3, Bellman × one
	030 deg 1,000 × 50yd	Dispersals:	6 × Double Fighter Pen,
	160 deg 1,000 × 50yd		3 × Circular (20ft diam)
		Personnel:	Officers – 132 (4 WAAF)
			Other Ranks – 911 (214 WAAF)

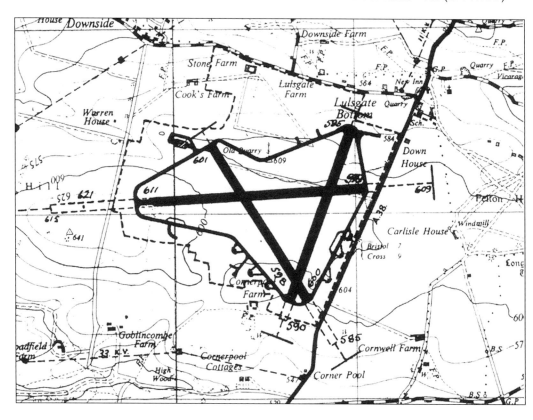

need for fighter bases in this area had gone. Army co-operation Lysanders of 286 Squadron moved in from Colerne and stayed for a few months but, on 1 June 1943, the station was transferred to Flying Training Command's No.23 Group. Flying training remained the rationale of Lulsgate Bottom into the post-war period; first occupants were No.3 (Pilots) Advanced Flying Unit from South Cerney, with Lulsgate operating as a satellite. Two Flights of Oxfords moved in and were joined in April by No.1540 Beam Approach Training Flight, which formed here and was affiliated with the PAFU, who continued to use Lulsgate as an RLG to September. The BATF's Oxfords continued in residence to work with the new

training unit that arrived in October. The attraction for the move of No.3 Flying Instructors School from Castle Combe was the runways at Lulsgate, as these would permit a more comprehensive flying operation than the limited grass of their previous base. However, the facilities at Lulsgate were not given any major improvements, as the servicing of the school's aircraft was undertaken at Hullavington. The FIS disbanded in July 1945 and Lulsgate became a satellite for No.7 FIS at Upavon, although nothing seems to have happened, as this unit was undergoing other changes. The net effect was that Lulsgate Bottom went into Care and Maintenance; however, this was short-lived as, by 1947, the decision had been taken to dispose of the site. It was taken-over by the Ministry of Civil Aviation, who at the time were considering options for the future civil airport for Bristol.

Whilst the debates were going on, the airfield was used by the Bristol and Gloucestershire Gliding Club but, with the 1954 decision in favour of developing Lulsgate, the gliders had to move out, although it was 1956 before the move to Nympsfield was completed.

Bristol Lulsgate Airport was opened in 1957 by the Duchess of Kent and, over the next ten years, passenger numbers steadily grew and the airport underwent a number of expansions to runway and terminals. The collapse of Court Line caused a blip in the growth but, after a few difficult years, the overall growth trend continued. As with all major civil airports there were frequent developments and the occasional change of owner or name. It was not until March 1997 that it became Bristol International Airport; the same year that Bristol Council sold a controlling stake to FirstGroup, retaining a 49 per cent stake. Ownership changed again in January 2001 with Macquarie Bank and Cintra taking control and continuing to invest in developing facilities. Passenger figures jumped to 3.8 million in 2003, with predictions of 12 million by 2030. Although Bristol International Airport (EGGD) is dominated by the east/west runway of 2,011m, the original wartime layout of runways can still be seen, although very little of the RAF site survives and there does not appear to be a memorial of any description. It always seems a shame (to put it mildly) that airports do not recognize their origins.

UNITS

1939–1945

286Sqn	24 Jan 1942–26 May 1942+	various
10 EFTS	Sep 1940–Jun 1941	Tiger Moth
1540Flt	15 Apr 1943–6 Feb 1945	
3 FIS	1 Oct 1943–18 Jul 1945	Oxford, Harvard

LYNEHAM

County: Wiltshire

UTM/Grid: OS Map 173 – SU015785
Lat/Long: N51°30.18 W001°58.30
Nearest Town: Swindon 6 miles to north-east

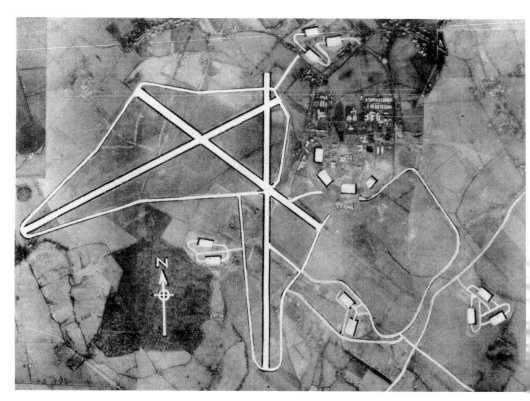

HISTORY

No.33 MU opened at Lyneham on 1 April 1940 in No.41 Group (SOM 270/40); however, this is a classic example of where official records can be in error, as this was apparently changed and the opening is later recorded as taking place on 5 June (SOM 497/40). This was the airfield's intended use and work on this hilltop site started in 1937; the site eventually extended from the village of Lyneham to the edge of the plateau, which at nearly 600ft was the highest point in the vicinity. Construction involved the demolition of a number of buildings plus the usual hedge removal, drainage work and site levelling, the result being a large grass landing area and a series of hangars on the north side for the MU, centred on four J-Types. By the time of the 1944 survey, Lyneham had forty-four hangars, thirty of these being Blister types. Also by the time of the survey, the original two grass strips had been replaced by three surfaced runways, two of 2,000 yards and one of 1,600 yards. Two of

these runways had entered service in 1942 and the third (356) was started in summer that year.

No.33 MU was an Aircraft Storage Unit and, by the end of June 1940, had thirty-eight aircraft in its care but, as with most MUs, it was not simply a matter of storing aircraft but also of carrying out modification work to install service equipment to prepare aircraft for issue to units. The Lyneham MU handled a very diverse array of aircraft, from Masters and Tiger Moths to Spitfires, Beaufighters and Wellingtons, to name but a few.

By late-summer 1940, the airfield was increasingly busy and, on 19 September, a German bomber scored a hit on one of the hangars, killing four workers (the MU was civilian manned). The MU continued to expand in 1941 and was using other airfields for dispersal, eventually making use of three satellite landing grounds for this purpose: No.45 SLG (Townsend, August 1941 to March 1943; No.2 SLG (Starveal

AIRFIELD DATA DEC 1944

Command:	Transport Command	Runway surface:	Tarmac on concrete
Function:	Airport	Hangars:	Blister × 30, Type L × 8, Type J × 4,
Runways:	252 deg 2,000 × 50yd		Type K × 2
	356 deg 2,000 × 50yd	Dispersals:	32 × Frying Pan, one × Concrete apron for
	135 deg 1,600 × 50yd		80 aircraft
		Personnel:	Officers – 301 (WAAF 11)
			Other Ranks – 2,751 (292 WAAF)

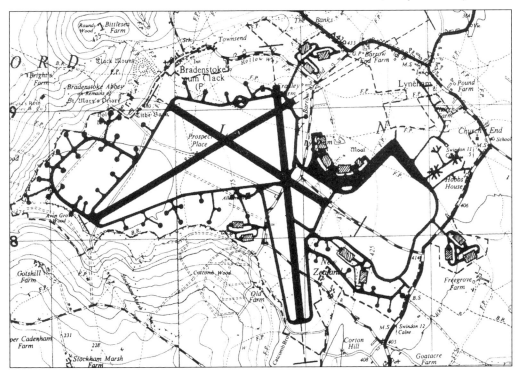

Farm) October 1941 to March 1942; and No.31 SLG (Everleigh) September 1942 to 1945. In the post-war period it made use of Yatesbury and Hullavington for a short period; the MU eventually disbanded at Lyneham on 31 December 1966.

August 1941 also brought the arrival of Lyneham's first based flying unit, when No.14 Service Flying Training School moved from Cranfield with its Oxfords – an impressive fleet of over 100 aircraft. Control of the airfield was transferred to Flying Training Command's No.23 Group and the circuit was soon humming with Oxfords, as pupil pilots learnt multi-engine flying skills as part of their training for bombers. RLGs were used at Long Newnton and Wanborough, but it was a brief stay for the SFTS and in January it moved to Ossington. The following month Lyneham was transferred to No.44 Group of

Ferry Command, as it had been chosen to act as a training unit for ferry crews. Over the next few months, a number of specialist Flights were formed, as were three Ferry Training Units. Of the Flights, perhaps the most interesting was No.1425 (Communications) Flight, which arrived from Honeybourne in April with three Liberators. These aircraft were used to fly a route to Cairo and were a critical link with the Middle East/Western Desert theatre of operations; the Flight flew other routes as well and was frequently carrying VIPs to key meetings. On 10 October 1942 the Flight was raised to squadron status as 511 Squadron, a unit destined to have a long and interesting career in the transport game, much of it spent at Lyneham. They were joined by a second transport squadron, 525 Squadron, in February 1944.

In October 1942, the FTUs had combined to form No.301 FTU and this remained active at Lyneham to March 1944. The station had come under the newly formed Transport Command in March 1943 and the units and roles outlined above continued, as did the detachment of BOAC Liberators that used one of the RAF hangars. The MU, too, had continued to evolve and, by mid-1943, its main type was the Spitfire, with an incredible 240 in store in June that year! This figure was paltry when you consider that Lyneham housed over 700 aircraft (mainly Spitfires) in 1946 – it was one of the MUs where the greatest number of unwanted airframes was gathered ready for disposal.

Lyneham remained one of Transport Command's main airfields and, as the unit list shows, it housed a variety of specialist Flights, such as No.1539 VIP Flight, and operational squadrons. By 1948, the three based squadrons (99, 206, 511) were operating Yorks and all played a role in Operation *Plainfare*, the Berlin Airlift. Over the next two decades, squadrons and aircraft changed (*see* unit list) and Lyneham operated the Hastings, Britannia and Comet. The arrival of the Comet in the mid-1950s meant yet another extension to the main runway, taking it to 2,600 yards; this extension also involved the destruction of three of the original hangars. In July 1967, the station received the first 'Fat Albert' for an RAF squadron – the C-130 had arrived and will soon celebrate forty years of operations from RAF Lyneham. If there is one aircraft that is truly associated with this airfield it is the Hercules; it has been operated here by a number of squadrons in a number of marks, the latest being the Hercules C.4 (C-130J). The Lyneham Wing comprises four operational squadrons, but the massive apron is seldom packed with aircraft, as the squadrons are amongst the busiest in the RAF, flying both tactical and strategic missions and playing key roles in global operations, from peace-keeping and humanitarian support to major conflicts such as the Gulf Wars. For many years Lyneham could safely claim to have been the most operational station in the RAF. Sadly, under present plans, it is scheduled for closure by the end of this decade, with all RAF transport resources being based at Brize Norton.

UNITS

1939–1945

159 Sqn	26 Apr 1942–7 Jun 1942	Liberator
160 Sqn	26 Apr 1942–11 Jun 1942+	Liberator
246 Sqn	11 Oct 1944–1 Dec 1944	Liberator, Halifax
511 Sqn	10 Oct 1942–1 May–Oct 1957+	various
525 Sqn	6 Feb 1944–15 Jul 1945	various
14 SFTS	16 Aug 1941–19 Jan 1942	Oxford, Harvard
1445Flt	27 Feb 1942–1 Nov 1942	Liberator
1Flt FTU	Mar 1942–3 Nov 1942	
2Flt FTU	Mar 1942–31 Jul 1942	
3Flt FTU	Mar 1942–20 May 1942	
1425 Flt	5 Apr 1942–10 Oct 1942	
1444 Flt	20 Jun 1942–1 Nov 1942	Hudson
301 FTU	1 Nov 1942–16 Mar 1944	
1 FCP	1 Aug 1943–14 Jan 1944	Wellington

Post-1945

24 Sqn	27 Nov 1950–9 Feb 1951	Valetta, Hastings
24 Sqn	5 Jan 1968–current	Hercules
30 Sqn	1 Feb 1971–current	Hercules
36 Sqn	1 Jul 1967–3 Nov 1975	Hercules
47 Sqn	1 Feb 1971–current	Hercules

Lyneham April 1944.

Ablemarle of 511 Squadron.

Hercules about to touch down; the Station operates a
four-squadron Hercules 'Wing'.

C-130 Hercules of 36 Squadron at Lyneham in September
1967, a few months after the squadron had equipped with
the type.

Britannia of Transport
Command on the apron at
Lyneham; the type was
operated from here by 99
and 511 squadrons.(via
Rod Priddle)

48 Sqn	1 Sep 1971–9 Jan 1976	Hercules
53 Sqn	9 Feb 1951–1 Jan 1957	Hastings
70 Sqn	15 Jan 1975–current	Hercules
99 Sqn	17 Nov 1947–16 Jun 1970	York, Hastings, Britannia
206 Sqn	17 Nov 1947–31 Aug 1949	York
216 Sqn	8 Nov 1955–30 Jun 1975	Valetta, Comet
242 Sqn	25 Jun 1949–1 May 1950	York, Hastings
511 Sqn	?–1 May Oct 1957	various
511 Sqn	15 Dec 1959–16 Jun 1970	Britannia
1409 Flt	10 Oct 1945–13 May 1946	Mosquito, Liberator
1359 Flt	1 Dec 1945–25 Feb 1946	York, Lancastrian
242 OCU	31 Oct 1975–1 Jul 1992	Hercules
HOEU	1996–?	Hercules

MEMORIALS

Lyneham has more memorials than any other RAF station; two of these are 'Gate Guard' aircraft: Comet C.2 XK699 Sagittarius and Dakota G-AMPO/KN566. The other memorials include a number of commemorative benches and:

1. Brick memorial with plaque showing a Britannia and the badges of Lyneham and the two 'Brit' squadrons with inscription:

Bristol Britannia Long Range Transport aircraft operated from Royal Air Force Lyneham from 19 March 1959 to 1 June 1970. To all who contributed to the successful operation of the Britannia. Presented by the Britannia Association 30 April 1994.

It also lists the registrations and names of all the aircraft.

2. Brick memorial with plaque inscribed: 'These 3 Lime trees were generously presented to RAF Lyneham by the Senate of the City of Berlin to mark the 40th anniversary of the involvement of 24, 30 and 47 squadrons in the Berlin Airlift 1948.'

3. Stained-glass window in St Michael and All Angels church to mark the 50th anniversary of RAF Lyneham, unveiled May 1990. The church also contains a number of RAF Standards.

MANNINGFORD

County: Wiltshire

UTM/Grid: OS Map 173 – SU130590
Lat/Long: N51°19.79 W001°48.88
Nearest Town: Devizes 7 miles to west

HISTORY

A white cross in a field was all that originally distinguished this as a relief landing ground rather than just another Wiltshire field. Close to Upavon and Alton Barnes the RLG was laid out on Mullen Farm, part Manningford Bohune Common, and was given no facilities when first brought into use. The site was also referred to as an ELG (Emergency Landing Ground) and this description was more accurate in terms of what Manningford had to offer, but did not reflect its routine use. Trainers from the Central Flying School at Upavon were the first users and this unit continued to visit Manningford to April 1942.

Use as an RLG/ELG by a variety of units (*see* unit list) continued to April 1947, but this was never a significant location; the most dramatic event, other

than a few training crashes, was an emergency landing by a Boston – for which the airfield was not really big enough. However, it got down in one piece and, after repair to a damaged wing (from hitting a hedge), it managed to get out again – with a light fuel load.

The airfield was abandoned in mid-1947 and was instantly a quiet Wiltshire field once more.

UNITS

Used as RLG/ELG by:

CFS (Upavon)	1939–Apr 1942
7 FIS (Upavon)	Apr 1942–Dec 1943
29 EFTS (Clyffe Pypard)	Nov 1942–?
2 EFTS (Yatesbury)	May 1946–?

MERRYFIELD
(Station 464) (HMS *Heron*)

County: Somerset

UTM/Grid: OS Map 193 – ST342186
Lat/Long: N50°57.45 W002°56.15
Nearest Town: Taunton 7 miles to north-west

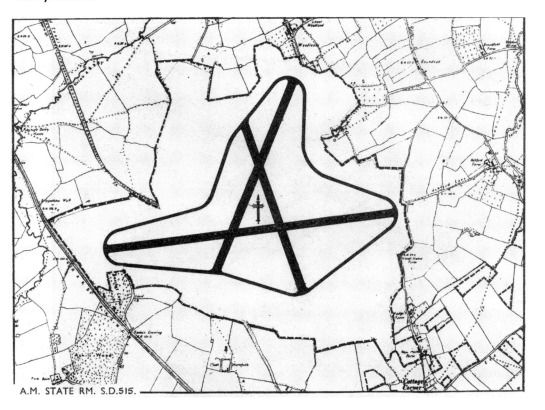

A.M. STATE RM. S.D.515.

HISTORY

The airfield opened as Merryfield on 9 February 1944, despite having been called 'Isle Abbots' during the planning phase it was allocated to the USAAF for a Transport Group and, as such, was referred to as Station 464. Development of the site had been lengthy, as it had originally been chosen in 1942 for a bomber operational station or OTU. In many respects it was a strange choice of site for, whilst the land was reasonably flat, the development work would involve removing a large section of an old canal on the west side, plus the closure of minor roads.

The four C-47 squadrons of the 441st Troop Carrier Group arrived in April from Langar and continued an intensive work-up in preparation for the airborne assault of Normandy. The Group's main training involved mass launches, formations and releases of Hadrian gliders, as it was critical to the

success of any air assault that the troops be dropped in the right place and as concentrated as possible. The target area for D-Day was St Mère Église and the Group contributed a number of combinations to the D-Day assault.

The ensuing days were taken-up with re-supply missions and the Group remained operational from Merryfield to September 1944. From early July the airfield received regular visits from aircraft of the 813th Air Evacuation Transport Squadron, bringing casualties from Normandy to the Field Hospital that had been established at Merryfield. In November 1944, the station was transferred to Transport Command, having officially been under Fighter Command (for some inexplicable reason) since August. January 1945 saw part of 232 Squadron become No.1315 Transport Flight, although two months later the Flight was en route to Australia. For

AIRFIELD DATA DEC 1944

Command:	Fighter Command	Runway surface:	Concrete surfaced with bitumen
Function:	Operational Satellite	Hangars:	T.2 × 2
Runways:	280 deg 2,000 × 50yd	Dispersals:	50 × Spectacle
	350 deg 1,400 × 50yd	Personnel:	Officers – 124
	040 deg 1,220 × 50yd		Other Ranks – 3,171 (216 WAAF)

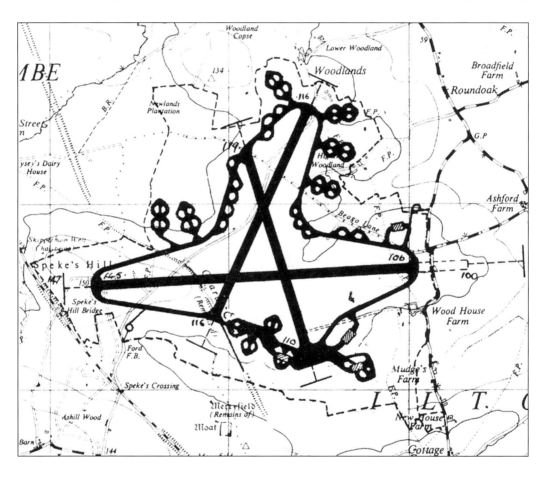

a few days in March, prior to its disbandment, the Halifax Development Flight was in residence. One of the few units to stay for more than a matter of weeks was 187 Squadron, which formed here on 1 February as a transport unit with Halifaxes (for a few weeks) and Dakotas. The unit absorbed the Halifax Development Flight and, eventually, moved to Membury in September.

With the closure of the airfield in 1946, following the major post-war review of airfields, Merryfield looked to have an uncertain future. As with most airfields, there was no immediate disposal plan and, in 1949, the site was adopted by Westland Aircraft as a flight test facility for the Wyvern. The company used the airfield for a number of activities, although the Wyvern was perhaps the most interesting. By the early 1950s, the airfield was reduced to two operational runways, with 17/35 being listed as 'closed'.

In November 1951, the RAF returned as part of the near panic increase in flying training brought on by the Korean War. The new occupants were No.208 Advanced Flying School and Merryfield whistled to the sounds of Vampires and Meteors for the next three years. As part of No.25 Group, the unit's role

Sea Venom XG663 of 809 Squadron, probably at Merryfield in 1957. (Ray Sturtivant)

was to train fighter pilots, some of whom were ex-World War Two veterans, whilst others were National Service. Merryfield was allocated Dunkeswell as an RLG and used this until December 1954; in June the school had been re-designated as No.10 Flying Training School – a designation that lasted one month before being changed to No.9 FTS. The end of the Korean War brought a run-down of training and, by February 1955, the Flying Training School had disbanded. The Meteors and Canberras of 'C (PR) Squadron' of No.231 OCU operated from Merryfield for a short period in the mid-1950s.

A year later, the Fleet Air Arm had need of the airfield as a bolthole whilst Yeovilton's runways were being worked on; first arrivals were 766 Squadron in November 1956, this unit remaining in residence to January 1958. The squadron was equipped with Sea Venoms and was, in effect, a training unit – as an All-Weather Fighter Pool. During the same period, other FAA squadrons made use of Merryfield, usually for short periods. The departure back to Yeovilton in 1958 put Merryfield, still in navy hands, into Care and Maintenance although, for most of 1960, the Fleet Requirements Unit, 700Sqn, operated from here. Indeed, it was one of their sub-units, 700XSqn responsible for Wasp trials, that brought rotary operations to the airfield – the role that Merryfield continues to retain with the Fleet Air Arm.

Such was the value of this airfield as an adjunct to Yeovilton, especially with the increasing employment of helicopters in the Fleet Air Arm, that it underwent a significant rebuild during the early 1970s, becoming HMS Heron on 22 May 1972, and Merryfield remains a vital satellite airfield for the very busy activities at Yeovilton. The airfield is primarily used by Yeovilton's helicopter squadrons and Lynx (702 and 815 Squadron) and Sea King (845, 846 and 848 Squadron) helicopters are frequent users of the immaculate airfield, whilst 847 Squadron Gazelles can also be seen. None of these are included in the unit list, as none are actually based at Merryfield. All three runways are still serviceable and the airfield is dotted with helicopter landing areas;

Sea Kings are a frequent site at Merryfield although no units are actually based at the airfield. (RNAS Yeovilton)

Merryfield is unusual for an active military airfield in that it does not have a four-letter ICAO code.

UNITS

1939–1945

53Sqn	17 Sep 1945–1 Dec 1945	Liberator
187Sqn	1 Feb 1945–17 Sep 1945	Halifax, Dakota
238Sqn	1 Dec 1944–22 Feb 1945	Dakota
243Sqn	6 Jan 1945–9 Mar 1945	Dakota
1315Flt	1 Jan 1945–9 Mar 1945	Dakota
HDF	Mar 1945	Halifax

USAAF Units
441st TCG
Squadrons: 99th TCS, 100th TCS, 301st TCS, 302nd TCS
Aircraft: C-47
Dates: 25 Apr 1944–8 Sep 1944

Post-1945

242Sqn	9 Dec 1945–7 May 1946	York
700Sqn FAA	5 Jan 1960–Oct 1960	
766Sqn FAA	24 Nov 1956–20 Jan 1958	Sea Venom
809Sqn FAA	Sep 1957–Jul 1958	Sea Venom
891Sqn FAA	Nov 1956–Mar 1958+	Sea Venom
893Sqn FAA	Feb 1957–Jan 1958	Sea Venom
894Sqn FAA	Sep 1957–Jan 1958	Sea Venom
1552Flt	9 Feb 1946–13 May 1946	Oxford
208 AFS	19 Nov 1951–1 Jun 1954	Vampire, Meteor
9 FTS	1 Jul 1954–16 Feb 1955	Vampire
231 OCU	May 1955–Oct 1956	Meteor, Canberra

Post-1972 extensive use by Yeovilton helicopters for training and exercises

MORETON-IN-MARSH

County: Gloucestershire

UTM/Grid: OS Map 163 – SP218328
Lat/Long: N51°59.59 W001°41.03
Nearest Town: Chipping Norton 7 miles to south-east

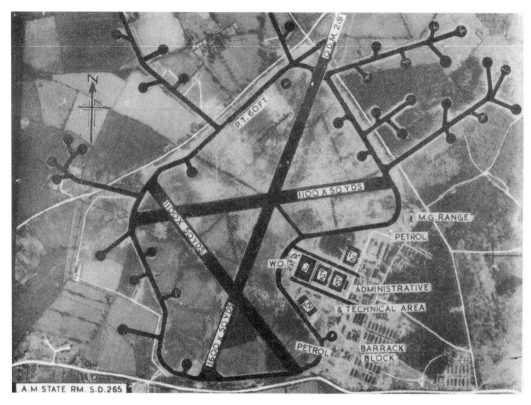

HISTORY

The airfield at Moreton-in-Marsh was laid-out on the east side of the village after which it took its name, on land that was acquired in late-1939, construction commencing early the following year for a standard three-runway airfield. The three runways were laid in a near-perfect triangular pattern, the longest being 1,600 yards (although originally built somewhat shorter than that). The runways were connected by a perimeter track and the airfield eventually had thirty heavy-bomber dispersals of frying-pan type, most of these on taxiway spurs from the north and east part of the perimeter track. The technical and admin area was on the south-east side, with four T.2s and one J-type hangar, along with various huts – most being rows of barrack blocks. The bomb dump was situated just to the east, in Wolford Wood. This description relates to the airfield as it was at the time of the 1944 survey and not all of this work was

complete when the station opened; indeed, when Moreton-in-Marsh opened in January 1941 it was far from complete. Although No.55 Operational Training Unit appears to have made some use of the airfield from late-1940, it was the arrival of a bomber training unit, No.21 OTU, in late-January 1941, that truly opened the station's RAF career. This Wellington OTU commenced training on 1 March 1941 and, over the next five years, trained hundreds of aircrew for Bomber Command.

The role of the Operational Training Units was a crucial one and, throughout the wartime life of Bomber Command, they maintained the flow of trained aircrew that was essential to the pace of the strategic bomber offensive; there were times when the loss rate amongst the operational squadrons threatened to overwhelm the capacity of the training units to provide replacements, which usually resulted

AIRFIELD DATA DEC 1944

Command:	Bomber Command	Runway surface:	Concrete and tarmac
Function:	Operational Training Unit, Parent	Hangars:	T.2 × 4, Type J × one
Runways:	218 deg 1,600 × 50yd	Dispersals:	30 × Heavy Bomber
	157 deg 1,100 × 50yd	Personnel:	Officers – 162 (12 WAAF)
	277 deg 1,100 × 50yd		Other Ranks – 2,361 (424 WAAF)

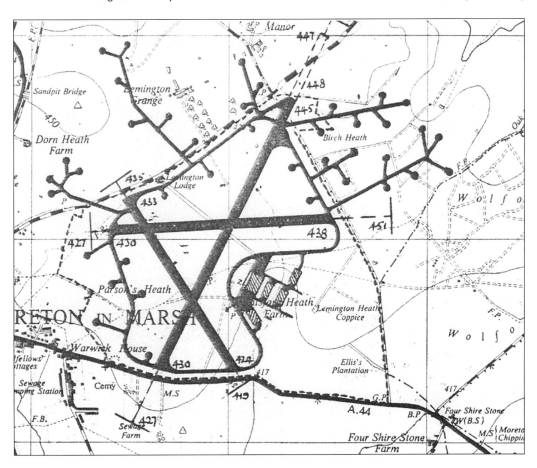

in a shortening of the training course. Many of the aircraft flown at the OTUs were worn-out operational aircraft and many of the instructors were men who had completed an operational tour and were on 'rest'. No.21 OTU, like others of its type, suffered numerous training accidents. The OTU had a particularly bad period for accidents in late-January–early February, with six aircraft being lost; the first incident occurred on 28 January when two aircraft collided over the Radwell bombing range, although all the crewmen except one managed to bale-out. On 4 February, a crew from No.19 Course crashed close to

the airfield, most being killed; they were one day from graduation. Most of the other crashes in this period also involved loss of life. Moreton may not have been an operational station, but it witnessed its share of tragedy. By August 1941, the unit's establishment was 40+14 Wellington and 14+4 Ansons, as well as two Lysanders. It appears to have maintained a strength of around fifty Wellingtons for most of its wartime career, with Mk Is later giving way to IIIs and Xs. As usual with some units, it also acquired a number of fighters, in this case four Hurricanes, for fighter evasion training. During its wartime career

The bomber OTUs flew leaflet-dropping sorties and also contributed to Main Force raids from time to time. This is probably not a Moreton shot.

Wellington LP713 of No.21 Operational Training Unit.

the station made use of a number of satellite airfields: Edgehill (Oct 1941–Apr 1943), Enstone (Apr 1943–Dec 1945), Honeybourne (Aug 1945–Oct 1945 when Enstone was not available).

The station was also required to contribute aircraft for operational missions, either as part of Main Force or with the introduction of a leaflet-dropping ('nickelling') sortie over an 'easy' target as part of the final weeks of training. Both activities resulted in losses. Perhaps the best-known such operational tasking came with the 1942 series of 'Thousand Bomber raids', when the new AOC of Bomber Command,

Arthur Harris, had to use the training units in order to reach his magic figure of 1,000 bombers – it was indeed an incredible achievement. Over the three raids Moreton contributed thirty-four aircraft, with only one failing to return. The OTU survived into the post-war period and eventually departed Moreton for Finningley in November 1946, where it became No.202 Advanced Flying School.

No.21 (Pilots) Advanced Flying Unit arrived in early December 1946 with its fleet of Oxfords, being joined the same month by No.1 Refresher School with Oxfords and Harvards. The two merged in August 1947 to become No.1 (Pilots) Refresher Flying Unit, with a mixed fleet of Harvards, Oxfords, Spitfires and Wellingtons. The training role continued, with the PRFU absorbing No.2 PRFU from Valley in April 1948, just before moving to Finningley. There was then a short lull before the station's final flying unit moved in; No.1 Flying Training School arriving from Oakington in October 1951. The school spent three years flying Harvards and Prentices from here, but the RLG at Edgehill was closed on 1 November and the final graduation parade at Moreton took place on 23 November 1954. The following year the site was handed to the Home Office and initial use was by RAF Class-H fire-fighting reservists. This role came to an end a few years later, but fire training was to be Moreton's future and, in 1967, a major building programme started. The new Fire Service Technical College was opened by HM The Queen in May 1974.

The village is home to the excellent little Wellington Aviation Museum (www.wellingtonaviation.org) founded by ex-wellington man Gerry Tyack. It contains various memorabilia and the front of the building includes a memorial.

Units

1939–1945

55 OTU	27 Nov 1940–22 Feb 1941	Blenheim, Defiant, Hurricane
21 OTU	21 Jan 1941–25 Nov 1946	Wellington, Anson
1446Flt	18 May 1942–1 May 1943	Wellington

Post-1945

21 OTU	?–25 Nov 1946	Wellington, Anson
21 (P)AFU	5 Dec 1946–6 Aug 1947	Oxford
1 RS	17 Dec 1946–6 Aug 1947	Oxford, Harvard
1 PRFU	6 Aug 1947–10 Jan 1948	various
1 FTS	31 Oct 1951–20 Apr 1955	Harvard, Prentice

Memorial

There is a memorial stone at the entrance to the Fire Service College; the engraved stone shows RAF wings and the plaque shows the RAF badge and the Fire Service badge with the inscription: 'The Fire Service College Moreton-In-Marsh. England. Royal Air Force Moreton-in-Marsh 1941–1959.' The memorial was dedicated on 3 September 1994.

MORETON VALENCE
(Haresfield)

County: Gloucestershire

UTM/Grid: OS Map 162 – SO796104
Lat/Long: N51°47.51 W002°17.83
Nearest Town: Gloucester 4 miles to north

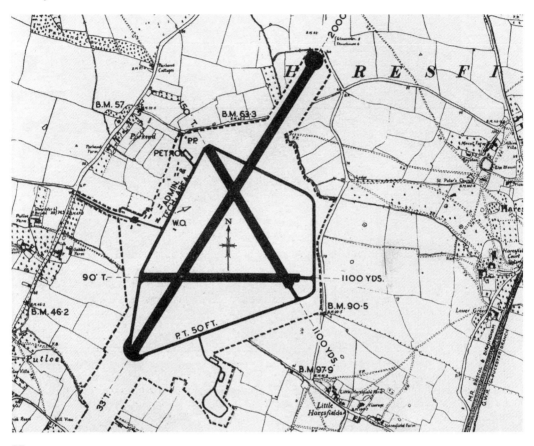

HISTORY

The Meteor was one of the classic jets of the 1950s and Moreton Valence was at the centre of its production, although the true military period of this Gloucestershire airfield involved flying training. Construction of the airfield to the south of Gloucester involved closure of a number of minor roads and the removal of hedges and ditches, along with a few buildings in the parish of Haresfield. When the airfield opened in November 1939 it was little more than a semi-developed relief landing ground for use by No.6 Air Observer and Navigation School at Staverton – it was known as Haresfield after the parish and the village just to the east. The school's Ansons made infrequent use of the landing ground, but it was enough to confirm that the site

was worth developing.

Rebuild work took place in 1941 and, from September, the 'new' airfield was known as Moreton Valence and was provided with three hard runways, perimeter track and a number of Blister hangars. Apart from the runways it was still a basic site, but the AONS based two Flights here, although major servicing was carried out at the parent station. On 1 May 1942, the Refresher Flying Training School formed at Moreton Valence, but it did little more than collect aircraft and personnel before moving to Kirknewton three weeks later. The Air Observer School and its successor OAFU remained at Moreton until December 1944, with Ansons as the main trainer. A few days later, the RLG was given to No.3 (Pilots) Advanced Flying Unit at South Cerney and

AIRFIELD DATA DEC 1944

Command:	Flying Training Command	Runway surface:	Concrete
Function:	Observers Advanced Flying Unit, Satellite	Hangars:	Extra-Over Blisters × 8,
Runways:	223 deg 2,100 × 50yd		Type B.2 (MAP) × 4,
	162 deg 1,000 × 50yd		Type A1 × one, Type B.1
	101 deg 1,000 × 50yd		(MAP) × one
		Dispersals:	Nil
		Personnel:	Officers – 95 (4 WAAF)
			Other Ranks – 351 (43 WAAF)

The Meteor was without doubt the most significant type to fly out of Moreton, although it was followed by the Javelin. Trio of Meteors of 616 Squadron.

the Oxfords made use of the airfield until July 1945. The final few months of 1945 were allocated for use by No.6 PAFU at Little Rissington, who also used Oxfords. With the exception of the Gliding School, which remained in residence to late-1946, this ended the RAF's use of Moreton Valence and allowed its other residents to expand.

The 'other residents' had been there since October 1943, when Glosters moved into a facility provided by the Ministry of Aircraft Production on the north-east corner, and included five B-Type (MAP) hangars. The other major development was an extension to the main runway to 2,100 yards. It was a highly classified location and the runway was needed for the development of jet aircraft, with Gloster moving the Meteor programme to the new site. Indeed, it is somewhat strange that the trainers were still allowed to use the airfield. The factory area gradually increased and, although the Meteor played little role in World War Two, it was a major part of the RAF's post-war fighter re-equipment and became a major export success. Although production and test flying

of Meteors dominated the post-war period of Moreton Valence, another classic British jet was born here. The prototype Gloster Javelin (WD804) flew from here on 26 November 1951 and, nearly eleven years later, it was a Javelin that made the last flight from the airfield. This flight took place on 25 July 1962 and the once busy production sheds were soon taken over for industrial use.

The airfield itself was cut in half by the construction of the M5 motorway and travelling south you could once clearly see the hangars and sheds, but this view has now gone, as the site has been re-developed.

UNITS

1939-1945

6 AONS	1939–Jun 1943	Anson
RFTS	1–23 May 1942	various
6 OAFU	Jun 1943–12 Dec 1944	Anson
3 PAFU	21 Dec 1944–12 Jul 1945	Oxford
6 PAFU	Jul 1945–Dec 1945	Oxford
83 GS	May 1944–13 Oct 1946	Cadet, Sedbergh

MOUNT BATTEN
(Cattewater)

UTM/Grid: OS Map 201 – SX483533
Lat/Long: N50°22 W004°08
Nearest Town: Plymouth

County: Devon

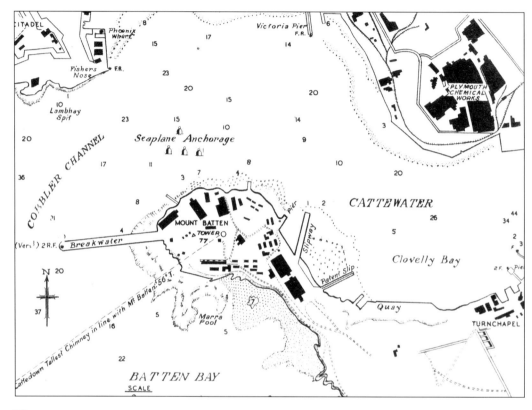

HISTORY

Plymouth being one of the Royal Navy's strongholds it was perhaps inevitable that an air station would be built in this area, although it was not until February 1917 that RNAS Cattewater opened as a seaplane base. The chosen site was a promontory to the south of Plymouth that divided Cattewater and the Batten Bay part of Plymouth Sound, the actual headland being known as Mount Batten Point. The RNAS also had an airship mooring-out station for two airships at nearby Chelson Meadow, known as RNAS Laira, but this was associated with RNAS Mullion.

The rugged peninsula sprouted slipways and various sheds and buildings, whilst the existing breakwater was used as a pier. The Navy based a few seaplanes here, but details are sketchy and it was only with the formation of the RAF in April 1918 that more details became available. The air station became RAF Cattewater and the new owners undertook develop-

ment work on hangars, slipways and other facilities. Two seaplane Flights, 347 and 348, formed in June and July, becoming part of 238 Squadron in August. The same month, 237 Squadron formed with Short 184 floatplanes. Patrols were flown to the end of the war and both squadrons survived into the post-war period, although 237 disbanded in May 1919. Although it was an important location, that did not save it in the immediate post-war period, but it was placed into reserve rather than being disposed of.

By the early 1920s, the RAF was already planning to bring the site back into use and this was eventually approved, along with authority to acquire land for expansion under the 'Cattewater Seaplane Station Bill'. Despite this intent, it was late-1928 before the station was back in operation with flying boats, No.482 (Coastal Reconnaissance) Flight forming on 8 October with Southampton flying boats as part of

AIRFIELD DATA DEC 1944

Command:	Coastal Command	Moorings:	Standard RAF FB moorings:
Function:	Flying Boat Station		Catte Water (9), Jennycliff Bay (6),
			Drake Island (4 emergency buoys)
		Slipways:	36 × 40ft
		Personnel:	Officers – 107 (7 WAAF)
			Other Ranks – 757 (257 WAAF)

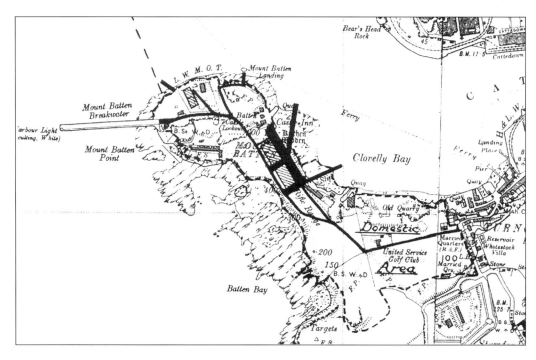

No.10 Group. The Flight was raised to squadron status as 203 Squadron on 1 January 1929 – but the following month left for the Persian Gulf. However, the same month, 204 Squadron formed with Southamptons and was joined the following year January by 209 Squadron, equipped with the Iris III.

On 1 October 1929, the site was renamed as RAF Mount Batten and its old name of Cattewater was soon forgotten. This major RAF flying-boat facility was now well-established and, overlooking the Sound in which the aircraft were moored, it was a delightful site although, as more development took place, it would become somewhat crowded.

With the plan to put catapult aircraft on major RN ships, the RAF, who still 'owned' naval aviation, formed a number of Catapult Flights and Mount Batten was chosen as one of the main shore bases. The moorings were occupied by Londons of 204 Squadron as the RAF entered 1939, although in February they were joined by the floatplane Sharks of

'D Flight' No.2 Anti-Aircraft Co-operation Unit to work with Devonport's Gunnery School. It was not until June that the squadron received its first Sunderland, but it was soon equipped with six of these large 'boats' and, in the days leading up to the outbreak of war, long-range patrols were instituted. Mount Batten's wartime career was very much linked to the activities of a single squadron, No.10 Squadron Royal Australian Air Force, one of very few units to operate in the UK under its RAAF number-plate rather than acquiring a number in the RAF sequence. The squadron arrived from Pembroke Dock on 1 April 1940 and spent the next five years operating from its Plymouth base, with notable success and, of course, inevitable losses. The operational record book of this squadron is a superb historic document, as it is detailed and includes photographs – and it does not appear to have been 'censored', as so many were by those who wrote or authorized them. During its time at Mount Batten the squadron operated four

Singapore or 209 Squadron; the squadron operated the type from Mount Batten in the early 1930s, although this is a September 1937 shot.

Groundcrew working on a 209 Squadron Iris.

Crew of 10 Squadron RAAF, January 1944; this Australian unit was the most significant (and successful) user of Mount Batten.

Damage caused by the German air raid of 27 November 1940.

marks of Sunderland: Mark I, Sep 39–Jul 42; II, Jun 41–Dec 43; III, Jan 42–Jun 45; V, May 44–Jun 45.

The squadron's operational score opened on 1 July 1940, when Flight Lieutenant Gibson and crew in P9603 sank the U-26; the U-boat, a Type 1A, was on its sixth war cruise. Over the next five years the squadron flew thousands of hours on patrol, most of which were notable for nothing more then endless horizons of grey sea. A number of sightings and attacks were made but, although claims for 'damage' were credited, it was not until May 1943 that the next confirmed destruction of a U-boat was made.

Confirmed U-boat 'kills' by 10 Squadron RAAF

1 Jul 40	U-26	10 RAAF, P9603	F/L W N Gibson
7 May 43	U-465	10 RAAF	F/L Rossiter
1 Aug 43	U-454	10 RAAF, W4020	F/L K G Fry
8 Jan 44	U-426	10 RAAF, EK586	F/O J P Roberts
8 Jul 44	U-243	10 RAAF, W4030	F/O W B Tilley

It was not all one-way traffic for Mount Batten and

the station was attacked a number of times by the Luftwaffe, the most effective raid taking place on 27 November 1940, which led to major damage to a hangar and the destruction of the Sunderland in the hangar – a dramatic picture as shown here – and one at the moorings. The squadron also operated a number of G-Class 'boats' on a courier service to the Middle East but, after the loss of one in 1941, the others were withdrawn. For a period in 1941, the station was without a based operational squadron, as it was considered that Plymouth Sound was too congested and, after another series of German air attacks that caused more damage to Sunderlands, it was too vulnerable. However, during this period, Mount Batten was used as a deployment base by Sunderlands and the overall decision was reversed with the return of 10 Squadron in January 1942. In April, the squadron was instrumental in helping form a second Australian Sunderland unit, 461 Squadron. The new unit was soon in action but, after a few weeks of ops, moved to Hamworthy in August.

The Australians of 10 Squadron RAAF finally left their Devon base in October 1945, after what, by any standards, had been a memorable period of operations. A few days later the station was placed in Care and Maintenance but, on 1 January 1946, it was transferred to Maintenance Command for use by No.238 MU. This unit remained to 17 October 1953, when it moved to Calshot, changing places with the Marine Craft Training School. Over the next few years Mount Batten acquired various parts of the RAF's Marine Craft organization, becoming one of the main centres of this activity.

To most RAF aircrew from the 1960s onwards, including the author, Mount Batten was known for only one thing – the RAF's School of Combat Survival and Rescue (SCSR). It was here that aircrew sat through lectures and, if it was a sea survival course, had the delights of being taken out in an RAF launch and dumped into the sea off Plymouth for dinghy drill – and perhaps pick-up by an SAR helicopter. Meanwhile, the nearby rugged landscape of Dartmoor was ideal for escape and evasion exercises.

The disbandment of the RAF Marine Branch in early 1986 marked the end of a fine career for the RAF's 'sailors', a career that has seldom received the recognition it deserves. This effectively spelled the death-knell for the station, as its remaining units, such as the SCSR, could hardly justify its continued existence. Closure finally came in 1992. The old RAF site was redeveloped in the late-1990s into a sailing and watersport centre, with a mix of new buildings and refurbished RAF buildings.

A 10 Squadron Sunderland monitors an oil streak – possible evidence of a U-boat, 8 May 1942.

The search and attack training room.

In its latter, post-aircraft, years, the station became a centre for the RAF Marine Craft Branch; this is not a Mount Batten shot.

UNITS

HQ Units at Cattewater/Mount Batten

No.2 Wing	15 May 1919–Apr 1920	238Sqn
No.72 (Ops) Wing	8 Aug 1918–May 1919	
No.4 (FB) Wing	2–3 Oct 1935	204, 230Sqn

Pre-1919

237 Sqn	Aug 1918–15 May 1919	Short 184
238 Sqn	20 Aug 1918–20 Mar 1922	H.16, Short 184, F.2A and F.3
347 (FB)Flt	15 Jun 1918–May 1919	H16, F3
348 (FB)Flt	15 Jul 1918–May 1919	H16, F3
349 (FB)Flt	15 Oct 1918–May 1919	H16, F3

1919–1939

203 Sqn	1 Jan 1929–28 Feb 1929	Southampton
204 Sqn	1 Feb 1929–27 Feb 1935	Southampton, Scapa
204 Sqn	5 Aug 1936–2 Apr 1940	Scapa, London, Sunderland
209 Sqn	15 Jan 1930–1 May 1935	various
238 Sqn	?–20 Mar 1922	H.16, Short 184, F.2A and F.3
482 Flt	8 Oct 1928–1 Jan 1929	Southampton
702 Flt FAA	15 Jul 1936–1 Jan 1938	Walrus, Seal
710 Sqn FAA	26 Aug 1939–1 Sep 1939	Walrus

712 Flt FAA	15 Jul 1936–1 Jan 1938	Osprey, Walrus
716 Flt FAA	15 Jul 1936–1 Jan 1938	Osprey, Seafox
720 Flt FAA	15 Jul 1936–1 Jun 1937	Walrus
FBDF	1 Jan 1924–1 May 1924	F5, Saro A7
2 AACU	16 Feb 1939–?	Shark

1939–1945

204 Sqn	?–2 Apr 1940	Sunderland
461 Sqn	26 Apr 1942–5 Sep 1942	Sunderland
10 Sqn RAAF	1 Apr 1940–31 Oct 1945+	Sunderland
771 Sqn FAA det	19–23 Aug 1939	Swordfish

MEMORIAL

There are a number of aviation memorials in Plymouth, the only one to recognize Mount Batten is a plaque on the Barbican Shopping Centre that shows Sunderland RB-W of 10 Squadron RAAF and the inscription: 'to the people of Plymouth with affection and admiration from members of 10 Squadron Royal Australian Air Force who operated from Mount Batten 1939–1945'. The squadron recognized the city – but the city has failed to recognize either the squadron or Mount Batten. There is an information board that gives a brief history of Mount Batten and four of its aircraft, although nearly half the board is concerned with TE Lawrence and mention of his period at the station.

Sunderland W4030 of 10 Squadron attacking, and sinking, U-boat U-243 on 8 July 1944.

NETHERAVON

County: Wiltshire

UTM/Grid: OS Map 184 – SU165494
Lat/Long: N51°14.30 W001°45.52
Nearest Town: Amesbury 4 miles to south

HISTORY

As can be seen from a glance at the unit list, Netheravon had a long, complex and interesting history that started in the earliest days of military aviation in Britain and is now the oldest airfield that is still operational. Salisbury Plain has long been a heartland of British military training and it was here that formal trials took place with aeroplanes – in 1912 at Larkhill – to determine the future production of military aircraft. There was also the need to find additional land for airfields to replace Larkhill and Netheravon, along with Upavon, was chosen.

The new airfield was constructed on land used for cavalry gallops and so was ideal for a landing ground; the first buildings, aircraft sheds and various huts, were put up in late-1912 and the site was laid out in two parts, with the upper aerodrome camp being the landing ground and operational buildings, and the lower aerodrome camp housing the domestic side and the training facilities, such as classrooms. The airfield was to be capable of accommodating two squadrons. The overall plan was impressive and a great deal of thought had been given to the building requirements and the overall layout.

Netheravon opened as an RFC flying station in June 1913 with the arrival of 3 Squadron from Larkhill, 4 Squadron flying in from Farnborough two days later. Both squadrons undertook trials to discover the most effective way to use aeroplanes in the army support roles for which they were intended, which included working with various army units as well as developing new ideas such as air-to-ground photography. In June 1914, the entire Military Wing of the RFC came to Netheravon for a major exercise, with tented areas springing up on the airfield. This

June 1914 with groundcrew about to hand-start a BE2c.

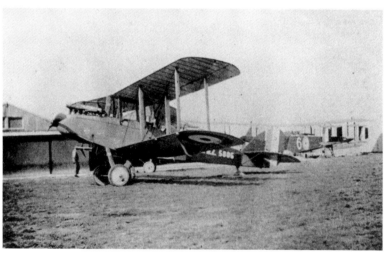

Snipe E6150 of No.1 FTS, c.1921.

was a major event that not only tested the use of aircraft but also showed the air strength (a maximum of thirty aircraft airborne) of the RFC – at a time when artillery was listed in hundreds of guns, this was not overly impressive! The Concentration Camp, as it had been called, dissolved in early July. A few weeks later World War One started and over the next four years military aviation would develop at an incredible pace. The operational squadrons departed and Netheravon's role in the war was to be primarily one of training, although some development work also took place, as did use of the airfield for forming of new squadrons.

In the first few months of war the Upavon-based Central Flying School used Netheravon as a satellite

but, in October, this detachment became No.3 Reserve Aeroplane Company, which departed to Shoreham in January 1915. As shown in the unit list, various squadrons passed through the airfield during the 1914–1917 period, some having been given training roles, others coming here to work-up for deployment to France or other operational theatres. By mid-1915 it had been realized that a more formalized training system was needed and Netheravon was selected to become a major training airfield, with two reserve squadrons, No.7 and No.8, forming here on 28 July, the former with Shorthorns and the latter with Henri Farmans. Under a designation change of May 1917, such squadrons became Training (Ex-Reserve) Squadrons but the role remained the same. The requirement for

AIRFIELD DATA DEC 1944

Command:	Fighter Command	Runway surface:	Grass
Function:	Operational, Parent	Hangars:	Flight Sheds × 3,
Runways:	E/W 2,000yd		Type A (250ft × 120ft) × 2,
	SE/NW 1,500yd		Cathedral × 2, Bessonneau × one
	NE/SW 1,400yd	Dispersals:	Nil
		Personnel:	Officers – 152 (10 WAAF)
			Other Ranks – 1,577 (375 WAAF)

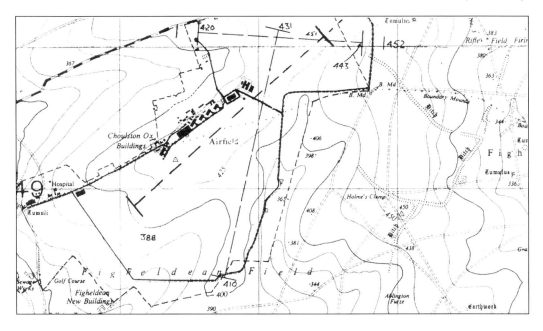

new pilots was constant as the RFC grew in strength and loss rates of operational pilots increased; there were also significant losses in training and no week went by at Netheravon without a spate of crashes, with injury or death of the crews all too frequent.

Spring 1918 saw Netheravon being used for the formation and work-up of a number of squadrons destined for the Independent Force – the RAF's strategic-bombing organization designed to attack German military and industrial targets. The main aircraft was to be the HP 0/400 but, as squadrons formed, they initially used a variety of aircraft until sufficient of the large bombers were available; for many of the squadrons this came just before or just after they left Netheravon.

The formation of the RAF on 1 April 1918 brought a number of organizational changes; for Netheravon this involved the amalgamation of training squadrons into Training Depot Stations, with No.8 and No.12 TDS forming here and both fulfill-

ing the same basic role. The Armistice month of November 1918 was marked by a fierce storm that destroyed a number of hangars and seventeen aircraft, including two 0/400s.

Training continued into 1919 but, in May, No.12 TDS was disbanded, leaving its sister-unit to become No.8 Training School to train new pilots. The school changed name twice more, becoming No.1 Flying Training School in December 1919. The school operated diversely over the next ten years and trained RAF and naval pilots; it disbanded in February 1931 and, for a short while, Netheravon was out of the training game. As the unit list shows, operational squadrons had been present at the airfield from the mid-1920s and this role increased in the 1930s – a role that included disembarked naval squadrons.

Training returned in the mid-1930s with the formation, in April 1935, of No.6 Flying Training School, to provide advanced training for qualified pilots by introducing them to service types and oper-

Airco DH9 at
Netheravon. (via Rod
Priddle)

ational considerations, such as formation and air-firing. The initial equipment of Hart and Audax was supplemented from late-1936 by Ansons and the school spent three years at Netheravon during this important phase of RAF expansion. When the school moved to Little Rissington in August 1938, its place was taken by No.1 FTS, equipped with Harts. The superlative Harvard trainer began to arrive in May 1939 and the school had a full establishment of thirty-two by September, as Netheravon entered its second war.

Training remained the rationale for Netheravon throughout the war but, from 1942, with the departure of the FTS, the station took on a major involvement with the still-evolving airborne-forces role. The FTS was a very busy unit and made use of a number of RLGs, including Castle Combe, High Post and Shrewton. No.1 FTS disbanded on 7 March 1942 and the airfield was transferred to Army Co-operation Command later that month, for use by No.38 Wing's 296 and 297 Squadrons. The latter had actually been here – as the Parachute Exercise Squadron – since the previous December. The two squadrons were central in the development of parachute and glider operations for airborne forces and worked closely with 6th Airborne Division, whose HQ was less than two miles away. The Glider Pilot Exercise Unit (GPEU) formed in August out of 296 Squadron to provide refresher flying for qualified Glider Pilot Regiment (GPR) personnel; as the unit list shows, a number of specialist flights and units were based at Netheravon in the latter half of the war and most of these were involved with airborne ops, and especially gliders. The old Whitley tugs were replaced in 295 Squadron by the far better Halifax from February

1943 and, as the station was becoming home to a large number of gliders, No.235 Maintenance Unit formed in January as a Mobile Repair and Salvage Unit, and No.1 Heavy Glider Maintenance Unit arrived from Hurn. The hectic pace of training and exercises continued and, in October, the Wing became No.38 (Airborne Forces) Group, retaining its HQ at Netheravon: in a further recognition of the growing importance of the airborne role, the Airborne Forces Tactical Development Unit (AFTDU) had formed on 1 December 1943, moving to Netheravon in January and becoming the Air Transport Tactical Development Unit (ATTDU).

The scale of exercises increased in early 1944; for example Exercise *Dingo* on the night of 6/7 May, which saw aircraft of No.38 Group release ninety Horsa gliders to 'assault' Netheravon. Although not a total success it was repeated two nights later with no lights on the landing zone. An even larger daylight event, Exercise *Exeter*, was staged on 19 May with 100 Horsa gliders, plus a number of Hamilcars, and 300 paratroops dropping onto Netheravon's north airfield. The exercise was witnessed by a large number of VIPs and it was, generally, a success.

The station remained in the airborne forces training and development role to the end of the war, the School of Air Transport having formed here on 4 November 1944 (eventually disbanding in March 1946). The ATTDU was renamed as the Transport Command Development Unit (TCDU) in August 1945 and departed to Harwell the following month. In the immediate post-war period, a number of Dakota squadrons spent short periods here, but the once hectic and crucial role of Netheravon had passed and the airfield went into decline.

Aerial shot dated
3 November 1927.
(via Rod Priddle)

Battle Trainer of No.1 SFTS, 1940.

The RAF left Netheravon in July 1963 and, after some twenty years as a transit camp for the ever-busy Salisbury Plain training ranges, aviation returned when the Army Air Corps took over part of the airfield. The whole site is now Airfield Camp Netheravon and the main flying unit is No.7 Regiment AAC, with the HQ and two squadrons – 658 and 666 – based here.

The English Heritage list of key airfields records Netheravon as:

Begun in 1912, Netheravon is the most complete of the sites that relate to the crucial formative phase in the development of military aviation in Europe, prior to the First World War. The domestic site retains a remarkably well-preserved group of single-storey barracks and mess buildings dating from 1913–14. The grass airfield remains intact.

DECOY SITE

Netheravon	SU1448

UNITS

HQ units at Netheravon

No.4 Wing	29 Nov 1914–23 Aug 1916; 10 Jan 1917–15 May 1919
No.38 Wing	19 Jan 1942–11 Oct 1943
No.38 (Airborne Forces) Gp	11 Oct 1943–12 Oct 1944
No.46 Gp Advanced HQ	Feb 1944–Jul 1945

Pre-1919

1 Sqn	13 Nov 1914–7 Mar 1915	various
2 Sqn	30 Jun 1914–5 Aug 1914	various
3 Sqn	16 Jun 1913–12 Aug 1914	various
4 Sqn	14 Jun 1913–13 Aug 1914	various
5 Sqn	28 May 1914–6 Jul 1914	various
6 Sqn	21 Sep 1914–4 Oct 1914	various
7 Sqn	Sep 1914–8 Apr 1915	various
10 Sqn	7 Apr 1915–27 Jul 1915	BE2c
11 Sqn	14 Feb 1915–25 Jul 1915	various
12 Sqn	14 Feb 1915–6 Sep 1915	Avro 504, BE2c
19 Sqn	31 Jan 1916–29 Mar 1916	various
20 Sqn	1 Sep 1915–15 Dec 1915	various
21 Sqn	23 Jul 1915–23 Jan 1916	RE7
26 Sqn	8 Oct 1915–23 Dec 1915	no aircraft
32 Sqn	12 Jan 1916–28 May 1916	HF F.20, FB.5
35 Sqn	3 Mar 1919–26 Jun 1919	cadre only
42 Sqn	26 Feb 1916–8 Aug 1916	Be2d, BE2e
42 Sqn	18 Feb 1919–26 Jun 1919	cadre only
43 Sqn	30 Aug 1916–9 Dec 1916	Scout
48 Sqn	15 Apr 1916–8 Mar 1917	Bristol F2a

52Sqn	18 Feb 1919–28 Jun 1919	cadre only
62Sqn	28 Jul 1916–8 Aug 1916	various
66Sqn	2–27 Jul 1916	BE2 series
72Sqn	8 Jul 1917–1 Nov 1917	Avro 505, Pup
97Sqn	31 Mar 1918–3 Aug 1918	HP 0/400
115Sqn	15 Apr 1918–17 Jul 1918	various, HP 0/400
118Sqn	15 Apr 1918–7 Aug 1918	various, HP 0/400
207Sqn	22 Apr 1918–13 May 1918	HP 0/400
208Sqn	9 Sep 1919–7 Nov 1919	Snipe
215Sqn	23 Apr 1918–13 May 1919	HP 0/400
7 TS	28 Jul 1915–30 Apr 1918	various
8 TS	28 Jul 1915–1 Apr 1918	various
24 TS	25 May 1916–30 Mar 1918	various
92 TS	15 Mar 1917–?	various
74 TS	21 Oct 1917–1 Dec 1917	various
59 TS	20 Nov 1917–6 Dec 1917	various
71 TS	28 Nov 1917–10 Dec 1917; Feb 1918–Apr 1918	various
8 TDS	1 Apr 1918–15 May 1919	various
12 TDS	1 Apr 1918–15 May 1919	various
8 TS	15 May 1919–29 Jul 1919	various

1919–1939

1 FTS	23 Dec 1919–1 Feb 1931	Avro 504, etc
11Sqn	31 May 1924–29 Dec 1928	Fawn, Horsley, Wapiti
13Sqn	23 Sep 1929–3 May 1935	Atlas, Audax
33Sqn	1 Mar 1929–14 Sep 1929	Horsley
57Sqn	20 Oct 1931–5 Sep 1932	Hart
99Sqn	1 Apr 1924–31 May 1924	Vimy
142Sqn	1 Jun 1934–3 Jan 1935	Hart
800Sqn FAA	3 Apr 1933–14 May 1934+	Nimrod, Osprey
801Sqn FAA	3 Apr 1933–1 Jun 1934+	Flycatcher, Nimrod, Osprey
802Sqn FAA	24 Jul 1934–21 Aug 1935+	Nimrod, Osprey
803Sqn FAA	3–26 Apr 1933	Osprey
822Sqn FAA	3 Apr 1933–5 Apr 1934+	Fairey IIIf
6 FTS	1 Apr 1935–26 Aug 1938	Hart, Tutor
1 FTS	26 Aug 1938–7 Mar 1942	Hart, Harvard, Battle

1939–1945

239Sqn	26–30 Sep 1941	Lysander, Tomahawk
295Sqn	3 Aug 1942–1 May 1943	Whitley, Halifax
296Sqn	1 Feb 1942–25 Jul 1942	Hector, Hart, Whitley
297Sqn	22 Jan 1942–5 Jun 1942	Whitley
1 FTS	?–7 Mar 1942	Harvard, Battle
GEU/GES	1 Feb 1942–?	Hector, Hotspur
GPEU	12 Aug 1942–Nov 1943+	Tiger Moth, Hector, Hotspur
1 HGMU	6 May 1943–25 Mar 1944	Horsa
ATTDU	14 Jan 1944–31 Aug 1945	various
1 HGSU	25 Mar 1944–31 Dec 1946	
1677Flt	1 Mar 1944–12 Oct 1944	Oxford
107 OTU det	Sep 1944	Dakota
TCDU	31 Aug 1945–20 Sep 1945	various

Post-1945

18Sqn	8–11 Dec 1947	
27Sqn	10 Jun 1950–10 Nov 1950	Dakota
53Sqn	1 Dec 1946–11 Dec 1947	Dakota
187Sqn	11 Oct 1946–1 Dec 1946	Dakota
VISTREFlt	16 Nov 1947–18 Nov 1950	Anson, Auster, Dakota
7 Regt AAC	1996–current	

MEMORIAL

There is no memorial as such – an amazing lack of consideration for this historic and important airfield – but the original RFC officers' mess still stands.

NEW ZEALAND FARM

UTM/Grid: OS Map 184 – ST974508
Lat/Long: N51°15 W002°03

County: Wiltshire

Nearest Town: Devizes 8 miles to north-east

Aerial shot dated May 1944. (via Rod Priddle)

HISTORY

New Zealand Farm died in the creation of the relief landing ground to which it gave its name in late-1940, although no doubt the ground personnel sent here would have preferred the barn, which they had to use for accommodation, to have been knocked down and the farmhouse left. The site was a replacement for a failed RLG at Market Lavington Hill and was needed for use by training units at nearby Upavon. The RLG came into use in early October and was used for both day and night training, although it gradually focused on the latter and was provided with gooseneck-flare paths – to be laid-out and maintained by the ground personnel sent out

from the parent station. The Oxfords and Masters made frequent use of the airfield, a normal routine for night flying being for aircraft to fly over from Upavon at last light and then operate from New Zealand Farm overnight before landing back at Upavon.

New Zealand Farm was provided with two grass strips, one east/west and one north/south, and it also had three Blister hangars, plus a hutted camp in a small wood adjacent to the landing area; there was even a small wooden watch-tower as flying control. Night flying was always a dangerous activity and a number of Masters and Oxfords crashed on or close to the airfield, all too often with fatal consequences.

The dim goosenecks were bright enough on 14 April 1941 to attract a prowling German bomber; fortunately nine of the ten bombs fell in an adjacent field and the one that landed on the airfield did no damage. When CFS disbanded in April 1942 it was, in part, used to form No.7 Flying Instructors School and this unit continued to operate at New Zealand Farm to late-1943. In August 1943, the school re-equipped with Magisters, but retained a number of Oxfords. New Zealand Farm looked set to continue its training role when a beam system was installed, as was a 'Darky' beacon but, in autumn 1943, the War Office declared its intent to expand the army training ranges and the RAF was given notice to quit – as were the residents of Imber village (the village is still there and is still used for urban battle training). New Zealand Farm closed on 17 December 1943.

Despite the closure, aircraft were back in March 1944, when the airfield was used by the L-4 Cubs of the 153rd Liaison Squadron, part of IXth Tactical Air Command. The squadron acted as a comms unit for the US First Army, stationed in the area and with HQ at Erlestoke Manor (two miles from the airfield). Stinson L-5s arrived the same month and the list of tasks performed by the squadron increased as D-Day approached. Crashes, and some fatalities, were once more part of the pattern at New Zealand Farm. The squadron departed to France in June, but its place was taken by the 125th Liaison Squadron, although this unit spent only a few weeks here before it, too, went to France.

In the post-war years the airfield was used as an out-station by the AAAE at Boscombe Down, as an observation point for weapon trials. This later involved turning the site into an air-to-ground range, with the addition of targets such as old vehicles and aircraft. The grass runways were maintained and, over the years, have been used by a variety of aircraft during exercise, involving RAF transport types such as Beverley, Andover and Hercules, and various Army Air Corps fixed-wing and rotary operations. New Zealand Farm is still an army base and is still used from time to time during exercises in the extensive range areas around Imber.

UNITS

1939–1945

CFS	Oct 1940–Apr 1942	Oxford, Master
7 FIS	Apr 1942–Dec 1943	Oxford, Master, Magister

USAAF units

153rd LS	13 Mar 1944–Jun 1944	L-4, L-5
125th LS	Jun 1944–Aug 1944	L-5

NORTHLEACH

County: Gloucestershire

UTM/Grid: OS Map 163 – SP110155
Lat/Long: N51°50 W001°50
Nearest Town: Cirencester 10 miles to south-west

AIRFIELD DATA DEC 1944

Command:	Flying Training Command	Runway surface:	Grass
Function:	Satellite Glider Training School	Hangars:	Blister (65ft) × 2
Runways:	E/W 1,050yd	Dispersals:	Nil
	N/S 750yd	Personnel:	Officers – 14
			Other Ranks – 89

HISTORY

Northleach was another of the RLGs that were so desperately needed by the training units and it was in this capacity that it entered service in late-summer 1941, the user unit being No.10 Elementary Flying Training School at Stoke Orchard. The airfield site was a large rectangular grass area, formed by removing hedge boundaries in order to provide practical take-off and landing runs in all directions, with eventually four equal-length grass runways being marked on the plan, although these do not appear clear on the aerial photograph and may not actually have been marked strips on the ground. Aircraft were dispersed along the hedgerow on the east side of the airfield and there were few facilities, other than a small hutted camp on the north-east corner.

The EFTS gave-up use of Northleach in November 1942 and was replaced by a detachment of No.3 Glider Training School, which had formed out of 10 EFTS at Stoke Orchard. The school primarily operated Masters as tugs and Hotspur training gliders and it was these combinations that now used the RLG. This continued to January 1945 but, with the departure of the GTS, there was no further need of Northleach and it was immediately abandoned.

UNITS

1939–1945

10 EFTS	Sep 1941–Nov 1942	Tiger Moth
3 GTS det	2 Nov 1942–15 Jan 1945	various

MEMORIAL

Memorials in church?

NORTH STOKE

County: Gloucestershire

UTM/Grid: OS Map 172 – ST717687
Lat/Long: N51°25 W002°26
Nearest Town: Bath 4 miles to south-east

HISTORY

During World War One the Royal Flying Corps had made use of the 'instant airfields' available by taking over horse-racing tracks; this option was not so usable in World War Two, but one of the exceptions was the Landsdown course at Bath. No.3 Flying Instructors School at Castle Combe was looking for an RLG in 1943 and, as suitable sites were hard to find in this region, someone suggested the Bath race-course. By summer 1943, this had been adopted as North Stoke and, other than the removal of the track's railings, it was ready to use, as the grandstands and other buildings provided adequate accommodation for an RLG.

Within weeks the unit's Oxfords were a regular sight and, whilst it was not an ideal airfield, it did permit pilots to practise circuits and landings. The FIS continued to use North Stoke until they were absorbed into No.7 FIS on 18 July 1945. The latter unit was parented at Lulsgate Bottom, Bristol and may have continued to use North Stoke for a few more weeks but, with the war over, the race-goers were keen to have their track back!

UNITS

1939–1945

3 FIS	late-1943–Jul 1945	Oxford
7 FIS	Jul 1945–Aug 1945	

OATLANDS HILL

County: Wiltshire

UTM/Grid: OS Map 184 – SU095408
Lat/Long: N51°09 W001°52
Nearest Town: Salisbury 7 miles to south

HISTORY

Oatlands Hill saw limited use during World War Two as a satellite for army co-operation units in the Salisbury Plain area. The site had been acquired in late-1940 for development into a satellite for Old Sarum (5 miles to the south-east) and was situated on the south side of the A303, not far from Stonehenge. The airfield was eventually given three grass runways, the longest being 1,600 yards, although these do not show as laid-out strips on

AIRFIELD DATA DEC 1944

Command:	Fighter Command	Runway surface:	Grass
Function:	Satellite	Hangars:	Blister × 4
Runways:	NE/SW 1,600yd	Dispersals:	Nil
	N/S 1,400yd	Personnel:	Officers – 5
	E/W 1,200yd		Other Ranks – 190

the air photos, with four Blister hangars, two of which were positioned on the hedge-line on the south side of the airfield, as were a number of other buildings. The first army co-operation unit to use Oatlands Hill was 239 Squadron, whose Tomahawks spent a few weeks here in summer 1941. More significant was the arrival, in September 1941, of elements of the newly formed (at Old Sarum) No.41 Operational Training Unit; initial training of AC pilots involved Lysanders and Tomahawks and the airfield was soon a hive of activity.

The Lysanders were phased out in March 1942 and, under a re-organization of the OTU, 'B Flight' (Tomahawks) and 'C Flight' (Mustangs) were based at Oatlands Hill, the Mustangs arriving from April. Both Flights departed in mid-November to Hawarden and the airfield had a quiet period until AOP Austers began to arrive.

The Austers of 658 Squadron spent three weeks here in August 1943, but it was February 1944 before Oatlands Hill had a major occupant. The Austers of No.43 OTU moved up from Old Sarum on 17 February and AOP courses started immediately. The unit had a number of Tiger Moths and Lysanders on strength, but its main type was the Auster, in various marks, and it had an establishment of 30+6 of these aircraft.

At the end of May a small American detachment arrived, the 47th Liaison Squadron being based here to carry out a comms role, including priority mail, for HQ Southern Base Section. The unit had six L-5s and they were kept very busy; priority mail was made somewhat faster when they acquired a P-47 – the 'hottest ship' to operate from Oatlands Hill. The Americans left in late-July and in August the OTU moved to Andover.

Oatlands Hill was put into Care and Maintenance, but was still used from time to time by AOP units; for example, Austers re-appeared in March 1945 when 665 spent a few weeks here before deploying to Holland. On 10 July 1945, the airfield was transferred to No.11 Group, but there was no intent to use the site and the following May it was closed. Very little trace survives of the airfield, although the farmer uses the sole remaining Blister hangar as a hay store.

UNITS

1939–1945

239 Sqn	summer 1941	Tomahawk
658 Sqn	6–29 Aug 1943	Auster
665 Sqn	17 Mar 1945–21 Apr 1945	Auster
41 OTU	Sep 1941–15 Nov 1942	Tomahawk, Lysander, Mustang
43 OTU	17 Feb 1944–10 Aug 1944	Auster

USAAF units

47th LS	30 May 1944–late July 1944	L-5, P-47

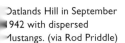

Oatlands Hill in September 1942 with dispersed Mustangs. (via Rod Priddle)

OKEHAMPTON
(Folly Gate)

County: Devon

UTM/Grid: OS Map 191 – SX575970
Lat/Long: N50°45 W004°01
Nearest Town: Okehampton 2 miles to south

HISTORY

The centre of the airfield was a trig point with a spot height of 784ft and this hill top at Five Oaks was certainly an unusual place to build an airfield; the only rationale for its existence was the proximity of the major army training ranges on Dartmoor (a few miles to the south) and the concentration of army camps near Okehampton. A landing ground was needed in the vicinity for army co-operation aircraft and the options were limited. The site appears to have been brought into use in 1928 and, at the time, was usually referred to as Folly Gate, a small group of buildings half a mile to the north of the airfield.

Summer detachments by AC squadrons, including 13 and 16 Squadrons, took place from 1928 and continued to the outbreak of the war, with the Bristol Fighter, Atlas, Audax and Lysander taking their turn on the field, with the squadron personnel in tents. With the squadrons off to war, the airfield was quiet for a few months but, with the fall of France, the AC units returned to the UK and Okehampton was back

AIRFIELD DATA DEC 1944

Command:	Maintenance Command	Runway surface:	Grass
Function:	Storage Unit	Hangars:	Nil
Runways:	NE/SW 840yd	Dispersals:	Nil
	N/S 840yd	Personnel:	Officers – (2 WAAF)
	SE/NW 840yd		Other Ranks – 154 (66 WAAF)
	E/W 830yd		

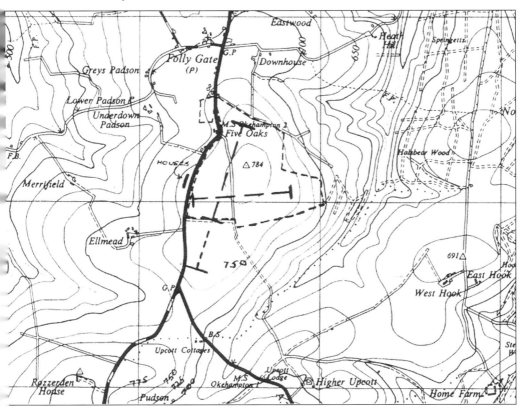

n use when 16 Squadron arrived in early August 1940 with its Lysanders. The squadron was at Okehampton as a complete unit or as a detachment until early 1942, although this was not a continuous presence, as the airfield was still not suitable for winter operations. After an initial invasion panic, during which the Lysanders flew coastal patrols and were ready to bomb-up and take-on the enemy, the routine settled into one of training with the army units in the ranges.

The airfield also served as No.73 Maintenance Unit from December 1942 to September 1945; this was officially a Static Equipment Park, one of those seemingly meaningless military phrases that, in RAF terms, meant it was not aircraft or MT – in other words it didn't move! The MU was the major occupant during this period, although there was occasional use by AC aircraft up to the early 1950s, Austers having become the more usual type since late-1943.

There is no significant trace of this airfield and if you mention Okehampton airfield the usual reaction is a blank stare or a suggestion that it may be on the moor somewhere.

UNITS

1939–1945

16Sqn	3 Aug 1940–early 1942+	Lysander
225Sqn det	1940–1941	Lysander

OLD SARUM (Ford Farm)

County: Wiltshire

UTM/Grid: OS Map 184 – SU153335
Lat/Long: N51°05.48 W001°46.58
Nearest Town: Salisbury 2 miles to south

Old Sarum is still a very active airfield; July 2001.

HISTORY

Old Sarum, on the outskirts of Salisbury and in the centre of one of the most historic regions of England, is a delightful airfield and, despite recent threats to its continued activity, is a vibrant general aviation airfield – and well worth a visit to sit at a picnic table in front of the clubhouse with an excellent lunch from the restaurant. The view over the grass airfield is now one of Cessnas, Jodels and the like, but it is still easy to imagine the days when this was *the* centre of army co-operation flying.

The field at Ford Farm, the original name for the airfield, was taken over by an advanced party of 99 Squadron in July 1917, when it was literally a field in which they erected their tents. The 182-acre site was rapidly developed, with the erection of a technical site on the north side – seven aeroplane sheds of 170 × 80ft, plus various other huts – and an adjacent domestic/admin site complete with messes and stores buildings. A number of the aeroplane repair sheds, with their impressive truss roofing, are still in use as

aircraft hangars. RFC Station Ford Farm opened in August with construction still underway and 98 and 99 Squadrons flew in from Harlaxton and Yatesbury respectively. They were joined a few days later by 103 Squadron from Beaulieu and Ford Farm was a very busy station, with various DH types (mainly DH4, DH6 and DH9) along with FK.8s undertaking intensive training. Three new squadrons (124, 125 and 126) formed at Old Sarum on 1 February 1918, all intended to equip with the DH9 and move to the Western Front as bombers; initially, they used whatever aircraft were available and, a month later, they moved to Fowlmere. By May 1918 the other squadrons had also left and the station had taken on a new role.

No.11 Training Depot Station formed here on 1 April 1918, the date coinciding with a name change to Old Sarum. The TDS operated from here until November 1918, when it moved to Boscombe Down. In the immediate post-war period three squadrons

This air photo is probably late 1943-early 1944; it was included in the 1944 RAF airfield survey.

appeared here, two of them as cadres, mainly with RE8s, but by late-1919 all had been disbanded.

However, the station was retained throughout the inter-war period, as it became home to the newly formed (at Stonehenge) School of Army Co-operation from January 1921. Throughout this period, Old Sarum underwent virtually no development. The school used Avro 504s and Bristol Fighters and the course concentrated on teaching qualified pilots the rudiments of AC flying, with reconnaissance, including photography (somewhere there must be a fantastic collection of photographs taken by pupils) and artillery co-operation being key subjects. The Co-operation Squadron of the school was re-designated as 16 Squadron on 1 April 1924 and this unit remained at Old Sarum until February 1940, operating, in turn, the Bristol Fighter, Atlas, Audax and Lysander. In addition to working with army units and assisting the school, the squadron also undertook various trials to develop the AC role, including trials with the autogyro.

Old Sarum received a number of visiting units for short stays, some on a regular basis, such as the summer camps by the Avro 504s of the Cambridge University Air Squadron. A Special Duties Flight was formed here in 1926, to work with the Experimental Gas School at Porton Down, and undertook air-delivery trials, moving these to Netheravon in September 1928. The varied work of the Old Sarum units continued into the 1930s, with new aircraft and ever-developing AC tactics; the school notionally lost the use of 16 Squadron in 1934, but the relationship appears to have continued to the outbreak of the war. As the unit list shows, the station's strength was increased to two squadrons with the arrival, in May 1935, of 13 Squadron, although they were replaced two years later by 107 Squadron and then 59 Squadron. Another aircraft under test by 16 Squadron was the Lysander, the first one of which was received in June 1936, but, despite the squadron's unfavourable report, the 'Lizzie' became the standard AC type for some years! In May 1938, the squadron was no doubt delighted to be issued with Lysander Is.

An Army Co-operation Pool (ACP) was formed on 25 September 1939 to provide a ready pool of trained and current crews for the operational squadrons – as quick replacements for losses. The main role of Old Sarum was still that of training and, in October (but with effect from December), the main unit became No.1 School of Army Co-operation; whilst still flying many of the delightful old types, such as the Audax and Hector, it also received Blenheims for training night-photography, as well as Lysanders. Old Sarum maintained its tradition of having minimal development and throughout World War Two, other than the laying of some Sommerfeld Track dispersal areas and the provision of pill-boxes, the old World War One infrastructure was simply adapted.

The departure of 16 Squadron in February 1940, after its long association with Old Sarum, was balanced later the same month by the arrival of 110 Squadron RCAF. The 'City of Toronto' Squadron was the first Canadian squadron to arrive in the UK and spent a few months at Old Sarum converting to the Lysander II; it had been joined in May by 112 Squadron RCAF, but both departed in June.

The airfield had Luftwaffe activity overhead twice in 1940 and on both occasions the enemy aircraft was shot down, although not at the airfield. A German aircraft shot down a Netheravon Hart in the Old Sarum circuit on 21 July, but was subsequently brought down by Hurricanes of 238 Squadron; on 21 October a Ju88 passed overhead – being pursued and then shot down by Spitfires of 609 Squadron. It was not until the night of 11/12 May 1941 that the airfield itself was attacked, a lone bomber causing damage to a hangar and other buildings.

59 Squadron operated Hectors at Old Sarum from June 1947.

Atlas J9531 over the Old Sarum castle site, close to the airfield. (via Rod Priddle)

A very neat and tidy airfield, dominated by the aeroplane sheds; probably 1920s. (via Rod Priddle)

AIRFIELD DATA DEC 1944

Command:	Fighter Command	Runway surface:	Grass
Function:	Operational Training Unit, Parent	Hangars:	GS Type (164 × 170ft) × 3,
Runways:	NE/SW 1,200yd		Blister × 2, 80 × 170ft × one
		Dispersals:	18 × Sommerfeld Track
		Personnel:	Officers – 179 (7 WAAF)
			Other Ranks – 1,476 (261 WAAF)

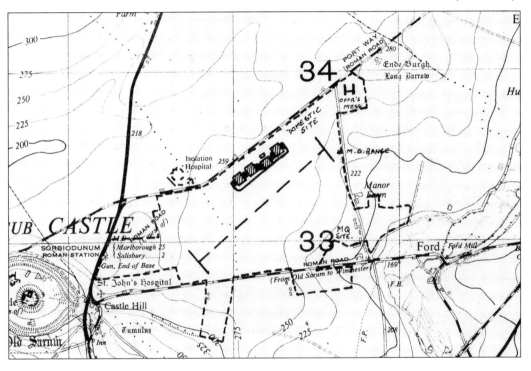

In another change of ownership the school passed to No.70 Group on 1 December 1940, but the role remained the same. A year later, No.41 Operational Training Unit formed here to train Tomahawk pilots, although it actually operated with a slightly broader remit of tactical training for Tomahawk and Lysander pilots. The Lysander role was soon dropped and the Tomahawk became the focus of attention, with Oatlands Hill being used as an RLG; by April 1942 it had a Tomahawk and a Mustang Flight at Oatlands Hill, although the former were gradually replaced by Hurricanes. The only Fleet Air Arm unit to have spent any appreciable period of time at Old Sarum was 879 Squadron, who were here from November 1942 to March 1943 for army co-operation training using Fulmars. Although they were a Fleet Fighter unit they were formed to work on combined operations, this work-up continuing when they

Spitfires of 140 Squadron at Old Sarum in November 1941.

moved to Scotland in March. When No.41 OTU left in November 1942, its place was taken by No.43 OTU and the role was subtly changed to that of Air Observation Post (AOP), for which the Auster was the main aircraft. The memorial at Old Sarum commemorates this period of training and the operational

Chipmunks position for a fly-by, date uncertain. (via Rod Priddle)

squadrons that formed here.

The unit list shows the dates that these 600-series squadrons were at Old Sarum. The OTU itself finally left in February 1944, moving to Oatlands Hill. Their place in the hangars was taken by hundreds of army vehicles and, for a few weeks, the main activity was preparing these vehicles for D-Day, although why Old Sarum was chosen – other than it being in 'army territory' – is a mystery.

Army co-operation training was still taking place and, after various name changes, the based unit had, by November 1944, become the School of Air Support, with RAF, army and navy participation. It operated two Wings – Offensive and Transport – and had a small but diverse fleet of aircraft. This unit continued into the post-war period, becoming the School of Land/Air Warfare in May 1947. This latter continued to operate from Old Sarum to 1963, when it became part of the Joint Warfare Establishment (JWE). There was, at times, a bewildering array of alphabet-spaghetti titles in the latter year of Old Sarum, with the likes of the AATTDC, AATDU, HDU and JHDU, to list the main ones. The Helicopter Development (HDU) had formed in June 1961 as part of the JWE and subsequently became a Joint unit, hence JHDU, with the navy.

Old Sarum eventually closed as a military airfield in 1979 but, two years later, and very much in keeping with the type of flying for which Old Sarum had made its name, a private venture took-over two of the hangars for design and build of the Edgley Optica 'spotter' aircraft. For a variety of reasons this was not a commercial success.

Old Sarum (EGLS) is still a very active flying field and is run by the Old Sarum Flying Club; it is a friendly location for those who arrive by air or by road and well worth a visit. The airfield operates a single grass strip (06/24) of 781m and the restaurant is excellent. In addition to the club there is a good array of private aircraft and there is every chance of seeing a Tiger Moth or Auster, to add a true historic perspective to the airfield. Over the years many of the wartime buildings have vanished, the guardroom being a recent victim, as the overall airfield site is not owned by the club. Indeed, there have been various threats of closure, as Salisbury continues to expand and the airfield is eyed-up by developers. Further details on the club can be found on www.oldsarumflyingclub.co.uk.

The English Heritage list of key airfields records Old Sarum as:

> 'The best-preserved flying field of the First World War period, bounded by one of the most complete suites of technical and hangar buildings of the period.'

DECOY SITE

| Q | Pitton | SU199319 |

UNITS

HQ units at Old Sarum
No.39 (R) Wing   20–25 Jun 1944

Pre-1919

7 Sqn	21 Sep 1919–9 Oct 1919	RE8
34 Sqn	3 May 1919–25 Oct 1919	cadre only
53 Sqn	15 Mar 1919–25 Oct 1919	cadre only
98 Sqn	30 Aug 1917–1 Mar 1918	various
99 Sqn	30 Aug 1917–25 Apr 1918	various
103 Sqn	8 Sep 1917–12 May 1918	DH9
124 Sqn	1 Feb 1918–1 Mar 1918	various
125 Sqn	1 Feb 1918–1 Mar 1918	various

| 126 Sqn | I Feb 1918–I Mar 1918 | various |
| II TDS | I Apr 1918–Nov 1918 | various |

1919–1939

13 Sqn	3 May 1935–16 Feb 1937	Audax
16 Sqn	I Apr 1924–17 Feb 1940	various
59 Sqn	28 Jun 1937–11 May 1939	Hector, Blenheim
107 Sqn	16 Feb 1937–15 Jun 1937	Hind
810 Sqn FAA	17 Sep 1938–27 Oct 1938	Swordfish
SoAC	Jan 1921–20 Sep 1941; Jun 1943–5 Nov 1944	
SDF	1926–12 Sep 1928	various

1939–1945

16 Sqn	17 Feb 1940	Lysander
98 Sqn det	spring 1940	Battle
225 Sqn	9 Jun 1940–1 Jul 1940	Lysander
651 Sqn	I Aug 1941–31 Jul 1942	Taylorcraft, Auster
652 Sqn	I May 1942–15 Jun 1942	Tiger Moth
653 Sqn	20 Jun 1942–8 Jul 1942	Tiger Moth
654 Sqn	15 Jul 1942–15 Sep 1942	Tiger Moth
658 Sqn	30 Nov 1942–22 Mar 1943+	Auster
660 Sqn	31 Jul 1943–21 Sep 1943	Auster
661 Sqn	31 Aug 1943–27 Nov 1943	Auster
662 Sqn	30 Sep 1943–4 Feb 1944	Auster
810 Sqn FAA	3–30 Jul 1940	Swordfish
879 Sqn FAA	18 Nov 1942–22 Mar 1943	Fulmar
SoAC	?–20 Sep 1941; Jun 1943–5 Nov 1944	various
ACP	25 Sep 1939–22 Oct 1940	various
DFlt	20 May 1940–3 Jun 1940	various
1471 Flt	I Apr 1942–10 Oct 1942	Tomahawk
8 AACU	6 Oct 1940–Mar 1943+	various
41 OTU	20 Sep 1941–15 Nov 1942	Lysander, Tomahawk, Mustang
43 OTU	19 Nov 1942–17 Feb 1944	Taylorcraft, Auster
84 Gp CF	20 Aug 1944–1 Dec 1944	Various
SAS	Nov 1944–1 May 1947	various
110 Sqn RCAF	25 Feb 1940–9 Jun 1940	Lysander
112 Sqn RCAF	29 May 1940–14 Jun 1940	Lysander

Post-1945

SAS	?–1 May 1947	various
SOL/AW	I May 1947–31 Mar 1963	various
HDU	I Jun 1961–1 Feb 1965	Sycamore, Whirlwind
JHDU	Feb 1965–Jan 1968	none on charge?
622 VGS	I Jul 1963–late-1978	various

MEMORIAL

Between two of the hangars is a stone cairn sur-

mounted by a bust of a pilot in flying jacket, plus bronze plaque with inscription:

This memorial is dedicated to the following AOP squadrons that were formed at Old Sarum during the Second World War and whose gallantry and tenacity were to play a vital role in the final victory. They flew light unarmed aircraft over enemy lines and many paid the ultimate price.
D Flight 1940-1941 – The Battle of France
651 AOP Squadron 1941 – North Africa, Sicily, Italy, Austria
652 AOP Squadron 1942 – Normandy, Belgium
653 AOP Squadron 1942 – Normandy, Belgium, Holland, Germany
654 AOP Squadron 1942 – North Africa, Sicily, Italy
655 AOP Squadron 1942 – North Africa, Italy
658 AOP Squadron 1943 – Normandy, Belgium, Holland, Germany
660 AOP Squadron 1943 – Normandy, Belgium, Germany
661 AOP Squadron 1943 – Normandy, Belgium, Holland, Germany
662 AOP Squadron 1943 – Normandy, Belgium, Holland, Germany
No.43 Operational Training Unit RAF. Their sacrifice was not in vain. This plaque was donated by members of the AOP Veterans Association and unveiled on 6th June 1993 by General Sir Martin Farndale KCB, The Master Gunner.

OVERLEY (No.14 SLG)

County: Gloucestershire

UTM/Grid: OS Map 163 – SO965046
Lat/Long: N51°44 W002°01
Nearest Town: Cirencester 4 miles to south-east

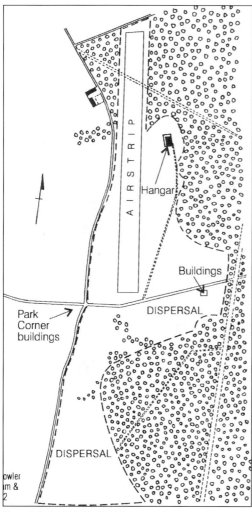

Plan of No.14 SLG (Airfield Research Group)

HISTORY

No.14 Satellite Landing Ground (SLG) opened in May 1941 at Overley Farm (or Overley Wood as it was sometime known) to the south-east of Cirencester and was allocated to No.20 Maintenance Unit at Aston Down. The site had been chosen in late-1940/early 1941 as it fulfilled the basic requirement of being within a reasonable distance of its parent airfield and it was suitable for the camouflaged dispersal of large numbers of aircraft. The other normal requirement was for a reasonable open area of well-drained grass for take-off and landing, but Overley was less suitable in this respect, as the runway ran through one corner of the woods. A single Robin hangar was provided, but very few other buildings, the idea being that aircraft would be taxied to the edge of the woodland and parked in the open.

The first aircraft arrived soon after the SLG opened and, over the next few years, it handled a variety of types, including four-engined bombers, such as the Stirling from late-1942, which necessitated an extension to the runway.

The site was also used as an RLG by No.3 SFTS from South Cerney on an opportunity basis in late-1942, although it was not one of that unit's official RLGs. No.14 MU remained the prime user throughout the war but No.10 MU (Hullavington) also stored aircraft here from April 1944. The records for Overley are poor and it is not clear just how busy the site was during the war; unlike other SLGs, it does not appear to have been inundated with aircraft at the end of the war.

The site was relinquished in October 1945 and, other than the old guard bungalow, a fairly standard design for SLG use, there is no real trace of the site, although pieces of steel-mesh track, once used for dispersals, can still be found.

OVERTON HEATH

County: Wiltshire

UTM/Grid: OS map 173 – SU180657
Lat/Long: N51°23 W001°44.4
Nearest Town: Marlborough 2 miles to north-east

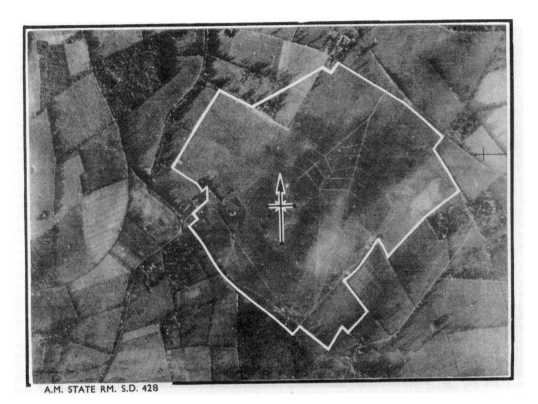

A.M. STATE RM. S.D. 428

HISTORY

Approval had been given in July 1939 for acquisition of land at Overton Heath for the construction of a RLG for Upavon. The actual site was on Clench Common and, whilst at first sight it appeared a good location, it was to prove very troublesome due to waterlogging. The original plan for opening in late-1940, from which time it was allocated to the Central Flying School at Upavon, had to be postponed, as the airfield was unusable that winter. Further drainage work led to an opening in April 1941, but the water-logging problem was to plague the site for its entire career.

Although allocated to CFS, it is uncertain how much use was made of the airfield, although in fine weather it was a perfectly adequate RLG. The school's Masters, Magisters and Oxfords would no doubt have made some use of the airfield but by the end of the year – and the approach of winter – this had pretty much come to an end.

The decision to develop Overton brought the con-struction teams back in early 1942, to lay two Sommerfeld Track runways; however, the intersec-tion of the runways was on a particularly wet spot and this had to be consolidated with stone ballast before the track could be laid – and this area was then given a tarmac covering to the track. Development also included buildings and Overton Heath was eventu-ally provided with seven Blister hangars and various buildings in an admin/domestic site on the south side of the airfield.

With the new improved runways, the airfield was allocated to No.7 Flying Instructors School, which had been created out of the CFS. The school appears to have used Overton Heath for about a year and, by spring 1943, it is no longer listed as an RLG and does not seem to have been allocated to anyone, although it may have been used by the Oxfords of No.1537 Beam Approach Training Flight. Other aircraft

Airfield Data Dec 1944

Command:	Flying Training Command	Runway surface:	Sommerfeld Track
Function:	Flying Instructor School RLG	Hangars:	4 × Blister (65ft),
Runways:	110 deg 1,700yd		2 × Blister (45ft),
	060 deg 1,500yd		one × Blister (69ft)
	270 deg 2,000 × 50yd	Dispersals:	Nil
		Personnel:	Officers – 2
			Other Ranks – 83

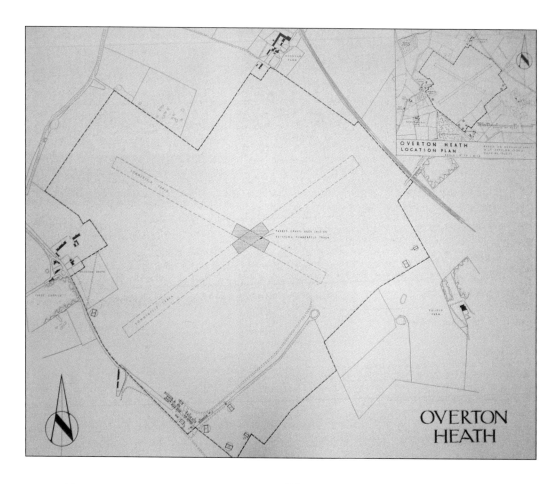

OVERTON HEATH

appeared from time to time, with, for example, a B-17 force-landing here on 1 January 1944.

With the end of the war, Overton was held in Care and Maintenance to 1948, following which it was retained by the Crown (as it still is) and leased out for farming. A number of buildings survive but there is little to see from the air.

Units

1939–1945

CFS	Sep 1940–Apr 1942	various
7 FIS	Apr 1942–Feb 1943	as RLG
1537 Flt	May 1943–Aug 1945	Oxford

PERRANPORTH

County: Cornwall

UTM/Grid: OS Map 204 – SW740528
Lat/Long: N50°19.38 W005°10.44
Nearest Town: Truro 8 miles to south-east

June 1003 view of Perranporth.

HISTORY

Authority was given on 4 July 1940 for land to be requisitioned at Perranporth for development as a satellite airfield for Portreath. The airfield was located on the cliffs adjacent to the village from which it took its name and was five miles south of its parent at Portreath. As the unit list shows, from its opening in spring 1941 to summer 1943, a large number of squadrons spent periods here and most of them flew Spitfires.

The airfield was originally designed for a single fighter-squadron and was laid on a flat strip of land between the road and the cliff – a dramatic site, if not an ideal one. Like the rest of the series of airfields along this stretch of the Cornish coast, it suffered weather problems, with the change from a fine sunny day to a thick sea mist occurring in a very short period. As a satellite airfield it was given few facilities other than its three runways, whose angles were not

ideal because of the constraints of the site, with connecting perimeter track and a number of Blister hangars, plus a single T-type hangar. Fighter-type dispersal pens were built at various parts of the peri track. This basic airfield structure was retained throughout the war, although minor runway modification were made and additional dispersals were added as the airfield became busier, including a series off a peri-track extension on the south-east corner of the airfield. As usual, all domestic and support sites were located off-airfield in small groups of huts, most of these being to the south.

The airfield opened in April 1941 and on the 27th of the month the Spitfires of 66 Squadron arrived from Exeter – no doubt unimpressed to exchange the 'delights' of Exeter and its neighbouring city for the rugged Cornish coast. The squadron stayed until December and were mainly involved in numerous

AIRFIELD DATA DEC 1944

Command:	Transport Command	Runway surface:	Tarmac
Function:	Parent Station	Hangars:	Over Blister × 4,
Runways:	058 deg 1,400 × 50yd		Extended-Over Blister
	100 deg 1,100 × 50yd		× 2, Teeside × one
	198 deg 1,100 × 50yd	Dispersals:	20 × Single-Engine
		Personnel:	Officers – 49 (1 WAAF)
			Other Ranks – 1,027 (41 WAAF)

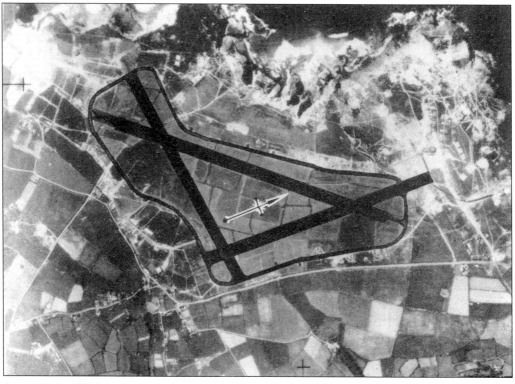

Portreath in June 2003.

fruitless patrols, although they were also called on to provide escort fighters on anti-shipping sorties. An Air-Sea Rescue Flight was formed here in May 1941 and operated a small number of aircraft on rescue work, until it became part of 276 Squadron in November and moved to Portreath.

The Czechs of 310 Squadron arrived in December and continued the routine of patrols and escorts; they departed the following May and Perranporth started to operate with two squadrons – at times, three squadrons. The periodic nature of the fighter detachments can be seen in the movements of 19 Squadron between their first appearance at Perranporth on 6 May 1942 and their final departure on 1 March 1943. During that time frame they spent periods of one to

two weeks at the Cornish base, with sojourns at Warmwell, Biggin Hill, Colerne and Southend in-between their visits.

No.145 (French) Wing formed here on 1 February 1944 within No.23 Wing of No.10 Group. It was allocated three Spitfire squadrons – 329, 340 and 341 – as part of the re-organization of air power for the invasion. The name was changed to No.145 Airfield on 12 April and the unit moved to Merston two days later.

Perranporth played a role in the anti-submarine element of D-Day and air strength was boosted in April 1944 with the arrival of three Fleet Air Arm squadrons who operated in this role, under the command of RAF Coastal Command, whose No.19

66 Squadron aircrew pose during their detachment to Perranporth in 1941.

Spitfires of 130 Squadron at the Cornish airfield in late summer 1942.

Group had taken control of the airfield in April. The Swordfish of 816 Squadron and the Avengers of 849 and 850 squadrons flew routine patrols and anti-shipping strikes, as part of the 'sweep the seas clear of enemy shipping' tactic; this was particularly vital in the hours of the actual invasion and the weeks of the build-up of the beachhead.

The departure of the naval aviators in August saw Perranporth reduced to Care and Maintenance on 1 September, although, in late-November, it was transferred to No.46 Group of Transport Command. This coastal airfield housed No.19 Terminal Staging Post from December 1944 to March 1945. Perranporth had a number of other involvements in this role: No.92 (Forward) Staging Post from mid-February to April 1945; No.120 (Major) Staging Post from November 1944 to April 1945; No.122 (Major)

Staging Post from December 1944 to April 1945; No.123 (Major) Staging Post from December 1944 to April 1945.

On 1 May 1945, the airfield was once more placed in Care and Maintenance, although the gliding school did not depart until June. Perranporth was closed as a military installation on 6 April 1946, but was not released for sale. There was a brief flurry of activity in 1951, when Newquay Council resurrected the airfield for commercial operations, the land being released for this purpose by the Air Ministry. Limited use was made of the airfield for a few months, but it was not a success and it was only the arrival of the Cornish Gliding Club in 1957 that allowed Perranporth to continue as an airfield, becoming a very successful gliding site.

Perranporth is still active as a GA airfield and the

only privately owned airfield in Cornwall with hard runways; parts of all three of the original runways are still in use, the maximum run being 860m on runway 05/23. This is a strictly 'prior permission required' airfield for anyone wishing to fly in: further details on www.perranporthairfield.co.uk. New owners took over in 1999 and have not only developed the commercial side of the airfield, encouraging flying visitors and holding events, but have also preserved the heritage of the airfield. Indeed, much of the surviving wartime structure has been scheduled by English Heritage and their report included the following summary:

> A 'Flight' comprised six Spitfires; there are four separate flight complexes – one at each corner of the airfield. Each flight complex comprised three dispersal pens, each housing just two fighters (to prevent the enemy from destroying lots of aircraft with any single bomb), along with a flight office, crew rest rooms, ancillary buildings and a hangar – or in one case access to a hangar. The two flight complexes at the north of the airfield also each had a night sleeping quarters for the aircrew. The living accommodation for the majority of the airfield personnel was located in four small hutted sites to the south of the airfield. Some of the individual features, such as the Battle Headquarters and the brick-built gun pits are rare. The aircraft dispersal pens, located at the north of the airfield, appear to be unique examples of early dispersal pens for single engine fighters. Overall, our survey has demonstrated that, as a group, these features represent a really important survival – one of the best-preserved fighter airfields anywhere in England.

DECOY SITE

Q   Penhal Sands   SW770567

UNITS

HQ units at Perranporth
No.145 Airfield   1 Feb 1944–14 Apr 1944

1939-1945

19 Sqn	6 May 1942–1 Mar 1943+	Spitfire
65 Sqn	29 Mar 1943–31 May 1943	Spitfire

66 Sqn	27 Apr 1941–14 Dec 1941	Spitfire
118 Sqn det	autumn 1941	Spitfire
130 Sqn	17 Jul 1942–30 Mar 1943+	Spitfire
132 Sqn	18 May 1943–20 Jun 1943	Spitfire
183 Sqn	18 Sep 1943–14 Oct 1943	Typhoon
234 Sqn	summer 1942–19 Jan 1943+	Spitfire
276 Sqn det	1942–1944?	various
286 Sqn det	spring 1942	various
302 Sqn	20 Jun 1943–19 Aug 1943	Spitfire
310 Sqn	29 Dec 1941–7 May 1942+	Spitfire
317 Sqn	21 Jun 1943–21 Aug 1943	Spitfire
329 Sqn	24 Mar 1944–17 Apr 1944	Spitfire
340 Sqn	9 Nov 1943–17 Apr 1944	Spitfire
341 Sqn	11 Oct 1943–14 Apr 1944	Spitfire
412 Sqn	13 Apr 1943–21 Jun 1943	Spitfire
453 Sqn	20 Aug 1943–15 Oct 1943	Spitfire
602 Sqn	20 Jan 1943–14 Apr 1943	Spitfire
610 Sqn	30 Apr 1943–26 Jun 1943	Spitfire
639 Sqn det	1944–1945	Henley, Hurricane
816 Sqn FAA	20 Apr 1944–1 Aug 1944	Swordfish
849 Sqn FAA	20 Apr 1944–9 Aug 1944	Avenger
850 Sqn FAA	23 Apr 1944–1 Aug 1944	Avenger
ASRF	May 1941–5 Nov 1941	Lysander
95 GS	Apr 1945–Jun 1945	Cadet

MEMORIAL

The on-airfield memorial consists of a stone cairn surmounted by a propeller plus a plaque with RAF roundel and inscription: 'In memory of those who lost their lives flying from RAF Perranporth and to commemorate all those who served here 1941–1945'

PORTLAND
(HMS *Sereptia*, HMS *Osprey*)

County: Dorset

UTM/Grid: OS Map 194 – SY682746
Lat/Long: N50°34.10 W002°26.46
Nearest Town: Weymouth 3 miles to north

Portland in 1997 with its very short 'runway' and tarmac area marked out with helicopter landing spots.

HISTORY

There are very few UK-based Royal Navy helicopter squadrons that have not spent some time at Portland as, for over four decades, this was one of the Fleet Air Arm's main helicopter bases, especially for training. The first RNAS base in the Portland area opened in September 1916 as HMS *Sereptia* and by early the fol-

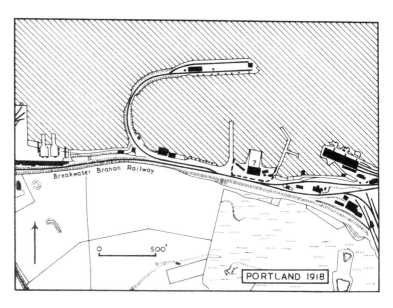

Short 184 at Portland in July 1918, operated by two Flights of 241 Squadron.

The Wright seaplane was one of a number of types flown from here on coastal patrols in the latter months of World War One.

lowing year was operating a Flight of Short 184 seaplanes on coastal patrol work. The main interest was in protecting shipping from the increasingly effective German U-boat campaign, a role that continued for the rest of the war. The RAF formed a new squadron at Portland in August 1918; No.241 Squadron comprised three Flights – 416, 417 and 513. The first two of these had been at Portland since forming in May and operated the Short 184 and the Campania, as well as a few converted Wrights. The third element, 513 Flight, was actually based at Chickerell and there is some disagreement as to whether this was actually part of 241 Squadron.

Although the station remained on the military books throughout the inter-war period there appears to have been little activity here, certainly very little flying activity and no based units. It was not until 1939 that Portland became an active flying station once more, with the formation of 771 Squadron on 24 May as a Fleet Requirements Unit (FRU). The squadron was initially equipped with fourteen Swordfish, some equipped as floatplanes, and a few Walruses and its task was to provide targets, including target-towing, and other services in the training of naval gunners. The unit was kept very busy as, in 1939, the navy had intensified its training in preparation for the, by then inevitable, war. 'X Flight' of the squadron had moved to Lee-on-Solent in late-June, whilst 'Y Flight' remained at Portland, with a brief period on HMS *Illustrious* and at Donibristle, to late-September. In that month it became 772 Squadron and, whilst its HQ was at Lee-on-Solent, its four floatplane Swordfish operated from Portland, still performing the FRU role. The squadron remained at Portland to July 1940, when it moved to Macrihanish in Scotland. However, the flying activity was only part of Portland's role, as it also housed the Anti-Submarine School, although this unit was moved out when it was deemed that Portland would be too vulnerable to attack. The airfield was held under Care and Maintenance for the rest of the war.

In the meantime, the navy had concentrated its anti-submarine warfare training at the Portland Naval Base and, in 1946, helicopter experiments were underway using the Sikorsky R-4B Hoverfly. Over the next few years other types were evaluated and a number of the navy's new helicopter squadrons used Portland Naval Base for trials and training. With the development of helicopters for the ASW role, there was a need for a new flying station at Portland. The site chosen for development was on the old playing fields and a number of nearby buildings were converted and others built, including a control tower. The site was commissioned as HMS *Osprey* on 24 April 1959 and, in addition to its primary training role, it was the shore base for Wasp small ships Flights from December 1964 to March 1988 and for Lynx Flights from July 1982 to its closure in 1999. The first training unit to form here in conjunction with the ASW School was 815 Squadron in April 1959; the squadron had reformed the previous October as an ASW helicopter unit with Whirlwinds to operate with the Naval Air Anti-Submarine School. The Whirlwinds, HAR.3s having replaced the unreliable HAS.7s, moved to Portland in April – but, in August, the squadron was disbanded to be re-designated as 737 Squadron. The new squadron was officially the Anti-Submarine Operational Flying School and continued to use Whirlwinds, which included a number of HAS.22s from February 1960 when SAR was added to the training task, although the latter passed to 771 Squadron when that unit reformed at Portland in July 1961. As the unit list shows, Portland's strength continued to grow and, as a result, the station itself underwent various stages of development with more landing areas, hangars and support facilities being added. Indeed, there was an almost constant development of the site over the next three decades.

The movements of naval helicopter units is invariably complex and, whilst the unit list given here shows major moves and units, it by no means reflects all the units that have made use of Portland. It does show that every naval helicopter type (and its sole V/STOL type, the Sea Harrier) has been seen here and in the early 1990s the expectation was that it would also see the next-generation type, the EH101, also grace its tarmac – but it was not to be as, under one of the many defence base closures of the 1990s, Portland was deemed surplus to requirements and was closed in 1999. The final unit to depart was 815 Squadron, which moved to Yeovilton on 12 February 1999.

The only subsequent based aviation activity has been by an SAR helicopter operated by Bristow Helicopters.

UNITS

Pre-1919

416Flt	May 1918–Mar/Jun 1919	Short 184, Campania
417Flt	May 1918–Mar/Jun 1919	Short 184, Campania

1919–1939

821Sqn FAA det	May–Jul 1937	Shark

1939–1945

771Sqn FAA	24 May 1939–Sep 1939	various
772Sqn FAA	28 Sep 1939–14 Jul 1940	Swordfish

Post-1945

700LSqn FAA	6 Jul 1990–17 Jul 1992+	Lynx
701Sqn FAA det	17–20 Sep 1958	Whirlwind
702Sqn FAA	19 Jul 1982–15 Jan 1999	Lynx
703Sqn FAA	22 Jan 1972–1 Jan 1981	Wasp
705Sqn FAA det	8 Feb 1950–12 Jul 1950	Dragonfly
706BSqn FAA	5 Feb 1964–8 Mar 1964	Wessex
737Sqn FAA	28 Aug 1959–7 Feb 1983	Whirlwind, Wessex, Sea King
771Sqn FAA	11 Jul 1961–1 Dec 1964	Whirlwind
771Sqn FAA	23 Jun 1967–4 Sep 1974	Wessex
772Sqn FAA	6 Sep 1974–Sep 1995	Wessex, Sea King
810Sqn FAA det	Nov 1985–Nov 1987+	Sea King
814Sqn FAA	7 May 1960–9 Sep 1960; det 1961–1966+	Whirlwind, Wessex
815Sqn FAA	14 Apr 1959–21 Nov 1959	Whirlwind
815Sqn FAA	19 Jul 1982–12 Feb 1999	Lynx
819Sqn FAA	29 Aug 1963–14 Feb 1964+	Wessex
820Sqn FAA	26 Nov 1959–29 Jan 1960	Whirlwind
824Sqn FAA	25 Sep 1961–Jan 1963+	Whirlwind
825Sqn FAA	9 Sep 1960–27 Jan 1961+	Whirlwind
829Sqn FAA	1 Dec 1964–26 Mar 1993	Wasp, Wessex, Lynx
845Sqn FAA det	10 Jan 1956–23 Apr 1956	Whirlwind
860Sqn FAA	Jun 1974–Feb 1975+	Wasp

PORTREATH (Station 504)

UTM/Grid: OS Map 204 – SW670460
Lat/Long: N50°16.02 W005°15.59
Nearest Town: Redruth 2 miles to south-east

HISTORY

Authority was given on 4 July 1940 for land to be requisitioned at Portreath for development as an operational station and it opened on 7 March 1941 as a fighter station for No.10 Group. The airfield was situated on Nancekuke Common, one of the few relatively flat areas along this coast, and its construction involved the closure of a number of roads, some of which were incorporated into the overall airfield layout. The small fishing village after which the airfield took its name was less than a mile to the south, but hidden in a steep valley. As a fighter base, the airfield was initially laid out with three short runways, although, unusually for an RAF airfield, a fourth runway was subsequently added, and all were given asphalt surfaces. The east/west runway was lengthened at some stage, but the maximum run was still only 1,800 yards – fine for the fighter types, but more of a problem for heavy types using Portreath. The runways were linked by a perimeter track, off which were a number of dispersal points, and at the height of its development the airfield had eight Blister

hangars and four T.2 All of the communal sites, which were quite extensive, were to the south of the main airfield site.

Whirlwinds of 263 Squadron were the first to appear, the twin-engined fighters arriving from St Eval in early March, but staying less than a month before their place was taken by the Spitfires of 152 Squadron. As the unit list shows, this routine of a few weeks or months saw many squadrons spend short periods at the Cornish airfield, the majority being fighter squadrons but, despite the presence of a Sector Room associated with Portreath, the main role of the squadrons was offensive operations over the Bay of Biscay or the coastal districts of France. The airfield and its units retained a defensive commitment, although on the few occasions that the airfield itself was attacked – a hit-and-run strafe attack or a small number of bombs – there was no defensive reaction. It was over the water that Portreath's units made their contribution, attacking shipping and U-boats or supporting other aircraft, by providing

AIRFIELD DATA DEC 1944

Command:	Fighter Command	Runway surface:	Asphalt
Function:	Sector Station	Hangars:	Extra-Over Blister × 8, Teeside × 4
Runways:	283 deg 1,800 × 50yd	Dispersals:	22 × Single-Engine
	242 deg 1,300 × 50yd	Personnel:	Officers – 169 (10 WAAF)
	194 deg 1,000 × 50yd		Other Ranks – 2,562 (495 WAAF)

fighter cover, or providing convoy cover to Allied shipping along the vulnerable south coast. What the unit list does not show is the large number of squadrons that used Portreath as an advanced refuel and re-arm base, either for a specific mission or whilst en route elsewhere. The airfield appears in a great many RAF operational record books in this capacity. The urgent need for aircraft in the Middle East led to the development of various ferry routes: one of these departed Land's End for a long over-sea flight via the Bay of Biscay, past neutral Spain and Portugal and then into the Mediterranean or Africa. Portreath became the 'hopping-off' point for much of this traffic, with aircraft taking on the maximum fuel-load before setting off on the hazardous flight.

In June 1941, the Overseas Aircraft Despatch Flight (OADF) – Unit (OADU) from August – at Kemble operated a detachment at Portreath as a No.44 Group lodger unit. The parent unit split in November and the OADU element moved to Portreath, becoming No.1 OADU the following January. Trebelzue (Newquay) had been used in late-1941 as a satellite, but it became No.2 OADU in January. The Unit remained at Portreath to October 1945 and handled hundreds of aircraft of virtually every operational type, as Portreath was well-placed as a departure point for aircraft ferrying to the Middle East and beyond.

One of the largest transfers took place in autumn 1942, to move aircraft to North Africa for Operation *Torch*, and involved both the RAF and USAAF. At some periods, Portreath had over 100 aircraft dis-

Beaufighters of 143 Squadron formed part of Portreath's striking power.

As a coastal station it was also involved in ASR, with Warwicks being one of the types operated in this role; this is probably not a Portreath-based aircraft.

persed around the airfield, often delayed because the weather forecast for the route was unsuitable. With the exception of the ASR aircraft of 276 Squadron, the airfield had no major based-units during this late-1942 to mid-1943 period and the OADU and associated activities certainly kept the airfield busy, as did the fact that its location made it a natural choice as a diversion airfield. Many damaged or lost aircraft sought sanctuary on Portreath's runways, often with dead or wounded crewmen.

In late-summer 1943, the operational squadrons returned and Portreath became home to two Beaufighter units, 143 and 235 Squadrons, whose major task was anti-shipping and fighter patrols over the Bay of Biscay and coastal areas. The battle over the Bay was still in full swing and the Allies were at last starting to cause the U-boats serious problems. February brought 248 Squadron, with its Tsetse Mosquitoes equipped with a 6-pounder cannon designed to punch through U-boat hulls. For the invasion period, No.153 (General Reconnaissance) Wing was formed at Portreath to command and control operations in a designated section of the English Channel, although the only operational units to be based at the airfield with the Wing during this period were 235 Squadron (Beaufighters) and 248 Squadron (Mosquitoes). There was an intense period of activity in summer 1944 but, when the Allies captured the west coast ports in France, the maritime threat that had occupied Portreath's units vanished and the squadrons left for new hunting grounds.

The remaining months of the war were quiet – even the ASR detachment had gone by the early part of the year – and the OADU was the main user. The Armament Synthetic Training Unit (ASDU) spent a short period at Portreath in 1945, before moving to St Mawgan; this is one of those strange units for which few details survive – the author has yet to uncover any significant information on the ASDU. It used Warwicks and Wellingtons, which appear to have been on its own charge rather than borrowed.

Portreath was transferred to Transport Command's No.44 Group in May 1945 but, by the autumn, it was obvious that the airfield was not really required and, in December, it was reduced to Care and Maintenance. It spent a few months the following year under Technical Training Command, whilst being used as a Polish Resettlement Unit.

In mid-1950 the airfield was taken over by the Ministry of Supply and became one of the most highly classified installations in the UK, as it was chosen to house a research and production facility for chemical warfare, such as the nerve agent Sarin. This work was carried out by the Chemical Defence Establishment and it was operated as an out-station for Porton Down. In 1956, the British Government stated that it was no longer developing offensive chemical agents and the CDE turned its attention to defensive agents and protective systems. The site was finally closed in 1980, the main activities having ceased two years before, and was handed back to the RAF in August that year. On 1 October 1980 RAF Portreath re-opened as an air defence control centre for GCI. The airfield structure is still intact and from the air looks much as it did in World War Two and many of the buildings also survive; the weather-covered radar head now dominates the centre of the airfield. Runway 06/24 is maintained in good condition, with a displaced threshold, but it is not declared as a usable runway.

Decoy Site

Q   Tehidy   SW622428

Units

HQ units at Portreath

No.330 (B) Wing 9–18 Dec 1942   142, 150Sqns
No.153 (GR) Wing 15 Apr 1944-14 Sep 1944 235, 248Sqns

1939–1945

66Sqn   14 Dec 1941–27 Apr 1942+Spitfire

130Sqn	16 Jun 1941–25 Oct 1941	Spitfire		400Sqn det	Dec 1942	Mustang
143Sqn	16 Sep 1943–12 Feb 1944	Beaufighter		414Sqn	4–20 Jun 1943	Mustang
152Sqn	9 Apr 1941–25 Aug 1941	Spitfire		613Sqn	20 Jun 1943–15 Jul 1943	Mustang
153Sqn	18–20 Dec 1942	Beaufighter		639Sqn det	summer 1944–1945	Henley,
234Sqn	27 Apr 1942–23 Aug 1942	Spitfire				Hurricane
235Sqn	29 Aug 1943–6 Sep 1944+	Beaufighter		OADU	Jan 1942–10 Oct 1945	
247Sqn	10 May 1941–18 Jun 1941	Hurricane		1478Flt	11–12 Jun 1943	
248Sqn	17 Feb 1944–12 Sep 1944	Mosquito		ASDU	1944–1945?	Wellington,
263Sqn	18 Mar 1941–10 Apr 1941;	Whirlwind				Warwick
	summer 1942					
264Sqn det	1942–1943	Mosquito				
275Sqn det	summer 1944–1945	various				
276Sqn det	winter 1942–Apr 1944	various				
276Sqn	4 Apr 1944–18 Sep 1944	various				
277Sqn det	late 1944–1945	various				
286Sqn det	spring 1942	various				
313Sqn	29 Nov 1941–15 Dec 1941	Spitfire				

MEMORIAL

A cairn or Cornish stone surmounted by the propeller blade from Spitfire R6642; plaque of slate with inscription: 'In memory of all those who served at RAF Portreath 14 March 1941–30 September 1945'.

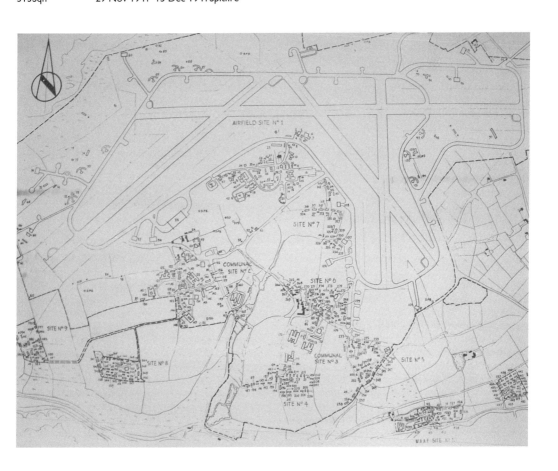

PREDANNACK

County: Cornwall

UTM/Grid: OS Map 203 – SW685162
Lat/Long: N49°59.58 W005°13.53
Nearest Town: Helston 6 miles to north

HISTORY

Authority was given on 4 July 1940 for 'land to be requisitioned at Mullion (Preddanack Downs) for development as a satellite airfield for Portreath'. Situated in the parish of Mullion and with various geographic features and groups of buildings carrying the Predannack name, it was the latter that was eventually adopted for the airfield when it opened in May 1941. Construction had been reasonably straightforward, despite the isolated location, and the airfield was laid out with four runways, an almost uniquely Cornish arrangement for RAF airfields, with the usual limited range of support structures for a fighter airfield. Predannack eventually had twelve Blister hangars and one Bellman, although one plan shows a variation on this hangar arrangement. Most of the communal sites were to the east of the airfield.

Situated close to Lizard Point, Predannack was one of the most southerly of major RAF airfields and, as

the unit list shows, this made it ideal for forward basing or refuel and re-arm use, which was also a main role of its parent at Portreath, some fifteen miles to the north. The Hurricanes of 247 Squadron were first to take up residence, moving down from Portreath on 18 June 1941 and remaining here until late-1942, although, in the latter months, as a detachment from the main base at Exeter. The squadron's main role was fighter sweep over France, this being the period when Fighter Command was taking the offensive, although with additional escort and defensive commitments. The difference for 247 was that the bulk of their sorties were at night, the Hurricanes being adept at the night-intruder role. Predannack's units specialized in the night role, with 600 Squadron bringing its Beaufighters here on detachment from June 1941 and moving in with the entire squadron in October. The Havocs and Bostons of No.1457

AIRFIELD DATA DEC 1944

Command:	Fighter Command	Runway surface:	Tarmac
Function:	Forward Airfield, Night Fighter	Hangars:	Over Blister × 6, Extra-Over
Runways:	238 deg 2,000 × 50yd		Blister × 6, Bellman × one
	282 deg 1,520 × 50yd	Dispersals:	11 × Twin-Engine, 7 × Single-Engine
	012 deg 1,380 × 50yd	Personnel:	Officers – 121 (3 WAAF)
	322 deg 1,000 × 50yd		Other Ranks – 1,936 (242 WAAF)

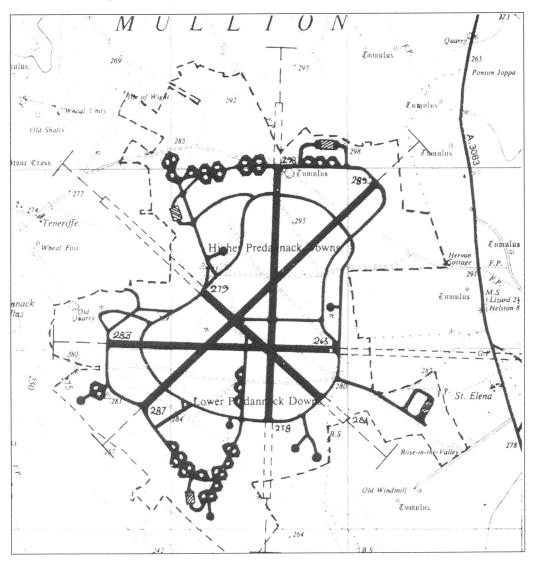

(Fighter) Flight moved in from Colerne in November 1941; some of the aircraft were Turbinlite equipped and were intended to operate as a hunter-killer team with a Hurricane. Despite the fact that, by this time, the tactic had been proven to have limited potential, it was persevered with; the Flight was given squadron

c.1944 aerial shot, or rather
an air shot with the operating
surfaces (runways etc)
enhanced.

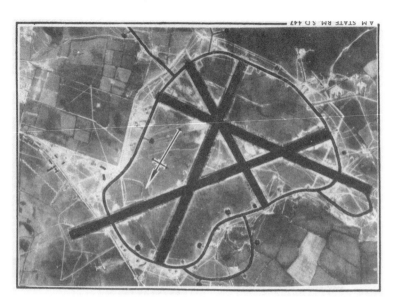

Wellington of 179 Squadron at Predannack in June 1944.

status as 536 Squadron in September 1942 and
moved to Fairwood Common the following month.

Predannack had been on the receiving end of
night-intruder ops twice in the latter part of 1941,
but with little damage caused and no casualties.

Although night ops were the main rationale for
the based unit, the airfield was used by a large number of detachments for a variety of fighter and fighter-
bomber activity; most of these spent very little time
here, perhaps one day, and are not included in the
unit list. By 1942, much of the effort was connected
with the Bay of Biscay battle, with the main focus
being attacks on U-boats or other shipping, or coun-
tering the increasingly aggressive Luftwaffe reaction

over the Bay. The latter part of the year also saw the
airfield, along with every other Cornish base, hosting
aircraft destined for North Africa and Operation
Torch. It was a similar story throughout 1943, with
offensive operations over the Bay and coastal districts
of France, but it was also a year in which more damaged aircraft landed here – the nearest friendly runway for many bombers, especially USAAF heavies,
with dead or wounded crewmen and badly shot-up
aircraft.

The runways were improved and, in most cases,
lengthened during 1943 to make the airfield more
suitable for larger aircraft, not so much with diversions of bombers in mind but for Coastal Command

use. Wellingtons of 304 Squadron were operated from here, by mid-December 1943, hunting U-boats and it is maritime operations that dominated the airfield's activities for the period leading up to and just beyond D-Day. No.152 (General Reconnaissance) Wing formed at Predannack on 15 April 1944 as part of the pre D-Day re-organization and was given command and control of operational units in a designated area of the Channel. Between April and the disbandment of the Wing in September, it had three squadrons under command: 179 (Wellington), 311 (Liberator) and 524, the latter not actually operating from Predannack. However, to add to the hectic nature of the airfield in this period, a two-squadron Spitfire Wing (1 and 165 squadrons) formed at the end of April and remained in residence to late-June. Predannack was a very busy airfield during the D-Day period and, whilst its fighter squadrons saw little combat, its maritime units attacked and sank a number of U-boats. With the Allied capture of the French ports the latter threat was no longer significant in this region and, indeed, the combat radius of the fighters also made Predannack unsuitable. The airfield became a rest and re-equipment base for fighter units and those squadrons listed as being here from September 1944 onwards were primarily here for this purpose. This remained the case to the end of the war.

On 1 June 1946 the airfield was reduced to Care and Maintenance and remained unused for a number of years, although not released for disposal. Barnes Wallis used Predannack for experiments on his Goose and Swallow swing-wing projects in the early 1950s, which included a ramp and rails to launch models with which to prove the concept. The project lasted some three years, but was eventually discarded by Vickers, who abandoned the airfield in October 1954.

The site was taken on by the Fleet Air Arm on 15 December 1954 for use as a satellite/relief landing ground for Culdrose, where helicopter training was starting to become a major role. Predannack (FGDO) remains in military use as an RLG for RNAS Culdrose and is used for helicopter training and exercises. The four runways are all serviceable but are now marked for helicopter use. The site is part-owned by English Nature as a Site of Special Scientific Interest (SSSI), because of its 'great natural beauty and the rare orchids and butterflies'. No.705 Squadron has been based at Culdrose since 1958 and, since then, has specialized in the helicopter training role; as such, it has been one of the main users of Predannack RLG. The RAF is still on site with No.626 VGS – the gliders having spent over twenty-five years at the Cornish airfield. Initial use by this unit had been from August 1965 to June 1966, when their parent base of Culdrose was not available.

Cadet glider of No.626 VGS; the unit now operates more modern types such as the Vigilant. (via 626 VGS)

However, in late-1968 the decision was taken to permanently move to Predannack, the move having been completed by October. The VGS has been in residence ever since, less a sojourn at St Mawgan from November 1990 to July 1991, and it now operates five Viking gliders.

DECOY SITES

Q	Goonhilly Downs	SW732185
Q	Kynance	SW676140
Q	Lizard	SW695135
QX	Traboe	SW735187

UNITS

HQ units at Predannack
No.152 (GR) Wing 15 Apr 1944–7 Sep 1944 179, 311, 524Sqns

1939–1945

1Sqn	29 Apr 1944–20 Jun 1944	Spitfire
25Sqn det	summer 1942	Havoc
33Sqn	15 Dec 1944–21 Feb 1945	Typhoon
64Sqn	9 Dec 1942–2 Jan 1943	Spitfire
66Sqn	26–29 Sep 1942	Spitfire
85Sqn det	summer 1943	Mosquito
118Sqn det	autumn 1941	Spitfire
120Sqn det	summer 1942	Liberator
141Sqn	18 Feb 1943–30 Apr 1943	Beaufighter
157Sqn	9 Nov 1943–7 May 1944	Mosquito
165Sqn det	summer 1942	Spitfire
165Sqn	2 Apr 1944–20 Jun 1944	Spitfire
179Sqn	28 Apr 1944–6 Sep 1944	Wellington
183Sqn	14 Oct 1943–1 Feb 1944	Typhoon
222Sqn	15 Dec 1944–21 Feb 1945	Spitfire, Tempest
234Sqn	24–31 Dec 1941	Spitfire
234Sqn	19 Jun 1944–28 Aug 1944	Spitfire

236Sqn det	late-1942–1943?	Beaufighter	626 VGS	Oct 1968–1990;	various
247Sqn	18 Jun 1941–Sep 1942	Hurricane		Jul 1991–current	Vigilant
248Sqn	18 Jan 1943–17 Feb 1944	Beaufighter, Mosquito			

MEMORIAL

263Sqn det	autumn 1942–spring 1943	Whirlwind
264Sqn	30 Apr 1943–7 Nov 1943+; 25 Sep 1944–30 Nov 1944	Mosquito
266Sqn det	autumn 1943	Typhoon
304Sqn	13 Dec 1943–19 Feb 1944	Wellington
307Sqn	Apr 1943–9 Nov 1943	Mosquito
310Sqn	9–11 Feb 1942	Spitfire
311Sqn	23 Feb 1944–7 Aug 1944	Liberator
349Sqn	16 Feb 1945–19 Apr 1945	Spitfire, Tempest
406Sqn	8 Sep 1942–8 Dec 1942	Beaufighter
410Sqn det	1943	Mosquito
414Sqn det	winter 1943	Mustang
456Sqn det	summer 1943	various
485Sqn	25 Feb 1945–19 Apr 1945	Tempest, Typhoon
536Sqn	8 Sep 1942–27 Oct 1942	Havoc, Hurricane
600Sqn	Jun 1941–2 Sep 1942	Beaufighter
604Sqn	7 Dec 1942–18 Feb 1943	Beaufighter
604Sqn	24 Sep 1944–5 Dec 1944	Mosquito
611Sqn	3–17 Jul 1944	Spitfire
618Sqn det	autumn 1943–1944	Mosquito
1457Flt	15 Nov 1941–8 Sep 1942	Havoc, Boston

Post-1945

151Sqn	17 May 1945–19 Apr 1946+	Mosquito
406Sqn	14 Jun 1945–1 Sep 1945	Mosquito

A large natural boulder bears a plaque with the RAF badge and inscription:

RAF Predannack. This memorial honours all ranks and nationalities that served here during World War II. While casting your eyes on this memorial spare a thought for those who flew from here and failed to return, many have no known grave. 'Like a breath of wind, gone in a fleeting second, only the memories now remain.' Simply Dedicated June 2002.

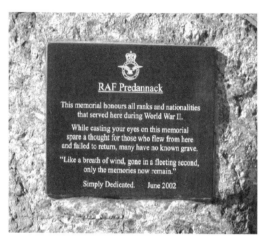

RAMSBURY (Station 469)

County: Wiltshire

UTM/Grid: OS Map 174 – SU278705
Lat/Long: N51°25.96 W001°36.08
Nearest Town: Marlborough 5 miles to west

19.7.42.

HISTORY

Land was requisitioned near Membury in 1941 for development as a satellite to Membury for use as a Bomber Command Operational Training Unit. Construction commenced in June for a standard bomber field with three runways, a main runway of 2,000 yards and two secondaries of 1,100 yards, the latter two positioned on the east side of the airfield. A connecting perimeter track was constrained on the north side by the airfield boundary and so all fifty dispersals, of frying pan and spectacle types, were built on the south side. It was a very unusual arrangement and because of that would have made a perfect target for marauding German aircraft. As usual with this type of airfield there was little provision for hangars – only two T.2s – and the poor ground-crew had to work in the open. The main technical area, such as it was, was on the east side and the communal sites were dispersed in the fields to the south-east.

The OTU plan came to nothing and, by the time the airfield was ready for occupation in 1942, the priority was airfields for the growing USAAF

strength; Ramsbury was allocated for their use in June 1942. The 64th Troop Carrier Group began to arrive in August and it was as home to TCGs that the airfield spent its operational career. Under the command of Colonel Tracey K Dorsett, four Troop Carrier squadrons moved into the still-unfinished station with their C-47s and C-53s and started intensive training in the airborne-forces role, as well as trying to get familiar with the British weather – and customs. The Group spent three months here before joining 12th Air Force and deploying to Gibraltar, on 9 November, to take part in Operation *Torch*, the invasion of North Africa. With the departure of the Americans, Ramsbury reverted to the RAF and Oxfords of No.15 (Pilots) Advanced Flying Unit, based at Andover, used the airfield as an RLG and satellite for a year. At times the airfield was very busy, especially in summer 1943, when much of the PAFU spent time here; inevitably there were crashes and fatalities – flying training and accidents went hand-

Airfield Data Dec 1944

Command:	RAF Fighter Command	Runway surface:	Concrete and tarmac
Function:	Operational Satellite	Hangars:	2 × T.2
Runways:	260 deg 2,000 × 50yd	Dispersals:	50 × Concrete, 2 × Steel Planking
	200 deg 1,100 × 50yd	Personnel:	Officers – 470
	320 deg 1,100 × 50yd		Other Ranks – 1,898

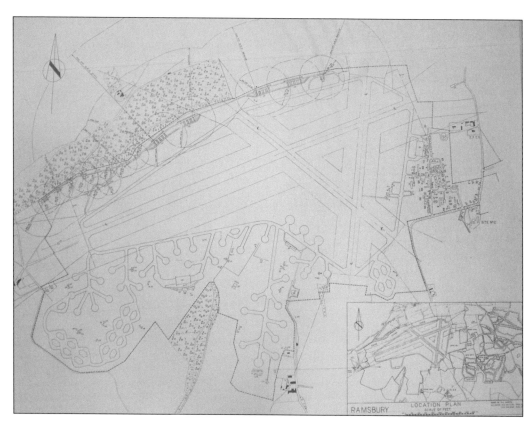

in-hand. The RAF's 'occupation' was only ever intended as an interim measure, as Ramsbury (Station 469) was still intended as an American TCG base and, in October 1943, they reclaimed the airfield. Elements of the 434th and 435th TCGs arrived in December 1943 and took part in training and exercises, but neither of these units was intended as the permanent resident and, in late-January, the real owners, the C-47s of the 437th TCG, flew in from Balderton, having arrived from the USA a week earlier. The Group's four squadrons were under the command of Colonel Cedric E Hudgens and his first order of priority was a rigorous training routine of formation flying, paratroop dropping and glider operations for the inexperienced Group. The 82nd

Airborne Division were often part of this training, so aircrews and soldiers were familiar with each other when the call to action came in early June 1944.

In the early hours of 6 June, the Group despatched fifty-two C-47s, each towing a Waco glider, as part of Operation *Detroit*. A second mission was flown later the same day and, over the next few days, the C-47s flew more men and material to the Normandy area; the Group was awarded a Distinguished Unit Citation (DUC) for its part in the D-Day operations. The Group sent much of its strength to Italy in mid-July to participate in the Allied invasion of Southern France, but operational strength at Ramsbury was maintained by detachments from other squadrons, although this was short-lived.

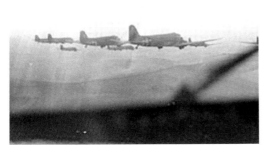

C-47s of the 437th Troop Carrier Group; the Group spent a year at Ramsbury and took part in a number of airborne operations.

Two American servicemen pose outside one of Ramsbury's Nissen huts.

No.15 PAFU operated Oxfords from Ramsbury in 1943.

In September the 101st Airborne moved into tented camps in the area – another airborne op was imminent. On 17 September, Ramsbury sent seventy combinations as part of Operation *Market-Garden*, dropping the 101st at Eindhoven, Holland. Re-sup-

ply missions took place over the next few days and, as with all transport bases, Ramsbury was involved in handling casualties brought back from the fighting area; as soon as possible the C-47s were using captured or semi-prepared strips and every return flight brought more casualties back to England, for which purpose many flights had a Flight Nurse on board from the 814th Air Evacuation Squadron.

The 437th TCG was one of the units flying air-supply missions to Allied forces during the German winter attack – the Battle of the Bulge – and their drop zones included the surrounded garrison of Bastogne. After a year of operations from Ramsbury, the 436th moved out in February 1945, flying to airfield A-58 in France. The USAAF retained control of Station 469 and used it for various rear echelon purposes, but they finally moved out on 11 June, handing the airfield back to the RAF. For the next year the airfield survived as an RLG, firstly for No.1336 Conversion Unit at Welford, then for No.22 Glider Pick-Up Training Unit and, finally, for No.7 Flying Instructors School from Upavon. On 2 May 1946, Ramsbury was put into Care and Maintenance and spent a few years under this status before being put up for disposal. Very little of the airfield survives.

UNITS

1939–1945

15 PAFU	Dec 1942–Nov 1943	Oxford
GP-UTF	29 Oct 1945–15 Nov 1945	Dakota, Hadrian

USAAF units

64th TCG

Squadrons:	16th, 17th, 18th, 35th, 54th TCS
Aircraft:	C-47
Dates:	Aug 1942–Nov 1942

437th TCG

Squadrons:	83rd, 84th, 85th, 86th TCS
Aircraft:	C-46, C-47
Dates:	5 Feb 1944–25 Feb 1945

MEMORIAL

Roll of Honour and memorial plaque in Holy Cross church, inscribed:

> Dedicated to the memory of those members of the 437th Troop Carrier Group, 9th Air Force, United States Air Force who gave their lives in World War II. Erected as a token of thanks for the friendship of the people of the Ramsbury area. January 1944 to February 1945.

ROBOROUGH (Plymouth)

County: Devon

UTM/Grid: OS Map 201 – SX503605
Lat/Long: N50°25 W004°06
Nearest Town: Plymouth 5 miles to south

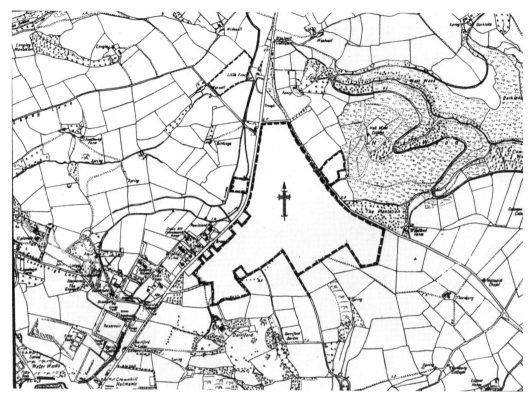

HISTORY

This site was first used as an airfield in 1923, as a substitute for the original Plymouth Aerodrome at Chelson Meadow. This use was short-lived, but a civil airport on the site opened in July 1931. Military interest began in the mid-1930s, with various detachments by the RAF and Fleet Air Arm. The 'RAF' had a brief stay at the Plymouth site in late-summer 1939, when No.46 ERFTS formed at the airfield, although like most of these schools it was civil operated, in this case by Portsmouth, Southsea and Isle of Wight Aviation Ltd. However, like all such schools it disbanded with the outbreak of war in September. As the plan shows, this was a very constrained site, as it was built in the triangle between two roads; its construction involved the closure of a number of roads and the removal of numerous field boundaries.

There was still some RAF movement, as the airfield was the base for the No.15 Group Headquarters Communication Flight; the Group HQ had moved to Mount Wise Barracks, Plymouth in June and Roborough was a convenient airfield for Magisters and Proctors, although the Flight usually only had three or four on strength. The Group moved to Liverpool in February 1941 and the Comms Flight moved to Hooton Park.

It was not until the fall of France in 1940 that the RAF found itself with an urgent need for operational airfields to cover the increased geographic area threatened by the Luftwaffe. In July 1940, Gladiators of 247 Squadron arrived and the unit flew the outdated biplane throughout the Battle of Britain, acting as fighter defence for Plymouth, eventually re-equipping with Hurricanes in December that year. The airfield was also being used by a detachment of No.2 Anti-Aircraft Co-operation Unit working with the Gosport naval ranges and was also used on a daily

AIRFIELD DATA DEC 1944

Command: Coastal Command
Function: Satellite for Mount Batten
Runways: NW/SE 720yd × 100yd
            NE/SW 780yd × 100yd
Note: handwritten undated amendment added
the following runways or runways extensions:
            NW/SE 800yd
            NE/SW 900yd
            E/W 600yd

Runway surface: Grass
Hangars: Civil Flying Club × 3, Blister × one
Dispersals: 4 × 3-bay concrete with brick walls
Personnel: Officers – Nil
              Other Ranks – 256 (66 WAAF)

The fighter defence of Plymouth included the Gladiators of 247 Squadron; N2306 seen at the airfield in August 1940. (Andy Thomas)

basis by other units, such as 225 Squadron at Tilshead for coastal patrols. The latter role was taken-over by a detachment of 16 Squadron Lysanders who, in addition to patrol work, were tasked with ASR. This latter task was removed when an Air-Sea Rescue Flight was formed in May 1941 and operated a small number of aircraft until absorbed into 276 Squadron in November, who then continued to operate a detachment from here.

Throughout the early part of the war, the airfield was under the control of the Admiralty, but it passed to the Air Ministry in May 1942. It had been used by the navy for gunnery practice since the start of the war and this use continued following the change of ownership. As part of this role, a Flight of No.2 Anti-Aircraft Co-operation Unit had been based at Roborough and, in February 1943, this became No.1623 Flight. It operated a small but mixed fleet comprising Defiants, Gladiators and Battles. At the end of the year it was renumbered again, becoming 691 Squadron. This unit, along with the No.19 Group's Comms Flight, remained at Roborough for the rest of the war.

When the war ended, flying occupation was limited to No.82 Gliding School, which had been here since forming in October 1953 with Cadet Is and IIs. The school remained at Roborough until February

1948, when it moved to Harrowbeer. Final RAF based presence was by No.19 Group's Communications Flight; the Group HQ had moved to Mount Batten in 1947 and Roborough was used by its Comms Flight from July the following year. The Flight disbanded at the airfield in April 1960.

The airfield returned to civilian operation in 1946 and various airlines and flying clubs have made use of it ever since, both for domestic flights and for some international services to Ireland and France. The airport has had various owners in the post-war years and has also been used by the military – for example, the Britannia Royal Naval College Air Experience Flight, operated by the airport owners, Airwork, from 1961, to provide air experience and pilot screening for officer cadets from Dartmouth. Tiger Moths were replaced by Chipmunks in 1966 which were used for twenty-five years, until replaced, under a new contract with Shorts, by Grob Tutors. The late-1960s also saw a detachment of helicopters at Roborough, initially the Air Troop of No.41 Royal Commando with three Sioux from April 1967, and later with No.45 Commando and No.95 Commando, as well as a brief spell with two Army Air Corps units, 8 Squadron (an interim designation) and 666 Squadron. All of this rotary activity had ended by

1972, although military helicopters continued to use the airfield on an opportunity basis. The Fleet Air Arm's newest squadron formed here in December 2001 as an air experience flight (to aid recruiting); it is part of the old RN Flying Training Flight.

Plymouth (City) Airport (EGHD) has had varying fortunes in recent years but, with the growth of low-cost carriers serving Europe, the market has increased and the airport is growing www.plymouthairport.com.

UNITS

1919–1939

801 Sqn FAA	26 Jul 1937–9 Aug 1937	Osprey
810 Sqn FAA	26 Jul 1938–6 Aug 1938	Swordfish
46 ERFTS	1 Aug 1939–3 Sep 1939	Hart, Audax

1939–1945

16 Sqn det	autumn 1941–1942	Lysander
247 Sqn	Aug 1940–May 1941	Gladiator, Hurricane
276 Sqn det	late 1941–1944?	various
691 Sqn	Dec 1943–Feb 1945	various
814 Sqn FAA	28 Aug 1939–10 Feb 1940+	Swordfish
815 Sqn FAA	12–21 Jun 1940	Swordfish
819 Sqn FAA	27 May 1940–21 Jun 1940	Swordfish
15 Gp CF	13 Jun 1939–1 Feb 1941	various
2 AACU det	1940–Feb 1943+	various
19 Gp CF	5 Feb 1941–15 Dec 1947	various
ASRF	May 1941–6 Nov 1941	Lysander
1623Flt	14 Feb 1943–1 Dec 1943	Defiant, Gladiator, Battle
82 GS	Oct 1943–19 Feb 1948	Cadet, Sedbergh

Chipmunks of the Royal Navy Air Experience Flight, which has had a variety if names, including the Grading Flight and the Britannia Royal Naval College AEF. The unit has been a long-term user of Roborough and was amongst the last operators of the Chipmunk. (Royal Navy)

Post-1945

727 Sqn FAA	6 Dec 2001–current	Tutor
82 GS	?–19 Feb 1948	Cadet, Sedbergh
19 Gp CF	?–15 Dec 1947; 27 Aug 1951–1 Apr 1960	various

ROLLESTONE

County: Wiltshire

UTM/Grid: OS Map 184 – SU095450 (Balloon station); SU088439 (Landing Ground)

Lat/Long: N51°12.24 W001°51.92 (Balloon station); N51°11.65 W001°52.52 (Landing Ground)

Nearest Town: Amesbury 4 miles to south-east

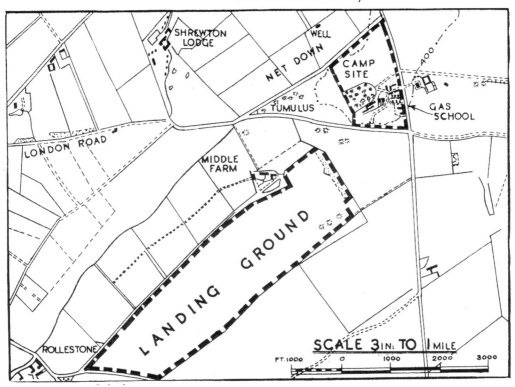

HISTORY

In July 1916, No.1 Balloon School moved from Manston to a new site adjacent to Rollestone Camp, an RFC 'station' having been established on a fifty-acre patch of land at Rollestone Bake Farm. The school was tasked with training observation balloon personnel and, over the next two years, it continued to expand, eventually covering around 180 acres, although facilities were always very limited – huts, tents, Bessonneau hangars and mooring masts. Training continued into the post-war period, with the school becoming No.1 Balloon Centre in 1919 and the School of Balloon Training from March 1920.

The school continued to operate in the period between the wars, usually having only two Type-R balloons on strength and with only a steady trickle of students. In 1932, the long-serving hangars were replaced with coupled airship-sheds, each one 105 × 40ft and 40ft high, of metal construction. The RAF

Balloon Centre was formed here on 3 November 1931, by which time the focus had started to shift from balloons for artillery observation to their use as barrage balloons. This was confirmed in 1935, with the formation of a Barrage Balloon Flight at Rollestone; this worked with the RAE's Research Department Flight to determine aircraft defence against balloons, which mainly involved systems to gather and then cut a balloon cable. One of the RDF's Wellingtons operated from Rollestone on such trials. The RAF Balloon Centre gave birth to No.2 Balloon Training Unit in November 1936 and this ran comprehensive courses in the handling and use of barrage balloons. The growing importance of this defensive system was recognized on 1 November 1938, with the formation of Balloon Command, with HQ in London and command of all barrage balloon units. The BTU moved to Cardington on 1 February 1939 and Rollestone's

Kite Balloons at Rollestone in January 1915. (via Rod Priddle)

involvement with this branch of the RAF was over.

In June 1939, the RAF's Anti-Gas School moved to the Rollestone area, using some of the buildings from the old balloon station but also a nearby landing ground that was laid out towards the end of the year. A rectangle of land 2,500 × 500yd was simply used as a landing ground for aircraft operating with the Anti-Gas School and there was no structural development. However, just before the outbreak of war the so-called 'Manby Screen' (named after Manby where it was first erected) was tested at Rollestone. The idea behind this 1,000-yard-long metal-mesh screen was to reduce the cross-wind effect and make it possible for aircraft to take-off safely in varying wind conditions, the practical use of which would be that airfields would not need multiple runways to cater for wind direction. Various trials took place to June 1940 and the results were mixed – but the screen was never adopted.

The first gas course started on 4 July and aircraft were used to simulate gas delivery as part of the training; the aircraft being provided by a variety of units, including the SDF, Old Sarum's Army Co-operation School, the Porton Down Chemical Defence Experimental Station and No.1 Flying Training School. The latter unit, based at Netheravon, also made use of Rollestone for night-flying training.

The only confirmed attack on this small airfield took place on 12 May 1941, when a lone German bomber released a stick of bombs and strafed the airfield, but with no result. The Rollestone Camp area was used for a number of ground courses and it is likely that the airfield was used by communications aircraft in connection with these courses, especially where senior officers – RAF and USAAF – were concerned.

The Anti-Gas School remained the main user of the airfield throughout the war, eventually leaving Rollestone on 12 October 1945. In the latter part of the war, the airfield had periods of use by the Operational and Refresher Training Unit (ex-Glider Pilot Exercise Unit) at Thruxton as an RLG, whilst No.43 OTU at Oatlands Hill used some of the accommodation, but not the airfield itself.

Post-war, the airfield housed Austers of 657 Squadron for a few weeks in late-1945 but, with their departure to Andover in late-January 1946, the Rollestone site was reduced to Care and Maintenance. The airfield was closed on 25 July 1946 and transferred to the army, who used it for a variety of purposes in connection with training on the Larkhill Ranges. The airfield area soon reverted to farmland but the camp area, along with many of the original buildings, has continued to be developed and is now the Rollestone Army Training Centre.

UNITS

Post-1945

657Sqn   16 Nov 1945–26 Jan 1946   Auster

ST EVAL (Station 129)

County: Cornwall

UTM/Grid: OS Map 200 – SW873685
Lat/Long: N50°28.41 W004°59.50
Nearest Town: Newquay 6 miles to south-west

A misty day for this over-flight of St Eval in June 2003.

HISTORY

The RAF's 1930s expansion plan included a requirement for a base to provide anti-submarine and anti-shipping patrols off the south-west of England. The site at St Eval was chosen as a Coastal Command base and work got underway in 1938; located about one mile from the coast, the requisitioned area of land was reasonably flat, but it included a number of roads and buildings – only the church survived from the village – and extensive field boundaries. Nevertheless, initial work progressed well and St Eval opened on 2 October 1939, but it was far from complete and it would be many months before all major construction work was finished. It was, eventually, a standard two-squadron airfield, with three hard runways and a technical area, on the east side, based on four C-Type hangars plus the usual support buildings, although runway construction did not start until mid-1940. Unlike many of the other Cornish airfields it was, therefore, well-equipped as a permanent station.

The Ansons of 217 Squadron began flight operations here in October 1939. Having arrived from Warmwell, the Ansons were immediately tasked with coastal patrols; the aircraft may have made its reputation later as a trainer but, in this early part of the war, it was one of Coastal Command's main operational types. Equipped with Tiger Moths and Hornet Moths, No.6 Coastal Patrol Flight formed in January 1940, to patrol the coastal waters from Land's End to Start Point, although the Flight only existed for a few months.

Bomber Command Whitleys joined the maritime war, with detachments at a number of airfields such as St Eval, the first of a number of such involvements, the most significant of which was when No.10 Operational Training Unit (Abingdon) ran an operational detachment attached to No.19 Group from 1942 to July 1943 as part of the U-boat campaign; during this operational period thirty-three Whitleys

AIRFIELD DATA DEC 1944

Command:	Coastal Command	Runway surface:	Part concrete/tarmac
Function:	Operational Parent	Hangars:	Blister (69ft) × 5,
Runways:	261 deg 1,980 × 50yd		Type C × 4, Blister (45ft) × 2,
	201 deg 1,970 × 50yd		T.2 × 2, Bellman × one
	320 deg 1,600 × 50yd	Dispersals:	48 × Spectacle
		Personnel:	Officers – 18
			Other Ranks – 1,284

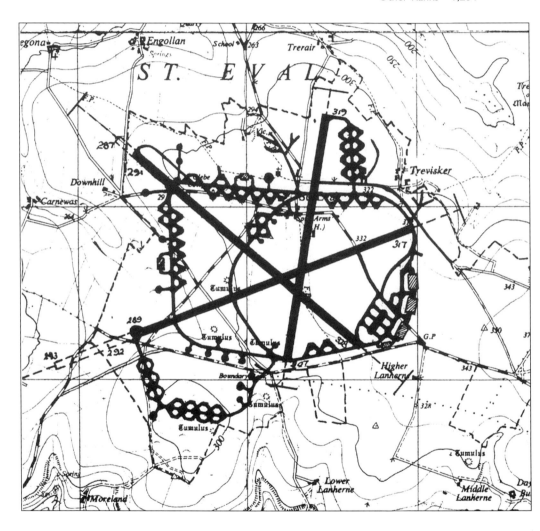

were lost.

With the arrival of Beauforts for 217 Squadron, the station acquired a more offensive aircraft, although the Beaufort with its poor performance was by no means an ideal anti-shipping aircraft for the waters around the UK. The squadron took some time to convert and the Ansons soldiered on to December 1940. During the latter months of 1940, the Mobile Torpedo Servicing Unit spent time at St Eval, providing the specialist support for detached torpedo-bomber units. As a Beaufort unit, 217 Squadron operated from St Eval to October 1941 and, after it

Beauforts used the airfield to mount anti-shipping attacks; in this case it was an attack by 86 Squadron on shipping in St Peter's Port.

Whitleys of No.10 detached to St Eval to help with the maritime war; one of their aircraft attacks a U-boat on 14 June 1943.

Detachment of 140 Squadron, September 1942.

had departed, the station was used by a number of other Beaufort units.

The first Fighter Command aircraft to move in were Spitfires of 234 Squadron, which arrived in mid-1940, charged with convoy patrols in the South-West Approaches and the English Channel and with a secondary role of defending the airfield and the surrounding area. The following month the Heston-based Photographic Reconnaissance Unit (PRU) formed its 'B Flight' at St Eval, to undertake recce of targets in Western France and particularly naval bases. 'B Flight' was replaced by 'D Flight' in October, which, in turn, was replaced by other PRU Flights until the detachments ceased in October 1942.

The fighter presence of Spitfires was not a great success, despite a Sector Ops Room having opened. Changes in the Luftwaffe's tactics soon led to increased night raids in the region and, as the Spitfires were not suited to the night-fighter role, 238 Squadron's Hurricanes took on the job. Indeed, the airfield itself was hit a number of times in late-summer 1940 and early 1941, causing damage and casualties. As the unit list shows, the main role of the station was that of an offensive Coastal Command base and, whilst some of this work was carried out by fighter types such as the Whirlwind, whose brief career was very much involved with anti-shipping and for which a detachment of 263 Squadron used St Eval for a few weeks in early 1941, it was the maritime types such as the Beaufort, Wellington and Liberator that played the major part.

Following the Battle of Britain, the airfield became almost the exclusive property of Coastal Command and was at the forefront in combating the U-boat menace in the North Atlantic and the Bay of Biscay. The unit list shows the movement of squadrons and aircraft types as St Eval remained an operational base throughout the war. On 6 April 1941, a small force of Beauforts from 22 Squadron, operating as a detachment from St Eval, launched an attack on the German cruiser, *Gneisenau*, in Brest Harbour. Only two of the attackers found the target; Flying Officer Kenneth Campbell dropped his torpedo but was immediately shot-down. A year later the story of his courageous attack was at last known and he was awarded the Victoria Cross; his citation read:

This officer was the pilot of a Beaufort aircraft of Coastal Command, which was detailed to attack an enemy battle cruiser in Brest Harbour at first light on the morning of 6th April, 1941. The aircraft did not return but it is now known that a torpedo attack was carried out with the utmost daring. The battle cruiser was secured alongside the wall on the north shore of the harbour, protected by a stone

Spitfire PRXI of 541 Squadron.

Whitleys, and a Spitfire, dispersed in one corner of the airfield in this January 1941 shot.

mole bending round it from the west. On rising ground behind the ship stood protective batteries of guns. Other batteries were clustered thickly round the two arms of land which encircle the outer harbour. In this outer harbour near the mole were moored three heavily armed anti-aircraft ships, guarding the battle cruiser. Even if an aircraft succeeded in penetrating these formidable defences, it would be almost impossible, after delivering a low-level attack, to avoid crashing into the rising ground beyond. This was well known to Flying Officer Campbell who, despite the heavy odds, went cheerfully and resolutely to the task. He ran the gauntlet of the defences. Coming in almost at sea level, he passed the anti-aircraft ships at less than mast-height in the very mouths of their guns, and skimming over the mole launched a torpedo at point-blank range. The battle cruiser was severely damaged below the water line, and was obliged to return to the dock whence she had come only the day before. By pressing home his attack at close quarters in the face of a withering fire on a course fraught with extreme peril, Flying Officer Campbell displayed valour of the highest order.

The formation in December 1940 of No.404 (later 1404) Meteorological Flight, with an initial establishment of 3+1 Blenheims, was significant, as the Flight was tasked to provide basic weather data on which the Command meteorologists could base their forecasts. This met role was highly important but seldom recognized, and it was a role that St Eval performed throughout the war, No.1404 Flight becoming 517 Squadron in August 1943.

Offensive operations continued into the crucial year of 1942, which was to be a turning point in the Battle of the Atlantic. Meanwhile, St Eval itself was still under attack, the Germans making a number of raids in May, causing damage to buildings and the destruction of aircraft. To boost the anti-submarine forces and to gain experience in this role, the

Americans began to use the airfield (as Station 129), with the B-24s of the 409th Squadron of the 93rd Bomb Group appearing in October 1942. The following month they were replaced by the 1st Anti-Submarine Squadron (Provisional), with a second such unit arriving a few months later. Both of these units moved to North Africa in March 1943 but, in July, were replaced by the two squadrons of the 479th Anti-Submarine Group. Again, this was a short-lived arrangement and the Group took its Liberators to Dunkeswell in August. Various US Navy units spent short periods at St Eval – further recognition of the part played by the station in the ASW role.

Every airfield has at least one tragic tale and for St Eval this came in August 1943 when a Whitley and Liberator collided on the runway, causing a massive explosion and the loss of aircraft and crews. The collision was, in large part, due to the poor runway layout, with a blind spot that hid one aircraft from the other. St Eval, like most major airfields, was under almost constant development during the war and underwent various improvements to its runways and facilities; by the time of the 1944 survey it had two long runways of almost 2,000 yards, in addition to the third shorter strip. The importance of the airfield was such that it was also given a FIDO installation, which became operational in early 1944. As a major coastal station, St Eval was destined to have a very busy first half of 1944 – the year of the Allied invasion – and was home to three RAF Liberator squadrons (53, 224, 547 Squadrons), all of which spent most of the year here. Many of these were equipped with the (by then) tried, tested and highly successful Leigh Light; in April a fourth squadron, 206 Squadron, arrived, giving the Cornish base one of the most powerful anti-submarine forces in the RAF. This force flew thousands of hours of patrols each month and was rewarded with a number of sightings, many of which

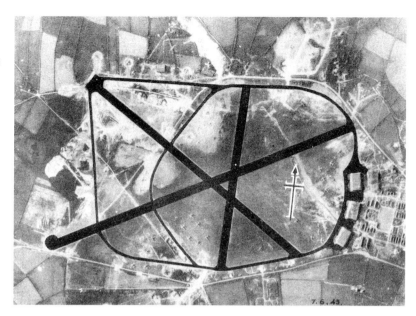

The 1944 survey picture; as with most of these it is an earlier air photo on which the main operating surfaces have been superimposed.

The reading room (whatever that was) of the 479th ASG; this American unit was here during 1943.

were converted into attacks and with at least three confirmed U-boat kills in June alone.

The Allied capture of the French ports meant that the U-boat threat was drastically reduced and also meant that the St Eval units would be better utilized elsewhere. By autumn, the station was a shadow of its former self in terms of operational units, although Wellington ASW squadrons were present until November 1944. The station was also used by ASR units, such as 282 Squadron, and both roles continued into the post-war period.

Maritime patrol work continued after the war and, by the early 1950s, the resident squadrons were using the Avro Shackleton. The airfield was also a major

site for diversions and a number of military and commercial aircraft made use of St Eval, mostly as a result of bad weather at their destination airfield. No.42 Squadron reformed at St Eval on 28 June 1952 to operate Shackletons, the first MR.1As arriving the same month; the squadron had operated a detachment of Beauforts at the airfield in 1941, but this time its association was somewhat longer. The squadron moved to St Mawgan in October 1958. Another Shackleton squadron formed in September; 206 Squadron had spent a number of periods at St Eval during the war. By July 1954, the station had a Wing of four Shackleton squadrons – 42, 206, 220 and 228 Squadrons, some with Mk.1s and some with Mk.2s. The St Eval Towed Target Flight was formed in September 1953 using the Mosquito TT.35, but only lasted two years before disbandment. The arrival of the Shackleton Mk.3 led to the maritime patrol squadrons moving to St Mawgan from late-1956 and St Eval was closed on 6 March 1959. No.626 VGS, which had arrived in June 1958, soldiered on at the airfield with its gliders until March 1963 but, by then, the airfield was already being returned to civil use, including the re-opening of long-closed roads. Like many Cornish airfields, the basic structure and layout is still there, seemingly little changed from its wartime layout, but many of the buildings have gone. The site is now an 'aerial farm' and various steel masts sprout from the grass between the runways.

DECOY SITES

Q   Colan   SW872585

| Q | Tregonetha Down | SW958631 |
| Q | Trelow Down | SW924683 |

UNITS

1939–1945

22 Sqn det	early 1941–Jun 1941	Beaufort
22 Sqn	28 Oct 1941–1 Feb 1942	Beaufort
42 Sqn det	1941	Beaufort
48 Sqn det	June 1940	Beaufort
53 Sqn	20 Mar 1941–17 Dec 1941+;	Blenheim,
	16 May 1942–3 Jul 1942	Hudson
53 Sqn	3 Jan 1944–13 Sep 1944	Liberator
58 Sqn	8 Apr 1942–30 Aug 1942;	Whitley,
	31 Mar 1943–29 Jun 1943	Halifax
59 Sqn det	1942–1943	Liberator
61 Sqn det	1942	Lancaster
86 Sqn	10 Jan 1942–5 Mar 1942	Beaufort
140 Sqn det	1942	various

For a short period in the immediate post-war years, the Lancaster was the main maritime type.

143 Sqn	28 Aug 1943–16 Sep 1943	Beaufighter
161 Sqn det	1942–?	various
179 Sqn	1 Nov 1944–30 Sep 1946	Wellington,
		Warwick
206 Sqn	30 May 1941–12 Aug 1941	Hudson
206 Sqn	12 Apr 1942–11 Jul 1944	Fortress
217 Sqn	2 Oct 1939–Mar 1942+	Anson,
		Beaufort
220 Sqn det	Nov 1940–Apr 1941	Hudson
221 Sqn det	Nov 1940–Sep 1941	Wellington
224 Sqn	20 Dec 1941–19 Feb 1942	Hudson
224 Sqn	23 Apr 1943–11 Sep 1944	Liberator
233 Sqn	16 Aug 1941–Jul 1942 +	Hudson
234 Sqn	18 Jun 1940–24 Feb 1941+	Spitfire
235 Sqn det	early 1943	Beaufighter
236 Sqn	Jul 1940–late-1941	Blenheim
238 Sqn	14 Aug 1940–10 Sep 1940	Hurricane
247 Sqn det	summer 1940–summer 1941	Gladiator,
		Hurricane
248 Sqn det	summer 1941	Blenheim
254 Sqn det	late-1940	Blenheim
263 Sqn	24 Feb 1941–18 Mar 1941	Whirlwind
280 Sqn det	autumn 1944–autumn 1945	Warwick
282 Sqn	19 Sep 1944–9 Jul 1945	various
304 Sqn	6 Mar 1945–9 Jul 1945	Wellington
407 Sqn	1 Oct 1942–10 Nov 1942;	Hudson,
	3 Nov 1943–2 Dec 1943	Wellington
415 Sqn	11 Apr 1942–late 1942	Hampden
489 Sqn det	May 1942–Jun 1942	Blenheim
500 Sqn	30 Aug 1942–5 Nov 1942	Hudson
502 Sqn	Feb 1942–Jun 1943+	Whitley,
		Halifax
517 Sqn	7 Aug 1943–25 Nov 1943	Hampden,
		Hudson
541 Sqn det	1943	Spitfire
543 Sqn det	late-1942–1943	Spitfire

Lancaster of 210 Squadron in the maritime role, October 1947.

547 Sqn	14 Jan 1944–1 Oct 1944	Liberator
612 Sqn	1 Nov 1943–3 Dec 1943	Wellington
796 Sqn FAA det	Aug–Sep 1948	Gannet
801 Sqn FAA	31 Jan 1941–6 Feb 1941	Skua
807 Sqn FAA	20–23 Aug 1949	Sea Fury
812 Sqn FAA det	Nov 1940–Dec 1940+	Swordfish
816 Sqn FAA det	Apr 1941–May 1941+	Swordfish
820 Sqn FAA	11–18 Nov 1944	Avenger
827 Sqn FAA	11 May 1941–4 Jun 1941	Albacore
829 Sqn FAA	7 Oct 1940–3 Nov 1940	Albacore
833 Sqn FAA	11 Mar 1943–15 Apr 1943	Swordfish
849 Sqn FAA	9–26 Aug 1944	Avenger
2 AACU det	?–Apr 1940	various
6 CPF	15 Jan 1940–27 May 1940	Tiger Moth
PRU	1 Jul 1940–Oct 1942+	various
404/1404Flt	24 Dec 1940–11 Aug 1943	Hampden, Blenheim, Hudson, Albemarle
8 AACU det	Mar 1941–Jun 1941	various
10 OTU det	1942–23 Jul 1943	Whitley

USAAF units
479th ASG
Squadrons:	4th, 6th, 19th, 22nd
Aircraft:	B-24
Dates:	8 Jul 1943–6 Aug 1943

Post-1945
42 Sqn	28 Jun 1952–8 Oct 1958	Shackleton
179 Sqn	?–30 Sep 1946	Wellington, Warwick
203 Sqn	16 Jan 1947–15 Aug 1952	Lancaster
206 Sqn	27 Sep 1952–14 Jan 1958	Shackleton
210 Sqn	1 Jun 1946–10 Sep 1952	Lancaster
220 Sqn	14 Nov 1951–4 Dec 1956	Shackleton
228 Sqn	1 Jun 1946–30 Sep 1946	Liberator
228 Sqn	1 Jul 1954–29 Nov 1956; 14 Jan 1958–6 Mar 1959	Shackleton
240 Sqn	27 May 1952–5 Jun 1952	Shackleton
95 GS	Jun 1945–31 Jan 1950	Cadet
19 Gp CF	29 Jul 1948–27 Aug 1951	various
TTF	Sep 1953–Sep 1955	Mosquito
626 VGS	1 Jun 1958–16 Mar 1963	Cadet

MEMORIAL

There are various memorials in St Uvelus church, including a Book of Remembrance, a memorial window (dedicated 1 October 1989) and a memorial to the crew of Shackleton VP254, who were killed in a crash off the coast of Borneo on 9 December 1958. The church itself is, in many ways, a memorial, as it was the central motif for the RAF St Eval badge and a well-known landmark to St Eval aircrew.

The Station badge featured St Uvelus church; the church now contains various memorials. This image is an extract of the St Eval page from the RAF Heraldry Trust project.

ST JUST

County: Cornwall

UTM/Grid: OS Map 203 – SW375292
Lat/Long: N50°06 W005°40
Nearest Town: Penzance 5 miles to east

HISTORY

St Just is the airfield for Land's End and was opened in September 1937, as Land's End Aerodrome, to provide an air link with the Scilly Isles by Channel Air Ferries. The large grass area was well-suited to the purpose, as most traffic was in the summer months with tourists visiting the Isles. The commercial services were reasonably successful and new routes were developed. In the early years of the war the commercial service was continued, but used for Government and military purposes until suspended in November 1941. Other than occasional detachments the airfield was not used for military purposes and the airfield was partially obstructed from mid-1941. The suspended service was re-started in 1942, but St Just was a little-used airfield despite the fact that the grass surfaces, whilst not wonderful in winter, would have been ideal for fighter-type aircraft.

Commercial services returned and were expanded after the war but, by the mid-1960s, this had declined and private flying became more significant, with the Land's End Aero Club taking over the airfield. It was not until 1984 that a viable commercial service was resumed, with Skybus operating the Britten-Norman Islander. The airfield (EGHC) has continued to develop and now operates four grass strips, the longest of which is 792m.

ST MARY'S

County: Scilly Islands

UTM/Grid: OS Map 203 – SV922104
Lat/Long: N49°54.44 W006°17.30
Nearest Town: Hugh Town 1 mile to west

HISTORY

Land's End Aerodrome opened in September 1937 and its main route was to the Scilly Isles, with the destination 'airport' being a stretch of grass on the golf course. The following year an area of land to the east of Hugh Town was leased for an airport and the new facility opened on 25 July 1939 with three grass strips, the maximum run being 2,000ft. The commercial air service was maintained after the outbreak of war and used for official and military purposes.

The airfield was used by a detachment of Hurricanes from 87 Squadron to provide some measure of air cover for the Scilly Isles; this detachment

AIRFIELD DATA DEC 1944

Command:	Fighter Command	Runway surface:	Grass
Function:	Operational Satellite	Hangars:	Nil
Runways:	NE/SW 666yd	Dispersals:	2
	N/S 600yd	Personnel:	Officers – 5
	NW/SE 593yd		Other Ranks – 73

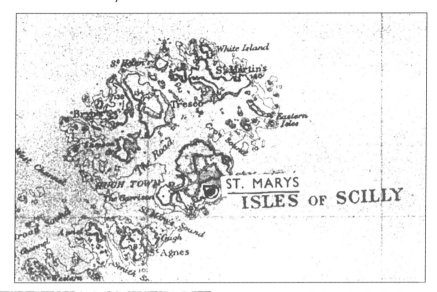

Hurricanes of 87 Squadron maintained a detachment presence at St Mary's in 1941–42; the telephone was the means by which the pilot was scrambled!

started in May 1941 and ran through to early 1942. The squadron usually rotated a Flight of four aircraft to the detachment, with pilots sitting at dispersal on standby with a telephone nearby, over which the scramble call would come. Facilities were poor, with tents being the main accommodation for those stuck on the airfield, although billets were also available in Hugh Town. The detachment met with some success and, in comparison to some airfields used by the peripatetic 87 Squadron, St Mary's was considered quite reasonable. The squadron detachment was replaced in mid-April 1942 by the cre-

ation of No.1449 (Fighter) Flight, this being made from the 87 Squadron Flight present at the time. The Flight had an establishment of 4+2 Hurricanes and remained as the islands' main air defence to September 1944.

At some point the NE/SW runway had been given a partial hard surface, although it was still listed in the 1944 survey as being grass. By late-September 1944 the airfield had been reduced to Care and Maintenance and, whilst retained for possible use, its only routine use was by the commercial service that had re-started in 1943. The post-war period saw the resumption of scheduled services, but these met with varying success and the airport had a number of owners. It was only the instigation of a viable helicopter service by BEA on 1964 that kept the route to Cornwall open. Various operators, both rotary and fixed-wing, have used the airfield since then and the infrastructure has been improved, with a new terminal building and apron areas. St Mary's Airport (EGHE) is now operated by the Council of the Isles of Scilly and has one tarmac runway (15/33), one tarmac/grass (half-length tarmac) runway and one grass runway.

UNITS

1939–1945

87Sqn det	May 1941–spring 1942	Hurricane
1449Flt	10 Apr 1942–17 Sep 1944	Hurricane

ST MAWGAN (Trebelzue) (Station 512)

UTM/Grid: OS Map 200 – SW870646
Lat/Long: N50°26.25 W005°00.30
Nearest Town: Newquay 2 miles to south-west

County: Cornwall

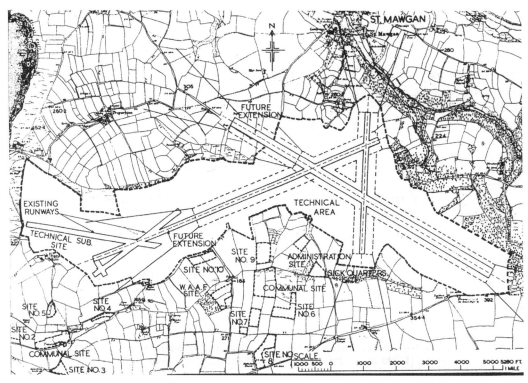

HISTORY

Trebelzue Big Field, on the cliff-top above Watergate Bay, just to the north of Newquay was used by aircraft from the mid-1930s, with a commercial service by Western Airways being started in May 1939. This was a small-scale operation but, like most commercial routes, it was closed on the outbreak of war and the RAF acquired the site as a satellite for St Eval. As Trebelzue, although also referred to as Newquay, the airfield did not open until September 1941, by which time it had been given two surfaced runways despite the constrained nature of the site. In December, it was transferred to Ferry Command's No.44 Group and No.2 Overseas Aircraft Despatch Unit (OADU), formed at Trebelzue on 26 January 1942 out of the OADU at Portreath, and, during the rest of that year, primarily handled Beauforts and Beaufighters en route to units in the Middle East. Within a very short time it was determined that the airfield was unsuitable and would need major work. It was this decision that led to St Mawgan's unusual lay-

out of, apparently, two airfields – for that is exactly what it was. The existing airfield simply could not be extended and so a new airfield was constructed on the eastern boundary, with one of Trebelzue's runways being extended as part of the new airfield (the plan makes this arrangement clear). Construction work started on 24 August 1942; whilst there was some use of Trebelzue during this period, it was restricted. 'O Flight' of No.1 AACU used Trebelzue from May to October 1942 whilst work on their home base of Cleave was underway, the Henleys of this unit flying target-towing for the gunnery school at Penhale. As the unit list shows, a number of other Flights – and even a detachment of Mustangs from 400 Squadron – used Trebelzue during this period. However, the station's name was changed from Trebelzue to St Mawgan on 24 February 1943 and one of the RAF's great maritime stations was born.

The units at Trebelzue remained at the new airfield, but the old runways gradually became parking

AIRFIELD DATA DEC 1944

Command:	Transport Command	Runway surface:	Concrete
Function:	Airport	Hangars:	T.2 × 2
Runways:	140 deg 3,000 × 100yd	Dispersals:	60 × Loop
	080 deg 2,000 × 50yd	Personnel:	Officers – 144 (12 WAAF)
	010 deg 1,400 × 50yd		Other Ranks – 2,381 (368 WAAF)

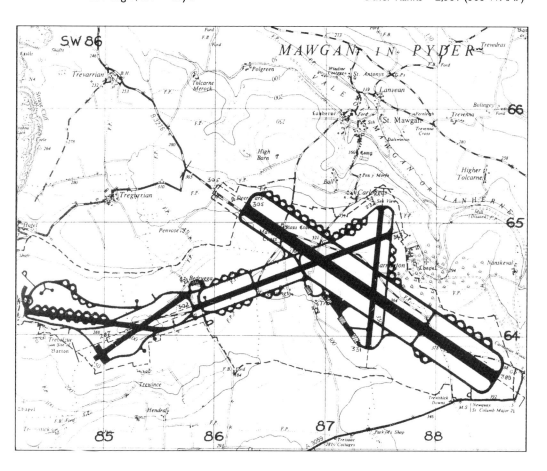

areas and were subsequently developed into dispersals; indeed, it was this latter facility and the station's location in the extreme south-west of England that appealed to the Americans. In June, the 491st Base and Air Base Squadron of the USAAF arrived at Station 512 and prepared to handle the large flow of aircraft expected to route via St Mawgan to North Africa as soon as the new runways were ready. The first runway was open on 1 July and the first landing was by a USAAF B-24. St Mawgan was also a receiving point for aircraft from America and when two Met Flights were based here, both with B-17s, the

American presence was dominant, as the RAF ferry work had all but ceased. The Met Fortresses stayed only a few weeks, but the ever-increasing number of dispersal points continued to house large numbers of transient American aircraft. It was not until early summer 1944 that the majority of the heavy construction work on runways and dispersals was complete and the airfield had its three runways, the longest of which was 3,000 yards. As there were few based aircraft there was little need for hangars and, at this time, the airfield only had two T.2s. The 1944 survey lists St Mawgan as a Transport Command Airport, a title

This aerial shot dated 5 April 1942 is labeled Newquay, all part of the confusion of names as the official name at the time was Trebelzue. The picture shows how close the airfield was to the coast and how constrained the site was.

given to very few wartime airfields but that certainly reflected the station's role. Even the limited services by BOAC/KLM routed via the Cornish airfield.

Oxfords of No.1529 Beam Approach Training Flight were in residence from December 1944 to early 1946. The Traffic Control School, which had formed here in November 1944, became No.1 Air Traffic School on 3 January 1945 as a No.44 Group lodger unit, but moved to Bramcote in November. Like its predecessor it was a ground training unit, but used the normal air traffic of the airfield for training. At some point in 1945 one of those strange small units arrived: the Armament Synthetic Development Unit (ASDU) arrived from Portreath with a small number of Warwicks and Wellingtons; the unit disbanded in June 1946. After the final use of the dispersals by 'redundant' aircraft en route back to North America, the once crucial airport was suddenly not required. St Mawgan was reduced to Care and Maintenance on 1 July 1947.

The Air-Sea Warfare Development Unit (ASWDU) moved to St Mawgan from Ballykelly in May 1951, the station having re-opened the previous

month, and, although the unit returned to its Northern Ireland base in 1958, the seven-year period was a fascinating one. The ASWDU had a very wide remit, from the obvious elements of the title, such as development work on weapons and tactics, to training of operational units, who sent aircraft and crews on short-term detachments to work with the experts. The list of aircraft operated by the ASWDU is a 'who's who' of maritime types, although some of the older types had vanished by the time it arrived in Cornwall and the focus was on the various marks of Shackleton. The Navy also had a keen interest in ASW development and 744 Squadron had reformed at Culdrose in March 1954 to work with the RAF's ASWDU; in October, the squadron moved to St Mawgan to co-locate with their RAF colleagues. The squadron operated a variety of types during its two years at the station.

St Mawgan's role in Coastal Command had increased in July 1954, with the formation here of the Coastal Command Modification Centre to carry out any modification work on the Command's Lancasters and Shackletons. However, in February 1956, the

The extensive hutted camp
at St Mawgan, 1951.

unit disbanded. The SAR Whirlwinds of 22
Squadron arrived from Thorney Island in June 1956
but, as usual with the SAR squadrons, the parent airfield was simply a HQ and engineering base, although
with one operational Flight, and the Whirlwinds
were dispersed to various airfields across southern
England. In April 1974, the squadron moved its parent location back to Thorney Island.

The maritime training role was enhanced in
January 1951 with the formation of the School of
Maritime Reconnaissance, initially equipped with
MR Lancasters and a few Hastings, although the latter were transferred to Lindholme for the radar
course. The school was part of No.19 Group and had
responsibility for all air-sea warfare training, for
which it worked with the ASWDU. When the
school disbanded in September 1956, its role was
taken on by the Maritime Operational Training Unit
(MOTU) at Kinloss (with No.18 Group); however, it
returned to St Mawgan in July 1965, by which time it
was equipped with Shackletons. Nimrods were taken
on charge from late-1969, but the following year the
MOTU became No.236 Operational Conversion
Unit. The OCU was responsible for training the
RAF's maritime Nimrod crews and, over the twenty-
two years it spent at St Mawgan, it trained hundreds
of crews on the 'Mighty Hunter'. During part of this
period it also carried the number-plate of 38
(Reserve) Squadron. The OCU spent a year or so at
Kinloss (1982–1983) whilst work was being done at
its home base but, ten years later, in October 1992, it
disbanded at St Mawgan, its training role being taken
on by 42 (Reserve) Squadron at Kinloss.

Operational squadrons, with Shackletons, had
arrived in 1956 but the two units, 220 and 228
Squadron were only in existence here for two years. A
change of number took place in October 1958, with

220 Squadron becoming 201 Squadron, the new unit
'taking over the aircraft and personnel as a going concern' and remaining with the 'Shacks' at St Mawgan to
July 1965, when they moved to that other bastion of
maritime ops, Kinloss in Scotland. The same month
that the renumbering took place saw the formation of
another Shackleton unit, 42 Squadron coming back to
life after five years of disbandment. Along with 206
Squadron, which had moved here from St Eval in
January 1958, this unit became the station's main
operational strength for the rest of its front-line maritime life and is the squadron most associated with St
Mawgan. The 'Shacks' gave way to Nimrods in August
1970 for 206 Squadron and April 1971 for 42
Squadron, but the routine of training, exercises and
detachments continued. It was only with the reduction in RAF maritime strength and the decision to
make Kinloss the sole operational maritime base that
brought the disappearance of the squadrons.

On 1 May 1972, a Canberra target facilities
squadron was formed at St Mawgan, primarily to work
with the various weapon ranges in the area and along
the south coast. No.7 Squadron's main type was the
Canberra TT.18, with its pair of Rushton winch targets that made it suitable for working with large-cali-
bre weapons, such as naval 4.5in guns and
surface-to-air missiles. The squadron spent the whole
of its Canberra period based at St Mawgan, disbanding in January 1982, but much of its time was taken up
with detachments to other airfields. The major structural change in the latter years of the station's life was
the construction of a HAS site on the west side of the
main airfield, St Mawgan being allocated as a forward
deployment base for air-defence aircraft, with various
Tornado F.3 squadrons exercising this facility.

Although the hectic days of maritime operations
are long gone, the station is still an active RAF air-

220 Squadron operated Shackletons from St Mawgan from 1956 to 1958.

Target-towing Canberra TT.18 of 7 Squadron.

The latter decades of the station's flying career involved the Nimrod.

field, although the only based flying is by 203 (Reserve) Squadron with three SAR Sea King helicopters; this squadron formed in October 1996, when the Sea King OCU was given a shadow number. The OCU itself had been very short-lived, having formed in April 1996 out of the Sea King Training Flight (SKTF), which itself had arrived from Culdrose in April 1993, when the RAF had taken its Sea King training back from the navy. The airfield now also looks after all RAF Sea King maintenance and has a number of other non-flying units, including two RAF Regiment squadrons: No.1 Squadron and No.2625 (County of Cornwall) Squadron RAuxAF.

In early 2005, it was announced that St Mawgan (EGDG) would be reduced to Care and Maintenance in April 2007, with the helicopter unit moving to

Valley. There is opposition to this plan from the council, as it will affect the operation of Newquay Cornwall Airport. This council-owned and subsidized commercial operation uses the military facilities, but has its own terminal. With an increasing number of flights by Ryanair, Skybus and Air Southwest, passenger numbers are around 25,000 a year – but it is far from being self-sustainable should the RAF pull-out go ahead.

UNITS

1939–1945

264Sqn det	1942	Mosquito
282Sqn det	late-1944–1945	Warwick, Walrus, Sea Otter
400Sqn det	early 1943	Mustang
2 OADU	26 Jan 1942–1944?	Various
I AACU	29 May 1942–27 Oct 1942	Henley
1529Flt	7 Dec 1942–27 Jan 1946	Oxford
1602Flt	14 Dec 1942–28 Feb 1943	Henley
1604Flt	14 Dec 1942–23 Mar 1943	Henley
I ATS	3 Jan 1945–20 Nov 1945	

USAAF units

Met Flt	Nov 1943	B-17

Post-1945

7Sqn	I May 1970–5 Jan 1982	Canberra
22Sqn	4 Jun 1956–I Apr 1974	Whirlwind
42Sqn	8 Oct 1958–?	Shackleton, Nimrod
201Sqn	I Oct 1958–I Jul 1965	Shackleton
203Sqn	I Nov 1996–current	Sea King
206Sqn	14 Jan 1958–?	Shackleton, Nimrod
217Sqn	I Feb 1958–13 Nov 1959	Whirlwind
220Sqn	4 Dec 1956–I Oct 1958	Shackleton
228Sqn	29 Nov 1956–14 Jan 1958	Shackleton
702Sqn FAA det	4–14 Feb 1991	Lynx
744Sqn FAA	23 Oct 1953–31 Oct 1956	various
849Sqn FAA det	3–12 Mar 1993	Sea King
ASDU	1945–23 Jun 1946	
16 FU	26 Apr 1946–15 Nov 1946	various
1552Flt	5 Jun 1946–29 Jul 1946	Oxford
SoMR	I Jan 1951–30 Sep 1956	Hastings, Lancaster
ASWDU	10 May 1951–I Sep 1958	various
1360Flt	I Aug 1957–I Feb 1958	Whirlwind
MOTU	7 Jul 1965–I Jul 1970	Shackleton, Nimrod
236 OCU	I Jul 1970–I Apr 1982, I Nov 1983–I Oct 1992	Nimrod
626 VGS	1990–1991	Viking
SKTU	2 Apr 1993–I Apr 1996	Sea King
SK OCU	I Apr 1996–I Nov 1996	Sea King

ST MERRYN
(HMS *Vulture*, HMS *Curlew*)

County: Cornwall

UTM/Grid: OS Map 200 – SW889714
Lat/Long: N50°30 W004°59
Nearest Town: Padstow 3 miles to north-east

St Merryn in June 2003; the basic airfield structure is still clear.

HISTORY

St Merryn was the most northerly of the three airfields of St Merryn, St Eval and St Mawgan, all within three miles of each other on this stretch of Cornish coast. Like St Mawgan (Trebelzue), it had its origins as a pre-war civil airfield, although it was little more than a large field with a single hangar that had been laid out in 1937. The site was examined by the Admiralty in early 1939 and chosen for development, work commencing at the end of the year on a standard four-runway naval air station. Construction involved the diversion of one major road and the closing of a number of minor roads, as well as substantial ground work, including levelling and the removal of field boundaries. The main technical area was on the west side of the airfield with a number of hangars and other buildings, with the main hutted camp in the same general area (*see* plan). The original provision was for four hangars, but this was increased and, by 1944, St Merryn had sprouted a variety of hangars, including the usual naval arrangement of Mains types at the dispersal points. The two main dispersal areas were to the south and north, the latter from an access taxiway that crossed the (diverted) main road.

Naval Air Station St Merryn (HMS *Vulture*) opened on 10 August 1940, with 792 Squadron forming here as an Air Target Towing Unit on 15 August, initially equipped with six Rocs and Skuas. This squadron, subsequently operating Defiants and Martinets, remained at St Merryn until January 1945, when it disbanded and its motto of 'We Suffer That Others May Learn' speaks volumes for the type of work the squadron had to do! September brought 774 Squadron from Evanton; this was an Armament Training Squadron for training of observers and

AIRFIELD DATA DEC 1944

Command:	Fleet Air Arm	Runway surface:	Tarmac
Function:	Care and Maintenance	Hangars:	Mains (60ft × 84ft) × 13, Mains
Runways:	15/33 3,810ft × 90ft		(60ft × 70ft) × 13, Teesside S × 4,
	10/28 3,090ft × 90ft		Pentad × 2, Callender Hamilton × one
	01/19 3,000ft × 90ft	Dispersals:	8 aircraft standings, 4 aprons
	06/24 3,000ft × 90ft	Personnel:	Officers – 220 (8 WRNS)
			Other Ranks – 1,101 (231 WRNS)

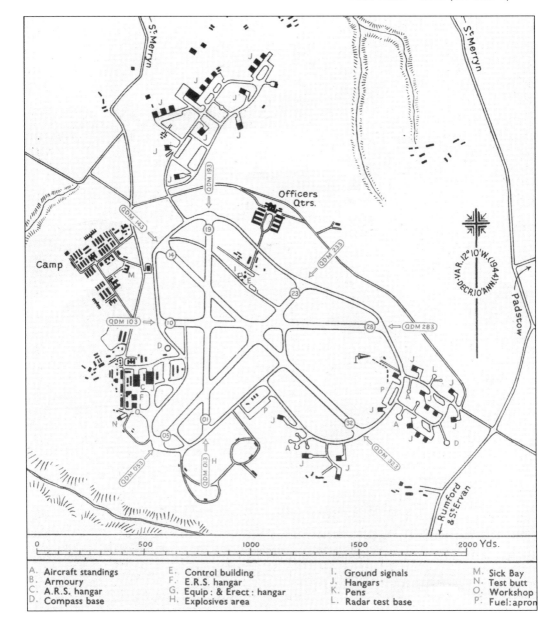

A. Aircraft standings	E. Control building	I. Ground signals	M. Sick Bay
B. Armoury	F. E.R.S. hangar	J. Hangars	N. Test butt
C. A.R.S. hangar	G. Equip : & Erect : hangar	K. Pens	O. Workshop
D. Compass base	H. Explosives area	L. Radar test base	P. Fuel:apron

telegraphist air gunners and it operated a variety of air-craft, adding Albacores to its diverse fleet on arrival at St Merryn. Aircraft types changed during its stay at the Cornish airfield, but the basic role remained the same until the squadron departed in late-October 1944. As the unit list shows, a large number of squadrons oper-ated from St Merryn, the majority of these in the train-ing role, as the airfield became one of the Fleet Air Arm's main training bases, with others in the support role, such as target-towing. As with all naval air sta-tions there were also brief appearances by operational squadrons, either for a specific operation or a shore-base period for rest, re-equipment or training.

The Luftwaffe had not failed to notice these three Cornish airfields in a neat row and St Merryn, like its colleagues, was attacked a number of times in late-1940, with single raiders making bomb or strafe attacks on 3, 9 and 14 October and 11 November. Some damage was caused, especially in the latter attack. The bombers were back in spring 1941, with raids in April and May, the latter, on 5 May, being the largest and most effective, when six He111s

caused damage to buildings and the destruction of a number of aircraft.

October 1942 saw the formation of 748 Squadron to operate as a Fighter Pool squadron, for which it held a diverse fleet that included Fulmar, Hurricane, Martlet and Spitfire for refresher flying. The follow-ing March it became an Operational Training Unit, as No.10 Naval OTU, a role it retained for the rest of its existence. However, the major development was the decision to base the School of Air Combat here and it was in preparation for this that the airfield was given the additional hangars and other buildings and an extension of the main runway to almost 4,000ft. The School of Air Combat, in typical Fleet Air Arm fashion, comprised numbered squadrons, each of which performed a particular role with the school. One of the first to take up residence was 736 Squadron, arriving from Yeovilton in September 1943 to become the Fighter Combat School. This unit was to remain at St Merryn to 1950 and eventu-ally absorbed a number of the other squadrons that had operated in the School of Air Combat. Three further

A typical large Fleet Air Arm base with four runways, although two are not very distinctive in this picture.

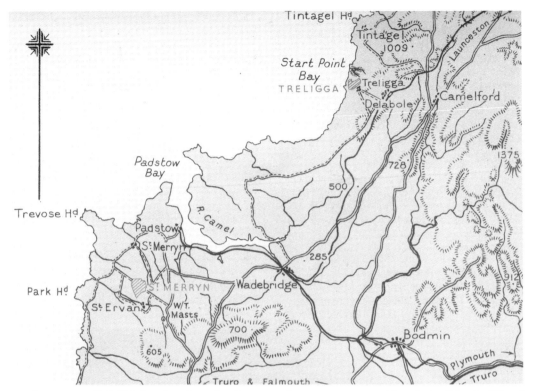

squadrons were added: 719 Squadron formed in June 1944, to run a Naval Air Firing course; 709 Squadron formed in September 1944, using Seafires and operating as a Ground-Attack School – the squadron also used Hellcats and Harvards and remained at the airfield until disbanding in January 1946. The training 'empire' at the station had continued to increase and, in August 1944, part of 736 Squadron was used to form 715 Squadron, the latter's task being a Fighter Air Combat course and a Fighter Leaders Course, for which it primarily used the Corsair and the Seafire. All of this made St Merryn an incredibly busy and important training base and placed strain on the airfield's infrastructure, with accommodation being a major problem, despite the growing collection of huts and the use of billets in towns such as Padstow. The airfield itself continued to develop, the major feature being the addition of yet more hangars.

By January 1945, the school had become the School of Naval Air Warfare and the first of its units disappeared when 719 Squadron disbanded. Training continued at an intense pace, with naval operations in the Pacific War becoming the focus of the Fleet Air Arm's activities. This remained the situation to the end of the war but, all of a sudden, the rush to train combat aircrew had gone; nevertheless, St Merryn continued to operate as a training unit, although with an increased emphasis on support roles

such as target-towing, although the School of Naval Air Warfare was also still in business. No.725 Squadron arrived in August 1945 to act as an Air Target Towing Unit; like other squadrons it was subsequently absorbed into 736 Squadron.

As the post-war unit list shows, St Merryn continued to be used by a variety of squadrons, including, in the early 1950s, Naval Reserve squadrons on annual weapon camp. The School of Air Warfare departed to Culdrose in March 1948, but was replaced by the Air Armament School, although this was closed in early 1952. This left only 796 as the based flying unit and, in April 1952, it was split to form 750 Squadron, the latter acquiring the Barracuda element. Together they operated as the Observer School. Again this was short-lived and, in November 1953, the school moved to Culdrose, although it was February the following year before the move of both squadrons was complete. In the meantime, the station had been paid off as HMS Vulture on 14 October 1953 and renamed as HMS Curlew. In the latter guise it was home to the School of Aircraft Maintenance and the Naval Air Ordnance School and the once busy flying station spent a further two years as home to these technical schools, the only airframes being 'dead' ones on which students could practise their skills. St Merryn was placed into Care and Maintenance in June 1955 and was finally closed on 10 January 1956.

817 Squadron operated the Firefly from here for a few months in 1950. (Ray Sturtivant)

There had been some debate as to the site's future, with suggestions that it could become an airport for Newquay (a role that eventually went to St Mawgan) or be used by the RAF Regiment as a depot and training base. These and other plans came to naught and the disposal of the site and its assets commenced in 1959. The large collection of buildings have undergone varied fortunes, some became a holiday camp, some have been taken over for industrial or agricultural use and some have been demolished – but, overall, much of the structure of St Merryn has survived. There has been some flying at the airfield since the late-1970s, most significantly by the Cornwall Parachute Centre.

UNITS

1939–1945

709 Sqn FAA	15 Sep 1944–6 Jan 1946	Seafire, Hellcat
715 Sqn FAA	17 Aug 1944–31 Mar 1946	Corsair, Seafire
719 Sqn FAA	15 Jun 1944–2 Jan 1945	Wildcat, Seafire, Master
736 Sqn FAA	2 Sep 1943–1 Feb 1950	various
748 Sqn FAA	12 Oct 1942–4 Feb 1944	various
762 Sqn FAA	15 Apr 1942–8 Sep 1942	Fulmar, Martlet, Master
774 Sqn FAA	17 Sep 1940–24 Oct 1944	various
787 Sqn FAA det	24 Feb 1943–1 Jul 1944+	various
792 Sqn FAA	15 Aug 1940–2 Jan 1945	various
794 Sqn FAA	2 Jan 1945–9 Aug 1945	various
801 Sqn FAA	17 Jan 1941–Feb 1941+; Oct–Nov 1941+	Skua, Sea Hurricane
804 Sqn FAA	22 Jun 1942–25 Jul 1942	Sea Hurricane

808 Sqn FAA	17 Mar 1942–18 Apr 1942	Spitfire
809 Sqn FAA	29 Mar 1941–10 Jun 1941; 21 Aug 1942–1 Oct 1942	Fulmar
828 Sqn FAA	25 Oct 1940–18 Nov 1940	Albacore
829 Sqn FAA	14 Sep 1940–7 Oct 1940	Albacore
836 Sqn FAA	26 Nov 1942–3 Dec 1942	Swordfish
837 Sqn FAA	19 Oct 1942–16 Nov 1942	Swordfish
879 Sqn FAA	1 Oct 1942–10 Oct 1942	Fulmar
880 Sqn FAA	1 Jul 1941–14 Aug 1941+	Martlet
882 Sqn FAA	3 Nov 1941–1 Dec 1941	Martlet
883 Sqn FAA	5–19 Dec 1941	Sea Hurricane
884 Sqn FAA	1 Jan 1942–7 Feb 1942	Fulmar
885 Sqn FAA	6 Feb 1942–10 Mar 1942	Sea Hurricane
885 Sqn FAA	19 Feb 1944–31 Mar 1944	Seafire
886 Sqn FAA	23 May 1942–22 Jun 1942	Fulmar
886 Sqn FAA	25 Apr 1944–4 May 1944	Seafire
887 Sqn FAA	25–28 Jul 1942; 3–22 Mar 1943	Fulmar, Seafire
888 Sqn FAA	29 Dec 1941–12 Jan 1942	Martlet
891 Sqn FAA	9 Sep 1942–8 Oct 1942	Sea Hurricane
893 Sqn FAA	23 Aug 1942–9 Sep 1942	Fulmar, Martlet
895 Sqn FAA	22 Mar 1943–3 May 1943	Seafire
897 Sqn FAA	5 May 1943–12 Jul 1943	Seafire
897 Sqn FAA	11–22 Apr 1944	Seafire

Post-1945

709 Sqn FAA	?–6 Jan 1946	Seafire, Hellcat
715 Sqn FAA	?–31 Mar 1946	Corsair, Seafire
725 Sqn FAA	4 Aug 1945–27 Dec 1945	various
736 Sqn FAA	?–1 Feb 1950	various
741 Sqn FAA	12 Aug 1946–25 Nov 1947	Firefly, Seafire
748 Sqn FAA	14 Aug 1945–11 Feb 1946	various
750 Sqn FAA	17 Apr 1952–30 Nov 1953	Anson, Barracuda, Firefly, Sea Prince
796 Sqn FAA	13 Nov 1947–9 Feb 1954	Firefly
807 Sqn FAA	May 1949–Apr 1950+	Sea Fury
810 Sqn FAA	May 1949–Jan 1950+	Firefly
813 Sqn FAA	8–15 Sep 1947	Firebrand
817 Sqn FAA	25 Apr 1950–Aug 1950	Firefly
820 Sqn FAA	31 Mar 1952–Jan 1953+	Firefly
825 Sqn FAA	5 Nov 1951–19 Jan 1952	Firefly
860 Sqn FAA	7 May 1946–27 Jul 1946	Firefly
1831 Sqn FAA	Jul 1951–May 1952; Jun 1953–Sep 1953	Sea Fury
1832 Sqn FAA	23 Jun 1950–8 Jul 1951	Sea Fury
82 GS	16 Aug 1950–1 Sep 1955	Cadet, Sedbergh

SANDBANKS
(HMS *Daedalus II*)

County: Dorset

UTM/Grid: OS Map 195 – SZ044877
Lat/Long: N50°41 W001°56
Nearest Town: Bournemouth 3 miles to north-east

Seafox of 765 Squadron at Sandbanks, one of a number of types operated by this diverse unit. (Ray Sturtivant)

HISTORY

The naval base at Sandbanks was opened on 15 May 1940 as HMS *Daedalus II*, to show its connection with Lee-on-Solent, for which it acted as a 'marine aerodrome'. It was laid out on a small site on the east side of Poole Harbour, close to Bournemouth, with the harbour being used for mooring and as an alighting area. The harbour was also in use by the RAF and BOAC, as well as a large amount of shipping, and it was a pretty congested area. From August 1940 to October 1943, Sandbanks housed 765 Squadron, which operated as the Basic Seaplane Training School and for which it used a variety of floatplanes, including Kingfisher, Roc, Seafox, Swordfish and Walrus. The station was equipped with one large hangar and the concrete apron of the hangar was sloped down to the water to also act as a slipway, although aircraft also used nearby beaches.

A second unit was added in July 1943, with the formation of 'W Flight' of 700 Squadron, which was formed specifically for the planned Azores operation and for which it held six Walrus and four Swordfish on charge. This special mission did not take place as planned and the unit moved to Machrihanish later in the month. By late-1943, the navy's need for a seaplane training base had gone and Sandbanks was reduced to Care and Maintenance.

UNITS

1939–1945

700WSqn FAA	12 Jul 1943	Walrus, Swordfish
765Sqn FAA	26 Aug 1940–25 Oct 1943	various

SHREWTON

County: Wiltshire

UTM/Grid: OS Map 184 – SU076460
Lat/Long: N51°13 W001°53
Nearest Town: Salisbury 10 miles to south-east

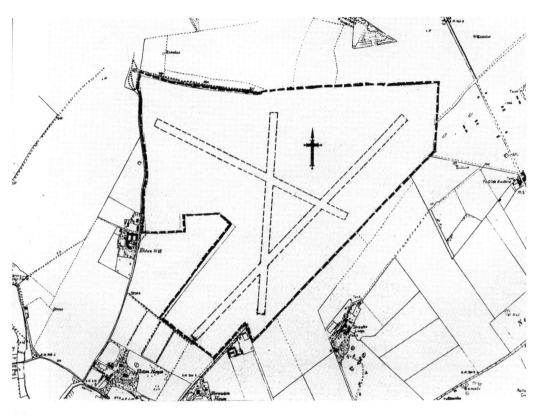

HISTORY

Situated in the centre of Salisbury Plain training areas, Shrewton would have been an ideal airfield for use by army co-operation aircraft and that was the original intention in early 1940, with No.3 School of Army Co-operation scheduled to form here, the authority for which was dated 20 April. The school did not, however, form and the new airfield was allocated as an RLG for Netheravon's No.1 SFTS.

Shrewton was laid out on an area of fields to the east of Elston Hall and, after the removal of hedges and some work on the grass surfaces, it provided reasonable runs in most directions, the plan showing three strips, but with some suggestion that in its early months it actually used four. As an RLG it did not require anything in the way of infrastructure, although a permanent flare path, using the standard gooseneck flares, was provided, as the airfield was predominantly used for night flying. The flares actually proved to be a problem, in that they attracted the

Luftwaffe; a number of attacks were made – with no result – in August 1940 and again, but with more success, in April and May 1941. There were no fatalities in these raids but Shrewton, like all training bases, had its share of fatal flying accidents.

The SFTS started using the airfield in July 1940 as one of a number of RLGs that this large and busy training school needed for training RAF and FAA pilots, the latter dominating the training in the early months of use. The Wiltshire field saw various aircraft in its circuit, from Harts, Hinds and Harvards to Battles and this unit remained the main user of Shrewton to March 1942, when the school disbanded. A number of army co-operation squadrons made use of the airfield in 1941 for specific exercises, but none were actually based here. The demise of the SFTS was caused by the creation of a new organization, the Glider Pilot Regiment and its associated training units, with the Salisbury Plain airfields being an obvi-

AIRFIELD DATA DEC 1944

Command:	Fighter Command	Runway surface:	Grass
Function:	Relief Landing Ground	Hangars:	Blister × 3
Runways:	NE/SW 1,500yd	Dispersals:	Nil
	WNW/ESE 1,300yd	Personnel:	Officers – 8
	270 deg 2,000 × 50yd		Other Ranks – 158

ous location for the airborne operations organization.

Shrewton was used as an RLG by the Glider Exercise Unit from Netheravon in early 1942 and by the Glider Pilot Exercise Unit from the autumn of that year to the end of the year. Keeping with the glider theme, the Heavy Glider Conversion Unit (HGCU) had formed here on 1 July 1942, with Whitley tow aircraft and Horsa gliders but, two weeks later, moved to Brize Norton. In December 1942, the airfield was handed to the Ministry of Works and, over the next few months, a number of structures were erected, including three Blister hangars on the north-east side and various accommodation buildings. It may have been at this period that the new runway layout was set, although the confusion is increased by the fact that the survey listed two runways but showed three on the plan. The re-built Shrewton re-opened on 24 March 1943 and was officially an emergency landing ground, which technically was a lower rating than an RLG!

The GPEU was back from autumn 1943 when, once more, Shrewton became a satellite for Netheravon. The GPEU became part of the Operational and Refresher Training Unit (ORTU) in December 1943 and the new unit, still with glider pilots as their 'customers', retained use of Shrewton

as a satellite; indeed, the Tiger Moth element of the ORTU was based at Shrewton from early 1944 to November that year. Anyone allowed to lean over the fence in January 1944 might have been surprised to see rocket projectiles fired across the airfield: the A&AEE used Shrewton for ground firing of RPs for a few weeks. Armament trials were an important aspect of the A&AEE's work and they occasionally used Shrewton as a landing ground in the late-1940s, when involved on trials in the Salisbury Plain ranges.

The end of the war had seen Shrewton reduced to Care and Maintenance and it was officially closed in April 1946, although it was kept on the books for some time and, as mentioned above, saw some use by the A&AEE. However, this was soon discontinued and the airfield site was returned to agriculture; there is now no significant remnant of the site.

UNITS

1939–1945

1 SFTS	Jul 1940–Mar 1942	various
HGCU	1–15 Jul 1942	Whitley, Horsa
GPEU det	8 Oct 1942–17 Dec 1942;	Tiger Moth
	29 Sep 1943–Nov 1943	
ORTU det	early 1944–Nov 1944	Tiger Moth

SOUTH CERNEY

County: Gloucestershire

UTM/Grid: OS Map 163 – SU056988
Lat/Long: N51°41.23 W001°55.20
Nearest Town: Cirencester 3 miles to north-west

HISTORY

South Cerney spent over thirty years as an RAF training base and, during that time, many thousands of aircrew and officers passed through its various courses, the most intensive period occurring during the middle years of World War Two. A large area of flat farmland to the south-east of Cirencester and adjacent to the main road was acquired in 1936 for the construction of a major training base. This was part of the RAF's expansion period planning, as it was already appreciated that training units would have to move from the airfields closer to the east coast – and Germany. The village after which the airfield was named was to the south, as was the nearest

railway station. Construction of the grass airfield was straightforward, with a large, oval, operating area, later encircled by a concrete perimeter track, and a comprehensive technical and administrative area on the north-west side. In addition to three C-Type hangars, this included the usual well-designed and laid-out selection of brick buildings, for everything from workshops and classrooms to barrack blocks and, of course, the architecturally attractive officers' mess. Although construction was simple it was a major project and, not unusually, the station was not complete when its first unit arrived.

The biplane trainers of No.3 Flying Training

AIRFIELD DATA DEC 1944

Command: Flying Training Command
Function: Parent (Pilots) Advanced Flying Unit
Runways: 190 deg 975yd
            270 deg 1,075yd

Runway surface: Sommerfeld Track
Hangars: Double Blister (69ft) × 8,
                  Blister (65ft) × 3, C Type × 3,
                  Bellman × 2, ARS × one
Dispersals: Nil
Personnel: Officers – 225 (13 WAAF)
                  Other Ranks – 2,152 (400 WAAF)

School arrived in August 1937 and the Harts, the main training type, were soon supplemented by Airspeed Oxfords. In September 1939 the unit became a Service Flying Training School and was given an establishment of thirty-one Harts and forty-four Oxfords, although the Oxford element continued to grow and, by late-summer 1940, the school had over 100 Oxfords on strength and had said farewell to the Harts – having given-up the single-engine pilot-training role. It was a busy unit and, as such, made use of Bibury and Long Newnton as RLGs. The SFTS was re-designated as No.3 (Pilots) Advanced Flying Unit on 1 March 1942 and became one of the busiest training airfields in this Region, which included operating a number of RLGs:

3 (P)AFU RLG Airfield	From	To
Bibury	1 Mar 1942	15 Nov 1944
Long Newnton	29 May 1942	30 Sep 1943
Lulsgate Bottom	1 Jun 1942	30 Sep 1943
Southrop	13 Jul 1942	22 Jan 1945
Chedworth	9 Feb 1943	Jun 1944
Babdown Farm	30 Sep 1943	30 Oct 1943
Fairford	Nov 1943	29 Mar 1944
Charmy Down	30 Oct 1944	17 Dec 1945
Moreton Valence	21 Dec 1944	12 Jul 1945

The PAFU was at its maximum strength in 1944 when the RAF's needs for pilots seemed to be endless and, at that period, it had almost 200 aircraft on strength, almost all of which were Oxfords. South Cerney's training role also included that of HQ No.23 (Training) Group, which moved here in October 1939 and, the following year, became part of Flying Training Command and had responsibility for all SFTS and PAFU units in the Cotswolds and the wider region of South and West England, as well as a number of specialist training and glider schools. The Group's Communication Flight was also based at the airfield. The unit list shows the comings and goings, including the presence of specialist Flights such as No.1539 BATF. Having been one of the RAF's largest and busiest flying training stations, the run-down of strength started in the latter part of 1944 and

accelerated in 1945, as the need for pilots rapidly decreased. The PAFU was still in existence in the immediate post-war period, but it was a shadow of its former self and, by the time it reverted to its original 3 SFTS title in December 1945, it had just a handful of aircraft.

The first post-war unit was the Flying Training Command Flying Instructors School, which arrived from Wittering in May 1946 but only survived to the following February. A number of ground-based, but flying-related, units then held sway at South Cerney until spring 1942, when flying training returned. From April 1948 to May 1952 the major occupant of the airfield was No.2 Flying Training School, which arrived with seventy trainers (Tiger Moths and Harvards) and ran basic flying training courses, for which they also used Blakehill Farm as a satellite. The creation of CFS (Basic) in 1952 came about from renaming the FTS and incorporating the CFS component that was present at the airfield. The Central Flying School (CFS) had made use of South Cerney from the early 1950s, with, initially, two Prentice squadrons and a Qualified Flying Instructor Refresher Flight being based here, with the parent CFS located at Little Rissington. Re-organization in May 1952 saw the South Cerney elements become CFS (Basic). The CFS Helicopter Flight was here from June 1955 to June 1957 but, in the latter month, most elements of CFS reunited at Little Rissington. Some records show a helicopter presence beyond this and that the CFS Helicopter Squadron incorporated, from December 1960, a Helicopter Communication Flight, for use by command staff of No.1 (British) Corps between the UK and Germany. July 1957 brought No.1 Initial Training School from Kirton-in-Lindsey; part of the role of the school was grading of aircrew officers and providing air experience, for which it had used a variety of types, eventually settling on the Chipmunk T.10. On 1 January 1967, this was renamed as the Aircrew Officers Training School; this unit moved to Church Fenton a year later. The longest-serving post-war flying unit was No.625 Volunteer Gliding School, which formed at South Cerney on 2 June 1958 and eventually left, for Hullavington, in June 1993. During its time at the airfield, it operated various types of glider, from the Cadet TX.3 to the Venture T.2, and gave air experience to thousands of cadet force personnel.

In 1971 this delightful Cotswold airfield was handed to the army and it still remains as an army base, with much of the airfield infrastructure, including the grass airfield and its perimeter track, still intact.

DECOY SITE

Q	Ashton Keynes	SU028927

UNITS

HQ units at South Cerney

No.23 Gp   Oct 1939–28 Sep 1946

1919–1939

3 FTS	16 Aug 1937–1 Mar 1942	Oxford, Hart

1939–1945

23 Gp CF	10 Oct 1939–1 Oct 1946	Magister, Hornet Moth
15 FTS	Jun 1940–Aug 1940?	Harvard, Oxford
3 FTS	?–1 Mar 1942	Oxford, Hart
1519Flt	Nov 1941–Dec 1941	Oxford
3 (P)AFU	1 Mar 1942–17 Dec 1945	Oxford, Harvard
1539Flt	15 Apr 1943–13 Jul 1943; 15 Nov 1944–1 Jun 1945	Oxford
3 FTS	17 Dec 1945–Apr 1946	Harvard

Post-1945

FTC ITS	25 May 1946–28 Feb 1947	
2 FTS	6 Apr 1948–1 May 1952	Tiger Moth, Harvard, Prentice
CFS	1951?–1 Jun 1957	various
1 ITS	22 Jul 1957–1 Jan 1967	Chipmunk
625 VGS	2 Jun 1958–30 Jun 1993	various
HCF	1 Dec 1960–5 Jan 1961	Dragonfly
AOTS	1 Jan 1967–21 Jan 1968	Chipmunk

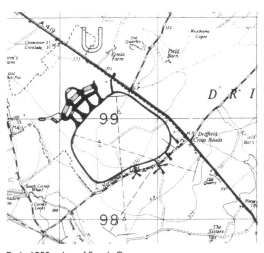

Early 1950s plan of South Cerney.

No.3 FTS operated a large number of Oxfords from South Cerney – at one time the unit had almost 200 aircraft on establishment.

SOUTH MARSTON

County: Wiltshire

UTM/Grid: OS Map 173 – SU181888
Lat/Long: N51°36 W001°45
Nearest Town: Swindon 3 miles to south-west

Aerial shot of South Marston dated 8 Sep 1943. (via Rod Priddle)

HISTORY

South Marston was one of the shadow aircraft factories built in the early part of the war to increase overall production and to disperse production to make it less vulnerable to air attack. Swindon was chosen, as it had good rail links and was home to a number of major engineering concerns, such as the GWR works, that could provide expertise and component manufacture. The initial plan was for a shadow factory for the Woodley-based Phillips and Powis Aircraft, whose most important product was the Miles Master trainer. The factory complex was constructed in late-1940 and production was underway late that year, with the first Master rolling off the line in March 1941. The production facility was on the west side of the airfield and the latter was eventually provided with two runways, the main one running east-west.

It was not long before others showed interest in South Marston; with Shorts having suffered from German attacks on its Rochester facility, the decision was taken to move Stirling production to Swindon – it was this decision that led to the building of the two surfaced runways. Building of the four assembly sheds (in pairs) for Stirlings, and this was assembly and not production, commenced in late-1940, on the opposite side of the airfield from the Phillips and Powis sheds, although the latter was also involved in production of Stirling components. Final assembly of Stirlings was underway by July 1941 and the four-engined bombers were soon a frequent sight, parked up awaiting flight-test or delivery.

By spring 1942, production of Masters had ended, the South Marston plant having turned out 1,000 of this important trainer; a plan to use the production capacity for Mosquitoes was shelved and Phillips and Powis relinquished their part of the factory to Vickers Armstrongs. The Castle Bromwich works took over this capacity and Spitfire work took place, with both production and modification, followed later by Seafire production. The following year Shorts departed, the Stirling production having ended, and their place was taken by Armstrong Whitworth, the intention being for that company to use the factory for its Lancaster contract. This plan was changed and was replaced by modification work for American types, to bring them up to the required RAF and FAA specifications, which meant a wide variety of American aircraft passed through South Marston.

In October 1945, Vickers bought the airfield and its production facilities and, in the immediate post-war period, undertook modification work on a variety of types from Wellingtons and Lancasters to Spitfires and Seafires. However, these were soon followed by the production of new jet-types, which also involved an extension to the main runway. Between 1950 and 1953, the factory produced 182 Attackers, a naval strike-attack aircraft that has received less attention than it deserves. This was followed by the Swift, an aircraft that acquired a poor reputation in RAF service. The prototype Swift (WJ960) first flew on 5 August 1951 and was the RAF's first swept-wing jet fighter to enter service; its introduction as a fighter was not a happy one, but subsequent marks developed for the fighter-reconnaissance role were more successful. The last type to leave the South Marston works was another naval jet, the Scimitar, the last of which flew in January 1961. Following the Scimitar, the works was primarily involved in component manufacture. After the final departure of Vickers in the late-1970s, the airfield remained in use for gliding and private flying, but it was obvious that this could not continue, as Swindon had now grown and was looking for more industrial development land. All flying ceased in April 1985 and the land was sold for development. Sadly, this wonderful piece of British aviation history has all but vanished – little of the airfield structure being visible within the complex that now houses a major car factory.

The various companies at the airfield undertook modification work on a range of American types prior to delivery to RAF units. (via Rod Priddle)

Line-up of Attackers; over 180 of these naval jets were produced here between 1950 and 1953. (via Rod Priddle)

SOUTHROP

County: Gloucestershire

UTM/Grid: OS Map 163 – SP190035
Lat/Long: N51°44 W001°44
Nearest Town: Cirencester 9 miles to west

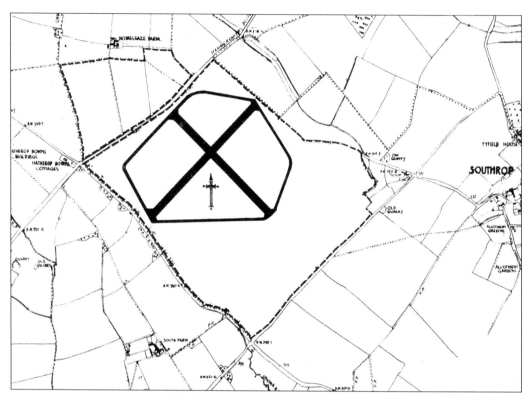

HISTORY

Southrop was one of a number of relief landing grounds in this region for use by flying training establishments, there being a concentration of this type of unit in this area. Land was acquired in early 1940, with a large flat area ideal for a grass training airfield. The layout was unusual, with two runways and a connecting concrete perimeter-track, with the grass areas outside this track being used for dispersal areas and on which a number of Blister hangars were constructed. The main technical area, with a single T-Type hangar and an assortment of other buildings was laid out on the north-west corner. The communal area included messes and a limited amount of accommodation.

First use of Southrop was as an RLG for 2 FTS (Brize Norton), from August 1940 to March 1942, although exactly how much use was made is uncertain. This continued into summer, when the school became No.2 (Pilots) Advanced Flying Unit. When this closed in July, use of Southrop passed to No.3 PAFU South Cerney and this unit continued to use the RLG until January 1945. Southrop was also used by No.1539 Beam Approach Training Flight from 1943 – and probably for most of the wartime period. The headquarters of No.27 (Signals Training) Group moved in from Lechlade in January 1945; this HQ had responsibility for all radio schools. Southrop was not, however, destined to survive for long in the post-war period. The airfield was used as an RLG by Little Rissington's No.6 FTS from December 1945 for four months, but there was little need of yet another very basic airfield and the final flying operations were by the Group's Communications Flight. The Flight moved to Fairford in autumn 1946 and the Group HQ moved out the following year.

AIRFIELD DATA DEC 1944

Command:	Flying Training Command	Runway surface:	Grass; E/W of Army Track
Function:	Satellite (Pilots) Advanced Flying Unit	Hangars:	Blister × 9, T.1 × one
Runways:	230 deg 1,020yd	Dispersals:	Nil
	330 deg 930yd	Personnel:	Officers – 74 (4 WAAF)
	E/W 1,150yd		Other Ranks – 872 (122 WAAF)

UNITS

HQ units at Southrop

No.27 (Signals Training) Gp	22 Jan 1945–18 Sep 1947		1539Flt	early 1943–1945?	Oxford

1939–1945			**Post-1945**		
2 FTS	Aug 1940–Mar 1942	Harvard, Oxford	6 FTS	Dec 1945–Apr 1946	Harvard
3 PAFU	13 Jul 1942–22 Jan 1945	Oxford	27 Gp CF	22 Jan 1945–autumn 1946	various

STAVERTON

County: Gloucestershire

UTM/Grid: OS Map 162 – SO887218
Lat/Long: N51°53.65 W002°10.03
Nearest Town: Gloucester 3 miles to south-west

Oblique view of Staverton dated 29 April 1941.

HISTORY

The Gloucester/Cheltenham Airport opened in late 1936, work having commenced on a 160-acre site in open land between the two towns in 1934. Commercial services were operated by Railway Air Services but growth of the airport was slow, although the Cotswold Aero Club had moved from the original 'airport' site (Down Hatherley). With its mid-1930s expansion the RAF was searching for airfields and training schools to conduct basic flying training. The Air Ministry signed a user agreement with the airport operators for development and future use of the airfield and, in September 1938, contracted Surrey Flying Services to operate No.31 Elementary and Refresher Flying Training School (ERFTS). The school operated Tiger Moths for a year, but was disbanded on the outbreak of war. In the meantime, another civil-run training unit had moved it; the Airwork Civil School of Air Navigation arrived from Shoreham in May 1939 and used Rapides to teach basic navigation to RAF observers. On 6 August, the school became No.6 Civil Air Navigation School; it and its successor units remained at Staverton to December 1944.

In April 1939, Rotol established a flight test department at Staverton and, throughout the war, this used a variety of aircraft types on propeller and associated trials, important and often ignored work. On 10 September 1939, the airfield officially became RAF Staverton and, over the next few years, its role as a training base and as a home to flight test departments kept it very busy. In early August 1940, No.2 Elementary Flying Training School (EFTS) moved to Staverton, but it was soon discovered that the airfield's surfaced runways were not ideal for the school's Tiger Moths and that a grass RLG would be needed. The choice fell on Worcester and every morning ground staff and pupil pilots would bus to the RLG, whilst instructors and pupils flew the Tigers across from Staverton. A full day's training would be followed by reversing the procedure. Summer 1940 also saw the formation of No.7 School of Technical Training to run courses for flight mechanics and riggers; in February, the school moved to Innsworth. The headquarters of No.44 (Ferry) Group was at Barnwood, Gloucester from August 1941 and their Communications Flight used Staverton from 15 August 1941 to August 1946.

As the unit list shows, the main flying organization at Staverton was No.6 Air Observer and Navigation School, which, in turn, dropped the 'Navigation' part of the title and then finally became No.6 (Observers) Advanced Flying Unit. During this five-year period,

AIRFIELD DATA DEC 1944

Command: Flying Training Command
Function: Parent (Observers) Advanced Flying Unit
Runways: 210 deg 1,000yd × 50yd
270 deg 1,000yd × 50yd
170 deg 1,000yd × 50yd

Runway surface: Concrete and tarmac
Hangars: Bellman × 6, Bellman (MAP) × one, Extra-Over Blister × one
Dispersals: Apron 300ft × 80ft
Personnel: Officers – 40 (4 WAAF)
Other Ranks – 792 (249 WAAF)

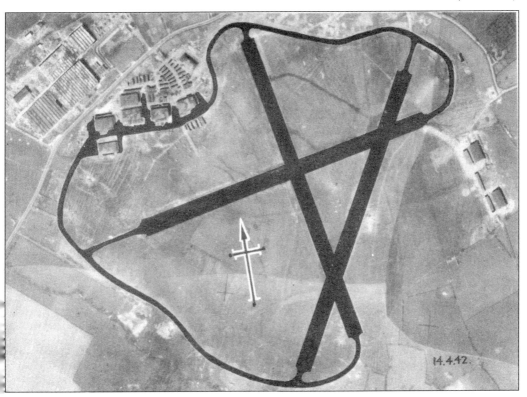

the school operated a variety of aircraft types and used a number of RLGs. As the AONS, it had an establishment of twenty Ansons and four Dominies and was still operated by Airwork; by the time it had become No.6 (O)AFU it had an establishment of seventy-two Ansons and was manned by RAF personnel. Staverton was kept busy day and night and, like all training schools, there were accidents and losses.

The flight test aspect of Staverton eventually involved four companies, with Rotol (Dowty) being joined by Folland, Gloster and Flight Refuelling. These were a mix of true testing of new concepts and flight-testing of new aircraft pre-delivery.

Folland had moved in during late-1940, Gloster had started using Staverton in mid-1941 to ease the

pressure on its main airfield at Brockworth and Flight Refuelling arrived in 1942. The latter was heavily involved in developing its in-flight refuelling concepts and, in February 1944, received a contract to provide systems for 600 Lancasters, this type having been involved in flight trials for some time as both tanker and receiver. Staverton was only attacked once by the Luftwaffe, a lone bomber causing damage and fatalities on the night of 12 July 1941.

The closure of the AFU in late-1944 left the airfield without an RAF unit but, as the aircrew training system was in decline as numbers in training reduced, there was no further need of Staverton for this purpose; with the exception of the Group Comms Flight, RAF flying interest in the airfield ended. In the immediate post-war period the Quedgeley-based

During its time at Staverton, Flight Refuelling undertook air-to-air refueling trials with various aircraft, and was even awarded a contract to provide equipment for 600 Lancasters, although this was subsequently cancelled.

No.7 Maintenance Unit used a number of sub-sites – Staverton was one of these from June 1945 to August 1953.

By mid-1946 the only flight test element left at the airfield was Rotol (Dowty), but the airfield was used by a number of RAF ground units before being de-requisitioned on 29 September 1950. The subsequent three decades were difficult ones for the airport, with a struggle to secure viable commercial operations. Private flying by clubs and owners helped keep it open and the presence of the Skyfame Museum (from 1963) made the airfield well-known amongst those with an interest in aviation history – but did little to help pay the running costs of the airport. The local councils took-over the running of the airport in 1962, but investment was always a problem and the infrastructure deteriorated. Major improvements, or at least restoration of most of the airfield, took place in the late-1990s and Gloucester/Staverton, or Gloucestershire Airport (EGBJ) as it now prefers to be known, is one of the best-equipped General Aviation airfields in the UK. All three wartime runways are usable, although 18/36 is restricted in length and width, and other parts of the old RAF airfield are still distinctive, although a great many newer buildings are also evident. The name change from the well known, and still often used, Gloucester/Staverton to Gloucestershire Airport was a political one, as the airport serves both Gloucester and Cheltenham and the latter were not happy with it being known as sim-

ply Gloucester. The airfield is home to a number of flying schools and helicopter operators, plus engineering and other facilities.

UNITS

1919–1939

31 ERFTS	29 Sep 1938–3 Sep 1939	Tiger Moth, Hart

1939–1945

6 CANS	15 May 1939–1 Nov 1939	Anson
6 AONS	1 Nov 1939–17 Jan 1942	Anson
2 EFTS	3 Aug 1940–1 Nov 1941	Tiger Moth
24 Gp CF	autumn 1940–early 1941	various
44 Gp CF	15 Aug 1941–9 Aug 1946	various
6 FIS	1 Nov 1941–18 Apr 1942	Tiger Moth, Magister
6 AOS	17 Jan 1942–11 Jun 1943	Anson
6 (O)AFU	11 Jun 1943–12 Dec 1944	Anson

MEMORIAL

The Jet Age Museum has been successful in its bid for Lottery funds and is in the process of developing a new museum at the airport. Whilst the museum is primarily focusing on Gloucestershire's aviation heritage in general it will no doubt include items specific to the airfield – www.jetagemuseum.org.

STOKE ORCHARD

County: Gloucestershire

UTM/Grid: OS Map 163 – SO925275
Lat/Long: N51°55.7 W002°06.6
Nearest Town: Cheltenham 3 miles to south-east

29.7.43

HISTORY

Authority was given in February 1940 to requisition land at Stoke Orchard for use as an RLG by the EFTS at Cheltenham (SOM 106/40), with construction taking place later that year and into 1941. The airfield was somewhat sandwiched between the main railway line and the River Severn, just south of the village and, whilst it was a large flat area, there were some problems with drainage, especially on the west side near the river. As an RLG for trainer types, the main requirement was a large grass area and Stoke Orchard certainly provided that, even when the RLG status was changed to that of a training airfield. The main technical area was constructed on the south-east side and was centred on four Bellman hangars, along with assorted huts and temporary brick buildings for workshops and other purposes, all neatly laid out alongside a pattern of roads. There was also an encircling concrete 'road' around the landing area to connect the various Blister hangars, which were positioned mainly to the north and east.

No.10 Elementary Flying Training School moved in to Southrop in late-September 1941 with Tiger Moths, with the first course commencing in the latter part of the month. The school soon had over fifty Tiger Moths at Stoke Orchard and the airfield proved almost ideal for this type of flying, as long as pupils were careful to avoid nearby Cleeve Hill. It was a busy airfield and, to ease congestion in the circuit, use was made of Northleach. The following summer, the school was disbanded to provide personnel – and an airfield – for glider training. The next main user of the airfield was No.3 Glider Training School (GTS), which formed here on 21 July 1942 from a core of the EFTS. The school belonged to No.23 Group and its initial establishment was 23+11 Masters and 31+15 Hotspur gliders, along with a few Oxfords and Tiger Moths. This was a very busy unit and trained basic-glider pilots and instructors, the Master-Hotspur combination remaining the main training medium throughout the life of the

AIRFIELD DATA DEC 1944

Command:	Flying Training Command	Runway surface:	Grass
Function:	Parent Glider Training School	Hangars:	Double Blister (69ft) × 7, Bellman × 4,
Runways:	NW/SE 1,200yd		Treble Blister (69ft) × one
	N/S 1,100yd	Dispersals:	Nil
		Personnel:	Officers – 50 (4 WAAF)
			Other Ranks – 796 (197 WAAF)

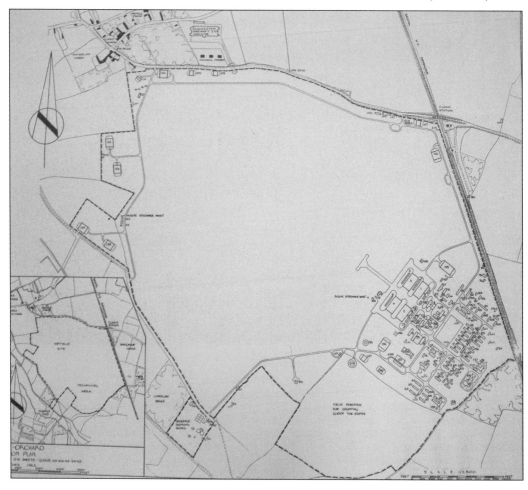

school. Relief landing grounds were essential and the school used, at various times, Aldermaston, Northleach and Wanborough. In July 1945, No.3 GTS moved to Wellesbourne Mountford, after which Stoke Orchard was reduced to Care and Maintenance, being closed early the following year. The site was probably disposed of in the late-1940s and, although it has long been back under agriculture, the basic layout is still clear from the air, as the new fields are long (the length of the airfield) rather than having the irregular pattern of the surround-

ing fields; also, the clutch of Bellman hangars have survived and are used for agricultural purposes.

UNITS

1939–1945

10 EFTS	22 Sep 1941–21 Jul 1942	Tiger Moth
3 GTS	21 Jul 1942–27 Jul 1945	Master, Oxford, Hotspur

TARRANT RUSHTON
(Station 453)

County: Dorset

UTM/Grid: OS Map 195 – ST946058
Lat/Long: N50°51.00 W002°04.30
Nearest Town: Blandford Forum 3 miles to west

Tarrant Rushton in July 2001.

HISTORY

Tarrant Rushton had two main periods of aviation activity: the intense few months in 1944 when it was a major airborne-forces base for the air assault on Europe and thirty years as home to Flight Refuelling.

The airfield was constructed in 1942, major work commencing in May, to the east of the small village after which it was named. The area was reasonably flat farmland but, as this was planned as a large airfield, it meant the closure of roads and tracks, the destruction of some farm buildings and the removal of various field boundaries to make way for the three surfaced runways and associated facilities. The main runway was oriented north/south and the other two were laid out in the near perfect 60-degree cut; the connecting perimeter track joined the ends of the runway and, in some places, ran close to the airfield boundary. Tarrant was intended as an airborne forces

airfield from the outset and was built to handle large aircraft and gliders, for which it was provided with numerous spectacle dispersals, mainly grouped on the south and east sides of the airfield. There were four T.2 hangars dispersed around the perimeter track but, other than the control tower, there were few substantial buildings on the airfield itself, the communal sites being to the north-east. Construction took a year and Tarrant Rushton was declared ready on 17 May 1943, although it did not fully open until October, as its planned units were not ready to form.

Operational flying began in late-1943, with the formation here, on 4 November, of 298 Squadron, with 295 Squadron (at Hurn) providing a Flight around which the new squadron formed. The new unit was, initially, equipped with the Halifax V and its first task was to assist in the operational develop-

AIRFIELD DATA DEC 1944

Command:	Fighter Command	Runway surface:	Concrete and wood chippings, grass extension
Function:	Operational Parent		
Runways:	010 deg 2,000 × 50yd, grass overshoots 200yd north and 400yd south	Hangars:	T.2 × 4
	080 deg 1,400 × 50yd, grass extension 200yd each end	Dispersals:	50 × Special Loop
		Personnel:	Officers – 200 (10 WAAF)
	130 deg 1,400 × 50yd		Other Ranks – 2,511 (376 WAAF)

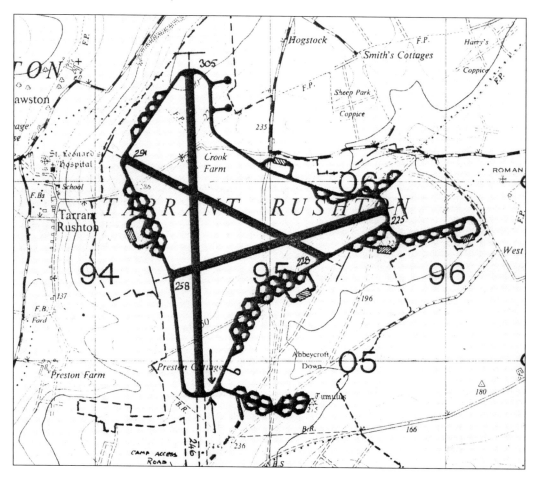

ment of this type for airborne warfare. The development task was also the primary role of the new Airborne Forces Tactical Development Unit (AFTDU), which formed here on 1 December 1943 with a diverse collection of types, from the Albemarle to the Halifax and Horsa glider. However, in mid-January 1944, the unit moved to Netheravon to continue its important task, leaving Tarrant for further development as an operational airfield.

No.196 Squadron arrived at Tarrant from Leicester East in early January 1944 and continued its re-equipment from Wellingtons to Stirlings, the latter finding a new lease of life as an airborne-warfare aircraft, having been found wanting in the bomber role. The squadron left again in March, but Tarrant Rushton's operational strength of two squadrons was maintained, as 644 Squadron had formed in February from a nucleus provided by 298 Squadron, the latter squadron having grown to forty plus Halifaxes. This gave the station two Halifax units and both of these remained in residence for the rest of the war. As gliders were very much part of the role, the station became home in March 1944 to No.14 and No.15 Glider Servicing Echelons of No.1 Heavy Glider Servicing Unit at Netheravon, with the Hamilcar being Tarrant's main type.

Training was intense in this early part of 1944, as it was only a matter of time before a major airborne operation was mounted as part of the long-anticipated invasion of Europe.

On the eve of D-Day the airfield was nose-to-tail with tug-glider combinations (as shown in the photographs); the first aircraft were airborne on the evening of 5 June, as part of a special force to drop gliders on key bridges. This mission included six of Tarrant's aircraft and was followed on 6 June by participation in the two main airborne drops over Normandy, during which two aircraft were lost. The next three weeks saw the squadrons flying supply missions but, by late-June, they had primarily reverted to training, as the bulk of airborne forces had been withdrawn to re-fit and prepare for any future operation. Tarrant's aircraft still flew operational sorties, with bombing missions and special sorties on behalf of the Special Operations Executive (SOE) or SAS. It was three months later that the next big airborne operation took place, with the daring drop of a 'carpet' of airborne troops in Holland in an attempt to secure a route to, and bridge over, the Rhine. Operation *Market-Garden*,

The impressive line-up of Halifax tugs plus Horsa and Hamilcar gliders for the D-Day operation, June 1944.

Halifax V of 644 Squadron; the unit formed here in February 1944 and remained in residence to December 1945.

No.298 Squadron makes use of the size of the Halifax wing to provide an impressive group photo.

the former being the airborne element, saw 298 and 644 squadrons airborne on 17 September with forty-one combinations, fourteen of which were the large Hamilcar gliders. The gliders were dropped over Arnhem and, although re-supply missions were flown over the next few days, it was ultimately a heroic failure, as the 'Bridge Too Far' was not captured.

The squadrons returned to training, also re-equipping with Halifax IIIs, as well as continuing to fly SOE-type operations. There was one final airborne assault in World War Two, Operation *Varsity*, the crossing of the Rhine in March 1945, but the two squadrons deployed to Woodbridge for this particular operation. Having returned to their Dorset base, they concentrated on special operations in Scandinavia, it being feared that the Nazi leadership would attempt to use Scandinavia as a final bastion. In May 1945, the squadrons flew Allied liberation forces to towns in Norway, to disarm German forces. The war with Japan was still going on and 298 Squadron was sent to India in July 1945, with 644 Squadron leaving in November for Palestine.

The Halifax-equipped 190 Squadron (at Great Dunmow) was renumbered as 295 Squadron, with the new squadron forming at Tarrant Rushton on 21 January 1946. Equipped with Halifax A.7s in the transport role, it was the briefest of existences, with a further renumbering to 297 Squadron taking place in April. The squadron was still working-up, although also flying transport missions, when it moved to Brize Norton in September. With the departure of the flying units Tarrant Rushton was reduced to Care and Maintenance in September and, fifteen months later, was declared surplus to requirements and offered for disposal. It was acquired the following June by Flight Refuelling Ltd, who brought their various development and test departments from places such as Ford and Staverton. The company spent the next thirty years at Tarrant Rushton and, in that time, developed not only in-flight refuelling equipment, for which it was and still is a world leader, but a range of other aerospace products, including pilotless aircraft and target equipment (the Rushton winch of the Canberra TT.18 was named after the airfield at which it was developed).

August 1952 saw No.210 Advanced Flying School form at Tarrant, as part of No.25 Group, to train jet pilots for the Meteor and Vampire. This was part of the Korean War and Cold War panic re-building of the RAF and was short-lived, the school disbanding in April 1954. The maintenance and support of the school had been carried out by Flight Refuelling and the RAF continued to support the airfield with infrastructure developments when it was adopted as a V-bomber dispersal airfield. Flight Refuelling continued to grow its business and undertook refurbishment and modification work on a variety of types.

The last flight from Tarrant Rushton took place on 30 September 1980, the company moving to Hurn to share rather than own an airfield, and, following its closure, the airfield was rapidly turned back into agricultural land by its new owners, the Crichton Estate; this work involved the demolishing of over 300 buildings and, today, little survives of the airfield, other than the basic structure of the operating surfaces, which are still very distinct from the air. One of Tarrant Rushton's operational aircraft has 'survived' – Halifax NA337 was pulled out of a Norwegian lake and is under restoration in Canada.

UNITS

1939–1945

196 Sqn	7 Jan 1944–14 Mar 1944	Stirling
298 Sqn	4 Nov 1943–5 Jul 1945	Halifax
644 Sqn	23 Feb 1944–1 Dec 1945	Halifax
AFTDU	1 Dec 1943–14 Jan 1944	various
1677 Flt det	Nov 1944–Dec 1944	Oxford

Post-1945

295 Sqn	21 Jan 1946–1 Apr 1946	Halifax
297 Sqn	1 Apr 1946–5 Sep 1946	Halifax
210 AFS	5 Aug 1952–29 Apr 1954	Meteor, Vampire

MEMORIAL

Granite memorial near main gate, inscribed: 'This memorial commemorates all who operated from Tarrant Rushton airfield 1943–1980. Unveiled 6th June 1982'. A second plaque reads: 'To honour all who served with 298 and 644 squadrons RAF, C Squadron Glider Pilot Regiment'.

THRUXTON (Station 407)

County: Wiltshire

UTM/Grid: OS Map 184 – SU280455
Lat/Long: N51°12.32 W001°35.59
Nearest Town: Andover 5 miles to east

Thruxton in September 2002.

HISTORY

Authority was given in mid-September 1940 for land to be requisitioned at Thruxton for development into a satellite airfield for Middle Wallop (SOM 880/40). The airfield was laid out on an area of land acquired from Thruxton Manor Estate and immediately west of the village. It was surrounded by roads and there was just sufficient space for a standard three-runway airfield, although the runway lengths were limited, with the longest being 1,560 yards rather than the standard 2,000 yards. One of the main dispersal areas had to be built on the other side of the road on the west side, with the bomb-dump being in a small wood in the same area. The airfield was given only one T.2 hangar, on the south side on a peri-track loop, although further provision was later made with a single Bessonneau and nine Blisters.

Although intended for Middle Wallop, the airfield actually opened in summer 1941 for use by Andover as an army co-operation airfield, the first occupants

being the Lysanders of 225 Squadron. The same month a detachment from Andover's No.42 Operational Training Unit arrived; its Ansons and Blenheims continued to use Thruxton to October 1942, when the parent unit moved to Ashbourne. We do not usually record 'one-off' missions, but it is worth mentioning Thruxton's involvement in two such 'specials'. The brief presence of 51 Squadron Whitleys in late-February 1942 was connected with Operation *Biting*, a daring and highly successful mission to capture German radar technology from the *Wurzburg* radar at Bruneval. The paratroops dropped from the all-black Whitleys on the night of 27 February and, this special task complete, the squadron returned to its home base at Lindholme.

Thruxton became a gathering place for medium bombers in August 1942, when it was used by three squadrons involved in Operation *Jubilee*, the raid on Dieppe. Bostons were flown by 226 Squadron and

AIRFIELD DATA DEC 1944

Command: Fighter Command
Function: Operational Station
Runways: 257 deg 1,560 × 50yd
    315 deg 1,150 × 50yd
    024 deg 1,000 × 50yd

Runway surface: Concrete and wood chippings
Hangars: Blister × 9, T.2 × one, Bessonneau × one
Dispersals: 23 × Frying Pan (125ft), 9 × Blenheim
Personnel: Officers – 56
    Other Ranks – 1,068

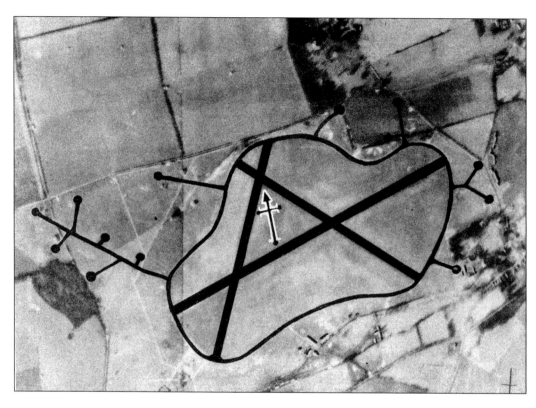

Blenheims by 13 and 614 squadrons, the primary task being smoke-laying, to conceal the amphibious assault from shore batteries. Unlike *Biting*, Operation *Jubilee* was not a success, although many valuable lessons were learned that would pay dividends in June 1944.

The Whitley-equipped 297 Squadron at Hurn provided a nucleus of aircraft and crews in August 1942 to form 298 Squadron at Thruxton. However, the new unit was still in the process of training and building up to full strength when, in mid-October, the plan was cancelled and the squadron disbanded. However, the Whitleys of 297 Squadron moved in from Hurn in October 1942 and this squadron stayed for almost a year, having acquired Albemarles to supplement the airborne operations role.

The Glider Pilot Exercise Unit (GPEU) arrived in

Bostons of 226 Squadron spent a brief period here in August 1942 as part of the air built-up for the Dieppe operation; this 226 Squadron aircraft was actually on a sortie to Ostend on 7 May 1942.

September 1943 from Netheravon, but its Master tugs and Hotspur gliders had barely settled in before they moved back to Netheravon. This gave room for the three squadrons of No.123 Airfield but they, too, stayed only a few weeks, before going to Sawbridgeworth, with the GPEU coming back and, in December, becoming the Operational and Refresher Training Unit. The ORTU departed in March and Thruxton became Station 407 for the USAAF. The P-47s of the 366th Fighter Group, IXth Air Force moved in as part of the re-distribution of tactical air power for the invasion build-up. The Group flew its first ops from Thruxton on 14 March 1944 and, over the next few months, was heavily involved in ground-attack missions over the Normandy area, bombing and strafing a wide range of targets. This routine intensified in the days following the landings, but the Group was amongst the first IXth Air Force units to move to forward airfields in France, departing Thruxton on 20 June.

With the departure of the Americans there was very little flying at Thruxton; the air ambulance Ansons of No.1311 Flight soon merged into the No.84 Group Communications Squadron, which itself worked closely with the Group Support Unit. The Austers of No.43 OTU made some use of Thruxton but its main role in the latter months of the war was for storing gliders against possible future need. In the event, there were far more gliders lying around at various airfields than were required for the final, March 1945, airborne operation and the fate of Thruxton's gliders was to be broken up as surplus to requirements. The airfield itself soon had the same

tag and it was put up for disposal in 1946. It was leased the following year by the Wiltshire School of Flying and this general aviation use of Thruxton has continued ever since. In the late-1950s, the Thruxton Jackaroo appeared – a conversion of the Tiger Moth into a four-seat aircraft, although only limited numbers were produced. In August 1963, the first Isaacs Fury flew from Thruxton – not perhaps noteworthy except to homebuilders, as this 7/10-scale replica of the RAF's famous biplane fighter was designed to be built from plans for private use. The aircraft was developed by John Isaacs and was based on a Currie Wot homebuild; the 'definitive' Fury II was designed for the Lycoming O-290 engine and a limited number were built. The 1960s were perhaps more 'notable' at Thruxton for the transition of the site from 'bleak wartime airfield to permanent motor racing facility' and it is as a racing circuit that Thruxton is now best known. The circuit, based on the old taxiway pattern, is approximately 2.4 miles long and, over the years, has witnessed many spectacular races – cars and bikes.

Aviation has, however, retained its hold on the airfield and Thruxton airfield (EGHO) is an active general aviation location, with a variety of fixed-wing and helicopter operators and private owners. The wartime runway layout is no longer in use but is still evident, although a stretch of 07/25 is still in use with an asphalt surface (770m long), with a grass strip alongside the old runway 13/31. The airfield is operated by Western Air (Thruxton) Ltd.

UNITS

HQ units at Thruxton

No.36 (T) Wing	8 Oct 1917–23 Jun 1918
No.123 Airfield	10 Oct 1943–12 Nov 1943

1939–1945

Unit	Dates	Aircraft
12 Sqn det	autumn 1940	Wellington
13 Sqn det	summer 1942	Blenheim
16 Sqn	25 Sep 1941–3 Oct 1941	Lysander
63 Sqn	8–12 Nov 1943	Mustang
168 Sqn	15 Oct 1943–12 Nov 1943	Mustang
170 Sqn	10–25 Oct 1942; 16 Oct 1943–12 Nov 1943	Mustang
225 Sqn	29 Jul 1941–31 Aug 1942+	Lysander
226 Sqn det	summer 1942	Boston
268 Sqn	15 Oct 1943–8 Nov 1943	Mustang
297 Sqn	24 Oct 1942–25 Aug 1943	Whitley, Albemarle
298 Sqn	24 Aug 1942–19 Oct 1942	Whitley
614 Sqn	14–24 Aug 1942	Blenheim
42 OTU det	Jul 1941–19 Oct 1942	Anson, Blenheim

Unit	Dates	Aircraft
1526 Flt	11 Nov 1941–26 Feb 1944	Anson, Blenheim, Oxford
1427 Flt	13 Dec 1941–18 May 1942	Stirling, Halifax
GPEU	29 Sep 1943–14 Oct 1943; 14 Nov 1943–1 Dec 1943	Tiger Moth, Hector, Hotspur
ORTU	9 Dec 1943–1 Mar 1944	Whitley, Tiger Moth, Horsa
84 Gp SU	10 Jul 1944–21 Nov 1944	
1311 Flt	10 Jul 1944–21 Jul 1944	Anson
43 OTU det	Aug 1944–?	

USAAF units

366th FBG

Squadrons:	389th FS, 390th FS, 391st FS
Aircraft:	P-47
Dates:	1 Mar 1944–12 Jun 1944
First mission:	14 Mar 1944

TILSHEAD (Station 539)

County: Wiltshire

UTM/Grid: OS Map 184 – SU025480
Lat/Long: N51°13.87 W001°57.93
Nearest Town: Warminster 9 miles to west

HISTORY

Tilshead appears in the World War One records as both a balloon out-station and a landing ground; the former was located on the edge of the village (at SU038479) and was used by No.1 Balloon School at Rollestone for training purposes from 1916. The nearby landing ground appears to have been in use from late-1917 to the end of the war but records are sketchy.

With the growth of army co-operation as a role in the 1920s and the importance of the Salisbury Plain area, a new site was adopted just to the west of the village. This appears to have come into use around 1925, but was simply a 'suitable field' on which AC squadrons could spend some time, with personnel living in tents. Tilshead Practice Camp was mainly involved with live artillery shoots, as part of annual exercise and manoeuvres, and various AC squadrons would have spent time here in the late-1920s and early 1930s, with confirmed use by 13 and 16 Squadrons during this period.

The landing ground appears to have gone out of use in the late-1930s but was re-activated in June 1940, the Lysanders of 225 Squadron arriving the following month. Tents were still the order of the day and there was no real attempt to improve the 'airfield', as its use was still considered to be temporary. This was the period of the invasion scare and every available aircraft was patrolling for signs of enemy infiltration or landing, the Tilshead Lysanders covering a large slice of the south coast down as far as Lizard Point. Two of the squadron's Lysanders engaged an enemy bomber on 13 August 1940 – the unusual aspect of this being that the aircraft were on the ground at Tilshead and the bomber was making a run over the airfield! A number of bombs were dropped, causing damage to aircraft and the loss of a few tents.

The squadron soldiered on at Tilshead despite

Lysanders of 225 Squadron operated from Tilshead from July 1940.

problems with waterlogging in the winter of 1940/41, during which Tilshead Lodge was taken over as accommodation, but it was clear that the airfield was unsuitable. In July, the squadron moved to Thruxton, although it continued to use Tilshead as a detachment base for a few months before the site was handed to the army.

From January to September 1943, the Glider Pilot Regiment had a ground-training set-up at Airborne Camp, Tilshead, a hutted camp just north of the village and not associated with the old landing ground. This was really a 'boot camp' and aviation played no part in the regime.

UNITS

1939–1945

16Sqn det	autumn 1940, summer 1941	Lysander
225Sqn	1 Jul 1940–29 Jul 1941	Lysander

MEMORIAL

The only memorial is one to the 8th (Midland Counties) Parachute Battalion and is located at Airborne Camp.

TOWNSEND (No.45 SLG)

UTM/Grid: OS Map 173 – SU070725
Lat/Long: N51°27 W001°53

County: Wiltshire

Nearest Town: Marlborough 8 miles to east

HISTORY

This field just to the north of the village of Yatesbury was in use as a practice forced-landing strip from mid-1938 by No.10 Elementary and Refresher Flying Training School, which formed at Yatesbury in February1938. The Tiger Moths of this school, which had become simply No.10 EFTS on the outbreak of war, continued to use the Townsend field until September 1940, when the unit moved to Weston-super-Mare.

The usefulness of the site had been noted and with the search for satellite landing grounds (SLGs) for the aircraft storage Maintenance Units, Townsend was taken on for this use from October, being allocated to No.10 MU at Hullavington. The first occupants, a Wellington and three Bothas, were in residence by early November and the estate parkland with its wooded areas was ideal for dispersal of aircraft. At this period usage was restricted and the site never had more than ten to twenty aircraft. However, it became No.45 SLG with effect from 1 August 1941, for use by No.33 MU at Lyneham.

The field proved unsuitable in winter, because of waterlogging, and it was not until spring 1942 that storage was re-commenced, with Spitfires being the main

residents, although Wellingtons also appeared. Unlike some SLGs, where large numbers of aircraft came and went, activity at Townsend was always restricted and a typical month might involve not more than ten or twelve aircraft in either direction. The site had a single grass strip and four main dispersal areas, with few other facilities. Attempts to improve drainage, including some use of steel track, proved ineffective and the site was emptied of aircraft in late-1942, before the onset of winter. The closure date of the SLG is uncertain, some records suggesting spring 1943 and others suggesting that it was retained by the Ministry of Aircraft Production, but not used, into 1944.

The field was still used for PFLs (Practice Forced Landings) and as a satellite by the Proctors of No.2 Radio School at Yatesbury, although the level of use is uncertain. The Fleet Air Arm inspected the site in summer 1944 with a view to using it once more for aircraft storage, but this was eventually rejected. Final closure of the site is uncertain and may have occurred in 1945, or perhaps as late as 1947. There is now no sign of this unsuccessful and little-used SLG.

TRELIGGA
(HMS *Vulture II*)

UTM/Grid: OS Map 200 – SX047848
Lat/Long: N50°38 W004°46

Nearest Town: Camelford 3 miles to east

County: Cornwall

HISTORY

Treligga Down was a pre-war gliding site and was developed by the navy into an air-to-ground range, with an air-to-sea element just off the coast; it opened in 1940 as HMS *Vulture II*, indicating its connection with St Merryn (HMS *Vulture*). As the air photo shows, the landing ground curved around the arc on which the line of air-to-ground targets were laid out and its primary purpose was as an emergency field for aircraft that suffered problems whilst using the range – as suitable unprepared fields were few and far between in this area. The road from the village at Treligga led to a small group of buildings on one side of the site.

The landing area was laid out with three grass strips: 04/22 (700 × 100yd), 10/28 (730 × 100yd) and 16/34 (800 × 100yd). These were used from time to time by aircraft in trouble and even looked good

A. Aircraft standings
B. Armoury
C. A.R.S. hangar
D. Compass base
E. Control building
F. E.R.S. hangar
G. Equip: & Erect: hangar
H. Explosives areas
J. Ground signals
J. Hangars
K. Pens
L. Radar test base
M. Sick Bay
N. Test butt
O. Workshop

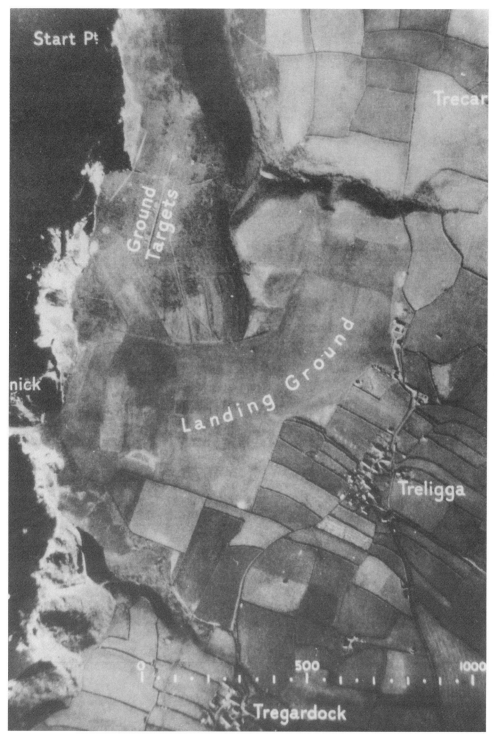

enough to attract an 8th Air Force B-17! The range area was intensively used and, in itself, had a fascinating history – from its all-female staff to its recreation of a Japanese island . . . But that falls outside the scope of this entry. The range continued in use by the navy and the RAF into the 1950s.

UPAVON

UTM/Grid: OS Map 184 – SU152542
Lat/Long: N51°17.24 W001°46.17
Nearest Town: Amesbury 8 miles to south

County: Wiltshire

Recent aerial shot of Upavon taken by No.622 VGS.

HISTORY

Of all the units to have operated from Upavon most important was the Central Flying School (CFS), which formed here on 3 May 1912 to train instructor pilots for the military (army) and naval flying wings – right at the beginning of British military aviation it was realized that a specialist organization would be needed to train instructors and maintain their standards; CFS has been performing that task ever since, although not always under that name. Between June and September 1917, four squadrons were formed at Upavon from within CFS; none of these remained for more than a few weeks and it is uncertain if they took any aircraft with them or simply borrowed CFS aircraft during their initial formation.

The CFS has spent various periods of its life at Upavon; the initial phase lasted right through World War One until it was re-designated as the Flying

Instructors School in December 1919. This lasted a mere four months before CFS was reborn at Upavon in May 1920, moving to Wittering on 7 October 1926 and not returning to Upavon until summer 1935. This period, too, ended in a renaming, with the unit becoming No.7 Flying Instructors School in April 1942, on the creation of the Empire Central Flying School at Hullavington. One of the sub-units of CFS was the Handling Flight, a small but highly-important unit whose task it was to fly every service type and produce the pilots' notes, to ensure safe and efficient operation of each type. Upavon was unsuitable for many of the aircraft types now being used by the CFS/ECFS and the unit never returned to its place of origin.

The site for this very early airfield was, perhaps, a little surprising: a stretch of not very ideal farmland

BE2d of the Central Flying School.

Impressive line-up of BE2s of the CFS, Upavon 1914.

Illustrating a diverse collection of types (and uniforms), the CFS in 1912; the unit formed here in May that year.

on the north edge of Salisbury Plain, close to the village from which it took its name and only a few miles north of that other early airfield, Netheravon. It was a rolling landscape and the size of the landing area was constrained by the small amount of reasonably flat land available, this being the major reason why future development of the airfield was impossible. The advanced party arrived at the airfield in June 1912, soon followed by the first pupil pilots for No.1 Course CFS, by which time a number of wooden buildings had been erected along the road on the north side of the site; these included eight aeroplane sheds, various workshops, stores and support buildings – including a two-bed (!) hospital – and messes. The airfield underwent almost constant change for a number of years, with more aeroplane sheds being built, with a tarmac apron in front, some temporary structures being made permanent and more accommodation being provided. With the exception of the hangars, most of the building was on the far side of the public road that ran alongside the airfield. By 1917, the station covered over 3,300 acres of land, an impressive size for a World War One airfield, although the operating surface was still from ideal because of its slopes and dips.

The first CFS course graduated at the end of December, thirty-four of its thirty-six students successfully passing the course, having flown a variety of machines and, surprisingly, having suffered few accidents and no fatalities, a situation that did not, of course, continue. Course lengths changed and aircraft types varied, but the basic routine remained the same for Upavon throughout the war. The only addition was for CFS to take on trials and evaluation, for which a number of sub-units were formed, such as the Experimental Flight in November 1914 to conduct trials on aircraft and weapons. This was the forerunner of the AAEE and also of the use of the CFS for specialist purposes, in addition to its training role. As the unit list shows, a number of operational squadrons formed here in 1917, but spent only days at Upavon before moving out; the main role of CFS had changed from training of instructors to training of pilots for front-line squadrons, such was the urgent need at the Front. By spring 1918 the CFS had four squadrons: 'A Squadron' with SE5s and 'B Squadron' with Camels for advanced training; and 'C Squadron' and 'D Squadron' with Avro 504s for basic training. The unit expected to graduate some 600 pilots that year.

Training continued in the inter-war period, with Avro 504s and Snipes for basic and advanced work. The Snipes of the recently formed 3 Squadron moved in from Manston at the end of April 1924 and this unit was to remain at Upavon for ten years. When the Snipes had arrived from Manston it was essentially a change from bomber to fighter, as the Vimy-equipped 9 Squadron, which had formed at Upavon at the beginning of April, went to Manston on the 30th of the month. A second fighter unit, 17 Squadron, arrived from Hawkinge in October 1926 with Woodcocks. Over the next few years, the two squadrons operated a number of classic inter-war biplane fighters, such as the Siskin, Gamecock and Bulldog, the latter entering service with both units in late-1929. A number of the original aeroplane sheds were demolished in the mid-1920s, as part of an improvement programme, the major difference being the construction of two A-type hangars. In the late-1930s, a number of C-types were also erected in the same area. However, in May 1934, both squadrons moved to Kenley and CFS was once more back in control at Upavon, although, as the unit list shows, for a brief spell in 1934–1935 the airfield was used as a shore base by a number of Fleet Air Arm units.

The training workload increased as the RAF's expansion plans took effect and CFS was busier than ever, a situation that continued into the early war years. A number of RLGs were used during the early war years, including New Zealand Farm and Overton Heath. There were various developments of the airfield in World War Two, including the addition of ten blister hangars and the laying of Sommerfeld Tracking over the main runway, along with its eventual extension to 3,500ft. By September 1942, this runway was encircled by a concrete perimeter track. There was a second runway nearly one kilometre to the east although, perversely, they appear to have been known as the south and north airfields. This latter strip was still shown on the 1950s plan, but it appears to have been little used after the war.

With the disbandment/renaming of the CFS in April 1942, the main unit at Upavon became No.7 Flying Instructors School and, with an impressive establishment of some 120 trainers, continued the work of creating flying instructors. The establishment comprised 31+14 Oxford, 26+13 Master, 14+7 Magister and 1+1 Dominie although, as usual with such establishments, the actual strength often varied in terms of numbers and types. Nevertheless, it was a very busy training base, turning out hundreds of instructors. In August 1942, Magisters became the main type, as Oxfords were passed to No.3 FIS at Castle Combe although, by early 1944, this had been reversed and Upavon's unit had become primarily an Oxford operator, with around sixty aircraft. A Beam

Dual-control Siskin of CFS.

Gamecock J8089.

Briefing pupils on the blind-flying panel – note the canvas hood that can be drawn over the rear cockpit; Tiger Moth c.1935. (via Ron Priddle)

Approach Training Flight, No1537 Flight, formed out of and then worked with No.7 FIS from May 1943 to May 1946, operating up to ten Oxfords. The FIS remained in residence for the rest of the war, finally moving to Little Rissington in April 1946.

The post-war period was a strange one for Upavon, when its main role was as headquarters connected with Airborne Forces and Air Transport; as the unit list shows, various Group and Command HQs were based here from May 1946 to November 1983. There was very little based flying activity during this period, with the exception of the No.38 Group Communication Flight from May 1946 to February 1951 and the Transport Command Communications Flight (later Squadron) from 1946 to April 1964. The few weeks of York operations in 1953 by No.1310 (Transport) Flight must have been interesting: the aircraft were supporting guided-weapons trials and, as these were primarily to take place in Australia, the Yorks departed in May 1953. The short take-off and landing capability of the Pioneer and Twin Pioneer were useful when 230 Squadron operated from Upavon between April 1959 and May 1960.

A number of Joint Service Trials Units were established at Upavon in the late-1950s and early 1960s but, in most cases, these appear not to have involved actual flying at the airfield, any flying trials being conducted elsewhere: No.13 JSTU, 1 Jun 1959–1 Feb 1962; No.14 JSTU, 2 Nov 1959–?; No.15 JSTU, 1 Dec 1959–22 Aug 1961; No.17 JSTU, 1 Oct 1960–1 Apr 1964.

The Western Communications Squadron at Andover kept a detachment here for the Air Support Command HQ from August 1967 to February 1969 and it is possible that the WCS successor, 21 Squadron, did likewise.

The RAF handed over its heritage-rich airfield to the army in 1993 and the final RAF unit to depart was No.626 VGS, the gliders eventually moving to Hullavington in the late-1990s. RAF aircraft still appear, for example, Lyneham's Hercules used this as one of a number of strips for grass-landing practice, along with visitors such as Army Air Corps helicopters. The only 'based flying unit' is the Army gliding club.

The English Heritage list of key airfields records Upavon as:

> Founded in 1912 as the Royal Flying Corp's Central Flying School, Upavon comprises one of three sites around the Army training ground at Salisbury Plain which relate to the crucial formative phase in the development of military aviation in Europe, prior to the First World War. Several buildings of the 1913/14 period survive here among later development.

DECOY SITE

Q	All Cannings	SU080608

UNITS

HQ units at Upavon

No.38 (Airborne Forces) Gp	31 May 1946–1 Feb 1951
Transport Command	21 Apr 1952–1 Aug 1967
No.38 (Air Support) Gp	1 Jan 1960–17 May 1960; 10 Nov 1975–17 Nov 1983

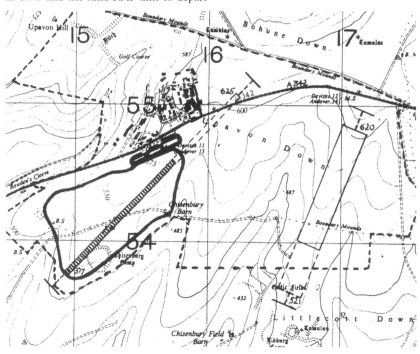

Air Support Command   1 Aug 1967–1 Sep 1972

Pre-1919

72 Sqn	28 Jun 1917–8 Jul 1917	various
73 Sqn	2–10 Jul 1917	various
85 Sqn	1–10 Aug 1917	various
87 Sqn	1–15 Sep 1917	various
CFS	13 May 1912–23 Dec 1919	
Experimental Flt	May 1916	
FIS	23 Feb 1919–26 Apr 1920	F2b
FOS	14 Aug 1919–10 Sep 1919	
CFS	26 Feb 1920–7 Oct 1926	

1919–1939

3 Sqn	30 Apr 1924–10 May 1934	Snipe, Woodcock, Gamecock, Bulldog
9 Sqn	1 Apr 1924–30 Apr 1924	Vimy
17 Sqn	14 Oct 1926–10 May 1934	Woodcock, Gamecock, Siskin, Bulldog
800Sqn FAA	13 Jul 1934–10 Jun 1935+	Nimrod, Osprey
801Sqn FAA	23 Oct 1934–16 Aug 1935+	Nimrod, Osprey
802 Sqn FAA	1 May 1934–24 Jul 1934	Nimrod, Osprey
810 Sqn FAA	25 Mar 1935–7 May 1935	Baffin
820 Sqn FAA	28 Jul 1934–20 Aug 1934	Seal
821 Sqn FAA	14 Jul 1934–Aug 1935+	Seal
823 Sqn FAA	1 May 1934–26 Jul 1934	Fairey IIIf
824 Sqn FAA	8 Oct 1934–8 Nov 1934	Fairey IIIf
CFS	Sep 1935–1 Apr 1942	
HF	8 Dec 1938–8 Nov 1940	

1939–1945

CFS	?–1 Apr 1942	various
HF	8 Nov 1940	
7 FIS	1 Apr 1942–24 Apr 1946	Master, Oxford, Magister
1537 Flt	4 May 1943–May 1946	Oxford

Post-1945

230 Sqn	30 Apr 1959–30 May 1960	Pioneer, Twin Pioneer
1310 Flt	31 Mar 1953–May 1953	York
38 Gp CF	31 May 1946–1 Feb 1951	
TCCF/S	May 1946–1 Apr 1964	various
WCS det	1 Aug 1967–3 Feb 1969	various
622 VGS	1978–1997?	various

MEMORIAL

1. There are various memorials on and around the airfield, the majority of which relate to individuals rather than the airfield itself. The one real exception is a plaque at the HQ building with inscription:

> This plaque was unveiled by Marshal of the Royal Air Force His Royal Highness The Prince Philip, Duke of Edinburgh KG KT GBE on 16th June 1962 to mark the 50th anniversary of the Royal Flying Corps and of Upavon.

2. The original CFS Regimental Office is now the Trenchard Museum and includes material on the 'founder of the RAF' as well as the CFS and Upavon. Visits by appointment only.

UPOTTERY
(Station 462)

County: Devon

UTM/Grid: OS Map 192 – ST188101
Lat/Long: N50°53 W003°09
Nearest Town: Honiton 5 miles to south-south-west

Upottery in June 1944.

HISTORY

Originally intended for use by a USAAF medium-bomber Group and one of the latter series of major airfield constructions in connection with the invasion of Europe, the airfield at Upottery was started in mid-1943 and completed early the following year. Laid out on a small plateau to the west of the village of Smeatharpe, the name that locals invariably called the airfield, it was an area just large enough for a standard three-runway airfield. The main runway was oriented east/west with the technical area on the north-east side, centred on two T.2 hangars (although only one was built, the second being constructed on the south side of the airfield), and with the communal sites further to the north-east. As it was intended for a three-squadron Bomb Group there were three main dispersal areas, each comprising a series of spectacle dispersals along the perimeter track. The bomb-dump was located on the west side. The station opened on 17 February 1944 as Station 462 for the USAAF, but was placed under Care and Maintenance whilst decisions were made on final basing of air units.

In April 1944 the 438th Troop Carrier Group of IXth Troop Carrier Command moved in, the decision having been made to focus airborne operations in this area. The three squadrons of the group were equipped with C-47s and C-53s and their primary role was the delivery of airborne forces by parachute or glider; the latter included Hadrians and Horsas, and the Group was soon involved in intensive training and exercises. On the evening of 5 June 1944 the Group despatched eighty-one aircraft to drop members of the 101st Airborne Division in the area around St Mère Église. The recent TV mini-series

AIRFIELD DATA DEC 1944

Command:	Fighter Command	Runway surface:	Concrete and tarmac
Function:	Operational Satellite	Hangars:	T.2 × 2
Runways:	270 deg 2,000 × 50yd	Dispersals:	50 × Spectacle
	210 deg 1,400 × 50yd	Personnel:	Officers – 124
	330 deg 1,400 × 50yd		Other Ranks – 2,378 (324 WAAF)

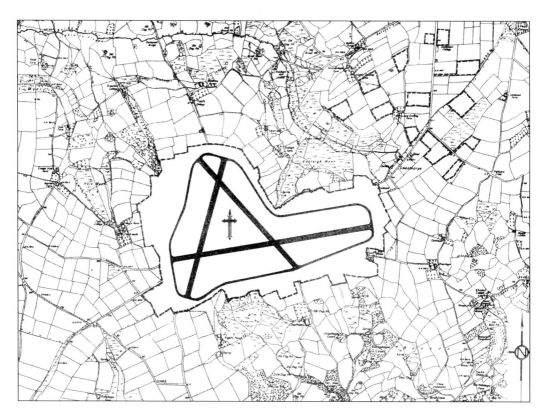

Band of Brothers dealt with the 506th Parachute Infantry Regiment and the lanes around this Devon airfield and the role of Upottery in the D-Day assault suddenly became well-known. The Group despatched glider sorties and supply missions over the next few days, as Upottery contributed to the Allied build-up during these critical first days of the invasion. By August, the intense period of activity was over and, by September, the Group had moved. On 1 October, it became a satellite for Weston Zoyland but was actually used as a detachment base by the US Navy units at Dunkeswell. This temporary arrangement became permanent in January 1945, when the US Navy took control of Upottery and moved in two anti-submarine squadrons, the 107th and 112th of the 479th Anti-Submarine Group.

The squadrons operated the PB4Y-1 version of the Liberator and their main role was anti-submarine patrols although, by the time they moved to Upottery, the main part of the U-boat war was all but over.

The long range of the Liberators meant they could search large areas and a number of sightings were made, but with no confirmed results. The end of the war in Europe brought an immediate abandonment by the Americans and most aircraft and personnel had returned to the United States by July. The airfield was transferred to Coastal Command, but this was a paperwork transaction as they had no need of the airfield.

The only post-war use of Upottery was as a sub-site for two Maintenance Units: No.265 MU at Kidlington from August 1945 to July 1948; No.267

This C-47 of the 91st TCS of the 439th TCG is carrying out a glider snatch to recover a glider in France after D-Day. (US National Archives)

MU at Croughton from November 1946 to September 1948.

The airfield at Upottery was closed in November 1948 and was put up for disposal in the first *tranche* of airfields in the early 1950s. Agriculture has now reclaimed the site, although the basic airfield layout is still quite clear from the air and a number of buildings, in various stages of ruin, can still be seen at the communal sites. You now drive over what were the southern taxiway and the NE/SW runway, as these are public roads.

UNITS

1939–1945
USAAF Units
439th TCG

Squadrons:	91st TCS, 92nd TCS, 93rd TCS, 94th TCS
Aircraft:	C-47
Dates:	26 Apr 1944–8 Sep 1944

479th ASG

Squadrons:	107th, 112th
Aircraft:	PB4Y-1
Dates:	Jan 1945–Jun 1945

MEMORIAL

There is a memorial in the village of Smeatharpe; a brick 'sentry box' on one wall of which is a plaque that gives a brief history of the airfield and lists the units based here and the operations undertaken by the airborne regiments.

WARMWELL (Woodsford) (Station 454)

UTM/Grid: OS Map 194 – SY760885
Lat/Long: N50°41.41 W002°20.26
Nearest Town: Dorchester 3 miles to north-west

County: Dorset

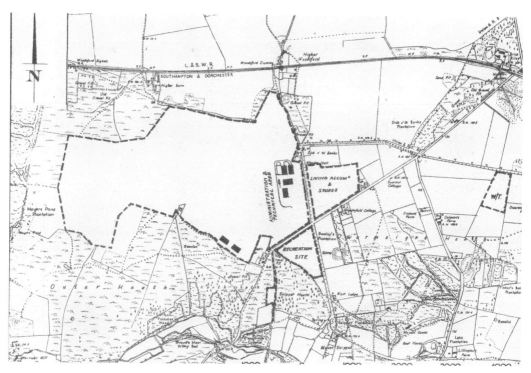

HISTORY

The original name of the airfield was Woodsford and it was established as No.6 Armament Training Camp (ATC) to work with the ranges at Chesil Bank, less than ten miles away. The station officially opened on 1 May 1937 as part of Armament Group, but it was little more than a large field with very limited facilities; squadrons that deployed to use the ranges were expected to stay in tented camps. The target-tow Flight formed a few weeks later with Tutors and Wallaces and the first two squadrons, 206 and 220, arrived for a brief period of exercise and gunnery. These were the first of a number of squadrons to cycle through the airfield both before and during World War Two, the majority staying for a few days or a few weeks at most – just enough time to use the ranges. The unit list does not include the pre-war detachments of units.

The ATC became No.6 Armament Practice Station on 1 April 1938 but the role remained the same, as did the aircraft in the tow Flight, and it was around this time that the airfield was renamed RAF Warmwell. An admin and technical site was constructed on the east

side of the airfield, with an additional two hangars on the south side, although the exact date of these constructions is uncertain. In essence, Warmwell remained a large grass area with a reasonably good operating surface. With the outbreak of war, the Ansons of 217 Squadron moved in to fly coastal patrols, the location of the airfield close to the south coast was what eventually made it a forward fighter airfield. However, the main role still remained that of training and, on 1 January 1940, No.10 Bombing and Gunnery School (BGS) was formed here by renaming No.10 AOS, which had been in place since the previous September, although it departed to Dumfries in July. Warmwell took on a new role as a fighter satellite for Middle Wallop. The first fighter detachment was by 609 Squadron, but this was short-lived and was normally a daytime deployment from their home base. Of more significance was the arrival of 152 Squadron from Acklington with Spitfire Is. This unit proved to be one of the longer-term residents for Warmwell, the Spitfires eventually moving to Portreath in April 1941.

AIRFIELD DATA DEC 1944

Command:	Fighter Command	Runway surface:	Grass
Function:	Forward Airfield	Hangars:	Blister × 8, Bellman × 2
Runways:	NE/SW 900yd	Dispersals:	12 × twin-engine, 6 × single-engine
	WNW/ESE 1,680yd	Personnel:	Officers – 107 (4 WAAF)
	NW/SE 900yd		Other Ranks – 1,568 (212 WAAF)

Warmwell's contribution to the Battle of Britain was made by these two Spitfire squadrons and they scored a number of successes and suffered a number of losses; the airfield itself was targeted once, with a formation of Ju88s causing damage on 25 August 1940.

In 1941, No.10 Group gradually started to go on the offensive and the various squadrons based at Warmwell made regular forays into northern France to attack German targets. Throughout this period the airfield was frequently targeted in German air raids. As

Spitfire of 152 Squadron; the airfield played host to a large number of fighter units.

245 Squadron was one of a number of Typhoon operators to pass through Warmwell; this is a January 1945 posing of aircrew.

The Typhoons of 257 Squadron spent various periods at Warmwell in 1943.

can be seen from the impressive list of units detailed below, many squadrons spent short periods of time there, either on offensive detachments or on refresher weapons training. The Central Gunnery School, which had formed here in November 1939 to 'upgrade the standard of RAF gunnery', finally departed for the quieter pastures of Castle Kennedy in June 1941.

By late-1943, the Americans had begun operations from Warmwell, flown first by P-47s of the 4th FG using the airfield as a refuel and re-arm base and then by the based P-38-equipped 474th Fighter-Bomber Group. As the Allies advanced further into Europe, the Americans moved to the Continent and the RAF returned to the airfield, which by this time had resumed its role as a base for gunnery practice. From September 1944 the station was home to two Armament Practice Camps, No.14 and No.17. Both were equipped with Martinets and Masters and both disbanded on 4 October 1945.

Rapidly wound down when the war ended, Warmwell initially reduced to Care and Maintenance in November 1945, but was soon abandoned. The control tower has survived, heavily modified, in the form of a large house, but most of the site has disappeared as a result of extensive gravel extraction.

Decoy Sites

Q	Knighton	SY812866
	Winfrith Heath	SY805865

Units

1919–1939

217 Sqn	28 Sep 1938–10 Oct 1938	Anson
6 ATC	1 May 1937–1 Apr 1939	Wallace
6 ATS	1 Apr 1938–3 Sep 1939	

1939–1945

2 Sqn	6–20 Jul 1945	Spitfire
3 Sqn	1–17 Apr 1945	Tempest
19 Sqn	1–14 Jun 1942	Spitfire
26 Sqn	29 Aug 1941–1 Sep 1941	Lysander, Tomahawk
41 Sqn	7–18 Mar 1945; 20 Aug 1945–6 Sep 1945	Spitfire
56 Sqn	8–23 May 1945	Tempest
66 Sqn	8–22 Feb 1942; 1–14 Nov 1942	Spitfire
80 Sqn	19 Apr 1945–7 May 1945	Tempest
118 Sqn	9–18 Apr 1941; 23 Feb 1942–7 Mar 1942	Spitfire
130 Sqn	30 Nov 1941–5 Dec 1941; 12–17 Jul 1942; 21–31 Oct 1942	Spitfire
137 Sqn	7–19 Mar 1945	Typhoon
152 Sqn	12 Jul 1940–9 Apr 1941	Spitfire
164 Sqn	20 Jun 1943–6 Aug 1943	Hurricane
174 Sqn	1–21 Sep 1942; 10–21 Nov 1944	Hurricane, Typhoon

175 Sqn	3 Mar 1942–10 Oct 1942	Hurricane		CGS	6 Nov 1939–23 Jun 1941	
181 Sqn	12 Jan 1945–3 Feb 1945	Typhoon		10 BGS	1 Jan 1940–13 Jul 1940	Whitley,
182 Sqn	3–21 Feb 1945	Typhoon				Battle
184 Sqn	4–18 Dec 1944; 7–28 May 1945	Typhoon		ASRF	May 1941–21 Oct 1941	Lysander
217 Sqn	25 Aug 1939–2 Oct 1939	Anson		10 Gp TTF	16 Jul 1941–8 Dec 1941	Lysander
234 Sqn	24 Feb 1941–5 Nov 1941	Spitfire		1487 Flt	30 Oct 1941–Sep 1943	Lysander,
238 Sqn det	Jun 1940–?	Hurricane				Master
245 Sqn	17–23 Nov 1941	Hurricane		14 APC	Sep 1944–4 Oct 1945	Martinet
	19 Dec 1944–6 Jan 1945	Typhoon		17 APC	Sep 1944–4 Oct 1945	Martinet
	16 Jun 1945–4 Jul 1945	Typhoon				

USAAF units

474th FBG

247 Sqn	21 Feb 1945–7 Mar 1945	Typhoon
257 Sqn	8 Jan 1943–20 Jan 1944+	Typhoon
263 Sqn	19–23 Dec 1941;	Whirlwind
	summer 1942–Dec 1943+	
263 Sqn	6–19 Mar 1944	Typhoon
266 Sqn	21 Sep 1942–8 Jan 1943	Typhoon
274 Sqn	3–7 Sep 1945	Tempest
275 Sqn	20 Apr 1944–7 Aug 1944	Spitfire,
		Anson
276 Sqn det	Jan 1942–?	various
277 Sqn det	1944	various
286 Sqn det	1942	various
302 Sqn	5 Sep 1941–11 Oct 1941;	Hurricane,
	27 Apr 1942–1 May 1942	Spitfire
310 Sqn	8–21 Mar 1942	Spitfire
312 Sqn	19–31 May 1942;	Hurricane,
	20 Feb 1943–14 Mar 1943	Spitfire
313 Sqn	23–29 Nov 1941	Spitfire
340 Sqn	6–17 Sep 1945	Spitfire
350 Sqn	5–15 Apr 1942	Spitfire
401 Sqn	24 Oct 1944–4 Nov 1944	Spitfire
402 Sqn	6 Nov 1941–4 Mar 1942	Hurricane
402 Sqn	14 Jan 1945–2 Feb 1945	Spitfire
403 Sqn	4–14 Jan 1945	Spitfire
411 Sqn	15–23 Oct 1944;	Spitfire
	24 May–7 Jun 1945	
412 Sqn	6–20 Nov 1944	Spitfire
414 Sqn	23 Jun–6 Jul 1945	Spitfire
421 Sqn	14–28 Jun 1942;	Spitfire
	6–18 Dec 1944	
430 Sqn	23 Jul–2 Aug 1945	Spitfire
438 Sqn	19 Mar 1945–3 Apr 1945	Typhoon
439 Sqn	3–22 Apr 1945	Typhoon
440 Sqn	23 Apr 1945–8 May 1945	Typhoon
442 Sqn	14–25 Nov 1944	Spitfire
443 Sqn	18 Dec 1944–3 Jan 1945	Spitfire
500 Sqn	30 Jul 1939–13 Aug 1939	Anson
501 Sqn	25 Jan 1942–7 Feb 1942	Spitfire
604 Sqn	12–23 Aug 1942	Beaufighter
609 Sqn	2 Oct 1940–24 Feb 1941	Spitfire
610 Sqn	21 Feb 1945–3 Mar 1945	Spitfire
793 Sqn FAA det	14–24 Aug 1940	Roc
794 Sqn FAA det	6 Mar 1943–7 Jul 1943	various
810 Sqn FAA	15 Jun 1939–3 Jul 1939	Swordfish
814 Sqn FAA	2–29 Jun 1939	Swordfish
10 AOS	3 Sep 1939–1 Jan 1940	Harrow,
		Seal, Battle

Squadrons: 428th FS, 429th FS, 430th FS
Aircraft: P-38
Dates: Feb 1944–Mar 1944

MEMORIAL

Stone on village green, inscribed:

Royal Air Force Station Warmwell formerly Woodsford 1937–1946. A memorial dedicated to those men and women who whilst serving with the Royal Air Force, United States Army Air Force, Military and Allied Forces at RAF Warmwell, made the supreme sacrifice in defence of freedom. Lest we forget 11th June 1989

WESTON-SUPER-MARE

County: Somerset (Avon)

UTM/Grid: OS Map 182 – ST344603
Lat/Long: N51°20.14 W002°56.14
Nearest Town: Weston-super-Mare 2 miles to north-west

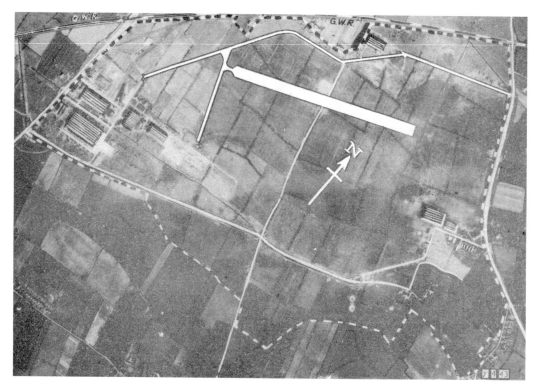

HISTORY

The civil airport for Weston-super-Mare, Weston Airport, opened in May 1936 with a Railway Air Services route between other airfields in South-West England. The airport was on the far side of the GWR railway line on the south-east side of the town close to the village of Locking. The latter subsequently became the site for an RAF School of Technical Training – about a mile from the airfield – and this has caused confusion and the impression that the school was at the airfield itself; the school did however operate a Station Flight at Weston for communications and staff training. The airport site comprised a large central grass landing area with a hangar and other buildings on the east side. Commercial services expanded over the first two years and, in July 1939, the main operators, the Straight Corporation, started an Air Ministry contract to run No.39 Elementary and Reserve Flying Training School, one of a number operated by the Straight Corporation. The Tiger Moths and Harts

had hardly warmed up their engines before the school was disbanded on the outbreak of war, although its place was taken by No.5 Civil Air Navigation School, also operated by Straight.

Ansons became the main type at Weston but, in August 1940, No.5 Air Observer and Navigator School, as the CANS had become, moved to South Africa, as part of the mass emigration of flying training. Western Airways, owned and operated by Straight, had taken on modification and overhaul work of RAF trainers. By late-1940 the airfield had also started to produce Beaufighters, a Bristol shadow factory having been constructed on the west side of the airfield near Old Mixon. After initial problems with production, the factory settled down and at its peak production in 1944 was turning out over eighty aircraft a month. The final Beaufighter left the factory in September 1945. It was the presence of the shadow factory and the need for flight testing that led to the laying of a 4,200ft runway, the old grass surface

AIRFIELD DATA DEC 1944

Command:	Technical Training Command	Runway surface:	Tarmac
Function:	Satellite	Hangars:	MAP × 4, Over Blister × 2
Runways:	254 deg 1,000yd × 50yd	Dispersals:	Nil
		Personnel:	Officers – Nil
			Other Ranks – 120

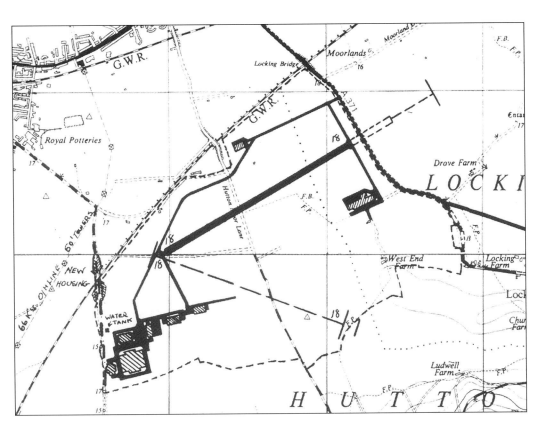

being susceptible to waterlogging and deterioration.

Flying training had returned to the airfield in September 1940, with the arrival of No.10 EFTS from Yatesbury with its Tiger Moths. The school was operated by the Bristol Aeroplane Co. and the hectic pace of training meant that RLGs were used at Lulsgate Bottom and Northleach, especially after the school was raised to Class A status in January 1941. No.10 EFTS moved out in September and, with the exception of the Locking Station Flight, the airfield was virtually deserted.

A final burst of flying activity took place between October 1942 and November 1943, when 286 Squadron arrived from Colerne with its diverse fleet of aircraft for target-towing and support work. The main types included Defiants, Hurricanes, Martinets,

Masters and Oxfords. In summer 1943, the station was transferred to Technical Training Command and the Equipment Training School arrived in July, although this did not signify a real interest by this Command. The shadow factory remained the main user and, from 1944, a detachment of the Air Torpedo Development Unit (ATDU), based at Gosport, used Weston for torpedo-dropping trials in the Bristol Channel. This role may have continued to 1948–1949; the original reason for the detachment was to work closely with Bristols on the Beaufighter Xs.

Although Beaufighter production ended in late-1945, Bristols continued to use the Old Mixon site, the original plan being to produce the Brabazon airliner, although it was decided that Weston was unsuitable as

Anson GR.1s operated from Weston as navigation trainers; this may not be a Weston shot.

an airfield and this plan was abandoned. Production switched, instead, to helicopters, with Sycamores and Belvederes rolling off the production lines in the 1950s. The Bristol Helicopter Division was taken over by Westland Aircraft in March 1960 and the factory continued to produce helicopters and parts until the company transferred all its work to the Yeovil factory.

Weston had transferred to the Ministry of Civil Aviation in 1946, with the return of commercial services, but these were small scale and not very successful; the Bristols presence and even the RAF's use of the airfield remained more significant. The Radio School at Locking based a small number of Varsity radar trainers at the airfield from 1959 to 1966; the last RAF unit to leave the airfield was No.621 Volunteer Gliding School, which had formed here in September 1955 and left, nearly forty years later, for Hullavington. By the time the gliders left, the airfield was in a sorry state, Westland had owned and operated the airfield since 1978 and had no interest in maintaining the runway and, a few years later, the condition of the surfaces meant that all fixed-wing flying had to move out, the private owners departing to Lulsgate. This coincided with discussions on the future of the airfield, with a plan for housing and other amenities leading Westland to sell the site. The company's impact was not all negative and, since 1978, the airfield has been home to a helicopter museum, which, since it became the International Helicopter Museum in March 1989, has acquired a truly amazing collection of helicopters, with a great deal of support from Westland.

DECOY SITE

| Q/QF | Bleadon | ST310567 |

UNITS

1939–1945

286 Sqn	10 Oct 1942–29 Nov 1943	various
39 ERFTS	3 Jul 1939–3 Sep 1939	Magister, Hind
5 CANS	2 Sep 1939–1 Nov 1939	Anson

Having specialized in helicopters, Westland produced a number of types at its Weston-Super-Mare facility, such as the Belvedere.

5 AONS	1 Nov 1939–22 Aug 1940	Anson
3 AONS	3 Jun 1940–12 Jun 1940	Anson
10 EFTS	7 Sep 1940–22 Sep 1941	Tiger Moth
Centaurus Flt	1942–30 Sep 1945	
ATTDU det	1944–1949?	Beaufighter

Post-1945

| 621 VGS | 1 Sep 1955–Jun 1993 | various |
| 1 RS | 1959–Oct 1966 | Varsity |

MEMORIAL

There is no memorial as such, but the International Helicopter Museum commemorates the role of Bristols and Westland in helicopter production at Weston-super-Mare.

WESTON ZOYLAND
(Station 447)

County: Somerset

UTM/Grid: OS Map 182 – ST365344
Lat/Long: N51°06.11 W002°54.23
Nearest Town: Bridgwater 4 miles to north-west

Summer Camp, for 100 Squadron, late 1920s.

HISTORY

From 1926 to 1936, a field to the east of the village of Weston Zoyland was brought into use each year for summer camps by aircraft detached to work with the coastal ranges in the Watchet area. As with other fields used for this purpose, it was a case of removing any livestock, checking the landing area and living in tents. This role was initially performed by the Horsleys of 100 Squadron but, from 1931, it was taken on by the newly formed (ex-Night Flying Flight) Anti-Aircraft Co-operation Flight (AACF), which detached to Westland every summer, usually between May/June and September. The AACF operated the Horsley, Moth and Wallace for this task and, in April 1936, was re-designated the AAC unit (AACU). The need for such units continued to increase and, by May 1937, the Westland Zoyland work was being undertaken by 'A Flight' of No.1 AACU, still on a summer camp basis. This changed in 1939, with the Flight taking up full-time residence.

Lysanders of 16 Squadron had been running detachments at Weston Zoyland since late-1939 on coastal patrols but, in August 1940, the whole squadron moved to the Somerset base, although continuing to operate detachments at a variety of airfields in the West Country. This squadron spent much of the time here between summer 1940 and summer 1943, although this was not a continuous period of residence. As the unit list shows, Weston Zoyland played host to a large number of units during World War Two, most on short detachments, most of these being army co-operation units with the Lysander, Mustang or Tomahawk. One of the exceptions was 286 Squadron, which arrived in November 1943 from Weston-super-Mare and remained until it disbanded in May 1945, although it was based elsewhere for a few months in summer 1944.

In December 1943, the three numbered target-towing Flights came together to form 587 Squadron and this unit, still with a varied fleet of aircraft, used

Airfield Data Dec 1944

Command: Fighter Command
Function: Anti-Aircraft Co-operation Unit
Runways: 285 deg 1,925 × 50yd
048 deg 1,188 × 50yd
343 deg 1,367 × 50yd

Runway surface: Concrete and wood chippings
Hangars: Blister × 9, T.2 × 2
T.2 (14-bay) × one, Bellman × one,
Bessonneau × one
Dispersals: 33 × Special Loop, 2 × Frying Pan (150ft)
Personnel: Officers – 134 (6 WAAF)
Other Ranks – 1,296 (162 WAAF)

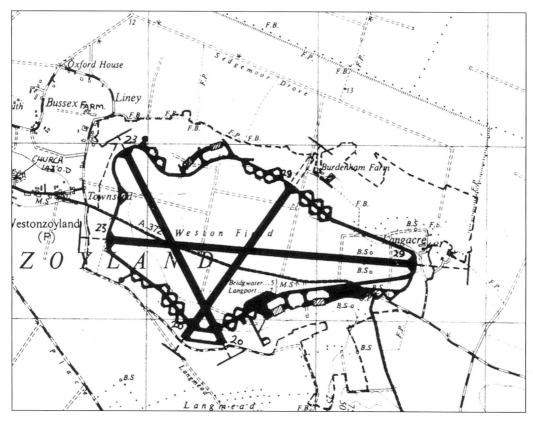

Weston Zoyland to June 1946, with a six-month absence in the middle of 1944.

As the importance of the airfield grew and it became a major army co-operation base as well as a major AACU airfield, various improvements were made to the runways and infrastructure. The major work in this respect took place in 1943, when three surfaced runways were laid, the longest oriented east/west and involving acquisition of more land at the east end. Hangar space was still limited, but there was a good provision of dispersals around the perimeter track.

The Americans took over the airfield, as Station 447, in May 1944, for use by a Troop Carrier Group as part of the assembly of airborne forces for D-Day. The first aircraft of the 442nd TCG arrived in late-May and participated in the D-Day drops of para-troops, although the full strength of the Group was not present until the middle of June. The 442nd remained at Weston Zoyland to October when they moved to Peray in France.

The RAF moved back in with a mix of training, support and operational units, as shown in the unit list, but, by 1947, these had all gone and the airfield was reduced to Care and Maintenance.

The Korean War and fears that it would spread to a

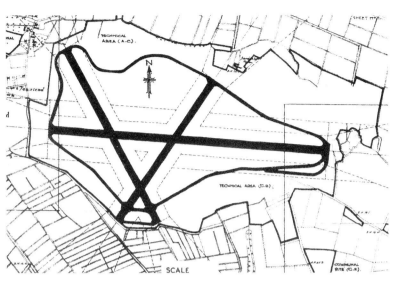

The airfield at Weston Zoyland was laid out over a large area of Somerset fens, having grown from being a temporary location for summer camps.

Aircrew of 140 Squadron at Weston in November 1941.

The special Canberras of 76 Squadron used the airfield as their home base but were frequently detached to other locations, especially for the nuclear weapon trials (hence the exotic location in the backdrop).

wider conflict gave renewed impetus to the RAF in terms of training – or in many cases re-training World War Two personnel – and Weston Zoyland was one of the airfields re-activated for this purpose, becoming home to No.209 Advanced Flying School in June 1952. This unit underwent a number of name changes and finally left in 1955 for Strubby. From 1955 to 1957, Weston Zoyland was home to the special Canberras of 76 Squadron; these were equipped with wing-tip pods for air sampling of nuclear tests and were deployed to the British tests in Australia, as well as flying 'sniffing' sorties to collect air samples from other tests. Other Canberra units also made brief appearances here. With the departure of the Canberras, the airfield was once again reduced to Care and Maintenance and then closed in January 1958. It was retained as MoD property for another ten years, finally being released in 1969.

The major road that had been closed when the airfield was built re-opened when the airfield closed and now bisects the old airfield from east to west, incorporating part of the old main runway. From the air, the basic airfield layout looks virtually intact and a number of hangars and other buildings have survived.

Units

1919–1939

100 Sqn	summer dets 1926–1930?	Horsley
AACF	Oct 1931–14 Apr 1936	various
AACU	Apr 1936–Sep 1936	
1 AACU	Feb 1937–Nov 1942+	

1939–1945

2 Sqn	4–10 Aug 1941	Lysander
16 Sqn	15 Aug 1940–22 May 1943	Lysander, Mustang

19 Sqn	29 Sep 1943–15 Oct 1943	Spitfire
26 Sqn	8–23 Feb 1942	Mustang
63 Sqn det	summer 1939	Anson, Battle
63 Sqn	6–13 Nov 1942	Mustang
122 Sqn	15 Oct 1943–3 Nov 1943	Spitfire
140 Sqn	29 Oct 1941–4 Nov 1941	Spitfire, Blenheim
168 Sqn	1–17 Mar 1943	Mustang
169 Sqn	12–18 Oct 1942	Mustang
170 Sqn det	late-1942; spring 1943	Mustang
171 Sqn	10–20 Sep 1942	Mustang
225 Sqn det	summer 1941	Lysander
231 Sqn	11–21 Jul 1943	Mustang
239 Sqn	6–13 Jul 1941	Lysander, Tomahawk
268 Sqn	21–27 Jul 1941	Tomahawk
285 Sqn	20–26 Jun 1945	Mustang
286 Sqn	29 Nov 1943–10 Apr 1944; 28 Sep 1944–16 May 1945	various
318 Sqn det	spring 1943	Hurricane
400 Sqn det	summer 1941–?	Tomahawk, Mustang
400 Sqn	8–22 Feb 1943	Mustang
414 Sqn	31 Jul 1943–10 Aug 1943	Mustang
430 Sqn	25 Apr 1943–5 May 1943	Mustang
525 Sqn	1 Sep 1943–6 Feb 1944	Warwick
587 Sqn	1 Dec 1943–10 Apr 1944; 1 Oct 1944–1 Jun 1946	various
613 Sqn det	late-1939–early 1940	Hind, Hector
614 Sqn det	late-1939–early 1940	Hind, Hector, Lysander
653 Sqn	6–17 Dec 1943	Auster

1492 Flt	18 Oct 1941–18 Oct 1943	Lysander, Master, Martinet
1600 Flt	1 Nov 1942–1 Dec 1943	Henley
1601 Flt	1 Nov 1942–1 Dec 1943	Henley
1 AAPC	20 Jan 1943–17 Jun 1943	Lysander, Martinet
1625 Flt	17 Jun 1943–1 Dec 1943	Lysander, Martinet
13 APC	18 Oct 1943–20 Nov 1943	Martinet
1540 Flt	6 Feb 1945–17 Dec 1945	Oxford

USAAF units
442nd TCG

Squadrons	303rd, 304th, 305th, 306th TCS
Aircraft	C–47, C–53
Dates	May 1944–Oct 1944

Post-1945

32 Sqn det	Jan 1957	Canberra
73 Sqn	early 1957	Canberra
76 Sqn	15 Nov 1955–1 Apr 1957	Canberra
151 Sqn	11 Jul 1946–10 Oct 1946	Mosquito
222 Sqn	5 Sep 1945–23 Oct 1945; 8 Jul 1946–28 Apr 1947	Tempest, Meteor
542 Sqn	15 Dec 1955–31 Mar 1957	Canberra
691 Sqn	29 Apr 1946–7 Jul 1946	various
209 AFS	23 Jun 1952–1 Jun 1954	Meteor, Vampire
12 FTS	1 Jun 1954–24 Jun 1955	Meteor
3 AWJRS	Jun 1955–? 1955	Meteor
1362 Flt	Oct 1955–?	Whirlwind

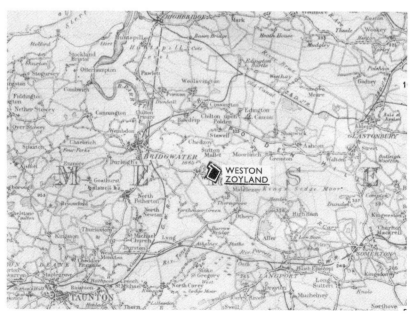

WHITCHURCH

County: Somerset (Avon)

UTM/Grid: OS Map 172 – ST595686
Lat/Long: N52°25 W002°35
Nearest Town: Bristol 2 miles to north

HISTORY

In 1929 the Bristol Corporation acquired 298 acres of land at Whitchurch for a new municipal airport. Bristol Airport opened in May 1930 for use by commercial operators and for private flying; indeed, it was largely at the instigation of the latter (the Bristol and Wessex Aeroplane Club) that the Corporation had undertaken the project. It was the third such municipal airport in the country and, over the next ten years, the number of routes expanded and it was handling 4,000 passengers a year – a trivial number by today's standards, but reasonable in 1939. In addition to the commercial routes and private flying, Whitchurch also housed an Airwork Service Depot.

In December 1938, No.33 Elementary and Reserve Flying Training School was formed at Whitchurch, its Tiger Moths being operated by Chamier, Gilbert Lodge and Co. The school undertook pilot training, until closed with the outbreak of war. By that time, Whitchurch's infrastructure had improved enough to be considered as a dispersal base for Imperial and British Airways, who had been told to look for alternatives to Croydon and Heston, as the London airfields were considered untenable in the event of war. Whitchurch was accepted in summer 1939 and, when war broke out, it became part of the National Air Communications network. By 1940, the major user was the newly formed British Overseas Airways Corporation (BOAC) and Whitchurch became a main base for the airline. It was also used by a detachment of No.3 Ferry Pilots Pool from February 1940, this becoming No.3 FPP in November to handle aircraft produce by Bristols at Filton and elsewhere. The

FPP remained at Whitchurch to September 1945.

By late-1941, the airfield had a 3,000ft paved east/west runway, a perimeter track and a variety of hangars and other buildings, some from the pre-war airport and others being wartime built. BOAC moved its activities to Hurn in November 1944, although they retained an engineering facility and, in the later part of 1945, were also using the airfield for pilot training. The Ministry of Civil Aviation took over the airfield in June 1945, as part of the plan of re-establishing commercial aviation at the earliest opportunity. Attempts to establish viable commercial routes were a failure and it was only the return of private flying that kept the airport open. This situation could not continue, especially as the site itself was under threat from the growth of the city and, in 1957, Bristol Airport closed in favour of the new Bristol Airport that had been developed from the old RAF station at Lulsgate Bottom.

UNITS

1919–1939

33 ERFTS	1 Dec 1938–3 Sep 1939	Tiger Moth, Hind

1939–1945

ATAS	1940–Oct 1940	
3 FPP det	Feb 1940–Nov 1940	
2 FPP	5 Nov 1940–Sep 1945	Anson, Argus

MEMORIAL

Memorial stone to the Air Transport Auxiliary (FPP) use of Whitchurch, unveiled April 1986.

Whitchurch hangar and dispersal area, probably late 1940s. (Rod Priddle)

Loading a BEA Dakota at Whitchurch. (Rod Priddle)

WINDRUSH

County: Gloucestershire

UTM/Grid: OS Map 163 – SP180120
Lat/Long: N51°48 W001°44
Nearest Town: Witney 10 miles to east

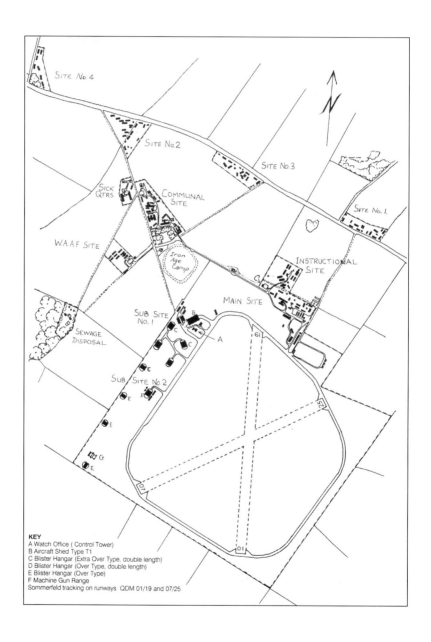

KEY
A Watch Office (Control Tower)
B Aircraft Shed Type T1
C Blister Hangar (Extra Over Type, double length)
D Blister Hangar (Over Type, double length)
E Blister Hangar (Over Type)
F Machine Gun Range
Sommerfeld tracking on runways QDM 01/19 and 07/25

AIRFIELD DATA DEC 1944

Command:	Flying Training Command	Runway surface:	Sommerfeld Track
Function:	(Pilots) Advanced Flying Unit satellite	Hangars:	Double (69ft) Blister × 5, Single
Runways:	011 deg 1,000yd		(69ft) Blister × 4, T.1 × one
	071 deg 1,053yd	Dispersals:	Nil
	270 deg 2,000 × 50yd	Personnel:	Officers – 52 (2 WAAF)
			Other Ranks – 2,046 (176 WAAF)

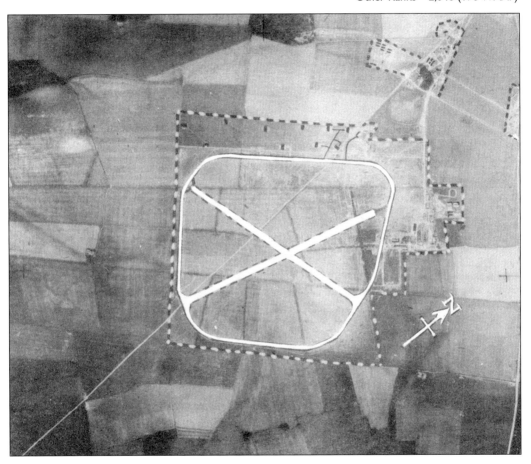

HISTORY

This small grass airfield spent its entire career from opening in early summer 1940 to closure in 1945 as a relief landing ground for day and night flying by training units based at Little Rissington. Unlike some RLGs, it did acquire both hangars, a series of Blister types on the east side, and an assortment of huts, as some ground instruction also took place here. The communal sites were just north of the actual airfield. In summer 1942, the two grass strips were overlain with Sommerfeld Track, as the continual circuits and bumps by Oxfords had begun to erode the surfaces. The main user throughout the airfield's life was No.6 Flying Training School, which became No.6 (Pilots) Advanced Flying Unit in April 1942 but continued the same basic role. If it was not for one event, then Windrush would barely have been remembered: that event took place on the night of 18 August 1940, when a He111 attacked the airfield; at some point

Painting of the incident
when an Anson collided
with (or rammed) a He
111 over Windrush.

during the attack it saw or was seen by the pilot of an Anson that was in the circuit. The two aircraft collided and it is usually recorded that the Anson pilot, Sergeant Hancock, rammed the enemy bomber, although it seems more likely that, having switched off his lights, he was attempting to evade when the collision occurred. The incident has been the subject of a painting and has entered RAF lore.

With the end of war, the airfield at Windrush was no longer required and it was amongst the first to be put up for disposal, with little left now to mark its existence.

UNITS

1939–1945

6 FTS	Jun 1940–1 Apr 1942	various
15 FTS	Jul 1940–Aug 1940	Oxford
6 PAFU	1 Apr 1942–12 Jul 1945	Oxford

WINKLEIGH (Station 460)

County: Devon

UTM/Grid: OS Map 191 – SS621094
Lat/Long: N50°53 W003°57
Nearest Town: Okehampton 8 miles to south

Winkleigh in June 2003.

HISTORY

Constructed on a small plateau just north-west of the village after which it took its name, this airfield was originally intended as a satellite for Chivenor but, by the time it was completed in late-1942, Coastal Command was no longer interested. It was a difficult site, as space was restricted, hence the unusual cruciform layout to fit two reasonable runways into the space available, and, although it was a plateau, the surface was subject to waterlogging, which caused major drainage and stabilization problems during construction. The main technical area, centred on a single T.2 hangar, was laid out on the north-west side, as were most of the dispersal areas, some of which were provided with Blister hangars. The admin area, a collection of huts, was on the south-east side and the communal areas were dispersed in fields to the south-east of the airfield.

It was not until 1 January 1943 that the new owners – Fighter Command – eventually accepted the airfield, additional fighter-type dispersals having been constructed late the previous year. It was a strange decision as, by 1943, the Command had little use for this type of airfield in a remote part of Devon and, although a few aircraft passed through, there was no plan for actual basing; in August the airfield was reduced to Care and Maintenance.

There was a burst of activity from October to November 1943, when Winkleigh became Station 460 for the USAAF and was used by a detachment of Spitfires from the 12th Photographic Reconnaissance Squadron. This was in connection with exercises being conducted on the North Devon coast as part of the build-up of capability for the invasion of Europe. The Americans retained an interest in the airfield into 1944 and the 74th Service Group handled various aircraft that staged through Winkleigh, the usual customers being C-47s. However, this had come to an end by late-February and Winkleigh was still in

AIRFIELD DATA DEC 1944

Command: Fighter Command
Function: Operational Station
Runways: 270 deg 1,550 × 50yd
             003 deg 1,500 × 50yd

Runway surface: Tarmac and concrete
Hangars: Over Blister × 8, T.2 × one
Dispersals: 9 × Open, 6 × Pens
Personnel: Officers – 92 (10 WAAF)
                 Other Ranks – 1,170 (190 WAAF)

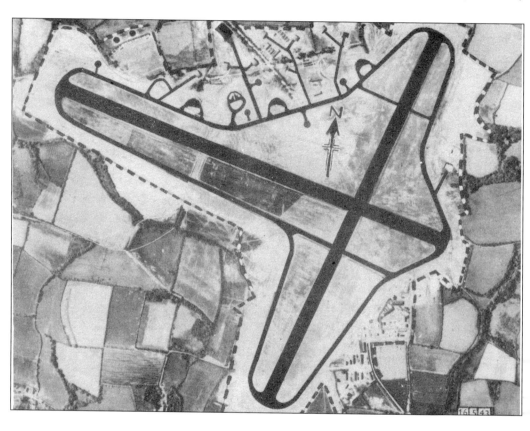

the hands of Fighter Command. At last, in April, the unloved station received a based unit, with the arrival of the Beaufighters and Mosquitoes of 406 Squadron from Exeter. The Canadians had been moved out because Exeter was needed for a USAAF Troop Carrier Group and Winkleigh was the nearest suitable airfield from which to maintain the night cover of the South Devon area, with its build-up of men and material for the invasion. By the end of April, the squadron had already made two confirmed 'kills' from Winkleigh. The night-fighter defence had been increased by a detachment from 286 Squadron, but this was still operating Defiants and Hurricanes in the role. Finally, the station acquired a night offensive capability with the arrival of a detachment from 415 Squadron,

whose Albacores and Wellingtons specialized in night anti-shipping work, the targets in this instance being the E-boats that harassed the south coast.

The Canadian night-fighters also took the offensive from time to time, flying intruder missions over France. The squadron eventually left Winkleigh in September, by which time they had claimed at least eight confirmed and a similar number damaged during their sojourn at the airfield, four of the 'kills' having come on the night of 14/15 May when they intercepted a raid aimed at Bristol. Summer 1944 had also seen the black Lysanders of 161 Squadron use Winkleigh for clandestine operations in France but, by late-September, the active period of the station was over and it was once more reduced to Care and Maintenance.

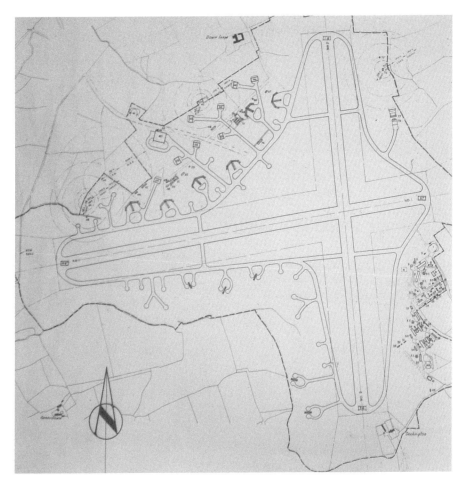

The airfield was used as the Norwegian Training Base from January 1945, which used Harvards and Oxfords to train pilots for the Royal Norwegian Air Force, which was officially reforming now that the end of the war was in sight. The unit also used a number of Cornell trainers – the only UK-based use of this standard American trainer. The task was officially declared over in November and the unit moved to Norway to continue the training task.

Winkleigh was handed to the Ministry of Agriculture and Fisheries in October 1948 for disposal and was quickly returned to agriculture, although it was requisitioned again in October 1956 for some strange reason and allocated as a satellite to Chivenor. Whatever the plan had been, it seemed to come to nothing and the site was released once more in December 1958. The major road that once crossed the site then re-opened and for many years learner drivers (the author included) turned off the road and on to the old runway for a spot of driving practice. The overall layout of the airfield is still distinctive from

the air and many of the buildings, including the T.2 and some blister hangars, survive in good condition. The future of the airfield site is currently the subject of much debate, with plans to turn it into a massive industrial centre, including a Biomass power station.

UNITS

1939–1945

161Sqn det	summer 1944	Lysander
286Sqn det	Apr 1944–?	Hurricane, Defiant
406Sqn	14 Apr 1944–17 Sep 1944	Mosquito
415Sqn det	May–12 Jul 1944	Albacore, Wellington
NTB	Jan 1945–10 Nov 1945	Harvard, Oxford

USAAF unit

12th PRS	Oct 1943–Dec 1943	Spitfire

WORTH MATRAVERS

County: Dorset

UTM/Grid: OS Map 194 – SY963770
Lat/Long: N50°35.56 W002°03.21
Nearest Town: Swanage 4 miles to east

HISTORY

In May 1940 the RAF element of the Telecommunications Research Establishment moved to Worth Matravers; TRE spent two years here and grew from a few hundred staff to over 2,000. One of the main items of equipment under development was IFF (Identification Friend or Foe) but, as far as the 'airfield' was concerned, it was the glider trials of 1940 that were important. The Worth Matravers site included a Special Chain Home (CH) site that consisted of one 240ft wooden tower and a 350ft steel tower for the antennae used in the trials. The flying side of the TRE, the Telecommunications Flying Unit, operated from Hurn and Christchurch and used a wide range of aircraft types, but the trial that involved the creation of a landing ground at Worth Matravers in summer 1940 was designed to see if Chain Home could detect gliders – it was feared that the German invasion would include glider landings at key locations. The landing ground – a basic field – was used by Avro 504s to tow wooden gliders out to sea, where they were then released to make their way back to the landing ground, whilst the radar attempted to pick them up. These trials took place from June to August 1940; when they were completed the Worth Matravers 'airfield' went out of use, except perhaps for the occasional communications flight.

WROUGHTON

UTM/Grid: OS Map 173 – SU138787
Lat/Long: N51°30.4 W001°48.2
Nearest Town: Swindon 4 miles to north

County: Wiltshire

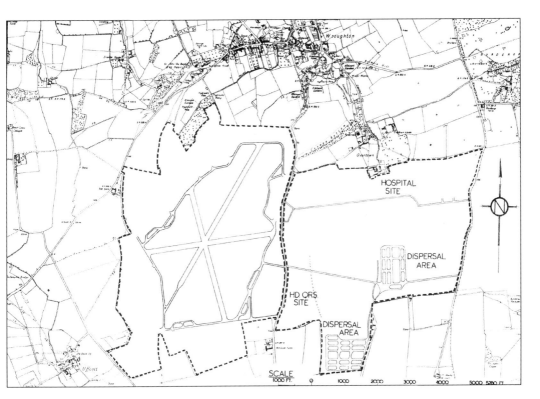

HISTORY

No.15 MU opened at Wroughton on 1 April 1940 in No.41 Group and over the next forty years this Wiltshire airfield was a major aircraft storage and refurbishment location, although the original intent when the site was chosen in the mid-1930s expansion plan was for it to be a training base. The airfield is named after the village just to the north and it was laid out with its main axis along one of the few level bits of ground – the airfield is impressively overlooked by an old Iron Age hillfort (Barbury Castle) to the south.

No.5 Electrical and Wireless School, part of No.26 Group, had been destined to form here, but this was cancelled in late-1938, by which time the site had already been acquired and initial grading work commenced. As a reasonably remote yet central (to South and Central England) site it was allocated instead as an Aircraft Storage Unit. Main construction work commenced in May 1939 and Wroughton was eventually to have three concrete runways and an impres-

sive collection of hangars, in six main groups. It took some while for the complete site to be finished and when the airfield received its first aircraft (Lysanders and Tiger Moths) it was far from complete. One of the site plans shows the main groupings of hangars around the airfield, whilst the other also includes the area to the east of the road with its two dispersal areas, complete with Robin hangars. Aircraft were also placed in open storage and a number of fields to the south and west were used for this purpose.

The MU was initially a service-manned Pool MU within No.41 Group, but this was quickly changed to a civilian-manned Aircraft Storage Unit with few uniformed personnel. It was, however, a busy site and, like all Parent MUs, it operated a number of other sites, initially being allocated Bicester (November 1940 to November 1941) and then, in rotation, three satellite landing grounds: No. 31 SLG (Everleigh) – Nov 1941–Sep 1942; No.1 SLG (Slade

AIRFIELD DATA DEC 1944

Command:	Maintenance Command	Runway surface:	Concrete
Function:	Parent Station	Hangars:	Robin × 27, L-Type × 7, D-Type × 4,
Runways:	220 deg 1,659yd × 50yd		C-Type × 3, B-Type × 2
	180 deg 1,376yd × 50yd	Dispersals:	55 × hardcore and asphalt 'roads'
	270 deg 1,333yd × 50yd	Personnel:	Officers – 15 (1 WAAF)
			Other Ranks – 283 (16 WAAF)

Much of the airfield is still in excellent condition, as evidenced by the hangars; some of the hangars are used by the Science Museum to store aircraft and exhibits.

Farm) – 1 Oct 1942–Feb 1943; No.12 SLG (Beechwood Park) – 17 Mar 1943–Apr 1945.

The airfield was essentially complete by 1941, in terms of storage and support facilities, most of the latter being wooden huts, but it was still using grass runways. Despite the drainage work during initial construction, waterlogging had been a problem and it was decided that the airfield needed hard runways; this work was started in 1941 and the runways were linked by a concrete perimeter track.

Although Wroughton was an ASU this does not define the true nature of its work. Whilst storage was part of the task, the more important element was modification and repair. A number of different types went through Wroughton, the first operational types being the Blenheim and Hurricane. Like many ASUs it took advantage of its fighter aircraft and test pilots to operate a Battle Flight, with occasional scrambles during the Battle of Britain. The airfield was attacked twice in August 1940 (13th and 19th) by single aircraft dropping a small number of low-calibre bombs.

A second MU was opened at Wroughton with the arrival of No.76 MU, a Packing Depot, from Cosford in May 1941, this unit remaining in place to 30 September

1946. The main role of this unit was to strip-down aircraft and box them for overseas shipment. American types were added to the mix, being handled at Wroughton from late-1941 and, during World War Two, the airfield handled over 7,000 aircraft, of sixty-two types, a large number of these being gliders. It was particularly important as an assembly and test facility for gliders and this became a primary role from late-1943. By summer 1944, there were 600 gliders on site.

One of the 'flying units' associated with the MU was the Glider Test and Ferry Flight, which formed in spring 1943 and was allocated fourteen Whitleys, although initial strength was only four. Albemarles gradually replaced the Whitleys and the unit undertook test and delivery for gliders from Wroughton and Brize Norton (No.6 MU), even though the latter had its own GTFF. The unit disbanded in August 1945.

The airfield's main role from summer 1944 was handling naval types, such as the Albacore, Barracuda, Firefly and Sea Otter, although a large number of Mosquitoes and Spitfires were also present, primarily in storage. In terms of modification work, the priority was for the Barracuda and the unit was tasked with modifying ninety aircraft a month. Summer 1944 also saw the formation of No.88 Gliding School, with its Cadet gliders giving air experience to the local ATC.

The end of the war brought a change of role and the S part of ASU became more relevant, although it could also now stand for 'scrapping', as Wroughton received redundant aircraft, including many Lancasters, for disposal. The last operational RAF Lancaster ended its life here when retired in October 1956 – only to be scrapped. Jets also appeared, with Meteors and then Vampires, for either storage or modification, as No.15 MU once more took on the modification role. Canberras arrived from 1953 and it was this type that was most associated with the airfield in its post-war RAF years; it was a Canberra than eventually sat as a Gate Guard at the nearby RAF Hospital.

The Group Test Pilots Pool for No.41 Group was located at Wroughton from April 1958 to summer 1959, when it was incorporated into the Maintenance Command Communications and Ferry Squadron at Andover. Earlier that year it had given birth to the Maintenance Command Jet Training Flight, but this moved in March to Lyneham. Helicopters were on-site from 1959 and Wroughton handled all the RAF's rotary types over the next few years, which was perhaps one reason why the navy became interested in the site. On 1 December 1962, Wroughton became an Aircraft Supply and Servicing Depot. Ten years later the RAF said farewell.

The RAF gave up the airfield on 31 March 1972, with Wroughton becoming a Royal Naval Aircraft Yard, handling various helicopters.

This was a short-lived venture and a run-down commenced in March 1976, with a view to closure in 1979; however, the plan was changed and the air yard remained operational to 1989. The Department of Naval Recruiting is still in place at Wroughton and the site is still used for aircraft storage, although this is now historic aircraft in the hands of the Science Museum, who took over a number of hangars in 1978. Wroughton made a name for itself in the early 1990s for the Great Warbirds air displays, the last of which took place in June 1994.

Most of the airfield is intact, although many of the temporary wartime buildings (the huts) have vanished and the dispersed sites are no longer connected to the airfield, although some of the Robin hangars are still there and being used for farm storage.

The English Heritage list of key airfield sites records Wroughton as:

'Opened in 1940, and after Kemble the best example of a landscape built as one of the Air Ministry's twenty-four Aircraft Storage Unit sites, with hangar types of parabolic form and concrete construction dispersed in groups around the flying field.'

YATE

County: Gloucestershire

Yate in June 1941.

HISTORY

The Western Aircraft Repair Depot formed at Yate on 31 May 1917, to provide flight test and delivery of aircraft produced in the Bristol area. The airfield was simply a large field adjacent to the road and was provided with four aeroplane sheds for erection of aircraft. In mid-October 1917, it was renamed as No.3 (Western) ARD and, under this designation, remained open to May 1920. The airfield was subsequently abandoned and was gently rotting away until acquired in 1925 by George Parnall and Co. for the design and production of aircraft; the only notable product was the Percival Gull – and that was not a Parnall design. In 1935, Parnall combined with a number of other small aircraft companies to become Parnall Aircraft, the Hendy Heck being the only

significant product – and that was produced in very small numbers. The company turned its attention to repair and overhaul work and involvement in powered gun turrets, both activities securing it contracts as the war approached.

The Parnall factory also became part of the Civilian Repair Organization (CRO) from August 1940, but it was gun turrets that had become the main focus of attention and the factory was a key supplier of these vital pieces of equipment. The Luftwaffe paid a number of visits to Yate in early 1941 and the threat, if not the effectiveness of the attacks, was sufficient for production to be dispersed. The airfield had no real function, it was the production facilities that were important and Yate was little

The Parnall Hendy Heck was one of the few 'successful' designs.

Spitfire wings under construction in the Yate workshops.

used from 1941 onwards.

Training gliders were operating from Yate by early 1944, following the formation of No.92 Gliding School, equipped primarily with Cadet Is and IIs.

No.94 Gliding School formed here by mid-1945 to take over the role from No.92 GS, which moved to Charmy Down.

UNITS

1939–1945

92 GS	Jan 1944–mid-1945	Cadet

Post-1945

94 GS	mid-1945–20 Feb 1948	Cadet, Grunau Baby

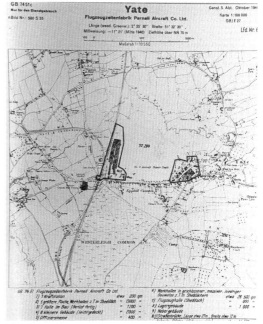

Luftwaffe target map of the Yate installation dated October 1940.

YATESBURY (Cherhill)

County: Wiltshire

UTM/Grid: OS Map 173 – SU055710
Lat/Long: N51°25.58 W001°54.08
Nearest Town: Calne 4 miles to west

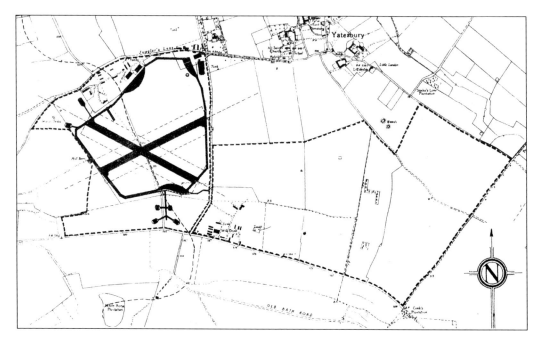

HISTORY

The area round Yatesbury is very popular with tourists, who visit the prehistoric stone circle at Avebury or search for the crop circles that 'magically' appear in this part of Wiltshire every summer. Most drive past Yatesbury with no knowledge that an important RFC and RAF airfield was once laid out over these fields. One of the confusing aspects with Yatesbury is that there were two adjacent airfields: No.1 (Western) Camp and No.2 (Eastern) Camp. Both were constructed in 1916 for the same purpose – as a base for two training squadrons. The land area was ideal, being flat and well drained; the western aerodrome was laid out on Cherhill Field (and in its non-flying post-World War Two period was referred to as RAF Cherhill from May 1954), whilst the eastern aerodrome was laid out on Yatesbury Field. Both were of a similar size, around 270 acres, and both were equipped with various hangars and sheds, as well as huts and other support buildings.

Yatesbury opened in November 1916 and its first training unit, No.55 Training (Ex-Reserve) Squadron arrived the same month from Filton, with the usual diverse fleet of types but with Avro 504s

and Bristol Scouts as the main training types. No.66 Training (Ex-Reserve) Squadron arrived from Wye in May 1917. The unit list shows the build-up of other training squadrons and Yatesbury's twin camps were becoming very busy.

In January 1918, the personnel and aircraft of No.32 TS became No.7 Training Squadron of the Australian Flying Corps – but, in essence, little changed in terms of role or equipment. A few months later, in July 1918, the two main Training Squadrons, 13 and 66, became No.36 Training Depot Station (No.2 Aerodrome) as part of 28th Wing, whose HQ had been at Yatesbury since May 1917. The TDS operated a variety of types, from the Avro 504K to the DH9 and RE8, and training continued at Yatesbury to May 1919, albeit the scale had been decreasing since late the previous year. No.1 Aerodrome played host to No.37 TDS for the same period.

In early 1919, five operational Camel squadrons arrived at Yatesbury as cadre units; three of these disbanded here whilst two, 28 and 66 Squadrons, spent only two weeks here before moving on. The airfield

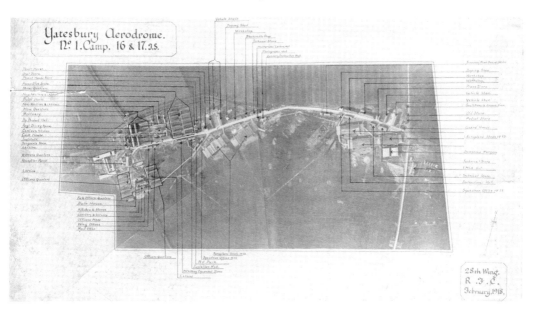

closed at the end of the year and the area was returned to its original owners. In the mid-1930s there was renewed interest in developing both old airfield sites. In 1935, the Bristol Aeroplane Co. bought part of the old western site, as they had been awarded a contract for a Reserve Flying Training School and needed an airfield. The Bristol School of Flying restored some of the surviving World War One buildings and added others, the result being a delightful aerodrome with well-equipped training facilities. The school commenced training in 1936 and, two years later, in February 1938, became No.10 Elementary and Reserve Flying Training School, using Harts and Tiger Moths. On the outbreak of war, it became No.10 EFTS and, in October 1939, this was raised to Class B status to handle ninety pupil pilots and was given a notional establishment of 36+18 Tiger Moths. However, the airfield was too busy and accommodation was in short supply so, in September 1940, the EFTS moved to Weston-super-Mare.

Meanwhile, the ERFTS had given birth in September 1938 to No.2 Civil Air Navigation School; the school was operated by the Bristol Aeroplane Company and the main training type was the Anson. A year later, in November 1939, the school changed name, but not function, to become No.2 Air Observer and Navigator School (AONS), still flying Ansons to teach basic air navigation. However, the school disbanded in December 1940.

A month after the CANS had formed, Yatesbury's main wartime unit also formed. No.2 Electrical and Wireless School formed in December 1938 but, whilst the basic course was under development and

teaching started, it was not until the following October that the first aircraft arrived. This unit had become the first occupants of the restored and rebuilt eastern airfield. The school became No.2 Signals School in August 1940. By this time, it had been joined by No.2 Radio School, which formed on 18 January 1940. The Bristol Wireless Flight formed in May 1940 to provide aircraft as flying classrooms for the pupils of the school, the DH.89 Dominie and the Proctor being the main types in which pupils practised the skills that they had learnt in the classroom. The Flight continued to provide this facility throughout the war, disbanding in July 1945.

As part of the seemingly endless changes of unit name that bedevilled Yatesbury's unit, the Radio School was renamed No.2 Radio Direction Finding (RDF) School in May 1942. In January, this became No.9 Radio School, to train ground radar operators, and it remained in this guise to 30 January 1946, when it disbanded. No.2 Radio School had been re-born in January 1943 by renaming the Signals School and for the rest of the war this was the largest single unit at the airfield. The aircraft fleet still comprised Dominies and Proctors, with the latter growing in numbers to a peak of over 100 aircraft.

The role of the school changed in July 1945 to focus on ground trades and the aircraft fleet was quickly dispersed. However, Tiger Moths took up residence in July 1945, when No.2 EFTS arrived from Worcester. Pupil pilots used the grass runways at Yatesbury for two years, with Manningford being used as a satellite, but the school finally disbanded in September 1947. Ground training continued at Yatesbury, with the Radio School remaining in resi-

AIRFIELD DATA DEC 1944

Command:	Technical Training Command	Runway surface:	Sommerfeld Track
Function:	Radio School	Hangars:	Blister × 11, Single Span × 3,
			Bellman × one, Northern Light × one
Runways:	210 deg 946yd	Dispersals:	concrete aprons one × 250 × 60yd,
	310 deg 972yd		one × 200 × 75yd, one × 200 × 50yd
		Personnel:	Officers – 225 (16 WAAF)
			Other Ranks – 7,635 (665 WAAF)

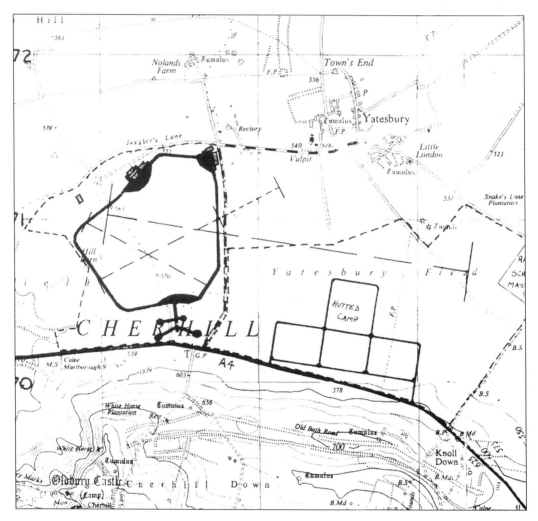

dence to the end of October 1965.

The HQ of No.27 (Signals Training) Group moved in from Colerne in July 1953; the Group had responsibility for the training of radio mechanics, fitters and operators and it remained at Yatesbury until disbanding in October 1958. A Casualty Evacuation Flight was formed in August 1956, but only lasted until December and there are few details as to why it was formed or its intended use.

Part of the airfield site is still used for aviation, as Yatesbury Field is the home to the Wiltshire Microlight Club, which operates a 410m grass strip.

F2b of No.37 Training Depot Station.

RE8 'The Coffin' at Yatesbury, 1918. (via Rod Priddle)

FE2b of No.66 Training Squadron, one of training units based here in World War One.

No.2 Training Camp, Yatesbury. (via Rod Priddle)

Many of the airfield buildings have survived, including some from World War One, but in many cases their condition is poor. There are planning applications in place for conversion of some buildings into commercial units in a 'sympathetic fashion', as some are Grade II listed.

The history of Yatesbury and its twin airfields is confusing and for those with a particular interest in this site the author recommends Rod Priddle's *Airfields of Wiltshire* book.

DECOY SITE

Q/QF	Easton Down	SU056663

UNITS

HQ units at Yatesbury

No.28 (Training) Wing	15 May 1917–15 May 1919
No.27 (Signals Training) Gp	20 Jul 1953–1 Oct 1958
No.215 Wing	Aug 1956–15 Jan 1957

Pre-1919

28 Sqn	23 Jul 1917–8 Oct 1917	various
99 Sqn	15–30 Aug 1917	various

55 TS	22 Nov 1916–23 Jul 1917	various
59 RS	30 Apr 1917–30 Oct 1917	various
62 RS	10 May 1917–1 Jun 1917	various
66 TS	10 May 1917–15 Jul 1918	various
13 TS	1 Jun 1917–15 Jul 1918	various
32 TS	1917–14 Jan 1918	various
37 TDS	15 Jul 1917–15 May 1919	various
7 TS AFC	14 Jan 1918–23 Feb 1918	various
36 TDS	15 Jul 1918–15 May 1919	various

1919–1939

28 Sqn	10 Mar 1919–29 Mar 1919	cadre Camel
54 Sqn	17 Feb 1919–25 Oct 1919	cadre Camel
65 Sqn	12 Feb 1919–25 Oct 1919	cadre Camel
66 Sqn	10 Mar 1919–29 Mar 1919	cadre Camel
73 Sqn	10 Feb 1919–2 Jul 1919	cadre Camel
BSoF	Jan 1936–1 Feb 1938	
10 ERFTS	1 Feb 1938–Sep 1939	
2 CANS	26 Sep 1938–1 Nov 1939	Anson
2 EWS	1 Dec 1938–26 Aug 1940	

1939–1945

2 EWS	?–26 Aug 1940	
10 EFTS	3 Sep 1939–7 Sep 1940	Tiger Moth
2 AONS	1 Nov 1939–14 Dec 1940	Anson
BWF	14 May 1940–Jul 1945	Dominie, Proctor

Tiger Moths at Yatesbury. (via Rod Priddle)

Dominie trainers of No.2 Radio School.

| 2 SS | 26 Aug 1940–1 Jan 1943 | various |
| GCAW | 1944 | |

Post-1945

| 2 EFTS | Jul 1945–30 Sep 1947 | Tiger Moth |

MEMORIAL

1. There are two memorials at the entrance to the current microlight airfield adjacent to the main road. A 'standing stone' carries a small plaque with the inscription: 'RFC RAF Yatesbury. In memory of those who served. 20th August 1996.' The brick pillar carries a metal plaque with a layout plan of RAF Yatesbury circa1946.

2. There are thirty-four associated graves in All Saints cemetery, Yatesbury.

YEOVIL

County: Somerset

Yeovil airfield, 1941.

HISTORY

Yeovil has played an important part in British aircraft manufacturing since World War One and, as such, is the longest-serving such airfield in Britain; it started life producing seaplanes under licence and is now part of the Agusta-Westland Company, a global leader in helicopters. Origins lay with a Yeovil engineering company, Petters Ltd, who decided to extend their production facilities in 1914 by acquiring Westland Farm. With the decision to build aircraft and an immediate contract for Short 184 seaplanes, the new part of the factory became Westland Aircraft Works. For the first few years the company built a variety of aircraft under licence and sent them by road to other locations for final assembly and flight-testing. It is surprising that it was not until 1917 that the decision was taken to build a flying field so that this work could be undertaken on site. By April 1917, the airfield had been laid out adjacent to the factory;

it was extended the following year when a contract for Vimy bombers was received.

Westland took the bold decision to remain in the aircraft business post-war and, after a difficult period, found success with adoption of the Westland Wapiti, the first notable design by the company and one that proved ideal for the inter-war 'colonial policing' with which much of the RAF was involved. The prototype Wapiti (J8495) flew in 1927; the type was eventually produced in a number of marks, with final production totalling over 500. Expansion of the factory took place to cope with production and also for the next successful product of the Westland design shop, the Lysander. The 'Lizzie' prototype (K6127) flew on 15 June 1936 and, a few months later, an initial contract for 155 aircraft was placed. By the time production ceased in January 1942, some 1,372 Lysanders had been built. Less successful, but nevertheless a fascinating aircraft, was the Whirlwind twin-engined fighter, which flew in late-1938. With ever-increasing wartime orders the factory continued to expand, but was not dispersed around the airfield. The Luftwaffe was well-aware of what went on at Yeovil and the factory was targeted a number of times, the first raid taking place on 15 July 1940. Damage and casualties were caused in this and subsequent raids in autumn 1940 and spring 1941, but none affected the

production at the factory. Throughout the war, Westland both produced its own designs and licence-built other types, including the Spitfire and Seafire, as well as acting as UK parent of Curtiss aircraft.

With the limited success of its own later designs, such as the Welkin and Wyvern, the company sensibly made the then bold decision to concentrate on helicopters, again in co-operation with American manufacturers. The first successful venture was the

The Westland Wapiti was the workhorse of RAF Colonial Policing in the 1920s.

The extensive Westland factory in 1944; in addition to its own products the company turned out Spitfires and Seafires, as well as being the UK parent for Curtiss aircraft.

Dragonfly, a licence-build of the Sikorsky S-51, with the first one flying in 1948. The RAF soon expressed an interest and the Dragonfly was the type that introduced the RAF to the potential of helicopters and provided Westland with a long-term future. The Dragonfly was produced in limited numbers, but the next type, the Whirlwind (based on the Sikorsky S-55), was far more successful and was employed by both the RAF and the Royal Navy. This has been followed by a succession of helicopters, including the Wessex, Sea King, Puma, Gazelle, Lynx, Apache and EH101 Merlin, many of these being collaborative projects.

DECOY SITE

Q/QF	Chinnock	193/ST496146

UNITS

1939–1945

81 GS	Oct 1943-Nov 1947	Cadet

The Whirlwind was one of the first truly successful helicopters produced by the Company.

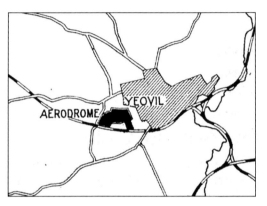

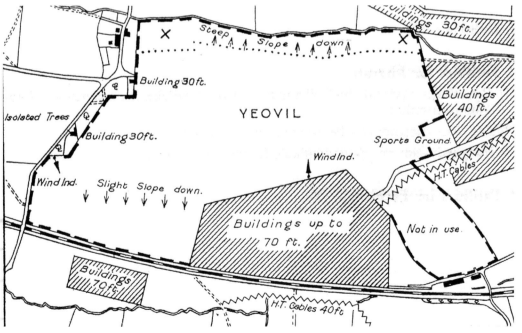

YEOVILTON (HMS *Heron*)

County: Somerset

UTM/Grid: OS Map 183 – ST550234
Lat/Long: N51°00 W002°38

Nearest Town: Yeovil 4 miles to south

In the mid 1960s the Fleet Air Arm's 'punch' was provided by Buccaneers, Sea Vixens, Scimitars and Hunters; this wonderful posed PR shot shows a lost heyday of British aviation.

HISTORY

The land for this naval air station was acquired in 1938 as part of the Admiralty's plan to re-establish the Fleet Air Arm (released from RAF control in 1937); Yeovilton was one of the first of the new series of naval air stations and its location made it ideal for work with the major naval bases on the south coast. It was intended as a training base but, as with all such bases, it would also act as a shore base for disembarked squadrons. As such, it was given the normal layout of four runways, all to the usual narrow naval specification and of around 1,000 yards length, with the main runway being slightly longer. All were connected by a perimeter track and there were three main dispersal areas, all on the south or east side. The main technical and admin area was laid out on the north-east corner and eventually comprised a large collection of hangars along with 'huts, various'.

The airfield was commissioned as HMS *Heron* on 18 June 1940, by which time the three squadrons of

the Naval Observer School had already arrived. Construction work was still not complete and, whilst the major infrastructure works were ready within months, Yeovilton, like most major airfields, underwent almost continual development during the war, with extra dispersal, runway lengthening and additional hangars and other buildings. No.1 Observers School (750, 751 and 752 squadrons) had moved from Ford because of its exposed position – it was only intended as a temporary arrangement, although it was late summer before all the squadrons had gone, two taking their training overseas. Yeovilton was intended for the new Naval Air Fighter School and the squadrons to form this started to gather in August, the formation of 794 Squadron being followed in September by the arrival of 759 and 760 squadrons. No.794 Squadron had formed as an Air Target Towing Unit with Rocs and Swordfish, later receiving various other types; the other two

Airfield Data c.1954

Command:	Fleet Air Arm	Runway surface:	Tarmac
Function:	HQ Flag Officer Flying Training	Hangars:	Bellman × 12, Mains (60ft × 70ft) × 7,
Runways:	09/27 7,500 × 150ft		ARS × one
	05/23 4,800 × 150ft	Dispersals:	Various
	36/18 3,300 × 150ft	Personnel:	Officers – 188 (15 WRNS)
			Other Ranks – 1,313

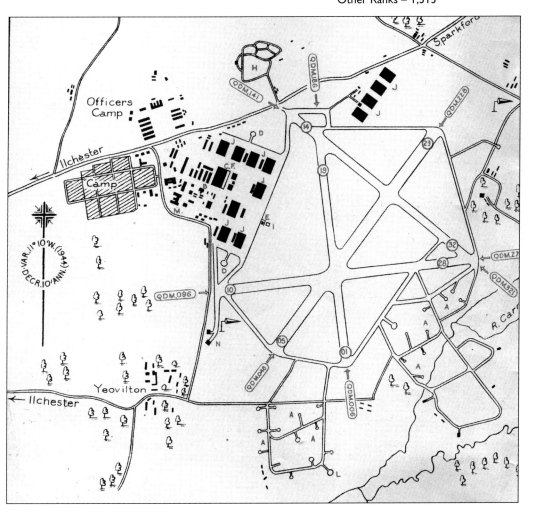

squadrons were the Fleet Fighter School, although in typical FAA fashion nomenclature kept changing and was, at times, somewhat confusing. Whilst 760 Squadron disbanded in December 1942, 759 continued to grow and, by May 1943, its strength comprised an impressive 113 aircraft, the majority (sixty-six) being Sea Hurricanes and the rest made up of Fulmars (twenty-four), Masters (fifteen) and Spitfires (eight).

This unit remained at Yeovilton throughout the war and, whilst aircraft types and numbers changed, the basic task remained the same; it eventually left for Zeals in September 1945, whilst work was carried out on Yeovilton's runways, but it didn't return.

Enemy aircraft appeared at Yeovilton in spring 1941, when a CR.42 and a Bf109 were used by 787 Squadron, the Fleet Fighter Development Unit, for comparative trials against naval fighters. This unit had formed here in March but, in June, it moved to Duxford to become the Naval Air Fighting Development Unit, alongside the RAF's AFDU.

Yeovilton continued to have a diverse history during the war, with training remaining the main occu-

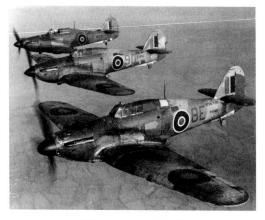

Sea Hurricanes of 760 Squadron, 1942. (Ray Sturtivant)

pation, but with a number of operational squadrons either forming and equipping here or passing through for short periods. It was also used by Westland Aircraft as a final assembly and flight test location for Spitfires and Seafires. The station also housed a number of ground units, perhaps the most important being the School of Fighter Control. It was such a busy airfield that it normally had at least one satellite or RLG in use; these included Hatston, Henstridge and Charlton Horethorne. The unit list shows the large number of squadrons to have made use of the Somerset base during the war.

By late-1945, the once crowded dispersals and hangars were all but empty and it was only when disembarked squadrons appeared that the station truly came to life. This was the period when the FAA was considering its post-war composition and the required basing; it was decided that Yeovilton would be developed into the major shore base for the new all-weather fighters. The main runway was lengthened to 2,300m to make it suitable for the new jets and one of the secondary runways was also lengthened, with both also being completely resurfaced. Other elements of the infrastructure were also

Vertical air photo dated 4 August 1945.

The FRADU operated a number of types, including various marks of Canberra; WH801 August 1985

For the past 25 years the Sea Harrier has dominated fixed-wing operations from Yeovilton.

improved and the rebuilt HMS *Heron* opened in November 1953. The station was now also home to Flag Officer Flying Training, another indication of the importance attached to the airfield.

The first new unit was 764 Squadron, which with Sea Hawks, Seafires and Fireflies operated as an Operational Flying School – although it disbanded in November 1954. Of more significance was the series of operational squadrons that formed or passed through Yeovilton to work-up with the new jets, starting with 809 Squadron and the Sea Venom, but with the Sea Vixen soon becoming the main type. The plan for the latter included yet more improvements to the airfield, which closed from late-1956 to January 1958 for this work. The same routine was followed a decade later, with airfield work in preparation for the F-4 Phantom, with 700P (for Phantom) Squadron becoming the first user of the new runway in early 1967. By the early 1970s, Yeovilton had taken on a major role with the Wessex helicopter used by the Royal Marines and this coincided with a reduction in fixed-wing usage, as the FAA looked set to lose all fixed-wing capability. This situation changed with the adoption of the Sea Harrier and Yeovilton became the main training and shore base for the V/STOL aircraft, the first Sea Harriers arriving for 700 Squadron in June 1979.

Yeovilton made one of the largest contributions to the Task Force that re-took the Falkland Islands in 1982 and, since then, its squadrons and personnel have been involved in every major operational commitment of the British military from Iraq to Bosnia, as well as various minor campaigns and peace-keeping operations. RNAS Yeovilton (EGDY) is now the Fleet Air Arm's main shore base and the only fixed-wing location. Two of the wartime runways are still in use, the main runway (09/27) now being 2,310m and the secondary (04/22) being 1,462m. Yeovilton is one of the busiest military airfields in the UK, often housing up to 150 aircraft and helicopters for nine

squadrons. Yeovilton is home to one of the best aviation museums in Europe, the Fleet Air Arm Museum. This is not connected with the history of the airfield but with British naval aviation in general, as well as other aspects of aviation. It is an absolute must for a visit. www.fleetairarm.com

DECOY SITE

King's Moor

UNITS

HQ units at Yeovilton

Flag Officer Flying Training	27 May 1953–Nov 1970
Flag Officer Naval Air Command	Nov 1970–?

1939–1945

736 Sqn FAA	24 May 1943–2 Sep 1943	various
748 Sqn FAA	11 Oct 1943–1 Oct 1944+	various
750 Sqn FAA	May 1940–Oct 1940	Shark
751 Sqn FAA	May 1940–19 Aug 1940	Walrus
752 Sqn FAA	May 1940–Sep 1940	Proctor
759 Sqn FAA	16 Sep 1940–19 Sep 1945	various
760 Sqn FAA	16 Sep 1940–31 Dec 1942	various
761 Sqn FAA	1 Aug 1941–10 Apr 1943	various
762 Sqn FAA	23 Mar 1942–15 Apr 1942; 8 Sep 1942–9 Jun 1943	various
787 Sqn FAA	5 Mar 1941–18 Jun 1941	various
794 Sqn FAA	1 Aug 1940–1 Jul 1943	various
800 Sqn FAA	30 Jun 1941–12 Jul 1941	Fulmar
801 Sqn FAA	1 Aug 1941–6 Oct 1941	Sea Hurricane
804 Sqn FAA	Feb 1941–Jun 1942+	Fulmar, Sea Hurricane
807 Sqn FAA	9 Dec 1940–4 Feb 1941; 12 Jul 1942–24 Aug 1942	Fulmar
808 Sqn FAA	18 Apr 1942–30 May 1942	Fulmar
825 Sqn FAA	Sep 1943	Swordfish

827 Sqn FAA	15 Sep 1940–2 Nov 1940	Albacore
880 Sqn FAA	17 Jul 1941–Oct 1941+	various
882 Sqn FAA	1–15 Dec 1941	Martlet, Sea Hurricane
883 Sqn FAA	10 Oct 1941–Jan 1942	Sea Hurricane
884 Sqn FAA	7 Feb 1942–Mar 1942	Fulmar
885 Sqn FAA	1 Dec 1941–Mar 1942	Sea Hurricane
886 Sqn FAA	22 Jan 1942–Jul 1942	Fulmar
887 Sqn FAA	1 Jun 1942–10 Jul 1942	Fulmar
888 Sqn FAA	14–16 Nov 1943	Martlet
1770 Sqn FAA	10 Sep 1943–14 Dec 1943	Firefly
1771 Sqn FAA	1 Feb 1944–3 Mar 1944	Firefly

Post-1945

700 Sqn FAA	1 Apr 1946–30 Sep 1949	various
700 Sqn FAA	19 Sep 1958–3 Jul 1961	Gannet
700A Sqn FAA	26 Jun 1979–31 Mar 1980	Sea Harrier
700L Sqn FAA	1 Sep 1976–16 Dec 1977	Lynx
700P Sqn FAA	30 Apr 1968–31 Mar 1969	Phantom
700X Sqn FAA	Oct 1959–Jun 1961	Wasp
700Y Sqn FAA	4 Nov 1958–1 Jul 1959	Sea Vixen
702 Sqn FAA	3 Jan 1978–19 Jul 1982	Lynx
707 Sqn FAA	15 May 1972–9 Feb 1995	Wessex, Sea King
766 Sqn FAA	18 Oct 1955–24 Nov 1956; 20 Jan 1958–10 Dec 1970	Sea Venom, Sea Vixen
767 Sqn FAA	8 Sep 1949–31 Mar 1955	various
799 Sqn FAA	13 May 1948–3 Dec 1951	Sea Fury
764 Sqn FAA	23 Sep 1953–23 Nov 1954	Firefly, Seafire, Sea Hawk
801 Sqn FAA	28 Jan 1981–current+	Sea Harrier
802 Sqn FAA	12 Dec 1948–25 May 1950	Sea Fury
803 Sqn FAA	8 Dec 1961–1962	Scimitar
806 Sqn FAA	28 Feb 1946–May 1946	Seafire
809 Sqn FAA	10 May 1954–1 Feb 1955	Sea Hornet
809 Sqn FAA	8 Apr 1982–17 Dec 1982+	Buccaneer
810 Sqn FAA	24 Mar 1949–May 1949	Firefly
811 Sqn FAA	Jul 1955–Sep 1955	Sea Hawk
814 Sqn FAA	12 Dec 1948–Jan 1949	Firefly

There are various memorials around Yeovilton, one of the most interesting is the Fleet Air Arm church of St Bartholomew.

815 Sqn FAA	1 Jan 1981–19 Jul 1982	Lynx
845 Sqn FAA	May–Jun 1962; Sep 1972–Jun 1977+	Wessex
846 Sqn FAA	Mar 1977–current+	Wessex, Sea King
848 Sqn FAA	Dec 1972–current+	Wessex, Sea King
849B Sqn FAA	May 1966–Sep 1966	Gannet
890 Sqn FAA	20 Mar 1954–6 Aug 1971+	Sea Venom, Sea Vixen
891 Sqn FAA	8 Nov 1954–Nov 1956+; 25 Apr 1960–27 Jul 1961+	Sea Venom
892 Sqn FAA	4 Jul 1955–Jul 1956; 1 Jul 1959–Jul 1972+	Sea Venom, Sea Vixen, Phantom
893 Sqn FAA	6 Feb 1956–Aug 1956; Jun 1958–14 Jul 1970+	Sea Venom, Sea Vixen
894 Sqn FAA	3 Dec 1958–17 Dec 1960+	Sea Venom
899 Sqn FAA	1 Feb 1961–current+	Sea Vixen, Hunter, Sea Harrier
899 OEU Sqn	Sep 1993–current+	Sea Harrier
81 GS	Nov 1947–Jul 1948	Cadet

ZEALS (Station 450)
(HMS *Humming Bird*)

County: Wiltshire

UTM/Grid: OS Map 185 – ST780327
Lat/Long: N51°05 W002°19
Nearest Town: Wincanton 4 miles to south-west

September 2003 view of Zeals.

HISTORY

Authority was given in early August 1940 for land to be requisitioned at Zeals for development into an, as yet, unspecified airfield (SOM 749/40). The 530 acres that made up Zeals were acquired from St Martin's Farm and Manor Farm to the north of the village after which the airfield was named. Construction involved closure of a number of roads and the demolition of a few buildings, as well as the usual drainage and hedge-removal work. The airfield was laid out as a grass oval and eventually had an encircling concrete perimeter track (still visible from air) from which sprang the dispersal points. A number of the dispersal points on the south side were provided with Blister hangars and all the technical and support buildings were also on the south side; the communal areas were dispersed in the fields to the south. Zeals opened on 21 May 1942 and was allo-

cated as a forward-operating airfield for Fighter Command's No.10 Group. Although 286 Squadron was first to arrive, they left in August to leave Zeals for the two Spitfire squadrons from Ibsley, 66 and 118. The Spitfires flew offensive sorties over France and the Low Countries on fighter sweeps and *Rhubarbs*, as well as the occasional bomber escort for *Circus* missions. Both departed in December, when the grass surfaces of Zeals became impractical.

There was little activity until February 1943, when the airfield had dried out enough to house the three squadrons of No.122 Airfield, which initially deployed here for the large-scale Exercise *Spartan*, one of the most important exercises to evaluate army co-operation and the employment of tactical air-power – essential pre-invasion training. The airfield was then allocated to the USAAF, becoming Station

AIRFIELD DATA DEC 1944

Command:	Balloon Command	Runway surface:	Grass
Function:	Storage	Hangars:	Over Blister × 8, T.1 × one
Runways:	N/S 1,600yd	Dispersals:	30 × Twin-engine, 12 × Sommerfeld Track
	E/W 1,417yd	Personnel:	Officers – 26 (6 WAAF)
	SE/NW 1,417yd		Other Ranks – 2,100 (236 WAAF)

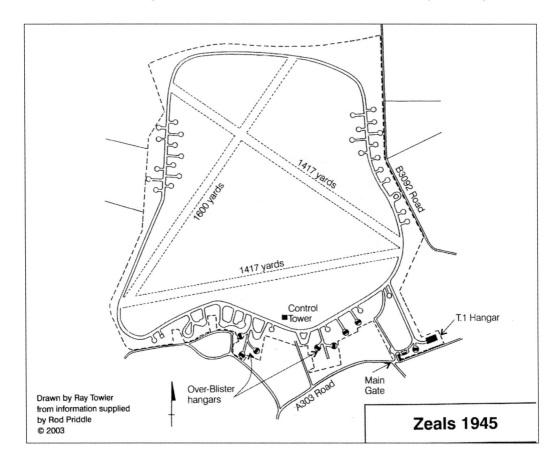

Drawn by Ray Towler
from information supplied
by Rod Priddle
© 2003

Zeals 1945

450, but, despite various attempts to improve the airfield surface, the wet spring and summer was winning and Zeals was considered unusable. There was a brief appearance by a P-47 Group in December 1943, but they soon moved on and further attempts were made to improve the airfield.

The station eventually re-opened on April 1944 and Zeals became home to the night fighters of 488 Squadron in May. This was part of a plan to increase the night defences of the South-West to protect the build-up of men and material for the invasion and prevent the Luftwaffe attacking the increasingly attractive targets. Within days of their arrival, the

Mosquitoes had scored their first successes and Zeals had at last contributed to the war. With the invasion underway, the squadron, along with 410 Squadron, which had arrived in mid-June, was tasked with night patrols over the beachhead area. By the end of June they had become No.149 (Long-Range Fighter) Wing and were joined by a Flight of 604 Squadron for a short while in July, giving Zeals a potent night-fighter capability. However, at the end of July they moved out and Zeals took up a training role with the return of 268 Squadron and the arrival of No.3 Glider Training School. This detachment was replaced the following January by the Glider Pick-Up

RAF Dakota on snatch pick-up at Zeals, part of the training by the GPTU.

November 1945 and a Corsair of 760 Squadron comes to grief. (via Rod Priddle)

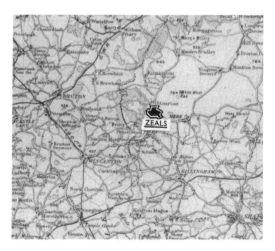

Training Flight, but they soon moved on to Ibsley.

The Admiralty took-over the airfield as HMS *Humming Bird*, the first FAA unit, 790 Squadron, arriving from Charlton Horethorne on 1 April, which some would have considered an appropriate date to arrive at what was still a pretty poor airfield! No.704 Squadron

of the Fleet Air Arm formed at Zeals on 11 April 1945, as a Naval Operational Training Unit for Mosquito crews; the squadron moved to Thorney Island in September. They were replaced at Zeals by 759 Squadron, one of the units displaced from Yeovilton when the latter's runways were being worked on. A number of other FAA units spent a short period at Zeals but, by autumn 1945, it was no longer required and it was paid-off by the Admiralty on 1 January 1946. The land was almost immediately released for disposal, the fields once more sprouted crops and the road across the centre of the airfield re-opened.

Although the airfield layout is clear from the air there is little to see from the ground, other than the old control tower; like a number of other towers this one has survived because it was turned into a house.

UNITS

HQ units at Zeals

No.122 Airfield	12–25 Feb 1943; 13 Mar 1943–4 Apr 1943
No.147 Airfield	11–12 May 1944
No.147 (NF) Wing	12 May 1944–29 Jun 1944
No.149 (LRF) Wing	29 Jun 1944–28 Jul 1944

1939–1945

66 Sqn	24 Aug 1942–23 Dec 1942+	Spitfire
118 Sqn	24 Aug 1942–23 Dec 1942	Spitfire
132 Sqn	28 Feb 1943–5 Apr 1943	Spitfire
174 Sqn	12 Mar 1943–Apr 1943	Hurricane
184 Sqn	12 Mar 1943–Apr 1943	Hurricane
263 Sqn	19 Jun 1943–12 Jul 1943	Whirlwind
286 Sqn	26 May 1942–31 Aug 1942; 28 Jul 1944–28 Sep 1944	various
410 Sqn	18 Jun 1944–28 Jul 1944	Mosquito
421 Sqn	Oct 1942–Nov 1942	Spitfire
488 Sqn	12 May 1944–29 Jul 1944	Mosquito
604 Sqn	25–28 Jul 1944	Mosquito
704 Sqn FAA	11 Apr 1945–Sep 1945	Mosquito
759 Sqn FAA	19 Sep 1945–7 Jan 1946	Seafire
760 Sqn FAA	10 Apr 1945–12 Sep 1945	various
771 Sqn FAA	25 Jul 1945–12 Sep 1945	Corsair, Wildcat
790 Sqn FAA	1 Apr 1945–30 Aug 1945	various
3 GTS det	21 Oct 1944–Dec 1944?	
GPTF	8 Jan 1945–19 Mar 1945	Dakota, Hadrian

MEMORIAL

There is no memorial to the airfield but, on 14 August 1999, a memorial was unveiled on Beech Knoll by ACM Sir John Gingell. This commemorates the loss of Dakota TS436 and its crew. They were one of the crews to graduate from the first RAF Glider Pick-Up course and were returning to their home base of Leicester East when they hit the hill in bad weather.

World War One Airfields and Landing Grounds

Although a number of the airfields in the previous alphabetical listing saw use in World War One as well as World War Two and beyond, there were a great many recorded sites in Britain whose history is restricted to the Great War. The problem with providing histories of these sites is that records are often very poor, especially when it comes to the landing grounds taken into use by the Home Defence squadrons, as these were seldom more than a field.

Most Home Defence squadrons had a list of approved, and one assumes surveyed and checked, fields of this nature and often the only reference occurs in the squadron records but, again, these tend to be poor for World War One. With many of the following entries, therefore, information is poor and at times unconfirmed; there are, no doubt, many more sites that qualify for inclusion.

LAKE DOWN

County: Wiltshire
UTM/grid: OS Map 184 – SU105390
Lat./Long.: N51°09.00 W001°51.07
Nearest Town: Salisbury 7 miles to south-east

Lake Down was used by a number of operational and training squadrons in 1917-1918. (via Rod Priddle)

History

The airfield at Lake Down was situated adjacent to the large house of Druid's Lodge, which in late-1918 was the HQ for 33rd Wing (the same house was taken-over again in World War Two for use by the instructors based at Oatlands Hill). A 160-acre area was requisitioned in early 1917 for the construction of a training airfield and the erection of aeroplane sheds – eventually six were provided in three pairs – and various workshops and other buildings was soon underway. The buildings were concentrated on the east side of the aerodrome, the hangars on the aerodrome side of the main Salisbury road and most other buildings on the other side of the road, leaving a diamond-shaped grass landing area. A number of Bessonneau hangars were also added as Lake Down's aircraft strength grew, but lines of 'army tents' were still much in evidence.

No.2 Training Depot Station formed at Lake Down on 15 August 1917 to undertake day-bomber training for RFC and USAS personnel, for which it used BE2c, DH4s, FK8s and RE8s. Training commenced immediately, even though the airfield was still not complete; indeed, it was still not finished when the TDS moved to Stonehenge in December. The early part of December 1917 brought three squadrons to Lake Down, all operating a diverse collection of aircraft but, in May/June 1918, re-equipping with DH9s. A fourth squadron had formed on 1 April 1918; it had been planned that 136

Squadron also equip with the DH9, but this did not take place and the squadron was disbanded in July. All the squadrons came under No.14 TDS when it formed in June, but the TDS also had its own establishment of aircraft for training, including Avro 504s and DH4s and 9s. Although the squadrons had gone by August, either disbanded or sent elsewhere, the training role of the TDS continued to the end of the war and beyond. There is some debate as to when the TDS departed, with some records suggesting it was at Boscombe Down by late-1918.

Lake Down was closed at the end of 1919 and, by the following year, most of the buildings had been removed.

Units

Pre-1919

107Sqn	2 Dec 1917–5 Jun 1918	various, DH9
108Sqn	2 Dec 1917–14 Jun 1918	various, DH9
109Sqn	2 Dec 1917–19 Aug 1918	various, DH9
136Sqn	1 Apr 1918–4 Jul 1918	various
201Sqn	17 Feb 1919–2 Sep 1919	cadre only, Snipe
2 TDS	15 Aug 1917–2 Dec 1917	various
14 TDS	6 Jun 1918–Sep 1919?	various

LEIGHTERTON

County: Gloucestershire
UTM/grid: OS Map 162 – ST825935
Lat./Long.: N51°38 W002°15
Nearest Town: Stroud 7 miles to north

HISTORY

This World War One landing ground was laid out on a rolling part of the Cotswolds and opened in February 1918 as No.2 Station of 1st Wing, Australian Flying Corps (AFC). The site was some 170 acres and was provided with four large (170ft × 100ft) GS sheds as hangars, plus an assortment of wooden huts on both the technical and domestic site, the latter being at the north end of the airfield. Along with Minchinhampton this was one of the main training bases for the AFC and, from February 1918, it housed two training squadrons, No.7 TS and No.8 TS, both equipped with a variety of types. No.8 Squadron focused on training of future fighter pilots and, in addition to Avro 504s, operated Pups and Camels, whilst No.7 Squadron focused on aircrew for Corps Reconnaissance squadrons and used BE2s and RE8s, in addition to the stalwart Avro 504.

For the remainder of the war training was intense and Leighterton witnessed the usual array of crashes, some humorous and some tragic. With the end of the war, the training regime continued at a much reduced level, until the two squadrons disbanded in May 1919. The airfield was abandoned by the military and most buildings had soon vanished, although the old officers' mess eventually became the Aerodrome Garage. Some private flying continued on the field over the next two decades and, in March 1940, the site was allocated to No.9 SFTS at Hullavington for use as an RLG, although this does not appear to have been taken-up.

UNITS

Pre-1919

7 TS AFC	23 Feb 1918–May 1919	various
8 TS AFC	25 Feb 1918–May 1919	various
6 TS	Aug 1919–Sep 1919	?

MERIFIELD

County: Cornwall
UTM/grid: OS Map 201 – SX433566
Lat./Long.: N50°23.30 W004°12.34
Nearest Town: Plymouth 1 mile to east

HISTORY

Situated close to the important naval dockyard at Devonport, the site at Merifield (Maryfield) was in use from early 1918 to the end of the war as No.16 Balloon Base for the operation of kite balloons. Six balloon sheds were erected, each 100ft × 36ft, for the six kite balloons allocated to the station and a variety of support buildings were erected on Looking Glass Point, although accommodation for personnel was in an anchored 'hulk', HMS *Valiant*. The balloons were used for convoy protection, but there are few details of the activity at Merifield. The site was abandoned almost as soon as the war ended.

MORETON

County: Dorset
UTM/grid: OS Map 194 – SY762898
Lat./Long.: N50°42 W002°20
Nearest Town: Dorchester 4 miles to west

HISTORY

Work on this planned World War One airship station was still underway at the end of the war and was immediately halted and the site cleared.

MULLION

County: Cornwall
Country: UK
UTM/grid: OS Map 203 – SW705102
Lat./Long.:
Nearest Town:

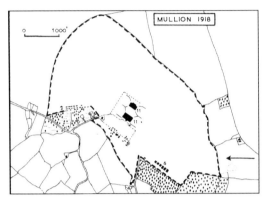

HISTORY

The Lizard Airship Station, subsequently known as
RNAS Mullion, opened in June 1916 and was
destined to become a major airship-base with a
number of out-stations. A 320-acre site had been
acquired for the station and its location was ideal for
the provision of much-needed coastal patrols to help
counter the increasingly effective German submarine
campaign. One large airship shed (300ft × 100ft ×
70ft high) was constructed, along with a hutted camp
and, by the end of June, two airships were in
residence. By early 1917, additional buildings had
been provided and the site was fulfilling a dual role as
an airship and land-plane base, with a number of
Sopwith 1½ Strutters arriving. The latter were
withdrawn in August and it was nearly a year before
any aircraft were again based here.

Meanwhile, the airships (C2 and C9 being
Mullion's usual occupants) continued the often
monotonous task of flying long patrols over the sea in
search of U-boats; Mullion crews made a number of
sightings and recorded a few attacks although, with
the anti-submarine bombs then in use, the successful
outcome of such attacks was doubtful.

With the formation of the RAF there was a re-
organization of units and a return of fixed-wing
aircraft to Mullion; the RAF had settled on the DH6
as its main anti-submarine type and a Special Duty

Flight was formed at Mullion on 16 May 1918; a
second Flight was formed the following month and
they became 515 and 526 Flights respectively, as part
of 254 Squadron. In August 1918, they were
transferred to 236 Squadron; this latter unit also took
over No.493 (Light Bomber) Flight, which had
formed at Mullion in May with the DH9 and
Sopwith 1½ Strutter. This organization survived until
early 1919, with disbandment probably taking place
in May.

By mid-1918 the airfield infrastructure had
expanded to include a number of additional aircraft
sheds, including six Bessonneau hangars, and
workshops and, with the closure of the site, most of
these were removed, leaving only a few huts and the
large concrete mooring blocks used by the airships.

Out-Stations
Bude (Cornwall). The out-station at Bude was in a
heavily wooded valley at Langford Bottom, where
breaks in the trees were made to accommodate two
Coastal-type airships in early 1918. The airships flew
coastal patrols between St George's Channel and the
Bristol Channel, a role that continued to the end of
the war. The site was abandoned in early 1919.

Laira (Devon). Located in Saltram Park near
Plymouth, the out-station at Laira opened in May
1918, with provision for two airships – SS or Coastal
type. As the site was adjacent to the old Plymouth
Racecourse, no additional buildings were provided. It
seems that two SS types were based here until late-
1918, flying coastal patrols with no apparent result.
The site was probably abandoned early in 1919.

Toller (Dorset). The airship out-station at Toller
near Bridport (and sometimes referred to as such) was
constructed in spring 1918 and in use later that year
for a single SS type detached from Mullion. The site
was abandoned at the end of 1918 and disposed of the
following year.

Upton (Dorset). The sub-station at Upton was in
the grounds of Upton House, where the estate's trees
provided suitable cover for the SS type deployed here
from Mullion. The site appears to have been in use
from mid-1918 to the end of the war and then was
immediately abandoned.

UNITS

Pre-1919

515Flt	16 May 1918–15 May 1919	DH6
516Flt	Jun 1918–15 May 1919	DH6
439Flt	30 May 1918–Mar 1919?	DH9

NEWLYN

County: Cornwall
UTM/grid: OS Map 203 – SW469281
Lat./Long.: N50°06 W005°32
Nearest Town: Penzance 2 miles to north

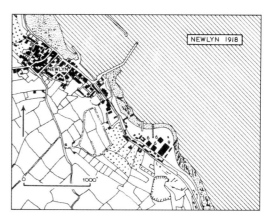

HISTORY

Situated on the shore just south of the village after which it takes its name, Newlyn opened as an RNAS seaplane station in early 1917. The available area was small and, as shown in the plan, it was a tight fit, even for the small number of buildings provided, the largest of which was the 180 × 60ft seaplane shed, along with three Bessonneau hangars. The station was allocated six Short 184s, which were probably operational by spring. They flew coastal patrols hunting for U-boats, making a number of sightings and at least one attack, as well as flying convoy patrols.

Two Special Duties Flights (424 and 425) were formed in May 1918, when the RAF took control of the station. As part of No.4 Group, they operated the Short 184s taken over from their predecessors; both Flights joined 235 Squadron when this formed in August and remained at Newlyn to February 1919.

Post-war, the site was retained but unoccupied and the only record of further military interest was an assessment visit by the Seaplane Development Flight in August 1922; with a 'not suitable' report, the site was finally put up for disposal.

UNITS

Pre-1919

424Flt	20 May 1918–22 Feb 1919	Short 184
425Flt	20 May 1918–22 Feb 1919	Short 184

PADSTOW

County: Cornwall
UTM/grid: OS Map 200 – SW898765
Lat./Long.: N50°33 W004°58
Nearest Town: Padstow 1 mile to south-east

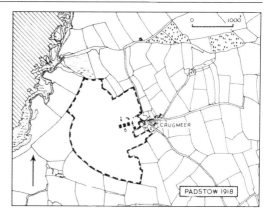

HISTORY

The landing ground of Padstow was located adjacent to the small village of Crugmeer and was often referred to by that name, as well as by Trevose Head, a landmark not far from the cliff-top on which the LG was laid out. The site was chosen in 1917, as part of a series of new airship stations and landing grounds to provide air cover for coastal convoys and to operate anti-submarine patrols. It was a far from ideal location but, after the removal of hedge boundaries and some grading of the site, it was adequate for the operation of DH6s for this role. As the plan shows, a line of four Bessonneau hangars was set up on the east side of the site near to the village but there was little else in the way of facilities.

Opened as RNAS Padstow in March 1918, it became part of the new RAF the following month and two Special Duties Flights (500 and 501) formed at the end of May, both equipped with the DH6. Both were part of 250 Squadron and they flew coastal patrols and convoy escort to the end of the war. The squadron eventually disbanded in May 1919 and the station was closed.

UNITS

Pre-1919

500Flt	31 May 1918–15 May 1919	DH6
501Flt	31 May 1918–15 May 1919	DH6

PRAWLE POINT

County: Devon
UTM/grid: OS Map 201 – SX778368
Lat./Long.: N50°13.11 W003°42.85
Nearest Town: Salcombe 3 miles to north-east

HISTORY

The landing ground at Prawle Point was opened in April 1917 as part of the network of south-coast locations for coastal patrols. The site was small and ill-equipped, but a number of Sopwith 1½ Strutters was in residence within weeks and flying patrols. With the aircraft needed elsewhere, operations ceased in August and it was May 1918 before Prawle

Point was back in use. By this time, the RAF was in control and three Flights were formed here; the first of these was No.492 (Light Bomber) Flight equipped with DH9s, joined a week later by 517 and 518 Flights with the DH6. All were part of 254 Squadron and remained so until the squadron disbanded in February 1919. The station was not immediately closed and may have been used by an army co-operation unit for a few weeks in the summer. However, by early 1920, the site had been abandoned.

UNITS

Pre-1919

492Flt	30 May 1918–22 Feb 1919	DH9
517Flt	6 Jun 1918–22 Feb 1919	DH6
518Flt	6 Jun 1918–22 Feb 1919	DH6

STONEHENGE

County: Wiltshire
UTM/grid: OS Map 184 – SU115418
Lat./Long.: N51°11 W001°50
Nearest Town: Amesbury 3 miles to east

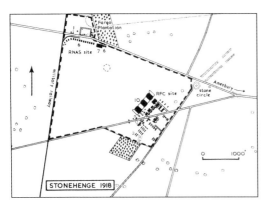

HISTORY

The name Stonehenge is best-known for the impressive prehistoric stone-circle that sits majestically alongside the A303; in the shadow of those stones the RFC laid out an aerodrome in 1917 on a 360-acre site. The technical site was provided with six paired GS Sheds, plus numerous huts for workshops and other purposes; there were also a number of Bessonneau hangars. With the decision to undertake Handley Page bomber training here, the aerodrome was also given two Handley Page sheds; these and the main technical

area were connected by a spur line to the Larkhill military railway. The domestic site included messes and barracks; there was a separate domestic area at the north end of the airfield near Fargo Plantation for use by the night crews of the Handley Pages – this site is shown on the plan as the RNAS site. The primary role of Stonehenge was to house two training units for day- and night-bomber training. The first occupants were 107 Squadron, which arrived from Catterick in October to equip and train. During its time at Stonehenge, it used a variety of type and it was only after it moved to Kenley, via a spell at Lake Down, that it eventually received its operational type, the DH9. A similar routine was followed by the next two squadrons; all had gone by December and Stonehenge was ready to receive its first true training unit, No.2 Training Depot Station, which arrived in December from Lake Down. On 5 January 1918, the TDS disbanded and part was used to form No.1 School of Aerial Navigation and Bomb Dropping (SoANBD), an accurate description of the role, if something of a

View of the extensive hutted and tented encampment at Stonehenge, September 1918.

mouthful. The school operated no less than sixteen types, from the HP 0/400 to the Avro 504. The RNAS Handley Page Training Flight arrived in January 1918, moving into the RNAS site on the north side, but it was already known that the RAF would shortly be formed and would take over all RFC and RNAS flying duties. It should be remembered that the RNAS and not the RFC were the great proponents of strategic bombing in the middle years of the war – hence their interest in the 'heavy' bombers.

Training continued at Stonehenge to September 1919, when the school moved to Andover and the air around the stone circle fell quiet. However, the School of Army Co-operation formed here in March 1920 and used Bristol Fighters to train pilots and observers in this role, as well as acting as a development unit to evaluate appropriate tactics. The intention had been for Stonehenge to be one of the limited number of permanent stations, but the plan was changed and, in January 1921, the school moved to Old Sarum and Stonehenge was closed. Many of the buildings survived for some time but, by the late-1920s, they were starting to be removed, some for use elsewhere and some simply demolished. The very controlled environment around the stone circle now contains no hint of this former usage.

Units

Pre-1919

97Sqn	21 Jan 1918–31 Mar 1918	various
107Sqn	18 Oct 1917–2 Dec 1917	various
108Sqn	12 Nov 1917–2 Dec 1917	various
109Sqn	12 Nov 1917–2 Dec 1917	various
2 TDS	2 Dec 1917–5 Jan 1918	various
SoANBD	5 Jan 1918–23 Sep 1919	various

1919–1939

SoAC	8 Mar 1920–Jan 1921

Memorial

The only memorial is a Celtic cross marking the death of Major Alexander Hewetson on 17 Jul 1913 in a Bristol aircraft from Larkhill.

TORQUAY

County: Devon
UTM/grid: OS Map 202 – SX919632
Lat./Long.: N50°27.51 W003°31.45
Nearest Town: At Torquay

History

Situated between two of the piers at the seaside town of Torquay, this seaplane station came into use in early 1918. The site consisted of a slipway and a number of Bessonneau hangars, plus a few sheds, and even this small provision was hard to fit-in between the foreshore and the road. An initial provision of six Short 184 floatplanes arrived and, in June, these became No.418 (Special Duties) Flight of the RAF. In August, this became part of 239 Squadron, but the plan to form a second Flight (419) was abandoned, as there simply wasn't room. The squadron continued to operate its single Flight on coastal patrol until at least spring 1919; with the disbandment of the squadron the site was sold-off.

Units

Pre-1919

418Flt	15 Jun 1918–May 1919	Short 184

TRESCO

County: Scilly Isles
UTM/grid: OS Map 203 – SV890149
Lat./Long.: N49°57 W006°20
Nearest Town: Hugh Town 3 miles to south

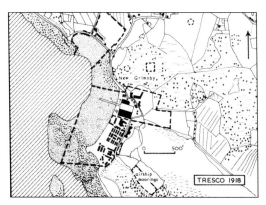

TRESCO 1918

HISTORY

The Scilly Isles were an obvious place at which to base maritime patrol aircraft and, with the urgent need to provide such cover in the face of U-boat attacks, a number of attempts were made to establish a base here. The first such took place in 1916, when a detachment of Short 184 floatplanes used temporary moorings near St Mary's harbour. This was not a great success and was soon abandoned. The next attempt was in February 1917, when Curtis H12 flying-boats used moorings near Port Mellon. Again the moorings were not ideal but, following a survey of the island, a site at Tresco was proposed. This was

established by spring 1917, with the flying-boats finding New Grimsby harbour an ideal stretch of water. Facilities on the shore-line at Tresco were expanded, to include hangars, slipways and support buildings, and the detachment of six flying-boats was able to carry out extensive patrolling, including a number of U-boat sightings and attacks.

When the RAF took control, the detachment became No.350 (Flying Boat) Flight at the end of May, being joined by 351 Flight in June. These both became part of 352 Squadron when it formed on 20 August 1918, as did two further Flights that formed in September. The squadron disbanded in May 1919 and at least two Flights were still in existence at that time.

UNITS

Pre-1919

350Flt	31 May 1918–May 1919	various
351Flt	30 Jun 1918–May 1919	various
352Flt	15 Sep 1918–May 1919	various
353Flt	30 Sep 1918–May 1919	various

Felixstowe F3 of 234 Squadron at Tresco in 1918.

WESTWARD HO!

County: Devon
UTM/grid: OS Map 190 – SS443307
Lat./Long.: N51°03 W004°13
Nearest Town: Bideford 1 mile to south

HISTORY

One of the late-period coastal-patrol landing grounds, Westward Ho! opened in spring 1918 using the golf course at Northam Burrows. The site was given minimum facilities, with the usual selection of Bessonneau hangars and a few huts, as an RAF coastal-

patrol base to operate two Flights (502 and 503) with the DH6, both of which formed in June 1918 within 260 Squadron. Within a few days, the squadron designation changed to 250 Squadron and it was with this unit that the Flights undertook coastal patrols to the end of the war; in the post-war period, in common with most coastal patrol units, they were involved in the search for mines as part of the 'clean-up' to make the sea-lanes safe. The squadron disbanded in May 1919 and the golf course was handed back to the golfers.

UNITS

Pre-1919

502Flt	6 Jun 1918–May 1919	DH6
503Flt	6 Jun 1918–May 1919	DH6

Airfield Location Maps

The location maps shown on these pages are those used in the RAF's airfield listing of 1944 and, rather than provide a sketch map of locations or add World War One locations to these maps, it has been decided to include the raw maps. They do not join together and some airfields are shown on more than one map.

The maps illustrate the density of airfields at the high point of 1944 and they also provide a useful indication of geographic location for anyone wanting to visit the site (but remember the warning about access, private land, etc).

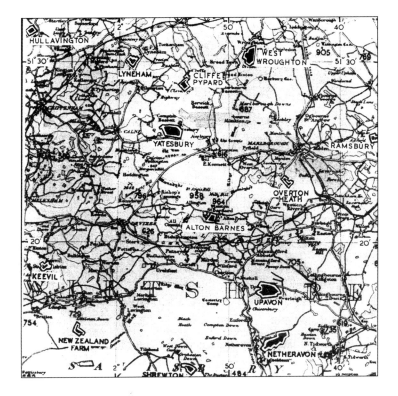

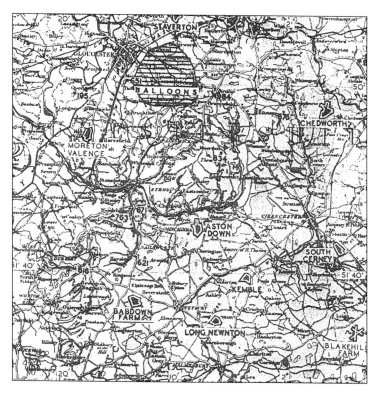

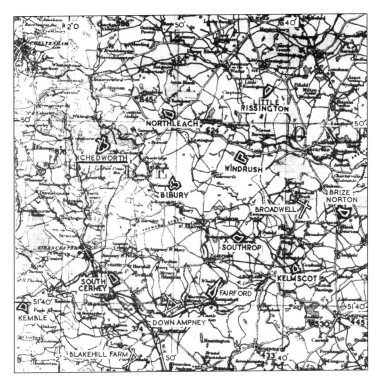

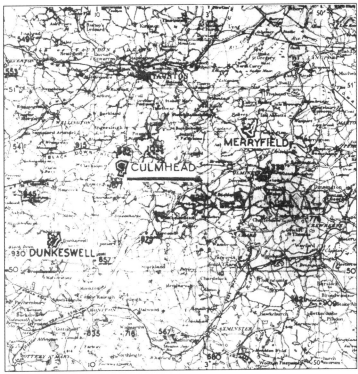

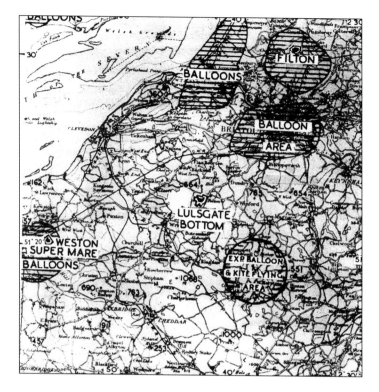

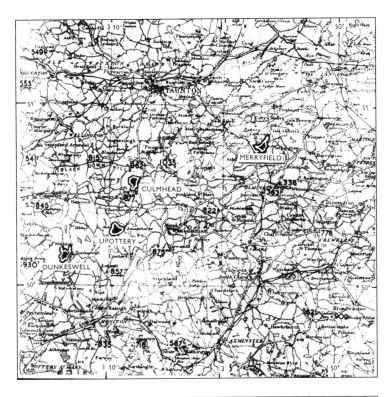

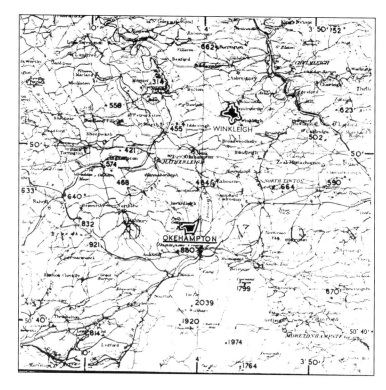

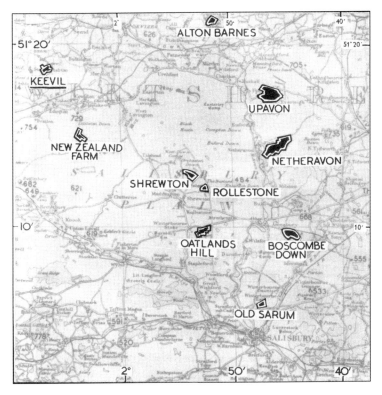

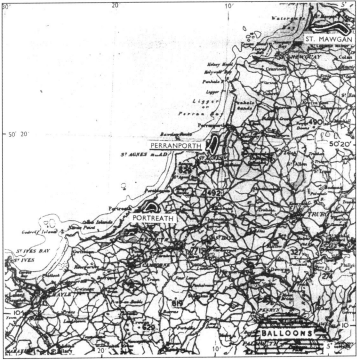

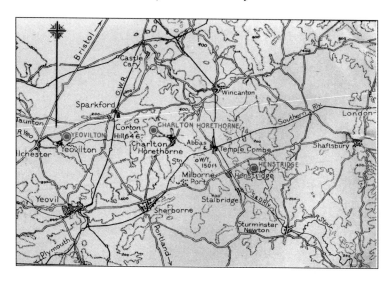

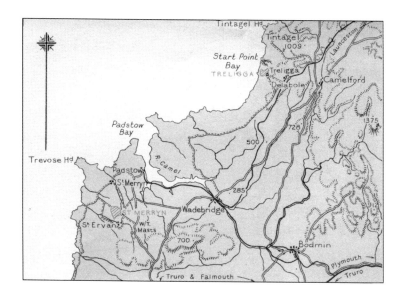

Abbreviations

All aspects of military aviation are crammed with abbreviations, especially when it comes to the designations of units. The following abbreviations have been used in this series, especially in the unit tables. This list is by no means exhaustive – at a rough estimate a complete list would run to 20,000 plus abbreviations! However, it does include the abbreviations most relevant to this series. There is an element of logic the reader can apply where an abbreviation is not listed; for example, 'CU' is most commonly used for Conversion Unit, hence a WCU could be a Wellington Conversion Unit . . . The down-side of this logic is that it could also be Washington or Wessex, and so context – i.e. which is most likely – must also be taken into account.

AAC	Army Air Corps	AOP	Air Observation Post
AACU	Anti-Aircraft Co-operation Unit	AOS	Air Observers School
A&AEE	Aeroplane and Armament Experimental Establishment	APC/S	Armament Practice Camp/Station
		ARD/S	Aircraft Repair Depot/Station
AAF	Auxiliary Air Force	ARW	Air Refuelling Wing
AAP	Aircraft Acceptance Park, Air Ammunition Park	ASF	Aircraft Servicing Flight
		ASP	Air Stores Park
AAS	Air Armament School	ASR(F)	Air Sea Rescue (Flight)
AASDF	Anti-Aircraft Special Defence Flight	ASRTU	ASR Training Unit
ABTF	Air Bomber Training Flight	ASS	Air Signallers School
ACCS	Airborne Control and Command Squadron	ASU	Aircraft Storage Unit
		ASW	Anti-Submarine Warfare
ACHU	Air Crew Holding Unit	ATA	Air Transport Auxiliary
ACIS	Air Council Inspection Squadron	ATC	Armament Training Camp, Air Traffic Control, Air Training Corps
ACS/W	Airfield Construction Squadron/Wing	ATDU	Air Torpedo/Transport Development Unit
ACU	Aircrew Holding Unit		
AD	Air Division	ATF	Autogiro Training Flight
ADF/U	Aircraft Delivery Flight/Unit	ATP	Advanced Training Pool
ADGB	Air Defence of Great Britain	ATW	Airship Training Wing
AEF	Air Experience Flight	AW	All-Weather
AF	Air Force	AWDS	All-Weather Development Squadron
AFDS/U	Air Fighting Development Squadron/Unit	AWFCS	All-Weather Fighter Combat/Conversion Squadron
AFEE	Airborne Forces Experimental Establishment	AWW	All-Weather Wing
AFS/U	Advanced Flying School/Unit	BAD	Base Air Depot
AGS	Air Gunnery School	BAFO	British Air Forces of Occupation
AIEU	Armament and Instrument Experimental Establishment	BANS	Basic ANS
		BAS	Beam Approach School
AIS	Air Interception School	BATF	Beam/Blind Approach Training Flight
ALS	Air Landing School		
AMC	Air Mobility Command	BBBLEE	Bomb Ballistics and Blind Landing Experimental Establishment
AMSDU	Air Ministry Servicing Development Unit		
		BB(M)F	Battle of Britain (Memorial) Flight
AMU	Aircraft Modification Unit	BBU	Bomb Ballistics Unit
ANS	Air Navigation School	BC	Bomber Command
AONS	Air Observer and Navigator School	BCBRU	BC Bombing Research Unit

BCDU	BC Development Unit
BCFU	BC Film Unit
BCIS	BC Instructors School
BCMS	BC Missile School
BDE	Balloon Development Establishment
BDU	Bombing Development Unit
BFTS	Basic Flying Training School
BG	Bombardment Group, Bomb Group
BGF/S	Bombing and Gunnery Flight/School
BLEU	Blind Landing Experimental Establishment
BS	Bombardment Squadron, Bomb Squadron
(BS)	Bomber Support
BSDU	Bomber Support Development Unit
BW	Bombardment Wing, Bomb Wing
CAACU	Civilian AACU
CAEU	Casualty Air Evacuation Unit
CBCS/F	Coastal Battery Co-operation School/Flight
CBE	Central Bomber Establishment
CBW	Combat Bomb Wing
CC	Coastal Command
CDTF	Coastal Defence Training Flight
CF/U	Conversion Flight/Unit; Communications Flight/Squadron
CFE	Central Fighter Establishment
CFS	Central Flying School
CGS	Central Gunnery School
CLE/S	Central Landing Establishment/School
CNS	Central Navigation School
CPF	Coast(al) Patrol Flight
CRO	Civilian Repair Organization
CSF	Central Servicing Flight
CSE	Central Signals Establishment
CSDE	Central Servicing Development Establishment
CTTO	Central Trials and Tactics Organization
deg	degrees
det	detachment
DF	Development Flight
DFCS	Day Fighter Combat School
DFLS	Day Fighter Leaders School
DUC	Distinguished Unit Citation
DWI	Directional Wireless Installation
EAB	Engineer Aviation Battalion
EAC	Enemy Aircraft Circus
ECU	Experimental Co-operation Unit
EF	Experimental Flight
EGS	Elementary Gliding School

E(R)FTS	Elementary (and Refresher) Flying Training School
FAA	Fleet Air Arm
FATU	
FB	Fighter-Bomber, Flying Boat
FBDF	Flying Boat Development Flight
FBS/W	Fighter-Bomber Squadron/Wing
FC	Fighter Command; Ferry Command
FCCRS	Fighter Command Control and Reporting School
FCPU	Ferry Command Preparation Unit
FEE	Fighter Experimental Establishment
FFU	Film Flight Unit
FG	Fighter Group
FIDO	Fog Investigation Dispersal Operation
FIS	Flying Instructors School
FIS/W	Fighter Interception Squadron/Wing
FIU	Fighter Interception Unit
FLS	Fighter Leaders School
Flt	Flight
F(P)P/U	Ferry (Pilots) Pool/Unit
FRS	Flying Refresher School
FSS	Flying Selection Squadron
FTF/U	Ferry Training Flight/Unit
FTS	Flying Training School
FW	Fighter Wing
FWS	Fighter Weapons School
FWTS	Fixed Wing Test Squadron
GCAOS	Ground-Controlled Approach Operators' School
GC/S	Gliding Centre/School
GCF	Gunnery Co-operation Flight
GIF/S	Glider Instructors Flight/School
GMDC	Groupe Mixte de Combat
GOTU	Glider OUT
GPR	Glider Pilot Regiment
GR&ANS	General Reconnaissance and Air Navigation School
GRF/U	Gunnery Research Flight/Unit
GSEU	Glider Storage and Erection Unit
GTF	Gunnery Training Flight
GTS	Glider Training School/Squadron
GWDS	Guided Weapon Development Squadron
HAS	Hardened Aircraft Shelter
HC	Home Command
HCF	Helicopter Communications Flight
HCU	Heavy Conversion Unit
HD	Home Defence
HDF	Halifax Development Flight
HG	Heavy Glider
HGCU	Heavy Glider Conversion Unit

HQ	Headquarters	NZ	New Zealand
HSF	High-Speed Flight		
HSL	High Speed Launch	OAF/PU	Overseas Aircraft Ferry/Preparation
HT	Heavy Transport		Unit
HTF	Heavy Transport Flight	OADU	Overseas Aircraft Delivery Unit
		OATS	Officers Advanced Training School
IDE	Instrument Design Establishment	OCF/U	Operational Conversion Flight/Unit
IE	Initial/Immediate	OEU	Operational Evaluation Unit
	Establishment/Equipment	OG	Observation Group
IRF/S	Instrument Rating Flight/Squadron	ORTU	Operational Refresher Training Unit
IRMB	Intermediate Range Ballistic Missile	OS	Ordnance Survey
ITF/S	Instrument Training Flight/Squadron	OTU	Operational Training Unit
ITW	Initial Training Wing		
		(P)AFU	Pilot Advanced Flying Unit
JASS	Joint Anti-Submarine School	PAS/U	Pilotless Aircraft Section/Unit
JATE	Joint Air Transport Establishment	PDC	Personnel Despatch Centre
JCF/U	Jet Conversion Flight/Unit	PFF	Pathfinder Force
JEFTS	Joint EFTS	PFU	Practice Flying Unit
JEHU	Joint Experimental Helicopter Unit	PoW	Prisoner of War
		PRDE/U	Photographic Reconnaissance
KES	Kestrel Evaluation Squadron		Development Establishment/Unit
KF	King's Flight	PRF/U	Pilot Refresher Flight/Unit
		PRU	Photographic Reconnaissance Unit
LAIS	Low Attack Instructors School	PRG	Photographic Reconnaissance Group
LAS	Light Aircraft School	PSP	Pierced Steel Planking/Plating
LCF/S	Lightning Conversion	PTS	Parachute Training School
	Flight/Squadron		
LFS	Lancaster Finishing School	QF	Queen's Flight
LG	Landing Ground	QRA	Quick Reaction Alert
LRDU	Long Range Development Unit		
LRF	Long Range Fighter	RAAF	Royal Australian Air Force
LUAS	London University Air Squadron	RAuxAF	Royal Auxiliary Air Force
		RAE	Royal Aircraft Establishment
MA	Midland Area	RAFC	Royal Air Force College
MAC	Military Airlift Command	RAFO	Reserve of Air Force Officers
MAEE/U	Marine Aircraft Experimental	RAFVR	Royal Air Force Volunteer Reserve
	Establishment/Unit	RAS	Reserve Aeroplane Squadron
MC	Maintenance Command	RASC	Royal Army Service Corps
MCS	Metropolitan Communications	RATS	Radio Aids Training Flight
	Squadron	RC	Reserve Command
MCU	Mosquito Conversion Unit	RCAF	Royal Canadian Air Force
METS	Multi-Engine Training Squadron	RCM	Radio Counter Measures
MOS	Marine Observers School	RE	Royal Engineers
MTU	Mosquito Training Unit; Mobile	RFC	Royal Flying Corps
	Training Unit	RFTS	Refresher Flying Training School
MU	Maintenance Unit	RFU	Refresher Flying Unit
		RLG	Relief Landing Ground
NA	Northern Area	RNAS	Royal Naval Air Service
NATO	North Atlantic Treaty Organization	RNZAF	Royal New Zealand Air Force
NCS	Northern Communications	ROC	Royal Observer Corps
	Squadron	RRE	Radar Research Establishment
NF	Night Fighter	RSU	Repair and Salvage Unit
NFF	Night Flying Flight	RS	Radio School
NFDW	Night Fighter Development Wing	RWE	Radio/Radar Warfare Establishment
NFLS	Night Fighter Leaders School	RWTS	Rotary Wing Test Squadron
NTU	Navigation/Night Training Unit		

SAC	Strategic Air Command	SoTT	School of Technical Training
SAD	Strategic Air Depot	SWA	South-West Area
SA(O)EU	Strike Attack (Operational) Evaluation Unit	SWO	School for Wireless Operators
SC	Support Command; Strike Command, e.g.:	T	Training
		TAF	Tactical Air Force
SCBS	Strike Command Bombing School	T/VASF	Transit/Visiting Aircraft Servicing Flight
SCF	Signals Co-operation Flight		
SD (F)	Special Duties (Flight)	TAW	Tactical Airlift Wing
SDU	Signals Development Unit	TC	Transport Command
SEF	Special Experimental Flight	TCF	Transport and Communications Flight
SF	Station Flight		
SFTS	Service Flying Training School	TCG/S/W	Troop Carrier Group/Squadron/Wing
SFU	Signals Flying Unit		
SHORAD	Short Range Air Defence	TDF/S	Torpedo Development Flight/Section
SHQ	Station Headquarters		
SHTTU	Support Helicopter Trials and Tactics Unit	TDS	Training Depot Squadron/Station
		TDY	Temporary Duty
SKTU	Sea King Training Unit	TEU	Tactical Exercise/Evaluation Unit
SLAIS	Specialist LAIS	TFS/U	Target Facilities Flight/Unit
SLG	Satellite Landing Ground	TFU	Telecommunications Flying Unit
SMT	Square-Meshed Track	TRE	Telecommunications Research Establishment
SOG	Special Operations Group		
SOM	Secret Organizational Memoranda	TRS/W	Tactical Reconnaissance Squadron/Wing
Sqn	Squadron		
SRCF	Short-Range Conversion Unit	TTF	Target Towing Flight
SRW	Strategic Reconnaissance Wing	TTS	Torpedo Training Squadron
STC	Strike Command	TTTE	Tri-national Tornado Training Establishment
STS	Seaplane Training Squadron		
SU	Support Unit	TU	Training Unit
Schools	N.B. the 'o' is often omitted or used in full 'of'	TW(C)U	Tornado/Tactical Weapons (Conversion) Unit
SoAC	School of Army Co-Operation; Airfield Construction	UAS	University Air Squadron
SoACCA	School of Aerial Co-operation with Coastal Artillery	UN	United Nations
		US(A)AF	United States (Army) Air Force
SoAG	School of Air Gunnery		
SoAN	School of Air Navigation	VC	Victoria Cross
SoAP	School of Air Pilotage	VE	Victory in Europe
SoAS	School of Air Support	VGS	Volunteer Gliding School
SoASR	School of Air Sea Rescue	VR	Volunteer Reserve
SoAT	School of Air Transport		
SoFC	School of Fighter Control; Flying Control	WA	Western Area
		WAAF	Women's Auxiliary Air Force
SoGR&AN	School of General Reconnaissance and Air Navigation	WEE	Wireless/Winterization Experimental Establishment
SoL(A)W	School of Land (Air) Warfare	W&O	Wireless and Observers
SoMR	School of Maritime Reconnaissance	WRS	Weather Research Squadron
SoNC	School of Naval Co-operation	WS	Wireless School
SoP	School of Photography	WTP	Wireless Testing Park
SoRF/T	School of Refresher/Flying Training	WTS	Washington Training Squadron
SoSF	School of Special Flying		